CORTI

CONVERSATIONAL
JAPANESE

ILLUSTRATED

Intended for self-study and for use in schools

With a Simplified System of Phonetic Pronunciation

By

RICHARD D. ABRAHAM, Ph.D.
MARTIN COLLEGE

and

SANNOSUKE YAMAMOTO

An Owl Book

HENRY HOLT AND COMPANY
New York

CORTINA LEARNING INTERNATIONAL, INC.
Publishers • WESTPORT, CT 06880

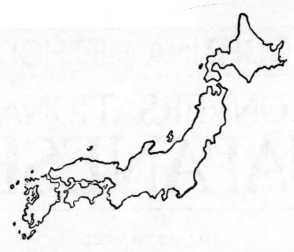

Cataloging Information

Cortina Method Conversational Japanese, intended for self-study and for use in
    schools, with a simplified system of pronunciation, by Richard D. Abraham
    and Sannosuke Yamamoto. New York, R.D. Cortina Co., 1980.
        248 p. 22cm.

        1. Japanese language—Conversation and phrase books.
I. Yamamoto, Sannosuke, joint author. II. Title. III.
Title: Conversational Japanese.
PL539.A5   1956   495.6242   56-58507
ISBN 0-8327-0009-6 (hardbound)
ISBN 0-8327-0016-1 (paperback)

PREFACE

There are many reasons why a practical knowledge of Japanese is both desirable and profitable for forward-looking Americans. During the postwar years the United States has developed far deeper political, economic, cultural and emotional ties with Japan than ever before in the history of our two countries. It is certain that American influence with the Japanese people will continue to be enormous for many years to come.

Japan at present is undergoing tremendous changes in her economic life. Since the war there has been a striking shift from low-quality, mass-produced goods to new industries manufacturing outstanding precision instruments, fine optical tools and solid household articles. America has played a prominent part in the development of these new and improved industries and will continue in a vital role, supplying a flow of trained people as well as equipment to Japan. Naturally, such high-quality products will find their place in American markets, providing new profitable contacts for enterprising Americans.

The economic and military conditions make it necessary for many Americans to live in or visit Japan. These contacts will have far-reaching effects in coming years, and it is clear that mutual understanding in these areas will be speeded up by a knowledge of each other's language. Nothing engenders confidence and respect so much as being able to converse with people in their own language. And naturally, the atmosphere thus created will make the American's stay in Japan more profitable, interesting and pleasant. Those who have a knowledge of the language are the best ambassadors for the United States in this important country.

Last, but not least, Japan offers enchantment, to the American tourist, with a variety of exotic scenery, quaint customs, fascinating local color in architecture, clothing, sculpture, religious habits, festivals and picturesque markets. Good hotel accommodations, delicious food, and meticulous service as only found in the Orient are all available at very low cost. And with a knowledge of Japanese you are free to travel to intriguing places that the ordinary tourist never sees.

All these are good reasons for studying Japanese, and the *Cortina Method* makes the study easy for you. The interesting lessons consist of normal, everyday conversations and a wealth of useful expressions. The exercises are based on the conversations and make you familiar with a wide variety of words and forms.

Language is habit! We are constantly expressing thoughts and ideas in speech, from habit, without paying attention to the words, phrases or idioms we use. When we say "How do you do?", "I've had a wonderful trip," "All right, let's go," we do so spontaneously. We are merely repeating a speech pattern that we have used so many times before that it has become automatic. Repetition, therefore, is the basis of language learning, and this is exactly the idea underlying the *Cortina Method:* to utilize the student's native language ability in the mastery of basic language patterns used in everyday topics, which the student absorbs and which encourage him to learn much faster than he would otherwise. The words are put to use right from the beginning, adding color and excitement to the lessons and engrossing the student's attention.

The lessons may be studied with little or no reference to grammar. However, a practical and easy-to-understand grammar is provided, which is tied closely to the lessons, for those who wish to use it.

For students wishing to accelerate their progress and master spoken Japanese in the easiest possible way, the *Cortina Academy* has recorded the Japanese text of this book. The vocabularies and conversations are spoken by native Japanese instructors whose voices have been chosen for their excellence of pronunciation and accent, clarity of speech and pleasing tonal quality. In classroom study too, *the phonograph method of learning languages* (originated by Cortina) has been found an invaluable aid to both student and teacher for oral practice and ear training.

INTRODUCTION

The lessons and exercises of this book provide the essential conversation for every-day living and at the same time progressively teach the basic features of Japanese speech. The book is divided into the following sections: Record Text, Exercises, Grammar, Japanese-English Dictionary and English-Japanese Dictionary.

The Grammar is both functional and systematic. As each new point appears, there is a superimposed number in the record text which indicates the section of the Grammar where that topic is discussed. The student may, if he likes, read the entire topic, but many will prefer to study only as much of the grammar topic as may be necessary to understand the particular sentence or phrase of the record text. In later lessons the student will in most cases be referred to this same topic again, and after reviewing the first part, he will continue reading more of the topic until he understands the further development of the point in question. In the Grammar after the examples quoted, there usually appears in parenthesis a roman numeral indicating the record and an arabic numeral indicating the line where that example occurs. Thus, points of grammar are presented as needed, and yet the Grammar is not merely a collection of isolated notes, but is classified and related to the work as a whole.

Beginning with section 104, there are many new charts which facilitate the understanding and use of the more important forms Sections 116 and 117 give the most widely used forms of every kind of verb in the Japanese language. The verbs are listed there alphabetically by their conclusive endings, so that the student has only to follow the chart to arrive at the tense, mood, or voice of any verb he may wish to use.

The Japanese-English Dictionary provided at the end of the book, page 219, is more than a vocabulary and should be consulted even when the text is perfectly clear, for not only are the words of the text included and their construction explained, but many other words related in form and meaning are given as well. This feature will aid the student in remembering the words he is learning and enable him to acquire a vocabulary of related words, and at the same time lead him to an understanding of Japanese word-formation.

The principal meanings of the words (not only the meaning of the word as used in the text and exercises) are given in the Dictionary. By consulting it, the student will learn the main concepts the word represents and he will know in what other senses it can be used if he desires to vary the sentences of the exercises. Also in this section of the work he will find all the inflected forms used in the text and notes as to how they are identified.

It is recommended, therefore, that the Dictionary be not neglected, but that it be studied along with the Grammar. Every word of the text appears there with an indication as to the record and line where it is used. If the student wishes to hear the pronunciation of any word, he should be able to find and hear it in a matter of a few seconds. The English-Japanese section of the Dictionary also gives all the words of the records, so that if a student forgets how to say a certain word he can find it there. If he wishes, he can then look in the Japanese-English section of the Dictionary and find out exactly where that word may be heard.

The English-Japanese Dictionary also gives many useful words with which the student may vary the exercise sentences.

In order not to confuse the student with too many diacritical marks, short or whispered vowels have been marked only in the record text while pitch is marked only in the Japanese-English section of the Dictionary. It is also important to note that an asterisk *after* a word in the Exercises indicates only that it appears in the Dictionary, but an asterisk *before* a word in the Dictionary itself indicates that the word is pronounced with level pitch.

Where a knowledge of the history of the various forms will clarify and relate them, the authoritative work of Sir George B. Sansom, *An Historical Grammar of Japanese*, published by the Oxford University Press, 1928, has been cited in the Grammar. This work has been referred to by the abbreviation HGJ.

Although the aim of this work is to teach spoken Japanese, the *katakana* syllabary with instructions for its use has been given in the Appendix. As this is the simplest form of writing and is known to all Japanese, it should prove useful in the writing and reading of brief notes.

The authors wish to express their gratitude to Sir George Sansom, who most kindly sent his own notes on his historical grammar, to Dr. Edwin B. Williams, Dean of the Graduate School, University of Pennsylvania, and general editor of the Conversaphone series, for invaluable aid in planning the work, to Mr. James Iannucci, head of the Language Department of St. Joseph's College, Philadelphia, for helpful suggestions, to Lt. Adam Cappello, Japanese language intelligence officer of the U. S. Army in Japan, for reading and correcting the manuscript and proofs, to Mrs. George Anderson for assistance in the construction of the dictionaries, to Mrs. William Goodis, for clerical aid, and to many students for help and advice.

R. D. A.
S. Y.

TABLE OF CONTENTS

Lesson	Subjects of Conversation	Subjects of Grammar	Page
I	Names of things and daily life. Greetings and taking leave	Declarative and interrogative constructions. Number. Word order. Use of postpositions **wa**, **ga**, and **to**. Affirmative and negative of the verb *to be* and of verbs in **-masu**	2
II	Names of people. Nationalities. Possession	Use of contraction **ja**. Postposition **mo**. Possessive relationship	6
III	Eating, drinking, reading, writing, and sending things	Formation of the past tense. Dative relationship and designation of the indirect object	12
IV	Wishes, ability and reasons. Sitting, Japanese style	Desiderative form of verbs. The periphrastic potential. The conclusive form of verbs. Classification of verbs. *Either . . . or.* Use of **kara**	18
V	School life. Taking and bringing people. Asking permission. Forbidding actions	Present progressive. Polite commands. Construction and use of the gerundial form in -te. Use of **mo** in asking permission. Use of **ikemasen** in prohibitions	26
VI	A social visit	Humble and honorific expressions. Form and use of adjectives. Adverbial form of adjectives. Comparative and superlative of adjectives. *Neither . . . nor.* Continuative form of the verb. Possession. Desiring things.	32
VII	Counting and telling time. Age. Preference. Suggestions. At the butcher shop. At the grocery	Noun form of the verb. Negative stem of the verb. Form of the adjective with **gozaru**. Use of cardinal and ordinal numbers of Chinese and native origin. Fractions. Probable present and future	38
VIII	At the baker's. At the fish store. Days of the week. Months of the year. Dates. Taking a rickshaw	Use of **sō desu**. Interrogative adjectives and pronouns. Numeral auxiliaries. Phonetic changes in numerals and auxiliaries	48
IX	Asking directions. Taking a street car. At a department store	Alternative questions. Approximate number. Use of attributive form of the verb with **tsumori** to express	58

intention. Use of **to** *if*. Direct discourse. Conditional meaning of the
verb in **-tara.** Use of **yŏ desu**

X   At the shoe store. Buying hats. Sea-   The verb **morau** meaning purchase.   68
       sons of the year. At the tailor's   Wearing clothes. Affixation of
                                                sugiru to adjectives. Expression of
                                                only. Temporal conjunctions. The
                                                verb **oku.** Negation and affirmation.
                                                The postposition **ya**

XI   Laundry. At a Japanese restaurant   Relative clauses. Simple form of the   78
                                                present, past, and future. Indef-
                                                inite adverbs. The interjection **yo**

XII   Stopping at a hotel. Taking a bath   Conditional. Potential form of the   88
                                                verb

XIII   A telephone conversation. Health. A   Transitive and intransitive verbs.   96
       visit from the doctor   Passive form of the verb. Causative
                                                form of the verb

XIV   At the bank. At the post office. Send-   Use of **tokoro.** Use of **suru** to make   106
       ing a telegram   verbs of nouns. The verb **shimau**

XV   At the barber's. Taking a train. A boat Use of the suffix **zu** to express *without*.   116
       trip. Customs   **Ni** with direct object of the verb **au**

XVI   Geography, religions, educational sys-   Stereotyped expressions. The prefix   126
       tem, sports and diversions of Japan   **ma.** *The former, the latter.* The suffix
                                                rashii

Grammar... 133

Appendix.. 213

Japanese-English Dictionary... 219

English-Japanese Dictionary... 239

Index... 247

KEY TO JAPANESE PRONUNCIATION

The Japanese ideographic writing can be transliterated, as in this book, with the Roman alphabet. The system of Romanization used is the Hepburn System, the one most widely accepted.

The sounds of Japanese are easy to master for English speakers. The instructions given below for the individual sounds will help the student greatly in acquiring a correct pronunciation.

VOWELS

The *short* vowels are:

a as in f*a*ther, but shorter
e as in m*e*t
i as in mach*i*ne
o as in n*o*rth
u as in r*u*le, but shorter

The vowels *i* and *u* between two voiceless consonants, and in some cases elsewhere, are whispered or not pronounced at all. They are usually marked short: ĭ and ŭ.

The *long* vowels, marked in the text by a short line above them, are pronounced as the corresponding short vowels but are held twice as long. Vowels followed by a nasal (*m* or *n*) in the same syllable are pronounced long. The long *ī* is written *ii*.

CONSONANTS

The consonants *b*, *k*, *m*, *n*, *p* and *w* are pronounced as in English.

The *w* of the postposition (*w*)*o* is not usually heard except after a word ending in *n·* It is therefore placed in parentheses, as are all letters which may or may not be pronounced.

D and *t* are pronounced as in English, but with the tongue touching the upper teeth.

G is always pronounced as in *g*ive or *g*o.

S approximately as in *s*ee
Sh　　"　　　"　" *sh*ip
Z　　　"　　　"　" *z*inc
Ts　　"　　　"　" ge*ts*
Ch　　"　　　"　" *ch*erry
J　　　"　　　"　" *j*eer

F, which occurs only before *u*, is pronounced with the lips close together.

H before *a*, *e* and *o* is pronounced as in English, but before *i* as a strong form of *h* (as *ch* in the German "*Ch*irurg" or *g* in the Spanish "*g*itano").

R is pronounced by a quick flapping of the tip of the tongue lightly touching the upper gums.

The double consonants *kk*, *mm*, *nn*, *pp*, *ss*, *ssh* (long *sh*), *tts* (long *ts*) and *tch* (long *ch*) are held twice as long as the single ones.

For further hints on pronunciation and accentuation, the student is referred to pages 133 to 136.

1

1

Dai[52] Ikk(w)a (Lesson I)

arigatŏ thank you
arimasen is not, are not, am not
asa morning
ban evening
desŭ is, are, am
empitsŭ pencil
fude (*writing*) brush
ga *a postposition used like* **wa** *but emphasizing the subject*
go language
gogo afternoon
hai yes
hon book
iie no
ikaga how
isu chair
ja *a contraction of* **de wa**; *used after nouns and pronouns before* **arimasen**

ka *an interrogative particle placed after the verb to make the sentence a question*
kakimasen do not write, does not write
kakimasŭ write, writes
kami paper
konnichi this day
kore this, these
mai every
manabimasen do not study, does not study
manabimasŭ *verb* study, studies
nani what
nichi day; —**gogo** afternoon
Nippon Japan; —**go** Japanese language
sayŏnara goodbye

shimasŭ do, does
shimbun newspaper
sŏ thus, so
tegami letter
to and; *a postposition connecting nouns and pronouns*
tsukue desk, table
wa *a postposition indicating that the preceding word is the logical subject of the sentence; may be translated by* as for
(w)o *a postposition usually indicating the preceding word as the object of the verb; has no English equivalent*
yasŭmi rest
yomimasŭ read, reads
zasshi magazine

Konnichi wa.	Good day.
Ikaga desŭ ka?	How are you?
Hai, arigatŏ.	Fine, thanks.
Nan(i) desŭ ka?[1]	What is it?
5 Empitsŭ[2] desŭ.	It is a pencil.
Nani desŭ ka?	What is it?
Pen desŭ.	It is a pen.
Nani desŭ ka?	What is it?
Hon desŭ.	It is a book.
10 Nani desŭ ka?	What is it?
Tegami desŭ.	It is a letter.
Nan(i) desŭ ka?	What is it?
Isu to tsukue desŭ.	It is a chair and a desk.
Nani desŭ ka?	What are they?
15 Zasshi to shimbun[4] desŭ.	They are magazines and newspapers.
Nan(i) desŭ ka?	What are they?
Kami to fude desŭ.	They are paper and a writing brush.
Kore wa[3] fude desŭ ka?	Is this a writing brush?
Hai, fude desŭ.	Yes, it is a brush.
20 Kore[4] wa hon desŭ ka?	Is this a book?

2

Hai, hon⁴ desŭ.　　　　　　　　　Yes, it is a book.
Kore wa empitsŭ desŭ ka?　　　　Is this a pencil?
Hai, sŏ desŭ.　　　　　　　　　　Yes, it is.
Kore wa tegami desŭ ka?　　　　　Are these letters?
25 Hai, sŏ desŭ.　　　　　　　　　Yes, they are.

Kore ga⁵ hon desŭ ka?　　　　　　Is *this* a book?
Iie, hon ja⁶ arimasen;⁸ shimbun desŭ.　No, it is not a book; it is a newspaper.
Kore ga empitsŭ desŭ ka?　　　　　Is *this* a pencil?
Iie, sŏ ja arimasen; pen desŭ.　　　No, it is not, it is a pen.
30 Kore ga tsukue desŭ ka?　　　　　Is *this* a desk?
Iie, sŏ ja⁶ arimasen; isu desŭ.　　　No, it isn't; it is a chair.

Mai asa nani (w)o³ shimasŭ⁷ ka?　　What do you do every morning?
Mai asa shimbun (w)o³ yomimasŭ.　Every morning I read the newspaper
Mai nichigogo nani (w)o shimasŭ ka?　What do you do every afternoon?
35 Mai nichigogo tegami (w)o kakimasŭ.　Every afternoon I write letters.
Mai ban nani (w)o shimasŭ ka?　　What do you do every evening?
Mai ban Nippon go (w)o manabimasŭ.　I study Japanese every evening.
Mai asa hon (w)o yomimasŭ ka?　　Do you read books every morning?
Iie, mai asa wa hon (w)o yomimasen.⁸　No, I don't read books every morning.
40 Mai nichigogo Nippon go (w)o mana-　Do you study Japanese every afternoon?
bimasŭ ka?
Iie, mai nichigogo wa Nippon go (w)o　No, I don't study Japanese every afternoon.
manabimasen.
Mai ban tegami (w)o kakimasŭ ka?　Do you write letters every evening?
45 Iie, mai ban wa tegami (w)o kakimasen.　No, I don't write letters every evening.
Mai ban wa zasshi (w)o yomimasen;　I don't read magazines every evening; I
Nippon go (w)o manabimasŭ.　　　study Japanese.
Sayŏnara.　　　　　　　　　　　Goodbye.
O-yasŭmi nasai.　　　　　　　　　Goodnight.

Exercises

Words followed by an asterisk appear in the Dictionary page 219.

Nani desŭ ka? Empitsu desŭ.　　　　**Nani desŭ ka? Empitsu to pen desŭ.**
　What is it? It is a pencil.　　　　　*What are they? They are a pencil and a pen.*
Nani desŭ ka? Pen desŭ.　　　　　　Nani desŭ ka? Hon to tegami desŭ.
Nani desŭ ka? Hon desŭ.　　　　　　Nani desŭ ka? Isu to tsukue desŭ.
Nani desŭ ka? Isu desŭ.　　　　　　Nani desŭ ka? Zasshi to shimbun desŭ.
Nani desŭ ka? Shimbun desŭ.　　　　Nani desŭ ka? Fude to kami desŭ.

Nani desŭ ka? Empitsu to pen to kami desŭ.
　What are they? They are pencils, pens, and paper.
Nani desŭ ka? Hon to shimbun to zasshi desŭ.　　Nani desŭ ka? Fude to empitsu to kami desŭ.
Nani desŭ ka? Tsukue to isu to tegami desŭ.　　Nani desŭ ka? Isu to zasshi to pen desŭ.

Kore wa nani desŭ ka? Hon desŭ.
What is this? It is a book.

Kore wa nani desŭ ka? Empitsu desŭ.

Kore wa nani desŭ ka? Tegami desŭ.

Kore wa nani desŭ ka? Kami desŭ.

Kore wa nani desŭ ka? Shimbun desŭ.

Kore wa tsukue to isu desŭ ka? Hai kore wa tsukue to isu desŭ.
Are these desks and chairs? Yes, they are desks and chairs.

Kore wa kami to tegami desŭ ka? Hai, kami to tegami desŭ.

Kore wa shimbun to zasshi desŭ ka? Hai, shimbun to zasshi desŭ.

Kore wa empitsu to fude desŭ ka? Hai, empitsu to fude desŭ.

Kore wa pen to fude desŭ ka? Hai, pen to fude desŭ.

Kore wa tsukue to isu to hon desŭ ka? Hai, sō desŭ.
Are these desks, chairs, and books? Yes, they are.

Kore wa kami to tegami to pen desŭ ka? Hai, sō desŭ.

Kore wa shimbun to zasshi to tegami desŭ ka? Hai, sō desŭ.

Kore wa empitsu to pen to hon desŭ ka? Hai, sō desŭ.

Kore wa fude to pen to kami desŭ ka? Hai, sō desŭ.

Kore wa shimbun desŭ ka? Iie, shimbun ja arimasen.
Is this a newspaper? No, it is not a newspaper.

Kore wa tegami desŭ ka? Iie, tegami ja arimasen.

Kore wa zasshi desŭ ka? Iie, zasshi ja arimasen.

Kore wa isu desŭ ka? Iie, isu ja arimasen.

Kore wa tsukue desŭ ka? Iie, tsukue ja arimasen.

Kore wa pen to empitsu to kami desŭ ka? Iie, sō ja arimasen.
Are these pens, pencils and paper? No, they are not.

Kore wa tegami to zasshi to shimbun desŭ ka? Iie, sō ja arimasen.

Kore wa tsukue to isu to hon desŭ ka? Iie, sō ja arimasen.

Kore wa kami to empitsu to pen desŭ ka? Iie, sō ja arimasen.

Kore wa fude to kami to hon desŭ ka? Iie, sō ja arimasen.

Kore wa hon desŭ; sō desŭ ka? Iie, shimbun desŭ.
This is a book, isn't it? No, it is a newspaper.

Kore wa empitsu desŭ; sō desŭ ka? Iie, pen desŭ.

Kore wa tegami desŭ, sō desŭ ka? Iie, kami desŭ.

Kore wa zasshi desŭ; sō desŭ ka? Iie, hon desŭ.

Kore wa pen desŭ, sō desŭ ka? Iie, fude desŭ.

Kore wa pen desŭ ka? Iie, pen ja arimasen; fude desŭ.
Is this a pen? No, it is not a pen; it is a brush.

Kore wa isu desŭ ka? Iie, isu ja arimasen; tsukue desŭ.

Kore wa hon desŭ ka? Hai, hon desŭ.
Is this a book? Yes, this is a book.

Kore wa zasshi desŭ ka? Hai, zasshi desŭ.

Kore wa pen desŭ ka? Hai, pen desŭ.

Kore wa fude desŭ ka? Hai, fude desŭ.

Kore wa tsukue desŭ ka? Hai, tsukue desŭ.

Kore wa empitsu desŭ ka? Iie empitsu ja arimasen; pen desŭ.

Kore wa shimbun desŭ ka? Iie, shimbun ja arimasen; zasshi desŭ.

Kore wa hon desŭ ka? Iie, hon ja arimasen; shimbun desŭ.

Mai asa nani (w)o shimasŭ ka? Mai asa, shimbun (w)o yomimasŭ.

What do you do every morning? Every morning, I read the newspaper.

Mai asa nani (w)o shimasŭ ka? Mai asa, hon (w)o yomimasŭ.

Mai asa nani (w)o shimasŭ ka? Mai asa, tegami (w)o yomimasŭ.

Mai asa nani (w)o shimasŭ ka? Mai asa, tegami (w)o kakimasŭ.

Mai asa nani (w)o shimasŭ ka? Mai asa, Nippon go (w)o manabimasŭ.

Mai nichigogo nani (w)o shimasŭ ka? Nippon go (w)o manabimasŭ.

What do you do every afternoon? I study Japanese.

Mai nichigogo nani (w)o shimasŭ ka? Tegami (w)o yomimasŭ.

Mai nichigogo nani (w)o shimasŭ ka? Hon (w)o yomimasŭ.

Mai nichigogo nani (w)o shimasŭ ka? Zasshi (w)o yomimasŭ.

Mai nichigogo nani (w)o shimasŭ ka? Tegami (w)o kakimasŭ.

Mai ban nani (w)o shimasŭ ka? Mai ban tegami (w)o yomimasŭ.

What do you do every evening? Every evening I read letters.

Mai ban nani (w)o shimasŭ ka? Mai ban hon (w)o yomimasŭ.

Mai ban nani (w)o shimasŭ ka? Mai ban shimbun (w)o yomimasŭ.

Mai ban nani (w)o shimasŭ ka? Mai ban Nippon go (w)o manabimasŭ.

Mai ban nani (w)o shimasŭ ka? Mai ban tegami (w)o kakimasŭ.

Mai nichi shimbun (w)o yomimasŭ ka? Iie, mai nichi wa yomimasen.

Do you read the newspaper every day? No, not every day.

Mai nichi tegami (w)o kakimasŭ ka? Iie, mai nichi wa kakimasen.

Mai nichi hon (w)o yomimasŭ ka? Iie, mai nichi wa yomimasen.

Mai nichi Nippon go (w)o manabimasŭ ka? Iie, mai nichi wa manabimasen.

Mai nichi zasshi (w)o yomimasŭ ka? Iie, mai nichi wa yomimasen.

Mai nichigogo tegami (w)o kakimasŭ ka? Iie, mai nichigogo wa kakimasen.

Do you write letters every afternoon? No, not every afternoon.

Mai nichigogo shimbun (w)o yomimasŭ ka? Iie, mai nichigogo wa yomimasen.

Mai nichigogo hon (w)o yomimasŭ ka? Iie, mai nichigogo wa yomimasen.

Mai nichigogo Nippon go (w)o manabimasŭ ka? Iie, mai nichigogo wa manabimasen.

Mai nichigogo zasshi (w)o yomimasŭ ka? Iie, mai nichigogo wa yomimasen.

Mai ban Nippon go (w)o manabimasŭ ka? Iie, mai ban wa manabimasen.

Do you study Japanese every evening? No, not every evening.

Mai ban shimbun (w)o yomimasŭ ka? Iie, mai ban wa yomimasen.

Mai ban zasshi (w)o yomimasŭ ka? Iie, mai ban wa yomimasen.

Mai ban tegami (w)o kakimasŭ ka? Iie, mai ban wa kakimasen.

Mai ban hon (w)o yomimasŭ ka? Iie, mai ban wa yomimasen.

Dai Ni K(w)a (Lesson II)

aikawarazu same as usual
Amerika-jin American (person)
anata *sg.* you
anatagata *pl.* you
ano *adj.* that, those (distant from the person spoken to)
are *pron.* that, those (distant from the person spoken to)
dare who
genki health
hĭto person; **kono —; sono —; ano —** he, she
hĭtotachi people; **kono —; sono —; ano —** they
Jirō *man's given name*

komban this evening
kono this, these
Matsumoto *a family name*
mina all, everybody, everything
mo also
no *particle indicating possession*
Nippon-jin Japanese (person)
onna woman
onna no hĭto woman; **kono —; sono —; ano —** she
onna no hĭtotachi women; **kono —; sono —; ano —** they (women)
otoko male, man

otoko no hĭto man; **kono —; sono —; ano —** he
otoko no hĭtotachi men; **kono —; sono —; ano —** they (men)
San Mr., Miss, Mrs.
Shina-jin Chinese (person)
sono, *adj.* that, those (near the person spoken to)
sore *pron.* that, that one, those (near the person spoken to)
Takahashi *a family name*
watakŭshi I; **—no** my, mine
watakŭshidomo we; **—no** our, ours

Komban wa.
Ikaga desŭ ka?
Arigatō gozaimasŭ. Aikawarazu.⁹⁸ Genki desŭ.
5 Anata wa Takahashi Jirō San desŭ ka?
Iie, watakŭshi wa Takahashi Jirō ja⁶ arimasen.

Good evening.
How are you?
Thank you. Same as usual. I am in good health.
Are you Mr. Jiro Takahashi?
No, I am not Jiro Takahashi.

Anata wa dare desŭ ka?
Watakŭshi wa Matsumoto⁹ desŭ.
10 Anata wa Nippon-jin desŭ ka?
Iie, Nippon-jin ja arimasen.
Ano¹⁰ onna no hĭto¹¹ wa Shina-jin desŭ ka?
Iie, sō ja arimasen.
Ano otoko no hĭto¹¹ wa dare desŭ ka?
15 Takahashi Jirō San⁹ desŭ.
Anatagata¹¹ wa Amerika-jin desŭ ka?
Hai, watakŭshidomo wa Amerika-jin desŭ.
Anata mo¹² Amerika-jin desŭ.
Ano hĭtotachi¹¹ wa mina Nippon-jin desŭ ka?
20 Iie, ano otoko no hĭtotachi¹¹ wa Nippon-jin desŭ; ano onna no hĭtotachi¹¹ wa Shina-jin desŭ.

Who are you?
I am (Mr.) Matsumoto.
Are you Japanese?
No, I am not Japanese.
Is she Chinese?
No, she is not.
Who is he?
He is Mr. Jiro Takahashi.
Are you Americans?
Yes, we are Americans. You also are an American.
Are they all Japanese?
No, those men are Japanese; those women are Chinese.

Kore¹⁰ wa dare no empitsŭ desŭ ka?
Sore¹⁰ wa watakŭshi no¹³ empitsŭ desŭ.

Whose pencil is this?
That is my pencil.

6

25 Sore wa dare no hon desŭ ka?	Whose book is that?
Kore wa sono[10] otoko no hĭto no hon desŭ.	This is his book.
Are[10] wa anata no shimbun desŭ ka?	Is that your newspaper?
Iie, watakŭshi no[13] ja arimasen; kono[10] onna no hĭto no shimbun desŭ.	No, it is not mine; it is her newspaper.
30 Kore wa anatagata no zasshi desŭ ka?	Are these your magazines?
Iie, watakŭshidomo no zasshi ja arimasen; ano otoko no hĭtotachi no zasshi desŭ.	No, they are not our magazines; they are their (those men's) magazines.
Kore wa dare no desŭ ka?	Whose is this?
Sore wa ano onna no hĭtotachi no desŭ.	That is theirs. (those women's)
35 Sore wa ano hĭtotachi no fude desŭ ka?	Are those their brushes?
Iie, ano hĭtotachi no ja arimasen; watakŭshidomo no desŭ.	No, they are not their brushes; they are ours.
Sore wa Takahashi San no[13] desŭ ka?	Are those Mr. Takahashi's?
Iie, Takahashi San no ja arimasen.	No, they are not Mr. Takahashi's.

Exercises

Anata wa ikaga desŭ ka? Arigatō gozaimasŭ. Aikawarazu. Genki desŭ.
How are you? Thanks. Same as usual. Fine.

Ano otoko no hito wa ikaga desŭ ka? Arigatō gozaimasŭ. Aikawarazu. Genki desŭ.
Ano onna no hito wa ikaga desŭ ka? Arigatō gozaimasŭ. Aikawarazu. Genki desŭ.
Anatagata wa ikaga desŭ ka? Arigatō gozaimasŭ. Aikawarazu. Genki desŭ.
Ano hitotachi wa ikaga desŭ ka? Arigatō gozaimasŭ. Aikawarazu. Genki desŭ.

Ano hito wa Takahashi San desŭ ka? Iie, Takahashi San ja arimasen.
Is he Mr. Takahashi? No, he is not Mr. Takahashi.

Ano hito wa Brown (Buraun) San desŭ ka? Iie, ano hito wa Brown San ja arimasen.
Ano hito wa Jones (Jonzu) San desŭ ka? Iie, ano hito wa Jones San ja arimasen.
Ano hitotachi wa Brown San to Jones San desŭ ka? Iie, ano hitotachi wa Brown San to Jones San ja arimasen.
Ano onna no hitotachi wa Takahashi San to Brown San desŭ ka? Iie, ano onna no hitotachi wa Takahashi San to Brown San ja arimasen.

Anata wa Takahashi San desŭ ka? Iie, watakŭshi wa Takahashi ja arimasen.
Are you Mr. Takahashi. No, I am not (Mr.) Takahashi.

Anata wa Brown San desŭ ka? Iie, watakŭshi wa Brown ja arimasen.
Anata wa Jones San desŭ ka? Iie, watakŭshi wa Jones ja arimasen.
Anata wa Harris (Harisu) San desŭ ka? Iie, watakŭshi wa Harris ja arimasen.
Anata wa Matsumoto San desŭ ka? Iie, watakŭshi wa Matsumoto ja arimasen.

Anata wa dare desŭ ka? Watakŭshi wa Matsumoto Jirō desŭ.
Who are you? I am Jiro Matsumoto.
Anata wa dare desŭ ka? Watakŭshi wa John (Jan) Brown desŭ.
Anata wa dare desŭ ka? Watakŭshi wa Tom (Tamu) Jones desŭ.
Anata wa dare desŭ ka? Watakŭshi wa Dick (Dikku) Harris desŭ.
Anata wa dare desŭ ka? Watakŭshi wa Harry Stone (Hari Sutōn) desŭ.

Ano hito wa dare desŭ ka? Ano hito wa Takahashi Jirō San desŭ.
Who is that person (he or she)? That person is Mr. Jiro Takahashi.
Ano hito wa dare desŭ ka? Ano hito wa John Brown San desŭ.
Ano hito wa dare desŭ ka? Ano hito wa Mary (Mēri) Jones San desŭ.
Ano hito wa dare desŭ ka? Ano hito wa Tom Harris San desŭ.
Ano hito wa dare desŭ ka? Ano hito wa Jane (Jein) Stone San desŭ.

Ano otoko no hito wa Amerika-jin desŭ. Ano onna no hito wa Nippon-jin desŭ.
He is an American. She is Japanese.
Ano otoko no hito wa Amerika-jin desŭ. Ano onna no hito wa Shina-jin desŭ.
Ano otoko no hito wa Shina-jin desŭ. Ano onna no hito wa Amerika-jin desŭ.
Ano otoko no hito wa Nippon-jin desŭ. Ano onna no hito wa Nippon-jin desŭ.
Ano otoko no hito wa Matsumoto San desŭ. Ano onna no hito wa Takahashi San desŭ.

Kono otoko no hito wa Takahashi San desŭ. Sono otoko no hito wa Matsumoto San desŭ.
He (near me) is Mr. Takahashi. He (near you) is Mr. Matsumoto.
Kono otoko no hito wa Matsumoto San desŭ. Sono otoko no hito wa Takahashi San desŭ.
Kono otoko no hito wa Brown San desŭ. Sono otoko no hito wa Jones San desŭ.
Kono otoko no hito wa Harris San desŭ. Sono otoko no hito wa Stone San desŭ.
Kono otoko no hito wa White (Waito) San desŭ. Sono otoko no hito wa Brown San desŭ.

Sono onna no hito wa Nippon-jin desŭ. Ano onna no hito wa Shina-jin desŭ.
She (near you) is Japanese. She (over there) is Chinese.
Sono onna no hito wa Amerika-jin desŭ. Ano onna no hito wa Shina-jin desŭ.
Sono onna no hito wa Shina-jin desŭ. Ano onna no hito wa Amerika-jin desŭ.
Sono onna no hito wa Nippon-jin desŭ. Ano onna no hito wa Nippon-jin desŭ.
Sono onna no hito wa Matsumoto San desŭ. Ano onna no hito wa Takahashi San desŭ.

Watakŭshi wa Shina-jin desŭ; Nippon-jin ja arimasen.
I am a Chinese; I am not a Japanese.
Watakŭshi wa Shina-jin desŭ; Amerika-jin ja arimasen.
Watakŭshi wa Amerika-jin desŭ; Shina-jin ja arimasen.

Watakŭshi wa Nippon-jin desŭ; Shina-jin ja arimasen.
Watakŭshi wa Nippon-jin desŭ; Amerika-jin ja arimasen.
Watakŭshi wa Amerika-jin desŭ; Nippon-jin ja arimasen.

Watakŭshi wa Amerika-jin desŭ; kono hĭtotachi wa Shina-jin desŭ.
I am an American; they (near me) are Chinese.
Watakŭshi wa Amerika-jin desŭ; kono hĭtotachi wa Nippon-jin desŭ.
Watakŭshi wa Nippon-jin desŭ; kono hĭtotachi wa Amerika-jin desŭ.
Watakŭshi wa Shina-jin desŭ; kono hĭtotachi wa Amerika-jin desŭ.
Watakŭshi wa Nippon-jin desŭ; kono hĭtotachi wa Shina-jin desŭ.

Kono hĭtotachi wa mina Nippon-jin desŭ ka? Iie, mina wa Nippon-jin ja arimasen.
Are they (these people) all Japanese? No, not all are Japanese.
Sono hĭtotachi wa mina Nippon-jin desŭ ka? Iie, mina wa Nippon-jin ja arimasen.
Ano hĭtotachi wa mina Shina-jin desŭ ka? Iie, mina wa Shina-jin ja arimasen.
Kono hĭtotachi wa mina Amerika-jin desŭ ka? Iie, mina wa Amerika-jin ja arimasen.
Sono hĭtotachi wa mina Shina-jin desŭ ka? Iie, mina wa Shina-jin ja arimasen.

Kono onna no hito wa Nippon-jin desŭ ka? Iie, sono onna no hito wa Nippon-jin ja arimasen.
Is she Japanese? No, she is not Japanese.
Kono otoko no hito wa Shina-jin desŭ ka? Iie, sono hito wa Shina-jin ja arimasen.
Kono hĭtotachi wa Nippon-jin desŭ ka? Iie, sono hĭtotachi wa Nippon-jin ja arimasen.
Kono onna no hĭtotachi wa Amerika-jin desŭ ka? Iie, sono hĭtotachi wa Amerika-jin ja arimasen.
Kono otoko no hĭtotachi wa Nippon-jin desŭ ka? Iie, sono hĭtotachi wa Nippon-jin ja arimasen.

Kono hĭtotachi wa mina Nippon-jin ja arimasen; kono otoko no hĭtotachi wa Nippon-jin desŭ; kono onna no hĭtotachi wa Shina-jin desŭ.
They (near me) are not all Japanese; these men are Japanese; these women are Chinese.
Sono hĭtotachi wa mina Amerika-jin ja arimasen; sono otoko no hĭtotachi wa Amerika-jin desŭ; sono onna no hĭtotachi wa Nippon-jin desŭ.
Ano hĭtotachi wa mina Shina-jin ja arimasen; ano otoko no hito wa Shina-jin desŭ; ano onna no hito wa Nippon-jin desŭ.
Kono hĭtotachi wa mina Nippon-jin ja arimasen; kono otoko no hito wa Shina-jin desŭ; kono onna no hito wa Amerika-jin desŭ.

Watakŭshidomo wa Takahashi to Matsumoto desŭ.
We are (Mr.) Takahashi and (Mr.) Matsumoto.
Watakŭshidomo wa Brown to Takahashi desŭ.
Watakŭshidomo wa Jones to Brown desŭ.

Watakŭshidomo wa Harris to Matsumoto desŭ.
Watakŭshidomo wa Jones to Harris desŭ.
Watakŭshidomo wa White to Stone desŭ.

Anata wa Amerika-jin desŭ. Watakŭshi mo Amerika-jin desŭ.
You are an American. I am also an American.

Anatagata wa Nippon-jin desŭ; watakŭshidomo mo Nippon-jin desŭ.
Ano otoko no hito wa Shina-jin desŭ. Ano onna no hito mo Shina-jin desŭ.
Ano onna no hĭtotachi wa Amerika-jin desŭ. Anata mo Amerika-jin desŭ.
Ano otoko no hĭtotachi wa Nippon-jin desŭ. Ano onna no hĭtotachi mo Nippon-jin desŭ.

Kore wa dare no fude desŭ ka? Watakŭshi no fude desŭ.
Whose brush is this? It is my brush.

Kore wa dare no empitsu desŭ ka? Watakŭshi no empitsu desŭ.
Kore wa dare no shimbun desŭ ka? Watakŭshi no shimbun desŭ.
Kore wa dare no tsukue desŭ ka? Watakŭshi no tsukue desŭ.
Kore wa dare no isu desŭ ka? Watakŭshi no isu desŭ.
Kore wa dare no tegami desŭ ka? Watakŭshi no tegami desŭ.

Kore wa anata no zasshi desŭ ka? Iie, watakŭshi no ja arimasen.
Is this your magazine? No, it isn't mine.

Kore wa anata no shimbun desŭ ka? Iie, watakŭshi no ja arimasen.
Kore wa anata no hon desŭ ka? Iie, watakŭshi no ja arimasen.
Kore wa anata no isu desŭ ka? Iie, watakŭshi no ja arimasen.

Kore wa ano hito no desŭ ka? Iie, sore wa anata no desŭ.
Is this his? No, that is yours.

Kore wa anata no desŭ ka? Iie, sore wa ano otoko no hito no desŭ.
Kore wa ano otoko no hito no desŭ ka? Iie, sore wa ano onna no hito no desŭ.
Kore wa ano hito no desŭ ka? Iie, sore wa watakŭshi no desŭ.
Kore wa kono otoko no hito no desŭ ka? Iie, sore wa ano otoko no hito no desŭ.

Sono hon wa Takahashi San no desŭ ka? Iie, Takahashi San no ja arimasen.
Are those books Mr. Takahashi's? No, they are not Mr. Takahashi's.

Sono empitsu wa anatagata no desŭ ka? Iie, watakŭshidomo no ja arimasen.
Ano shimbun wa ano otoko no hito no desŭ ka? Iie, ano otoko no hito no ja arimasen.
Sono zasshi wa sono onna no hito no desŭ ka? Iie, sono onna no hito no ja arimasen.
Sono tsukue wa Matsumoto San no desŭ ka? Iie, ano hito no ja arimasen.

Sono hon wa Takahashi San no desŭ ka? Iie, sō ja arimasen.
Are those books Mr. Takahashi's? No, they are not.

Sono tegami wa anata no desŭ ka? Iie, sō ja arimasen.
Sono tsukue wa ano onna no hito no desŭ ka? Iie, sō ja arimasen.
Sono isu wa Matsumoto San no desŭ ka? Iie, sō ja arimasen.
Sono kami wa watakŭshi no desŭ ka? Iie, sō ja arimasen.

Dai San K(w)a (Lesson III)

asahan breakfast
deshĭta was, were (*used to help form the negative past tense*)
gohan rice, meal
gyūnyū milk
hamŭ ham
hiruhan lunch
kōhĭ coffee

mimasŭ see
nani mo nothing (*with negative verb*)
niku meat
nomimasŭ drink
o-cha tea
okurimasŭ send
sakana fish

soshĭte and (*connecting clauses*)
tabemasŭ eat
tamago egg
tomodachi friend
watashimasŭ give, hand over
yasai vegetable
yūhan supper, dinner

Anata wa mai asa asahan ni[14] nani (w)o tabemasŭ ka? — What do you eat for breakfast every morning?

Watakŭshi wa hamŭ to[15] tamago (w)o tabemasŭ. Soshĭte kōhĭ (w)o nomimasŭ. — I eat ham and eggs. And I drink coffee.

5 Hiruhan ni nani (w)o tabemasŭ ka? — What do you eat for lunch?

Hiruhan ni wa[16] sakana to gohan[17] (w)o tabemasŭ.[11] Soshĭte gyūnyū (w)o nomimasŭ. — For lunch I eat fish and rice. And I drink milk.

Soshĭte yūhan ni wa nani (w)o tabemasŭ ka? — And what do you eat for dinner?

Niku to yasai (w)o tabemasŭ. Soshĭte o-cha 10 (w)o nomimasŭ. — I eat meat and vegetables. And I drink tea.

Anata wa yūhan ni nani (w)o tabemashĭta[18] ka? — What did you eat for supper?

Watakŭshi wa niku to yasai (w)o tabemashĭta. — I ate meat and vegetables.

15 Hiruhan ni wa nani mo[19] tabemasen deshĭta.[18] — I didn't eat anything for lunch.

Watakŭshi no shimbun (w)o mimashĭta ka? — Did you see my newspaper?
Hai, mimashĭta.[18] — Yes, I did.

Watakŭshi no zasshi (w)o mimashĭta ka? — Did you see my magazine?

20 Iie, anata no zasshi wa[20] mimasen deshĭta. — No, I didn't see your magazine.
Ano otoko no hĭtotachi no hon (w)o yomimashĭta ka? — Did you read their books?

Iie, yomimasen deshĭta. — No, I didn't.

Anata no tomodachi mo[12] yomimasen 25 deshĭta ka? — Didn't your friend read (them) either?

Iie, watakŭshi no tomodachi mo yomimasen deshĭta. — No, my friend didn't read (them) either.

Anata wa dare ni[14] ano tegami (w)o watashimashĭta ka? — To whom did you hand that letter?

30 Watakŭshi wa tomodachi ni[14] ano tegami (w)o watashimashĭta. — I gave that letter to (your) friend.

12

Takahashi San ni tegami (w)o kakimashĭta ka?

Did you write the letter to Mr. Takahashi?

Iie, Matsumoto San ni kakimashĭta.

No, I wrote (it) to Mr. Matsumoto.

35 Ano hĭto wa anata ni tegami (w)o kakimashĭta ka?

Did he (she) write a letter to you?

Iie, watakŭshi ni wa[16] kakimasen deshĭta.

No, he (she) did not write to me.

Watakŭshi no tomodachi ni kakimashĭta.

He (she) wrote to my friend.

Watakŭshi wa ano otoko no hĭto ni tegami
40 (w)o kakimashĭta.

I wrote a letter to him.

Ano onna no hĭto ni mo[16] tegami (w)o kakimashĭta.

I wrote a letter to her also.

Anatagata ni mo hon (w)o okurimashĭta.

I sent books to you also.

Ano hĭtotachi ni mo hon (w)o okurimashĭta
45 ka?

Did you send the books to them also?

Iie, ano otoko no hĭtotachi ni wa okurimasen deshĭta; ano onna no hĭtotachi ni wa okurimashĭta.

No, I didn't send (them) to those men; I sent (them) to those women.

Exercises

Mai nichi nani (w)o tabemasŭ ka? Mai nichi tamago (w)o tabemasŭ.
What do you eat every day? Every day I eat eggs.

Mai asa nani (w)o tabemasŭ ka? Mai asa hamŭ (w)o tabemasŭ.

Mai nichigogo nani (w)o tabemasŭ ka? Mai nichi gogo sakana (w)o tabemasŭ.

Mai ban nani (w)o tabemasŭ ka? Mai ban niku (w)o tabemasŭ.

Mai nichi nani (w)o nomimasŭ ka? Mai nichi kōhĭ (w)o nomimasŭ.
What do you drink every day? I drink coffee every day.

Mai asa nani (w)o nomimasŭ ka? Mai asa gyūnyū (w)o nomimasŭ.

Mai nichigogo nani (w)o nomimasŭ ka? Mai nichi gogo o-cha (w)o nomimasŭ.

Mai ban nani (w)o nomimasŭ ka? Mai ban kōhĭ (w)o nomimasŭ.

Asahan ni sakana (w)o tabemasŭ ka? Iie, asahan ni sakana wa tabemasen. Hamŭ to tamago (w)o tabemasŭ.
Do you eat fish for breakfast? No, I don't eat fish for breakfast. I eat ham and eggs.

Hiruhan ni niku (w)o tabemasŭ ka? Iie, hiruhan ni niku wa tabemasen. Sakana (w)o tabemasŭ.

Yūhan ni tamago (w)o tabemasŭ ka? Iie, tamago wa tabemasen. Niku to yasai (w)o tabemasŭ.

Asahan ni sakana (w)o tabemasŭ ka? Iie, asahan ni wa sakana (w)o tabemasen. Hiruhan ni tabemasŭ.
Do you eat fish for breakfast? No, I don't eat fish for breakfast. I eat (it) for lunch.

Hiruhan ni niku (w)o tabemasŭ ka? Iie, hiruhan ni wa niku (w)o tabemasen. Yūhan ni tabemasŭ.

Yūhan ni tamago (w)o tabemasŭ ka? Iie, yūhan ni wa tamago (w)o tabemasen. Asahan ni tabemasŭ.

Asahan ni o-cha (w)o nomimasŭ ka? Iie, asahan ni o-cha wa nomimasen. Kōhī (w)o nomimasŭ.
Do you drink tea for breakfast? No, I don't drink tea for breakfast. I drink coffee.

Hiruhan ni o-cha (w)o nomimasŭ ka? Iie, hiruhan ni o-cha wa nomimasen. Gyūnyū (w)o nomimasŭ.

Yūhan nī kōhī (w)o nomimasŭ ka? Iie, yūhan ni kōhī wa nomimasen. O-cha (w)o nomimasŭ.

Mai nichi o-cha (w)o nomimasŭ ka? Iie, mai nichi wa o-cha (w)o nomimasen. Gyūnyū (w)o nomimasŭ.

Asahan (w)o tabemashĭta ka? Hai, tabemashĭta.
Did you eat breakfast? Yes, I did.

Hiruhan (w)o tabemashĭta ka? Hai, tabemashĭta.

Yūhan (w)o tabemashĭta ka? Hai, tabemashĭta.

Anata wa mai nichi nani (wo) shimasŭ ka? Nani mo shimasen.
What do you do every day? I don't do anything.

Takahashi San wa mai asa nani (w)o shimasŭ ka? Ano hito mo nani mo shimasen.

Ano otoko no hito wa mai nichigogo nani (w)o shimasŭ ka? Nani mo shimasen.

Ano onna no hito wa mai ban nani (w)o shimasŭ ka? Ano onna no hito mo nani mo shimasen.

Anata wa mai nichi nani (w)o manabimasŭ ka? Nani mo manabimasen.
What do you study every day? I don't study anything.

Takahashi San wa mai asa nani (w)o nomimasŭ ka? Ano hito wa nani mo nomimasen.

Matsumoto San wa mai nichigogo nani (w)o yomimasŭ ka? Nani mo yomimasen.

Anata no tomodachi wa mai ban nani (w)o kakimasŭ ka? Nani mo kakimasen.

Anata wa asahan ni nani (w)o tabemashĭta ka? Watakŭshi wa hamŭ to tamago (w)o tabemashĭta.
What did you eat for breakfast? I ate ham and eggs.

Anata wa hiruhan ni nani (w)o tabemashĭta ka? Watakŭshi wa sakana to gohan (w)o tabemashĭta.

Anata wa yūhan ni nani (w)o tabemashĭta ka? Watakŭshi wa niku to yasai (w)o tabemashĭta.

Anata wa asahan ni niku to yasai (w)o tabemashĭta ka? Iie, niku to yasai wa tabemasen deshĭta.
Did you eat meat and vegetables for breakfast? No, I didn't eat meat and vegetables.

Anata wa hiruhan ni hamŭ to tamago (w)o tabemashĭta ka? Iie, hamŭ to tamago wa tabemasen deshĭta.

Anata wa yūhan ni sakana to gohan (w)o tabemashĭta ka? Iie, sakana to gohan wa tabemasen deshĭta.

Watakйshi no shimbun (w)o mimashĭta ka? Hai, mimashĭta.
Did you see my newspaper? Yes, I saw it.
Watakйshi no zasshi (w)o mimashĭta ka? Hai, mimashĭta.
Watakйshi no empitsu (w)o mimashĭta ka? Hai, mimashĭta.
Watakйshi no hon (w)o mimashĭta ka? Hai, mimashĭta.
Watakйshi no tomodachi (w)o mimashĭta ka? Hai, mimashĭta.
Watakйshi no fude (w)o mimashĭta ka? Hai, mimashĭta.

Watakйshi no zasshi (w)o yomimashĭta ka? Hai, yomimashĭta.
Did you read my magazine? Yes, I did.
Ano onna no hito no shimbun (w)o mimashĭta ka? Hai, mimashĭta.
Ano otoko no hito no hamŭ (w)o tabemashĭta ka? Hai, tabemashĭta.
Anata wa anata no hon (w)o okurimashĭta ka? Hai, okurimashĭta.

Watakйshi no zasshi (w)o mimashĭta ka? Iie, anata no wa mimasen deshĭta. Ano hito no (w)o mimashĭta.
Did you see my magazine? No, I didn't see yours. I saw his.
Ano otoko no hito no shimbun (w)o yomimashĭta ka? Iie, ano otoko no hito no wa yomimasen deshĭta. Ano onna no hito no (w)o yomimashĭta.
Kono onna no hĭtotachi no hon (w)o mimashĭta ka? Iie, sono onna no hĭtotachi no wa mimasen deshĭta. Ano otoko no hito no (w)o mimashĭta.
Watakйshidomo no hon (w)o okurimashĭta ka? Iie, anatagata no wa okurimasen deshĭta. Watakйshidomo no (w)o okurimashĭta.

Watakйshi wa kono hon (w)o yomimashĭta. Watakйshi no tomodachi mo yomimashĭta.
I read this book. My friend also read (it).
Ano otoko no hito wa kono tegami (w)o kakimashĭta. Ano onna no hito mo kakimashĭta.
Anata no zasshi (w)o mimashĭta. Watakйshi no mo mimashĭta.
Takahashi San no shimbun (w)o okurimashĭta. Matsumoto San no mo okurimashĭta.

Watakйshi wa zasshi (w)o okurimasen deshĭta. Ano hito mo okurimasen deshĭta.
I didn't send the magazine. He didn't send (it) either.
Watakйshi wa hon (w)o yomimasen deshĭta. Anata mo yomimasen deshĭta.
Anatagata wa asahan (w)o tabemasen deshĭta. Watakйshidomo mo tabemasen deshĭta.
Ano otoko no hĭtotachi wa o-cha (w)o nomimasen deshĭta. Ano onna no hĭtotachi mo nomimasen deshĭta.
Kono otoko no hito wa kono hon (w)o kakimasen deshĭta. Ano otoko no hito mo kakimasen deshĭta.
Ano hĭtotachi wa anata no zasshi (w)o mimasen deshĭta. Watakйshi mo mimasen deshĭta.

Anata wa dare ni ano tegami (w)o watashimashĭta ka? Watakйshi wa anata ni ano tegami (w)o watashimashĭta.
To whom did you give that letter? I gave that letter to you.

Anata wa dare ni ano᾿zasshi (w)o watashimashĭta ka? Watakŭshi wa ano otoko no hito ni watashimashĭta.

Anata wa dare ni ano shimbun (w)o watashimashĭta ka? Takahashi San ni watashimashĭta.

Anata wa dare ni ano fude (w)o watashimashĭta ka? Watakŭshi no tomodachi ni watashimashĭta.

Anata wa dare ni ano hon (w)o watashimashĭta ka? Anata ni ano hon (w)o watashimashĭta.

Anata wa dare ni ano empitsu (w)o watashimashĭta ka? Ano onna no hito ni ano empitsu (w)o watashimashĭta.

Watakŭshi ni ano hon (w)o watashimashĭta ka? Iie, anata ni watashimasen deshĭta.
Did you give that book to me? No, I did not give it to you.

Takahashi San ni ano empitsu (w)o watashimashĭta ka? Iie, Takahashi San ni watashimasen deshĭta.

Ano otoko no hito ni ano fude (w)o watashimashĭta ka? Iie, ano otoko no hito ni watashimasen deshĭta.

Ano onna no hito ni ano tegami (w)o watashimashĭta ka? Iie, ano onna no hito ni watashimasen deshĭta.

Watakŭshi ni wa ano shimbun (w)o watashimashĭta ka? Iie, anata ni wa watashimasen deshĭta. Matsumoto San ni watashimashĭta.
Did you give that newspaper to me? No, I didn't give (it) to you. I gave (it) to Mr. Matsumoto.

Ano otoko no hito ni ano zasshi (w)o watashimashĭta ka? Iie, ano otoko no hito ni wa watashimasen deshĭta. Ano onna no hito ni watashimashĭta.

Ano hĭtotachi ni ano hon wo watashimashĭta ka? Iie, ano hĭtotachi ni wa watashimasen deshĭta. Anatagata ni watashimashĭta.

Watakŭshidomo ni ano tegami (w)o watashimashĭta ka? Iie, anatagata ni wa watashimasen deshĭta. Anatagata no tomodachi ni watashimashĭta.

Ano hĭtotachi ni ano kami (w)o watashimashĭta ka? Iie, ano hĭtotachi ni wa watashimasen deshĭta. Kono hito ni watashimashĭta.

Ano hon (w)o ano otoko no hito ni watashimashĭta ka? Hai, watashimashĭta.
Did you give that book to him? Yes, I did.

Ano shimbun (w)o ano onna no hito ni okurimashĭta ka? Hai, okurimashĭta.

Anata wa kono tegami (w)o watakŭshi ni kakimashĭta ka? Hai, kakimashĭta.

Watakŭshidomo ni tegami (w)o kakimashĭta ka? Iie, kakimasen deshĭta.
Did you write the letter to us? No, I didn't.

Ano otoko no hĭtotachi ni tegami (w)o kakimashĭta ka? Iie, kakimasen deshĭta.

Ano onna no hĭtotachi ni tegami (w)o kakimashĭta ka? Iie, kakimasen deshĭta.

Ano otoko no hito ni tegami (w)o kakimashĭta ka? Iie, kakimasen deshĭta.

Ano onna no hito ni tegami (w)o kakimashĭta ka? Iie, kakimasen deshĭta.

Watakushi ni ano tegami (w)o kakimashĭta ka? Iie, anata ni wa kakimasen deshĭta.

Did you write that letter to me? No, I didn't write (it) to you.

Ano otoko no hito ni ano zasshi (w)o okurimashĭta ka? Iie, ano otoko no hito ni wa okuri-masen deshĭta.

Ano onna no hito ni ano hon (w)o okurimashĭta ka? Iie, ano onna no hito ni wa okurimasen deshĭta.

Matsumoto San ni ano empitsu (w)o watashimashĭta ka? Iie, ano hito ni wa watashimasen deshĭta.

Ano hĭtotachi ni zasshi (w)o okurimashĭta. Anatagata ni mo okurimashĭta.

We sent the magazines to them. We sent (them) to you also.

Ano otoko no hĭtotachi ni shimbun (w)o watashimashĭta. Ano onna no hĭtotachi ni mo watashimashĭta.

Ano otoko no hito ni tegami (w)o kakimashĭta. Ano onna no hito mo kakimashĭta.

Ano hito ni wa hon (w)o okurimasen deshĭta. Anata ni mo okurimasen deshĭta.

I didn't send the book to him. I didn't send (it) to you either.

Ano otoko no hĭtotachi ni wa zasshi (w)o watashimasen deshĭta. Ano onna no hĭtotachi ni mo watashimasen deshĭta.

Ano otoko no hito ni wa tegami (w)o kakimasen deshĭta. Ano onna no hito ni mo kakimasen deshĭta.

4

Dai Shi K(w)a (Lesson IV)

dekimasŭ can; is, are able
de mo even; ... de mo ... de
  mo either ... or
doko where
Eigo English (*language*)
hanashĭtai want to speak, say
hikōki airplane
ima now
isogimasŭ hurry, hasten
jidōsha automobile

kaitai want to buy
kakeru sit
kara because
keredomo but
kinō yesterday
koto thing, matter (*abstract*)
mawasu drive
nani ka something, anything
naze why
sŭkoshi little, few, somewhat

sŭmitai want to live
suru do
sŭwaritai want to sit (*Japanese fashion; i.e. squat*)
tachitai want to stand
tatsu stand
tobitai want to fly
to issho ni together, with
yoroshii good, all right

Nihon go (w)o hanashĭtai[21] desŭ ka?
Hai, Nihon go (w)o hanashĭtai desŭ.
Anata wa watakŭshi ni Nihon go de[22] hanashitai desŭ ka?
5 Iie, hanashitakŭ[21] arimasen.
Anata wa watakŭshidomo to issho ni sŭmitai desŭ ka?
Hai, sŭmitai desŭ.
Doko ni sŭmitai desŭ ka?
10 Tōkiō ni[14] sŭmitai desŭ; Nyū Yōkŭ ni wa sŭmitakŭ arimasen.
Nani (w)o shĭtai desŭ ka?
Nani mo shĭtakŭ arimasen.
Nani ka[23] tabetai desŭ ka?
15 Hai, arigatō. Niku to yasai ga tabetai desŭ, keredomo sakana wa tabetakŭ arimasen.
Soshĭte nani ka nomitai desŭ ka?
Kōhĭ de mo[24] o-cha de mo[24] yoroshii, keredomo gyūnyū wa nomitakŭ arimasen.
20 Ima tegami (w)o kakitai desŭ ka?
Iie, isogimasŭ kara.
Anata wa sŭwaritai desŭ ka? Tachitai desŭ ka?[24]
Sŭwaritakŭ arimasen.
25 Hikōki (w)o kaitai desŭ ka?
Iie, hikōki wa kaitakŭ arimasen, keredomo hikōki de[22] tobitai desŭ.

Do you want to speak Japanese?
Yes, I want to speak Japanese.
Do you want to speak to me in Japanese?
No, I don't.
Do you want to live with us
Yes, I do.
Where do you want to live?
I want to live in Tokio; I don't want to live in New York.
What do you want to do?
I don't want to do anything.
Do you want anything to eat?
Yes, thanks. I want to eat meat and vegetables, but I don't want to eat fish.
And do you want something to drink?
Either coffee or tea, but I don't want to drink milk.
Do you want to write a letter now?
No, because I am in a hurry.
Do you want to sit down or do you want to stand?
I don't want to squat.
Do you want to buy an airplane?
No, I don't want to buy a plane, but I want to fly in a plane.

Hikōki de tobu koto ga dekimasŭ[25] ka?
Hai, dekimasŭ, keredomo hikōki (w)o kau
30 koto ga dekimasen.[25]

Can you fly a plane?
Yes, I can, but I can't buy a plane.

Jidōsha (w)o mawasu[26] koto ga dekimasŭ ka?	Can you drive an automobile?
Hai, dekimasŭ.	Yes, I can.

Kinō niku (w)o taberu[26] koto ga dekima-shĭta[18] ka?	Could you eat meat yesterday?
Iie, dekimasen deshĭta.[25]	No, I couldn't.

Eigo (w)o hanasu koto ga dekimasŭ ka?	Can you speak English?
Hai, sŭkoshi[28] wa dekimasŭ.	Yes, I can a little.

---

40 Naze kono shimbun (w)o yomitakŭ arimasen ka?	Why don't you want to read this newspaper?
Nippon go (w)o yomu koto ga dekimasen kara.[29]	Because I can't read Japanese.
Ima wa nani mo suru[26] koto ga dekimasen, tatsu koto ga dekimasen kara.	I can't do anything now, because I can't stand up.
45 Sŭkoshi isogu koto ga dekimasŭ ka?	Can you hurry a little?
Hai, dekimasŭ.	Yes, I can.
Sŭwaru koto ga dekimasŭ[27] ka?	Can you sit (Japanese fashion)?
Iie, dekimasen. Watakŭshidomo Amerika-jin wa isu ni kakemasŭ.	No, I can't. We Americans sit on chairs.

Exercises

Nippon go (w)o hanashitai desŭ ka? Hai, Nippon go (w)o hanashitai desŭ.
Do you want to speak Japanese? Yes, I want to speak Japanese.

Nippon go (w)o yomitai desŭ ka? Hai, Nippon go (w)o yomitai desŭ.

Nippon go (w)o manabitai desŭ ka? Hai, Nippon go (w)o manabitai desŭ.

Nippon go (w)o kakitai desŭ ka? Hai, Nippon go (w)o kakitai desŭ.

Anata wa watakŭshi ni Nippon go de hanashitai desŭ ka? Iie, hanashitakŭ arimasen.
Do you want to speak to me in Japanese? No, I don't.

Anata wa ano otoko no hĭto ni Nippon go de hanashitai desŭ ka? Iie, hanashitakŭ arimasen.

Anata wa ano onna no hĭto ni Nippon go de hanashitai desŭ ka? Iie, hanashitakŭ arimasen.

Anata wa watakŭshidomo ni Nippon go de hanashitai desŭ ka? Iie, hanashitakŭ arimasen.

Anata wa ano otoko no hĭtotachi ni Nippon go de hanashitai desŭ ka? Iie, hanashitakŭ arimasen.

Anata wa Takahashi San ni Nippon go de hanashitai desŭ ka? Iie, hanashitakŭ arimasen.

Anata wa watakŭshidomo to issho ni sumitai desŭ ka? Hai, sumitai desŭ.
Do you want to live with us? Yes, I do.

Anata wa kono hĭto to issho ni sumitai desŭ ka? Hai, sumitai desŭ.

Anata wa kono hĭtotachi to issho ni sumitai desŭ ka? Hai, sumitai desŭ.

Anata wa watakŭshi to issho ni sumitai desŭ ka? Hai, sumitai desŭ.

Anata wa Matsumoto Jirō San to issho ni sumitai desŭ ka? Hai, sumitai desŭ.

Doko ni sumitai desŭ ka? Tōkiō ni sumitai desŭ.
Where do you want to live? I want to live in Tokio.

Doko ni sumitai desŭ ka? Nyū Yōkŭ ni sumitai desŭ.

Doko ni sumitai desŭ ka? Nippon ni sumitai desŭ.

Doko ni sumitai desŭ ka? Shina ni sumitai desŭ.

Doko ni sumitai desŭ ka? Amerika ni sumitai desŭ.

Tōkiō ni sumitai desŭ. Nyū Yōkŭ ni wa sumitakŭ arimasen.
I want to live in Tokio. I don't want to live in New York.

Nyū Yōkŭ ni sumitai desŭ. Tōkiō ni wa sumitakŭ arimasen.

Nippon ni sumitai desŭ. Amerika ni wa sumitakŭ arimasen.

Amerika ni sumitai desŭ. Nippon ni wa sumitakŭ arimasen.

Shina ni sumitai desŭ. Nippon ni wa sumitakŭ arimasen.

Nani (w)o shitai desŭ ka? Nani mo shitakŭ arimasen.
What do you want to do? I don't want to do anything.

Nani (w)o kaitai desŭ ka? Nani mo kaitakŭ arimasen.

Nani (w)o yomitai desŭ ka? Nani mo yomitakŭ arimasen.

Nani (w)o kakitai desŭ ka? Nani mo kakitakŭ arimasen.

Nani (w)o manabitai desŭ ka? Nani mo manabitakŭ arimasen.

Nani (w)o tabetai desŭ ka? Nani mo tabetakŭ arimasen.

Nani (w)o nomitai desŭ ka? Nani mo nomitakŭ arimasen.

Nani (w)o mitai desŭ ka? Nani mo mitakŭ arimasen.

Nani ka tabetai desŭ ka? Hai, nani ka tabetai desŭ.
Do you want to eat something? Yęs, I want to eat something.

Nani ka nomitai desŭ ka? Hai, nani ka nomitai desŭ.

Nani ka hanashitai desŭ ka? Hai, nani ka hanashitai desŭ.

Nani ka kakitai desŭ ka? Hai, nani ka kakitai desŭ.

Nani ka shĭtai desŭ ka? Hai, nani ka shĭtai desŭ.

Nani ka tabetai desŭ ka? Hai, arigatō. Niku to yasai (w)o tabetai desŭ, keredomo sakana wa tabetakŭ arimasen.
Do you want something to eat? Yes, thanks. I want to eat meat and vegetables, but I don't want to eat fish.

Nani ka nomitai desŭ ka? Hai, arigatō. Kōhī to o-cha (w)o nomitai desŭ, keredomo gyūnyū wa nomitakŭ arimasen.

Nani ka kaitai desŭ ka? Hai, kami to empitsu (w)o kaitai desŭ, keredomo fude wa kaitakŭ arimasen.
Nani ka yomitai desŭ ka? Hai, arigatō. Shimbun to zasshi (w)o yomitai desŭ, keredomo tegami wa yomitakŭ arimasen.

Nani ka nomitai desŭ ka? Hai, kōhī de mo o-cha de mo yoroshii, keredomo gyūnyū wa nomitakŭ arimasen.
Do you want something to drink? Yes, either coffee or tea, but I don't want to drink milk.
Nani ka tabetai desŭ ka? Hai, niku de mo tamago de mo yoroshii, keredomo sakana wa tabetakŭ arimasen.
Nani ka yomitai desŭ ka? Hai, zasshi de mo shimbun de mo yoroshii, keredomo hon wa yomitakŭ arimasen.
Nani ka kaitai desŭ ka? Hai, fude de mo pen de mo yoroshii, keredomo empitsu wa kaitakŭ arimasen.

Ima tegami (w)o kakitai desŭ ka? Iie, isogimasŭ kara.
Do you want to write a letter now? No, because I'm in a hurry.
Ima nani ka nomitai desŭ ka? Iie, isogimasŭ kara.
Ima zasshi (w)o yomitai desŭ ka? Iie, isogimasŭ kara.
Ima gohan (w)o tabetai desŭ ka? Iie, isogimasŭ kara.
Ima isu ni kaketai desŭ ka? Iie, isogimasŭ kara.

Anata wa sŭwaritai desŭ ka? Tachitai desŭ ka? Sŭwaritakŭ arimasen.
Do you want to squat or do you want to stand? I don't want to squat.
Anata wa tabetai desŭ ka? Nomitai desŭ ka? Tabetakŭ arimasen.
Anata wa sŭwaritai desŭ ka? Isu ni kaketai desŭ ka? Sŭwaritakŭ arimasen.
Anata wa yomitai desŭ ka? Kakitai desŭ ka? Kakitakŭ arimasen.
Anata wa manabitai desŭ ka? Hon (w)o okuritai desŭ ka? Manabitakŭ arimasen.

Hikōki (w)o kaitai desŭ ka? Iie, hikōki wa kaitakŭ arimasen, keredomo hikōki de tobitai desŭ.
Do you want to buy an airplane? No, I don't want to buy a plane, but I want to fly in a plane.
Pen (w)o kaitai desŭ ka? Iie, pen wa kaitaku arimasen, keredomo fude (w)o kaitai desŭ.
Zasshi (w)o kaitai desŭ ka? Iie, zasshi wa kaitakŭ arimasen, keredomo shimbun (w)o kaitai desŭ.
Kōhī (w)o nomitai desŭ ka? Iie, kōhī wa nomitakŭ arimasen, keredomo o-cha (w)o nomitai desŭ.
Tamago (w)o tabetai desŭ ka? Iie, tamago wa tabetakŭ arimasen, keredomo yasai (w)o tabetai desŭ.

Hikōki (w)o kau koto ga dekimasŭ ka? Hai, dekimasŭ.
Can you buy an airplane? Yes, I can.
Jidōsha (w)o kau koto ga dekimasŭ ka? Hai, dekimasŭ.
Shimbun (w)o kau koto ga dekimasŭ ka? Hai, dekimasŭ.
Gyūnyū (w)o kau koto ga dekimasŭ ka? Hai, dekimasŭ.
Kami (w)o kau koto ga dekimasŭ ka? Hai, dekimasŭ.

Tegami (w)o kaku koto ga dekimasŭ ka? Iie, dekimasen.
Can you write a letter? No, I can't.
Kono jidōsha (w)o mawasu koto ga dekimasŭ ka? Iie, dekimasen.
Ano hĭto (w)o miru koto ga dekimasŭ ka? Iie, dekimasen.
Kono niku (w)o taberu koto ga dekimasŭ ka? Iie, dekimasen.
Kono shimbun (w)o yomu koto ga dekimasŭ ka? Iie, dekimasen.
Kono hikōki de tobu koto ga dekimasŭ ka? Iie, dekimasen.

Ano hikōki (w)o miru koto ga dekimashĭta ka? Hai, dekimashĭta.
Could you see that airplane? Yes, I could.
Ano hon (w)o yomu koto ga dekimashĭta ka? Hai, dekimashĭta.
Ano jidōsha (w)o mawasu koto ga dekimashĭta ka? Hai, dekimashĭta.
Ano tegami (w)o kaku koto ga dekimashĭta ka? Hai, dekimashĭta.
Ano o-cha (w)o nomu koto ga dekimashĭta ka? Hai, dekimashĭta.
Sŭwaru koto ga dekimashĭta ka? Hai, dekimashĭta.
Eigo (w)o hanasu koto ga dekimashĭta ka? Hai, dekimashĭta.

Niku (w)o taberu koto ga dekimasen deshĭta ka? Iie, dekimasen deshĭta.
Couldn't you eat meat? No, I could not.
Nippon go (w)o hanasu koto ga dekimasen deshĭta ka? Iie, dekimasen deshĭta.
Tatsu koto ga dekimasen deshĭta ka? Iie, dekimasen deshĭta.
Hikōki de tobu koto ga dekimasen deshĭta ka? Iie, dekimasen deshĭta.
Jidōsha (w)o mawasu koto ga dekimasen deshĭta ka? Iie, dekimasen deshĭta.
Kōhĭ (w)o nomu koto ga dekimasen deshĭta ka? Iie, dekimasen deshĭta.

Eigo (w)o hanasu koto ga dekimasŭ ka? Hai, sŭkoshi wa dekimasŭ.
Can you speak English? Yes, I can (speak) a little.
Nippon go (w)o hanasu koto ga dekimasŭ ka? Hai, sŭkoshi wa dekimasŭ.
Shina go (w)o hanasu koto ga dekimasŭ ka? Hai, sŭkoshi wa dekimasŭ.

Nippon go (w)o yomu koto ga dekimasŭ ka? Hai, sŭkoshi wa dekimasŭ.
Can you read Japanese? Yes, I can (read) a little.
Eigo (w)o yomu koto ga dekimasŭ ka? Hai, sŭkoshi wa dekimasŭ.
Shina go (w)o yomu koto ga dekimasŭ ka? Hai, sŭkoshi wa dekimasŭ.

Shina go (w)o kaku koto ga dekimasen ka? Iie, Nippon go mo Shina go mo kaku koto ga dekimasen.
Can't you write Chinese? No, I can't write either Japanese or Chinese.
Eigo (w)o kaku koto ga dekimasen ka? Iie, Eigo mo Nippon go mo kaku koto ga dekimasen.

Naze kono shimbun (w)o yomitakŭ arimasen ka? Nippon go (w)o yomu koto ga dekimasen kara.
Why don't you want to read this newspaper? Because I can't read Japanese.
Naze kono tegami (w)o kakitakŭ arimasen ka? Tegami (w)o kaku koto ga dekimasen kara.
Naze sŭwaritakŭ arimasen ka? Sŭwaru koto ga dekimasen kara.
Naze kono jidōsha (w)o mawashitakŭ arimasen ka? Jidōsha (w)o mawasu koto ga dekimasen kara.
Naze kono hikōki de tobitakŭ arimasen ka? Hikōki de tobu koto ga dekimasen kara.

Naze Nippon go (w)o manabitai desŭ ka? Watakŭshi wa Nippon go de hanashitai desŭ kara.
Why do you want to study Japanese? Because I want to speak Japanese.
Naze ano isu ni kaketai desŭ ka? Watakŭshi wa sŭwaru koto ga dekimasen kara.
Naze sakana (w)o tabetai desŭ ka? Watakŭshi wa niku (w)o taberu koto ga dekimasen kara.
Naze gyūnyū (w)o nomitai desŭ ka? Watakŭshi wa kōhī (w)o nomu koto ga dekimasen kara.

Naze Nippon go (w)o manabitai deshĭta ka? Watakŭshi wa Nippon go de hanashitai deshĭta kara.
Why did you want to study Japanese? Because I wanted to speak Japanese.
Naze gyūnyū (w)o nomitai deshĭta ka? Watakŭshi wa kōhī (w)o nomu koto ga dekimasen deshĭta kara.
Naze sakana (w)o tabetai deshĭta ka? Watakŭshi wa niku (w)o taberu koto ga dekimasen deshĭta kara.
Naze ano isu ni kaketai deshĭta ka? Watakŭshi wa suwaru koto ga dekimasen deshĭta kara.

Naze ano jidōsha (w)o mawashitakŭ arimasen deshĭta ka? Watakŭshi no jidōsha ja arimasen deshĭta kara.
Why didn't you want to drive that auto? Because it wasn't my automobile.
Naze Nippon go de hanashitakŭ arimasen deshĭta ka? Watakŭshi wa Nippon go wa dekimasen deshĭta kara.
Naze sono hikōki de tobitakŭ arimasen deshĭta ka? Watakŭshi wa hikōki de tobu koto ga dekimasen deshĭta kara.
Naze sŭwaritakŭ arimasen deshĭta ka? Watakŭshi wa sŭwaru koto ga dekimasen deshĭta kara.

Naze kōhī (w)o nomitakŭ arimasen deshĭta ka? Watakŭshi wa kōhī (w)o nomu koto ga dekimasen deshĭta kara.
Naze niku (w)o tabetakŭ arimasen deshĭta ka? Watakŭshi wa niku (w)o taberu koto ga dekimasen deshĭta kara.

Ima wa nani mo suru koto ga dekimasen.
I can't do anything now.
Ima wa nani mo taberu koto ga dekimasen.
Ima wa nani mo yomu koto ga dekimasen.
Ima wa nani mo kaku koto ga dekimasen.
Ima wa nani mo miru koto ga dekimasen.
Ima wa nani mo kau koto ga dekimasen.
Ima wa nani mo hanasu koto ga dekimasen.
Ima wa nani mo okuru koto ga dekimasen.
Ima wa nani mo watasu koto ga dekimasen.
Ima wa nani mo manabu koto ga dekimasen.

Sŭkoshi isogu koto ga dekimasŭ ka? Hai, dekimasŭ.
Can you hurry a little? Yes, I can.
Sŭkoshi yomu koto ga dekimasŭ ka? Hai, dekimasŭ.
Sŭkoshi manabu koto ga dekimasŭ ka? Hai, dekimasŭ.
Sŭkoshi taberu koto ga dekimasŭ ka? Hai, dekimasŭ.
Sŭkoshi nomu koto ga dekimasŭ ka? Hai, dekimasŭ.
Sŭkoshi kaku koto ga dekimasŭ ka? Hai, dekimasŭ.
Sŭkoshi hanasu koto ga dekimasŭ ka? Hai, dekimasŭ.

Watakŭshidomo Amerika-jin wa Eigo (w)o hanashimasŭ.
We Americans speak English.
Anatagata Nippon-jin wa Nippon go (w)o hanashimasŭ.
Anatagata Shina-jin wa Shina go (w)o hanashimasŭ.
Watakŭshidomo Amerika-jin wa Shina go wa hanashimasen.
Anatagata Nippon jin wa Shina go wa hanashimasen.
Anatagata Shina jin wa Nippon go wa hanashimasen.

Anatagata Amerika-jin wa Eigo (w)o hanashimasŭ. Watakŭshidomo Nippon-jin mo hanashimasŭ.
You Americans speak English. We Japanese also speak (it).
Anatagata Shina-jin wa Shina go (w)o hanashimasŭ. Watakŭshidomo Nippon-jin mo hanashimasŭ.
Anatagata Nippon-jin wa Nippon go (w)o hanashimasŭ. Watakŭshidomo Amerika-jin mo hanashimasŭ.

Anatagata Nippon-jin wa Shina go wa hanashimasen. Watakŭshidomo Amerika-jin mo hanashimasen.

You Japanese do not speak Chinese. We Americans do not speak (it) either.

Anatagata Shina-jin wa Eigo wa hanashimasen. Watakŭshidomo Nippon-jin mo hanashimasen.

Anatagata Amerika-jin wa Nippon go wa hanashimasen. Watakŭshidomo Shina-jin mo hanashimasen.

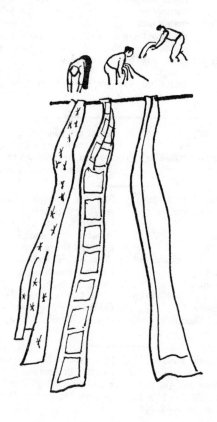

5 Dai Go K(w)a (Lesson V)

akeru open
arau wash
benjo toilet, latrine, W. C.
dōzo please
e to
hairu enter
ichi-do once, one time
ii good
iu *verb* say
ikemasen *pot.* of iku
imasŭ *pres.* of iru
kashĭkomarimashĭta all right, willingly (acceding to a request)

katakana *one of the Japanese syllabaries*
koko here
kudasai please, please give (me)
kuru come
mado window
matawa or
matsu wait
mŏ once more
motsu have, hold
motte kuru bring (come, having)
motte iku take (go, having)
renshū exercise

shimeru shut, close
shĭtsŭrei impoliteness
sumu live
takŭsan much, many
te hand
to door
tsugi next
tsuite following; —iku follow (there),—kuru follow (here)
tsurete accompanying; —iku take (conduct), —kuru bring (a person)
yukkuri slowly, deliberately
wakaru understand

Nani (w)o tabete[30] imasŭ ka?
Niku to yasai (w)o tabete imasŭ.[31]
Watakŭshi no hon (w)o mite[30] imasŭ ka?
Iie, nani mo mite imasen.[31]

What are you eating?
I am eating meat and vegetables.
Do you see my book?
No, I don't see anything.

---

5 Takahashi Jirō San, dōzo tatte kudasai,[32] soshĭte Nihon go de hanashĭte kudasai.
Kashĭkomarimashĭta.
Nani (w)o shĭte imasŭ ka?
Nani mo shĭte imasen.
10 Anata wa te ni nani (w)o motte imasŭ ka?
Empitsŭ (w)o motte imasŭ.
Koko e motte kite[37] kudasai.
Anata wa hon ni nani ka kaite imashĭta[31] ka?
Nani mo kaite imasen deshĭta.[31]
15 Anata no tomodachi e[33] kono hon (w)o motte itte[37] kudasai.

Mr. Jiro Takahashi, please stand up and speak in Japanese.
Certainly. With pleasure.
What are you doing?
I am not doing anything.
What do you have in your hand?
I have a pencil.
Bring (it) here.
Were you writing something in the book?
I wasn't writing anything.
Please take this book to your friend.

Sŭkoshi Nihon go (w)o yonde[30] kudasai. Mŏ sore de takŭsan desŭ. Watakŭshi ni wa wakarimasen deshĭta.[34] Nani go (w)o yonde
20 imashĭta ka? Eigo wo yonde imashĭta ka? Matawa nihon go wo yonde imashĭta ka?
Shĭtsŭrei shimashĭta.
Mŏ ichi-do yukkuri yonde kudasai.
Nani (w)o itte[30] imashĭta ka?
25 Nani mo itte imasen deshĭta.
Anata wa tomodachi ni nani (w)o itte imashĭta ka?

Please read a little Japanese. That's enough.
I didn't understand (you). What language were you reading? Were you reading English or were you reading Japanese?

I am sorry.
Please read once more slowly.
What were you saying?
I didn't say anything.
What were you saying to your friend?

26

Mado (w)o akete mo[35] ii n' desŭ ka?
May I open the window?

Hai, akete mo ii n' desŭ, keredomo to (w)o shimete wa ikemasen.[36]
Yes, you may open (it), but you must not close the door.

30 Sŭwatte kudasai.
Please sit down.

Katakana de tsugi no renshū (w)o kaite kudasai.
Please write the next exercise in *katakana*.

Te (w)o aratte mo ii n' desŭ ka?
May I wash (my) hands?

Hai, aratte mo ii n' desŭ.
Yes, you may wash (them).

35 Watakŭshi (w)o benjo e tsurete itte[37] kudasai.
Please take me to the lavatory.

Dōzo tomodachi (w)o tsurete[37] kite kudasai.
Please bring a friend.

Ano hĭto ni tsuite itte[37] kudasai.
Please follow him.

Watakŭshi ni tsuite[37] kite kudasai.
Please follow me.

40 Haitte[30] mo ii n' desŭ ka?
May I come in?

Iie, ima haitte wa ikemasen. Sŭkoshi matte[30] kudasai.
No, you mustn't enter now. Please wait a little.

Anata wa doko ni sunde[30] imasŭ ka?
Where do you live?

Tokio ni sunde imasŭ soshĭte anata wa?
I am living in Tokio, and you?

Watakŭshi wa Nyū Yōkŭ ni[14] sunde imashĭta, keredomo ima wa Chicago ni sunde imasŭ.
I used to live in New York, but now I am living in Chicago.

Anata wa isoide[30] imasŭ ka?
Are you in a hurry?

Iie, isoide wa imasen.
No, I am not in a hurry.

Exercises

Nani (w)o tabete imasŭ ka? Niku to yasai (w)o tabete imasŭ.
What are you eating! I am eating meat and vegetables.

Nani (w)o yonde imasŭ ka? Shimbun to zasshi (w)o yonde imasŭ.

Nani (w)o nonde imasŭ ka? O-cha to kōhĭ (w)o nonde imasŭ.

Nani (w)o kaite imasŭ ka? Tegami to renshū (w)o kaite imasŭ.

Nani (w)o shimete imasŭ ka? Mado to to (w)o shimete imasŭ.

Nani (w)o akete imasŭ ka? Hon to zasshi (w)o akete imasŭ.

Watakŭshi no hon (w)o mite imasŭ ka? Iie, nani mo mite imasen.
Do you see my book? No, I don't see anything.

Watakŭshi no niku (w)o tabete imasŭ ka? Iie, nani mo tabete imasen.

Watakŭshi no renshū (w)o manande imasŭ ka? Iie, nani mo manande imasen.

Watakŭshi no shimbun (w)o yonde imasŭ ka? Iie, nani mo yonde imasen.

To (w)o shimete imasŭ ka? Iie, nani mo shimete imasen.

Mado (w)o akete imasŭ ka? Iie, nani mo akete imasen.

Takahashi Jirō San! Dōzo tatte kudasai sōshĭte Nippon go de hanashĭte kudasai.
Mr. Jiro Takahashi! Please stand up and speak in Japanese.

Matsumoto Jirō San! Dōzo tatte kudasai sōshĭte Eigo de hanashĭte kudasai.
Jones San! Dōzo isu ni kakete kudasai sōshĭte Nippon go no tegami (w)o yonde kudasai.
Harris San! Dōzo suwatte kudasai sōshĭte Shina go (w)o kaite kudasai.,

Nani (w)o shĭte imasŭ ka? Nani mo shĭte imasen.
What are you doing? I am not doing anything.

Nani (w)o aratte imasŭ ka? Nani mo aratte imasen.
Nani (w)o akete imasŭ ka? Nani mo akete imasen.
Nani (w)o shimete imasŭ ka? Nani mo shimete imasen.
Nani (w)o tabete imasŭ ka? Nani mo tabete imasen.
Nani (w)o itte imasŭ ka? Nani mo itte imasen.
Nani (w)o yonde imasŭ ka? Nani mo yonde imasen.

Anata wa te ni nani (w)o motte imasŭ ka? Empitsŭ (w)o motte imasŭ.
What do you have in your hand? I have a pencil.

Anata wa te ni nani (w)o motte imasŭ ka? Fude (w)o motte imasŭ.
Anata wa te ni nani (w)o motte imasŭ ka? Pen (w)o motte imasŭ.
Anata wa te ni nani (w)o motte imasŭ ka? Kami (w)o motte imasŭ.
Anata wa te ni nani (w)o motte imasŭ ka? Shimbun (w)o motte imasŭ.

Anata wa nani ka kaite imashĭta ka? Nani mo kaite wa imasen deshĭta.
Were you writing something? I wasn't writing anything.

Anata wa nani ka yonde imashĭta ka? Nani mo yonde wa imasen deshĭta.
Anata wa nani ka tabete imashĭta ka? Nani mo tabete wa imasen deshĭta.
Anata wa nani ka itte imashĭta ka? Nani mo itte wa imasen deshĭta.
Anata wa nani ka nonde imashĭta ka? Nani mo nonde wa imasen deshĭta.

Anata no tomodachi e kono hon (w)o motte itte kudasai.
Please take this book to your friend.

Matsumoto San e kono zasshi (w)o motte itte kudasai.
Takahashi San e kono fude (w)o motte itte kudasai.
Watakŭshi no tomodachi e kono tegami (w)o motte itte kudasai.
Ano otoko no hĭto e kono gyūnyū (w)o motte itte kudasai.

Ano hon (w)o motte kite kudasai.
Please bring that book.

Ano tamago (w)o motte kite kudasai.
Ano empitsu (w)o motte kite kudasai.
Ano pen (w)o motte kite kudasai.
Ano kami (w)o motte kite kudasai.

Sŭkoshi Nippon go (w)o yonde kudasai.
Please read a little Japanese.

Sŭkoshi Eigo (w)o yonde kudasai.

Sŭkoshi Shina go (w)o yonde kudasai.

Sŭkoshi Nippon go (w)o hanashĭte kudasai.

Sŭkoshi Nippon go (w)o kaite kudasai.

Watakŭshi wa wakarimasen deshĭta. Nippon go wa wakarimasen.

I didn't understand. I don't understand Japanese.

Watakŭshi wa wakarimasen deshĭta. Eigo wa wakarimasen.

Watakŭshi wa wakarimasen deshĭta. Shina go wa wakarimasen.

Watakŭshi wa wakarimasen deshĭta. Katakana de kaite kudasai.

Eigo (w)o yonde imashĭta ka matawa Nippon go (w)o yonde imashĭta ka?

Were you reading Japanese or were you reading English?

Shina go (w)o hanashĭte imashĭta ka matawa Nippon go (w)o hanashĭte imashĭta ka?

Shina go (w)o kaite imashĭta ka matawa Nippon go (w)o kaite imashĭta ka?

Nippon go (w)o manande imashĭta ka matawa Shina go (w)o manande imashĭta ka?

Watakŭshi ni wa wakarimasen deshĭta. Mō ichido yukkuri yonde kudasai.

I did not understand. Please read once more slowly.

Watakŭshi ni wa wakarimasen deshĭta. Mō ichido yukkuri hanashite kudasai.

Watakŭshi ni wa wakarimasen deshĭta. Mō ichido kaite kudasai.

Mō ichido tatte kudasai.

Please stand up again.   Mō ichido watakŭshi ni tsuite kite kudasai.

Mō ichido suwatte kudasai.   Mō ichido koko e kite kudasai.

Nani (w)o itte imashĭta ka? Nani mo itte imasen deshĭta.

What were you saying? I wasn't saying anything.

Nani (w)o shĭte imashĭta ka? Nani mo shĭte imasen deshĭta.

Nani (w)o mite imashĭta ka? Nani mo mite imasen deshĭta.

Nani (w)o aratte imashĭta ka? Nani mo aratte imasen deshĭta.

Nani (w)o motte kite imashĭta ka? Nani mo motte kite imasen deshĭta.

Nani (w)o motte itte imashĭta ka? Nani mo motte itte imasen deshĭta.

Anata wa tomodachi ni nani (w)o itte imashĭta ka?

What were you saying to your friend?

Anata wa tomodachi ni nani (w)o kaite imashĭta ka?

Anata wa Matsumoto San ni nani (w)o okutte imashĭta ka?

Anata wa Takahashi San ni nani (w)o watashĭte imashĭta ka?

Mado (w)o akete mo, ii n' desŭ ka? Hai, akete mo, ii n' desŭ.

May I open the window? Yes, you may open (it).

To (w)o shimete mo, ii n' desŭ ka? Hai, shimete mo, ii n' desŭ.

Tegami (w)o kaite mo, ii n' desŭ ka? Hai, kaite mo, ii n' desŭ.

Renshū (w)o manande mo, ii n' desŭ ka? Hai, manande mo, ii n' desŭ.

Sŭwatte mo, ii n' desŭ ka? Hai, sŭwatte mo, ii n' desŭ.

Haitte mo, ii n' desŭ ka? Hai, haitte mo, ii n' desŭ.

Ima hiruhan (w)o tabete mo, ii n' desŭ ka? Hai, tabete mo, ii n' desŭ.

To (w)o shimete wa ikemasen.
You must not close the door.

Mado (w)o akete wa ikemasen.
Isu ni kakete wa ikemasen.
Ima aratte wa ikemasen.
Ano hon (w)o yonde wa ikemasen.
Ano o-cha (w)o nonde wa ikemasen.
Isoide wa ikemasen.
Eigo (w)o hanashīte wa ikemasen.
Haite wa ikemasen.

Sŭwatte kudasai.
Please sit down (Japanese fashion).

Isu ni kakete kudasai.
Tatte kudasai.
Haitte kudasai.
Isoide kudasai.
Aratte kudasai.
Tsuite kite kudasai.
Kono jidōsha (w)o mawashīte kudasai.
Ano hikōki de tonde kudasai.

Watakŭshi (w)o benjo e tsurete itte kudasai.
Please take me to the washroom.

Watakŭshi (w)o jidōsha e tsurete itte kudasai.
Watakŭshi (w)o hikōki e tsurete itte kudasai.
Ano hīto (w)o otoko no benjo e tsurete itte kudasai.
Ano onna no hīto (w)o onna no benjo e tsurete itte kudasai.

Nani (w)o shīte imashīta ka? Tomodachi (w)o jidōsha e tsurete itte imashīta.
What were you doing? I was taking my friend to the automobile.

Nani (w)o shīte imashīta ka? Ano otoko no hito (w)o benjo e tsurete itte imashīta.
Nani (w)o shīte imashīta ka? Matsumoto San (w)o hikōki e tsurete itte imashīta.
Nani (w)o shīte imashīta ka? Ano onna no hīto (w)o jidōsha e tsurete itte imashīta.

Anata wa tomodachi (w)o tsurete kite kudasai.
Please bring your friend.

Takahashi San (w)o tsurete kite kudasai.
Kono Nippon-jin (w)o tsurete kite kudasai.
Ano Shina-jin (w)o tsurete kite kudasai.
Ano onna no hito (w)o tsurete kite kudasai.

Dare (w)o tsurete kimashīta ka? Matsumoto San (w)o tsurete kimashīta.
Whom did you bring? I brought Mr. Matsumoto.

Dare (w)o tsurete kimashīta ka? Takahashi San (w)o tsurete kimashīta
Dare (w)o tsurete kimashīta ka? Tomodachi (w)o tsurete kimashīta.
Dare (w)o tsurete kimashīta ka? Nippon-jin (w)o tsurete kimashīta.

Watakŭshi ni tsuite kite kudasai.
Please follow me.

Ano otoko no hīto ni tsuite itte kudasai.
Ano onna no hīto ni tsuite itte kudasai.
Ano Nippon-jin ni tsuite itte kudasai.
Takahashi San ni tsuite itte kudasai.

Doko e ikimashïta ka? Ano Amerika-jin ni tsuite ikimashïta.
Where did you go? I followed that American.

Doko e ikimashïta ka? Ano otoko no hïto ni tsuite ikimashïta.

Doko e ikimashïta ka? Takahashi Jirō ni tsuite ikimashïta.

Doko e ikimashïta ka? Tomodachi ni tsuite ikimashïta.

Haitte mo, ii n' desŭ ka? Iie, ima haitte wa ikemasen. Sŭkoshi matte kudasai.
May I come in? No, you must not come in now. Please wait a little.

Itte mo, ii n' desŭ ka? Iie, ima itte wa ikemasen. Sŭkoshi matte kudasai.

Kite mo, ii n' desŭ ka? Iie, ima kite wa ikemasen. Sŭkoshi matte kudasai.

Tomodachi (w)o tsurete itte mo, ii n' desŭ ka? Iie, ima tsurete itte wa ikemasen. Sŭkoshi matte kudasai.

Takahashi San ni tsuite itte mo, ii n' desŭ ka? Iie, ima tsuite itte wa ikemasen. Sŭkoshi matte kudasai.

Anata wa doko ni sunde imasŭ ka? Tōkiō ni sunde imasŭ.
Where do you live? I live in Tokio.

Anata no tomodachi wa doko ni sunde imasŭ ka? Ōsaka ni sunde imasŭ.

Takahashi San wa doko ni sunde imasŭ ka? Nagasaki ni sunde imasŭ.

Ano otoko no hïtotachi wa doko ni sunde imasŭ ka? Yokohama ni sunde imasŭ.

Ano onna no hïtotachi wa doko ni sunde imasŭ ka? Nyū Yōkŭ ni sunde imasŭ.

Watakŭshi wa Nyū Yōkŭ ni sunde imashïta keredomo ima wa Shikago ni sunde imasŭ.
I used to live in New York, but now I am living in Chicago.

Ano otoko no hïto wa Yokohama ni sunde imashïta keredomo ima wa Tōkiō ni sunde imasŭ.

Ano onna no hïto wa Ōsaka ni sunde imashïta keredomo ima wa Nagasaki ni sunde imasŭ.

Watakŭshidomo wa Amerika ni sunde imashïta keredomo ima wa Nippon ni sunde imasŭ.

Anata wa isoide imasŭ ka? Iie, isoide wa imasen.
Are you in a hurry? No, I am not in a hurry.

Anata wa kaite imasŭ ka? Iie, kaite wa imasen.

Ano hïtotachi wa yonde imasŭ ka? Iie, yonde wa imasen.

Matsumoto San wa tabete imasŭ ka? Iie, tabete wa imasen.

Ano hïto wa manande imasŭ ka? Iie, manande wa imasen.

Anata wa tegami (w)o kaite imashïta ka? Iie, tegami wa kaite imasen deshïta.
Were you writing a letter? No, I wasn't writing a letter.

Anata wa shimbun (w)o yonde imashïta ka? Iie, shimbun wa yonde imasen deshïta.

Anata wa shimbun (w)o yonde imasŭ ka? Iie, shimbun wa yonde imasen.
Are you reading the newspaper? No, I'm not reading the paper.

Anata wa tegami (w)o kaite imasŭ ka? Iie, tegami wa kaite imasen.

Dai Rokk(w)a (Lesson VI)

hikui short, low	**okāsan** mother	**shĭkakŭ** square
kanai (my) wife	**ōkii** big, large	**shĭkan** officer (military)
kirei (na) beautiful	**okŭsan, okŭsama** (your) wife,	**shujin** master of the house,
marui round	madam	husband
nagai long	**otōsan** father	**tōi** far, distant
oishii tasty	**sei** stature	**yori** than, from

Gomen kudasai. Go-shujin[38] wa o-taku[38] desŭ ka?

Excuse me. Is the master of the house in?

Hai, irasshaimasŭ.[38] Anata wa donata de[39] gozaimasŭ[38] ka?

Yes, he is. Who are you?

5 Watakŭshi wa Buraun to[15] mōshimasŭ.

My name is Brown.

Sŭkoshi o-machi[38] kudasai. Sugu o-yobi[40] itashimasŭ[38] kara.

Please wait a moment for I'll call him at once.

Komban wa. O-matase[93] itashimashĭta.

Good evening. (I'm sorry) I made you wait.

Dōzo o-agari[41] kudasai.

Please come in.

10 Buraun Sama, watakŭshi no kanai[38] ni shōkai itashimashō.[50]

Mr. Brown, (may) I present my wife?

Hajimete o-me ni kakarimasŭ.[42]

I am pleased to meet you.

Dōzo yoroshikŭ o-negai itashimasŭ.[40]

I am very glad to know you.

Dōzo yoroshikŭ o-negai itashimasŭ. Ikaga de 15 gozaimasŭ ka?

Likewise. How are you?

Arigatō gozaimasŭ.

Fine, thank you.

Buraun San wa Amerika no[43] rikugun no shĭkan de,[44] Nyŭ Yōkŭ kara[45] o-ide ni narimashĭta.[38]

Mr. Brown is an American army officer and comes from New York.

20 Sō de gozaimasŭ ka? Anata no okŭsama[38] wa ima dochira ni irasshaimasŭ ka?

Is that so? Where is your wife now?

Tōkiō ni watakŭshi to issho ni[46] sunde imasŭ.

She is living with me in Tokio.

Takahashi San, ano shashin wa anata no 25 otōsan desŭ ka?

Mrs. Takahashi, is that your father's picture?

Hai, sō desŭ. Otōsan to okāsan wa ima Ōsaka e kembutsŭ ni itte imasŭ.

Yes, it is. My father and mother have now gone to Osaka to (go) sightseeing.

Ōsaka wa koko kara tōi[43] desŭ ka?

Is Osaka far from here?

Iie, amari tōkŭ[43] arimasen.

No, it isn't very far.

30 Koko kara Ōsaka e wa Kōbe e iku yori[47] tōi desŭ ka?

Is Osaka farther from here than Kobe?

Iie, Kōbe e yuku hodo[47] tōkŭ arimasen.

No, it's not as far as Kobe.

Anata wa kirei na[43] o-taku ni sunde imasŭ ne.[48]

You certainly live in a beautiful house.

35 Iie, sō de mo[24] gozaimasen. Kono uchi wa sŭkoshi chiisai desŭ kara, motto ōkii[47] uchi ga hoshii[21] desŭ ga . . .[5]

No, not at all. As this house is a little small, I want a bigger house.

32

O-taku wa kono atari de ichiban[47] ōkii desŭ ne.

Your home is the largest in this neighborhood, isn't it?

40 Iie, sō de mo arimasen.

No, not at all.

Kono uchi wa amari ōkiku mo chiisakŭ mo[24] gozaimasen. Anata ni wa[49] okosan ga arimasŭ ka?

This house is neither too big nor too small. Do you have any children?

Hai, musŭko to musŭme ga gozaimasŭ. 45 Musŭko wa kekkon shĭte,[50] watashidomo[11] to issho ni sunde imasŭ.

Yes, I have a son and a daughter. My son is married and he lives with us.

Musŭko wa sŭkoshi sei ga hikui desŭ ga musŭme hodo[47] hikukŭ arimasen.

My son is somewhat short, but he is not so short as my daughter.

Hanako San, sono shĭkakŭ no o-kashi no 50 hako (w)o motte kite kudasai.

Miss Hanako, please bring me that square candy box.

Okāsan, kono hako wa shĭkakŭ ja[39] arimasen. Shĭkakŭ no hako wa kara deshĭta kara, kono marui hako (w)o motte mairimashĭta.[38]

Mother, this box is not square. As the square box was empty, I brought this round box.

Amari oishikŭ arimasen ga, dōzo o-agari[41] 55 kudasai.

They are not very tasty, but please have some.

Arigatō gozaimasŭ.

Thank you very much.

Takahashi San, taihen nagai (w)o shĭte, shĭtsŭrei shimashĭta.

Mrs. Takahashi, I (stayed) very long and was impolite.

Mata dōzo chikai uchi ni o-ide kudasai.

Please come again soon.

60 Sayōnara.[89]

Goodbye.

Exercises

Gomen kudasai. Go-shujin wa o-taku desŭ ka?

Excuse me. Is the master of the house in?

Gomen kudasai. Brown San wa o-taku desŭ ka?

Gomen kudasai. Anata no okŭsan wa o-taku desŭ ka?

Gomen kudasai. Anata no musŭko San wa o-taku desŭ ka?

Gomen kudasai. Anata no musŭme San wa o-taku desŭ ka?

Anata wa donata de gozaimasŭ ka? Watakŭshi wa Brown to mōshimasŭ.

Who are you? My name is (Mr.) Brown.

Anata wa donata de gozaimasŭ ka? Watakŭshi wa Takahashi to mōshimasŭ.

Ano otoko no hĭto wa donata de gozaimasŭ ka? Ano hĭto wa Matsumoto San to mōshimasŭ.

Ano onna no hĭtotachi wa donata de gozaimasŭ ka? Ano hĭtotachi wa Jane Jones to Mary Harris to mōshimasŭ.

Ano rikugun no shĭkan wa donata de gozaimashĭta ka? Ano shĭkan wa White San to Stone San de gozaimashĭta.

Sŭkoshi o-machi kudasai.

Please wait a little.

Sŭkoshi o-hanashi kudasai.
Sŭkoshi o-yomi kudasai.
Sŭkoshi o-kaki kudasai.
Sŭkoshi o-agari kudasai.

Dōzo o-agari kudasai.
Please come in. (come up)

Dōzo o-hanashi kudasai.
Dōzo o-hairi kudasai.
Dōzo o-ide kudasai.
Dōzo o-kake kudasai.
Dōzo o-tachi kudasai.

Brown San, watakŭshi no kanai ni shōkai itashimasŭ.
Mr. Brown, I (want to) present you to my wife.

Takahashi San, watakŭshi no shujin ni shōkai itashimasŭ.
Matsumoto San, watakŭshi no musŭko (w)o anata ni shōkai itashimasŭ.
White San, watakŭshi no musŭme (w)o anata ni shōkai itashimasŭ.
Jones San, watakŭshi no otōsan ni shōkai itashimasŭ.
Harris San, watakŭshi no tomodachi no Yamamoto San ni shōkai itashimasŭ.

Anata no shujin ni Tōkiō de hajimete o-me ni kakarimashĭta.
I met your husband in Tokio.

Anata no musŭko San ni Nyū Yōkŭ de hajimete o-me ni kakarimashĭta.
Ano otoko no hĭto no otōsan ni Ōsaka de hajimete o-me ni kakarimashĭta.
Ano onna no hĭto no okāsan ni Yokohama de hajimete o-me ni kakarimashĭta.
Takahashi San ni Amerika de hajimete o-me ni kakarimashĭta.

Dōzo okŭsan ni yoroshikŭ itte kudasai.
Please remember me to your wife.

Dōzo otōsan ni yoroshikŭ kudasai.
Dōzo shujin ni yoroshikŭ kudasai.
Dōzo okāsan ni yoroshikŭ kudasai.
Dōzo Matsumoto San ni yoroshikŭ kudasai.

Brown San wa Amerika no rikugun no shĭkan de, Nyū Yōkŭ kara o-ide ni narimashĭta.
Mr. Brown is an American army officer and he comes from New York.

Takahashi San wa Nippon-jin de, Kōbe kara o-ide ni narimashĭta.
White San wa Amerika no shĭkan de, Nippon‧go (w)o manande irasshaimasŭ.
Harris San wa Nippon go (w)o manande, hon (w)o kaite irasshaimasŭ.
Matsumoto San wa to (w)o akete, Shina go de hanashĭte imasŭ.
Ano hĭto wa hiruhan (w)o tabete, o-cha (w)o nonde irasshaimasŭ.
Watakŭshi wa Ōsaka e itte, anata no okāsan ni o-me ni kakarimashĭta.

Anata no okŭsan wa ima dochira ni irasshaimasŭ ka? Tōkiō ni watakŭshi to issho ni sunde imasŭ.

Where is your wife now? She is living with me in Tokio.

Anata no shujin wa ima dochira ni irasshaimasŭ ka? Nyū Yōkŭ ni tomodachi to issho ni sunde imasŭ.

Anata no musŭme San wa ima dochira ni irasshaimasŭ ka? Kōbe ni watakŭshi no okāsan to issho ni sunde imasŭ.

Ano hĭto no otōsan wa ima dochira ni irasshaimasŭ ka? Kyōto ni musŭko to issho ni sunde imasŭ.

Ano onna no hĭto no musŭme San wa ima dochira ni irasshaimasŭ ka? Ano hĭto to issho ni sunde imasŭ.

Takahashi San, ano shashin wa anata no otōsan desŭ ka? Hai, sō desŭ.

Mr. Takahashi, is that your father's picture? Yes, it is.

Matsumoto San, kono shashin wa anata no okāsan desŭ ka? Hai, sō desŭ.

Brown San, sono shashin wa Stone San no musŭko San desŭ ka? Hai, sō desŭ.

Yamamoto San, ano shashin wa anata no okŭsan desŭ ka? Hai, sō desŭ.

Otōsan to okāsan wa ima Ōsaka e kembutsu ni itte imasŭ.

My father and mother have now gone to Osaka in order to go sightseeing.

Musŭko to musŭme wa Kyōto e kembutsu ni itte imashĭta.

Kanai wa Nihon e nihon go (w)o manabi ni itte imasŭ.

Watakŭshi wa Tōkiō e kembutsu ni kimashĭta.

Watakŭshi wa Tōkiō e Nippon go (w)o manabi ni kimashĭta.

Ano hĭto wa uchi e tegami (w)o kaki ni kaerimashĭta.

Kōbe e jidōsha (w)o kai ni ikimashĭta.

Kinō koko e shimbun (w)o yomi ni kimashĭta.

Watakŭshi wa hiruhan (w)o tabe ni koko e kimashĭta.

Tomodachi no uchi e shashin (w)o mi ni ikimashĭta.

Ōsaka wa koko kara tōi desŭ ka? Iie, amari tōkŭ arimasen.

Is Osaka far from here? No, it's not very far.

Kono empitsŭ wa nagai desŭ ka? Iie, amari nagakŭ arimasen.

Anata no musŭme San wa sei ga hikui desŭ ka? Iie, amari hikukŭ arimasen.

Kono o-kashi wa oishii desŭ ka? Iie, amari oishikŭ arimasen.

Ano hako wa kara desŭ ka? Iie, kara ja arimasen.

Koko kara Ōsaka e wa Kōbe e yuku yori tōi desŭ ka? Iie, Kōbe e iku hodo tōkŭ arimasen.

Is Osaka farther from here than Kobe? No, it is not so far as Kobe.

Koko kara anata no o-taku e wa ano otoko no hĭto no uchi e iku hodo chikakŭ arimasen.

Anata no fude wa Matsumoto San no yori nagai desŭ ka? Iie, ano hĭto no fude hodo nagakŭ arimasen.

Takahashi San no okŭsan wa Brown San no musŭme San yori sei ga hikui desŭ ka? Iie, ano hĭto no musŭme San hodo sei wa hikukŭ arimasen.

Kono hako wa sono hako yori ōkii desŭ ka? Iie, sono hako hodo ōkikŭ arimasen.

Anata wa kirei na o-taku ni sunde imasŭ ne. Iie, sō de mo gozaimasen.

You live in a beautiful house, I must say. No, not at all.

Anata wa chiisai o-taku ni sunde imasŭ ne. Hai, sō de gozaimasŭ.

Anata wa ōkii o-taku ni sunde imasŭ ne. Iie, sō de mo gozaimasen.

Anata ni wa ōkii musŭko San ga arimasŭ ne. Hai, sō de gozaimasŭ.

Kono uchi wa sŭkoshi chiisai desŭ kara, motto ōkii uchi ga hoshii desŭ ga . . .

As this house is a bit small, I want a bigger home and . . .

Kono shashin wa sŭkoshi ōkii desŭ kara, motto chiisai shashin ga hoshii desŭ ga . . .

Kono o-kashi wa amari oishikŭ arimasen kara, motto oishii o-kashi ga hoshii desŭ ga . . .

Yokohama wa sŭkoshi tōi desŭ kara, motto chikai machi e ikitai desŭ.

Kono hako wa amari kirei ja arimasen kara, motto kirei na hako ga hoshii desŭ ga . . .

O-taku wa kono atari de ichiban ōkii desŭ ne.

Your home is the largest in this neighborhood, isn't it?

Kono empitsŭ wa ichiban nagai desŭ ne?

Kono otoko no hĭto wa sei ga ichiban hikui desŭ ne.

Kono hako wa ichiban chiisai desŭ ne.

Kono uchi wa amari ōkikŭ mo chiisaku mo gozaimasen.

This house is neither too big nor too small.

Ano hĭto no uchi wa amari tōkŭ mo chikakŭ mo gozaimasen.

Kono hako wa amari ōkikŭ mo chiisakŭ mo gozaimasen.

Anata ni wa okosan ga arimasŭ ka? Hai, musŭko to musŭme ga gozaimasŭ.

Do you have any children? Yes, I have a son and daughter.

Anata ni wa okŭsan ga arimasŭ ka? Hai, kanai ga arimasŭ.

Anata ni wa ane* san ga arimasŭ ka? Hai, ane san ga arimasŭ.

Watakŭshidomo wa issho ni sunde imasŭ.

We live together.

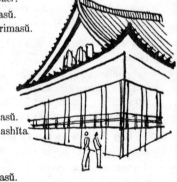

Watakŭshidomo wa issho ni sunde imashĭta.

Ano hĭtotachi wa issho ni sunde imasŭ.

Ano hĭtotachi wa issho ni sunde imashĭta.

Takahashi San to Matsumoto San wa issho ni sunde imasŭ.

Takahashi San to Matsumoto San wa issho ni sunde imashĭta.

Musŭko wa kekkon shimashĭta.

My son was married.

Anata wa kekkon shĭte imasŭ ka? Hai, kekkon shĭte imasŭ.

Ano otoko no hĭto wa kekkon shimashĭta ka? Iie, kekkon shimasen deshĭta.

Ano onna no hĭto wa kekkon shĭte imasŭ ka? Iie, kekkon shĭte imasen.

Ano hĭto wa donata to kekkon shimashĭta ka? Ano hĭto wa Matsumoto San to kekkon shimashĭta.

Musŭko wa sŭkoshi sei ga hikui desŭ ga musŭme hodo hikukŭ arimasen.

My son is a little short, but he is not so short as my daughter.

Koko kara Kōbe e wa sŭkoshi tōi desŭ ga Nagasaki e iku hodo tōkŭ arimasen.

Kono o-kashi wa sŭkoshi oishii desŭ ga sono o-kashi hodo oishikŭ arimasen.

Anata no empitsŭ wa nagai desŭ ga watakŭshi no hodo nagakŭ arimasen.

Takahashi San no uchi wa ōkii desŭ ga Matsumoto San no hodo ōkikŭ arimasen.

Kono hon wa chiisai desŭ ga are hodo chiisakŭ arimasen.

Hanako San, sono shikakŭ no hako (w)o motte kite kudasai.

Hanako, please bring me that square box.

Jirō* San, sono marui hako (w)o motte kite kudasai.

Hanako San, sono kirei na kami (w)o motte kite kudasai.

Jirō San, sono nagai fude (w)o motte kite kudasai.

Okāsan, kono hako wa shikakŭ ja arimasen.

Mother, this box is not square.

Otōsan, sono hako wa marukŭ arimasen.

Takahashi San, ano mado wa shikakŭ ja arimasen.

Hanako San, ano mado wa marukŭ arimasen.

Okŭsan, ano uchi wa kirei ja arimasen.

Okāsan, ano hako wa kara ja arimasen.

Amari oishikŭ gozaimasen ga . . .

They aren't very good . . .

Amari ōkikŭ gozaimasen ga . . .

Amari chiisakŭ gozaimasen ga . . .

Amari nagakŭ gozaimasen ga . . .

Amari hikukŭ gozaimasen ga . . .

Chikai uchi ni o-ide kudasai.

Please come in a little while.

Chikai uchi ni kaite kudasai.

Tomodachi wa chikai uchi ni Amerika e ikimashō.

Anata wa Amerika e chikai uchi ni ikimasŭ ka?

Ano hĭto wa chikai uchi ni Yokohama kara kimasŭ ka?

7

Dai Hichi K(w)a (Lesson VII)

Anata wa Nippon go de kazoeru koto ga dekimasŭ ka?
Hai, dekimasŭ: ichi, ni, san, shi, go, rokŭ, (s)hichi, hachi, k(y)u, jū.
5 Shĭkashi Nippon-jin wa ichi kara jū made[51] (w)o hĭtotsŭ, fŭtatsŭ, mittsŭ, yottsŭ, itsutsŭ, muttsŭ, nanatsŭ, yattsŭ, kokonotsŭ, tō[52] to[15] kazoemasŭ. Anata wa jū kara hyakŭ made tō zutsu[53] tonde kazoeru koto ga
10 dekimasŭ ka?
Hai, dekimasŭ.

Can you count in Japanese?

Yes, I can: one, two, three, four, five, six, seven, eight, nine, ten.
But the Japanese count from one to ten with *hĭtotsŭ, fŭtatsŭ, mittsŭ,* etc. ˙ (using another set of numerals) Can you count by tens to one hundred?

Yes, I can.

Sŭmisŭ San, ima kara,[45] kaimono ni ikimashō.[54]
Iie, watakŭshi wa imōto ga gakkō kara
15 kaeru no[55] (w)o mata[56]-nakereba narimasen[57] kara, sŭkoshi o-machi kudasai.
Imōto (w)o tsurete itte mo ii desŭ ka?
Ano ko wa iku sai[58] desŭ ka?
Jū issai desŭ.
20 Amari chiisai desŭ kara, tsurete ika-nai hō ga ii deshō.[59]
Sate, ima wa nan ji desŭ ka?
Gozen[63] jū ichi ji desŭ.
Watakŭshi wa gogo yo[52] ji han made ni uchi
25 e kaera[57]-nakereba narimasen.

Watakŭshi wa niku (w)o kawa[57]-nakereba narimasen ga kono kinjo ni niku-ya[60] ga arimasŭ ka?
Iie, arimasen. Koko kara san jitchōme[61]
30 no[52] tokoro ni ii niku-ya ga gozaimasŭ.
Nan ji ni dekakemashō ka?
Kanari tō[43] gozaimasŭ kara, ichi ji ni dekake-nakereba narimasen.
Niku-ya made wa dono kurai kakarimashō[42]
35 ka?
Han jikan[62] gurai kakarimashō.

Miss Smith, let's go shopping now.

No, as I have to wait for my younger sister to return from school, please wait a little.

Is it all right if I take my younger sister?
How old is the child?
She is eleven years old.
It would be better not to take her because she is too little.
By the way, what time is it now?
It is eleven A. M.
I must be back by four-thirty P. M.

I must buy some meat so is there a butcher shop in this neighborhood?

No, there is not. There is a good butcher shop on the thirtieth block from here.
What time shall we leave?
As it is quite far, we must leave at one o'clock.
How long does it take to (go) to the butcher store?
It takes about a half hour.

At the Butcher Shop

Niku-ya San, kono gyūniki wa ikŭra desŭ ka?
Ikkin[61] ichi yen rokŭ jissen[61] de gozaimasŭ.
40 Sore de wa kono gyūniku (w)o san gin[61] kudasai.

Butcher, how much is this beef?

It's one yen, sixty sen a *kin* (1.32 lb.).
Very well then, please give me three *kin* of this beef.

Kono tamago wa ikŭra desŭ ka?	How much are these eggs?
Sochira[10] wa hǐtotsŭ san sen desŭ, shǐkashi achira[10] no ōkii no[55] wa fŭtatsŭ hichi sen de 45 gozaimasŭ.	Those are three sen each, but those big ones are seven sen for two.
Dōzo, ichiban ii tamago (w)o ichi dāsŭ kudasai.	Please give me a dozen of the best eggs.

At the Grocery

Takahashi San, hayakŭ yao-ya e yukimashō, mō ni ji jippun[61] mae[63] ni narimashǐta kara.	Mr. Takahashi, let's go to the grocery store right away because already it's ten of two.
50 Kono ninjin wa ikŭra desŭ ka?	How much are these carrots?
Sore wa hǐto[52] taba shi sen desŭ.	Those are four sen a bunch.
Kono jagaimo wa ikŭra desŭ ka?	How much are these potatoes?
Sore wa rokkin[61] san jū go sen desŭ.	Those are thirty-five sen for six *kin*.
Motto o-yasui jagaimo wa arimasen ka?	Don't you have any cheaper potatoes?
55 Hai, kochira de gozaimasŭ.	Yes, here they are.
Sochira wa amari takō[43] gozaimasŭ kara, kochira[10] (w)o moraimashō.	As those are too expensive, I'll take these.
Kono suika wa oishii desŭ ka?	Are these watermelons sweet? (tasty)
Hai, taihen oishiū[43] gozaimasŭ.	Yes, they are very good.
60 Hambun morau[54] koto ga dekimasŭ ka?	May I take a half?
Hai, hambun de mo, sambun no ichi[52] de mo, yoroshiū gozaimasŭ.	Yes, either a half or a third is all right.
Hambun de takŭsan desŭ. De wa, Takahashi San, kore kara pan-ya e itte,[44] kashi (w)o 65 kaimashō.	A half will be enough. Well now, Mr. Takahashi, from here (after this) let's go to the bakery and buy some cake.

Exercises

Anata wa jū kara ni jū made kazoeru koto ga dekimasŭ ka? Hai, dekimasŭ: jū, jū ichi, jū ni, jū san, jū shi, jū go, jū rokŭ, jū hichi, jū hachi, jū ku, ni jū.

Can you count from ten to twenty? Yes, I can: ten, eleven, twelve, thirteen, fourteen, fifteen, sixteen, seventeen, eighteen, nineteen, twenty.

Anata wa tō zutsu tonde kazoeru koto ga dekimasŭ ka? Hai, jū, ni jū, san jū, shi jū, go jū, rokŭ jū, hichi jū, hachi jū, ku jū, hyakŭ.

Can you count by tens? Yes, ten, twenty, thirty, forty, fifty, sixty, seventy, eighty, ninety, one hundred.

Anata wa itsutsu zutsu tonde kazoeru koto ga dekimasŭ ka? Hai, go, jū, jū go, ni jū, ni jū go, san jū, san jū go, shi jū, shi jū go, go jū, go jū go, rokŭ jū, rokŭ jū go, hichi jū, hichi jū go, hachi jū, hachi jū go, ku jū, ku jū go, hyakŭ.

Anata wa hyakŭ zutsu tonde kazoeru koto ga dekimasŭ ka? Hai, hyakŭ, ni hyakŭ, sambyakŭ, shi hyakŭ, go hyakŭ, roppyakŭ, hichi hyakŭ, happyakŭ, ku hyakŭ, issen.

Anata wa sen zutsu tonde kazoeru koto ga dekimasŭ ka? Hai, issen, ni sen, san zen, shi sen, go sen, rokŭ sen, hichi sen, hassen, ku sen, ichi man.

Anata wa ichi man zutsu tonde kazoeru koto ga dekimasŭ ka? Hai, ichi man, ni man, samman, shi man, go man, rokŭ man, hichi man, hachi man, ku man, jū man.

Anata wa jū man zutsu tonde kazoeru koto ga dekimasŭ ka? Hai, jū man, ni jū man, san jū man, shi jū man, go jū man, rokŭ jū man, hichi jū man, hachi jū man, ku jū man, hyakŭ man.

Ima kara, kaimono ni ikimashō.
  Then let's go shopping now.

Ima kara, gakkō e ikimashō.
Ima kara, kembutsu ni ikimashō.
Ima kara, sakana-ya e ikimashō.
Ima kara, yao-ya e ikimashō.
Ima kara, niku-ya e ikimashō.
Ima kara, pan-ya e ikimashō.
Ima kara, shimbun (w)o kai ni ikimashō.

Ima kara, issho ni uchi e kaerimashō.
  Now let's go home together.

Ima kara, issho ni koko de machimashō.
Ima kara, issho ni Nippon go (w)o sŭkoshi manabimashō.

Mata-nakereba narimasen.
  I have to wait.

Gakkō e ika-nakereba narimasen.
Tegami (w)o kaka-nakereba narimasen.
Ano hikōki de toba-nakereba narimasen.
Nippon go de hanasa-nakereba narimasen.
Ima kara, hiruhan (w)o tabe-nakereba narimasen.
Uchi ni i-nakereba narimasen.
Uchi e kaera-nakereba narimasen.
Kore (w)o shi-nakereba narimasen.
Watakŭshi wa niku (w)o kawa-nakereba narimasen.

Watakŭshi wa imōto ga gakkō kara kaeru no (w)o mata-nakereba narimasen.
  I have to wait until my younger sister returns from school.

Watakŭshi wa okāsan ga niku-ya kara kaeru no˙(w)o mata-nakereba narimasen.
Watakŭshi no kanai ga pan-ya kara kaeru no (w)o mata-nakereba narimasen.
Watakŭshi no otōsan ga yao-ya kara kaeru no (w)o mata-nakereba narimasen.
Watakŭshi no tomodachi no Takahashi San ga kaeru no (w)o mata-nakereba narimasen.
Watakŭshi ga misę kara kaeru no (w)o matte kudasai.

Sakana-ya e ikimashō ka? Yao-ya e ikimashō ka?
Shall we go to the fish store or shall we go to the grocery?

Pan ya e ikimashō ka? Niku-ya e ikimashō ka?
Gakkō e ikimashō ka? Uchi e kaerimashō ka?
Tegami (w)o kakimashō ka? Nippon go (w)o manabimashō ka?
Yūhan (w)o tabemashō ka? Kembutsu ni ikimashō ka?

Ano ko wa iku sai desŭ ka? Jū issai desŭ.
How old is the child? She is eleven years old.

Anata wa iku sai desŭ ka? San jū shi sai desŭ.
Ano otoko no hĭto wa iku sai desŭ ka? Rokŭ jissai desŭ.
Ano onna no hĭto wa iku sai desŭ ka? Ni jū go sai desŭ.
Takahashi San no musŭko San wa iku sai desŭ ka? Jū hichi sai desŭ.

Ano ko wa ikutsu desŭ ka? Nanatsŭ desŭ.
How old is she? She is seven.

Ano ko wa ikutsu desŭ ka? Mittsu desŭ.
Anata no imōto San wa ikutsu desŭ ka? Itsutsu desŭ.
Matsumoto San no musŭko San wa ikutsu desŭ ka? Tō desŭ.

Tsurete ika-nai hō ga ii deshō.
Let's not take her with us.

Ima kara, ika-nai hō ga ii deshō.
Uchi e kaera-nai hō ga ii deshō.
Tsugi no renshū wa manaba-nai hō ga ii deshō.
Mata-nai hō ga ii deshō.
Eigo wa hanasa-nai hō ga ii deshō.
Amari niku wa tabe-nai hō ga ii deshō.

Ima wa nan ji desŭ ka? Jŭ ichi ji desŭ.
What time is it now? It is eleven o'clock.

Ima wa nan ji desŭ ka? Ichi ji desŭ.
Ima wa nan ji desŭ ka? Ni ji desŭ.
Ima wa nan ji desŭ ka? San ji han desŭ.
Ima wa nan jì desŭ ka? San ji go fun desŭ.
Ima wa nan ji desŭ ka? Ku ji jippun mae desŭ.
Ima wa nan ji desŭ ka? San ji go fun desŭ.
Ima wa nan ji desŭ ka? Jū ni ji roppun mae desŭ.
Ima wa nan ji desŭ ka? Yo ji sampun mae desŭ.

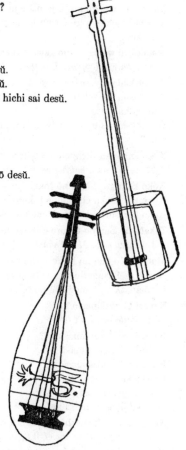

Watakŭshi wa gogo no yo ji han made ni uchi e kaera-nakereba narimasen.
I must be back home by four-thirty P. M.

Watakŭshi wa gozen no hachi ji han made ni kaimono ni ika-nakereba narimasen.

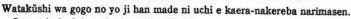

Anata wa gogo no rokŭ ji made ni kaera-nakereba narimasen.

Anata wa gozen no ku ji made ni koko e ko-nakereba narimasen.

Gogo no jū ni ji made ni ano hon (w)o motte ika-nakereba narimasen.

Watakŭshi wa kinō gogo no hichi ji made ni sore (w)o shi-nakereba narimasen deshĭta.

I had to do it by seven P. M. yesterday.

Ano hĭto wa gogo no jū ji made ni kaera-nakereba narimasen deshĭta.

Ano hĭtotachi wa gozen no hachi ji han made ni Tōkiō karà dekake-nakereba narimasen deshĭta.

Watakŭshi wa pan (w)o kawa-nakereba narimasen ga, kono kinjo ni pan-ya ga arimasŭ ka?

As I have to buy bread, is there a bakery in this neighborhood?

Watakŭshi wa yasai (w)o kawa-nakereba narimasen ga, kono kinjo ni yao-ya ga arimasŭ ka?

Watakŭshi wa sakana (w)o kawa-nakereba narimasen ga, kono kinjo ni sakana-ya ga arimasŭ ka?

Watakŭshi wa gyūniku (w)o kawa-nakereba narimasen, kono kinjo ni niku-ya ga arimasŭ ka?

Koko kara san jitchōme no tokoro ni yoi niku-ya ga gozaimasŭ.

There is a good butcher shop thirty blocks from here.

Koko kara go chōme no tokoro ni yoi pan-ya ga gozaimasŭ.

Koko kara rokŭ chōme no tokoro ni yoi sakana-ya ga gozaimasŭ.

Koko kara hichi-hachi chōme no tokoro ni yoi yao-ya ga gozaimashō.

Takahashi San no tokoro e ikitai desŭ.

I want to go to Mr. Takashashi's (house).

Matsumoto San no tokoro wa koko kara tōi desŭ ka?

Nan ji ni Takahashi San no tokoro e iku tsumori desŭ ka?

Kinō anata no tomodachi no tokoro e ikimashita ka?

Kanari tō gozaimasŭ ne?

It's quite far, isn't it?

Kanari chisō gozaimasŭ ne?

Kanari hikū gozaimasŭ ne?

Kanari ōkiū gozaimasŭ ne?

Kanari kirei de gozaimasŭ ne?

Kara de gozaimasŭ ne?

Shikakŭ de gozaimasŭ ne?

Nan ji ni dekakemashō ka? Ichi ji ni dekake-nakereba narimasen.

What time shall we leave? We must leave at one o'clock.

Nan ji ni kaimono ni ikimashō ka? Go ji ni ika-nakereba narimasen.

Nan ji ni yūhan (w)o tabemashō ka? Hichi ji han ni tabe-nakereba narimasen.

Anata wa nan ji ni dekakemasŭ ka? Rokŭ ji ni dekake-nakereba narimasen.

Nan ji ni uchi e kaerimashō ka? Jū ichi ji ni kaera-nakereba narimasen.

Niku-ya made wa dono gurai kakarimashō ka? Ni jū go fun gurai kakarimashō.
About how long does it take to the butcher shop? It takes about twenty-five minutes.
Anata no gakkō made wa dono gurai kakarimasŭ ka? Jippun gurai kakarimasŭ.
Koko kara Kōbe made hikōki de nan jikan kakarimashō ka? San jikan gurai karkarimashō.
Otōsan no o-taku made wa dono gurai kakarimashō ka? San jippun gurai kakarimasŭ.
Jidōsha de Tōkiō kara Kōbe made wa nan jikan kakarimashō ka? Ku jikan gurai kakarimashō.

Koko kara Tōkiō made dono gurai arimasŭ ka?
How far is it from here to Tokio?
Tōkiō kara Ōsaka made dono gurai arimasŭ ka?
Koko kara yoi pan-ya made dono gurai arimasŭ ka?
Koko kara Nagasaki made dono gurai arimasŭ ka?

Niku-ya San, kono gyūniku wa ikŭra desŭ ka?
Butcher, how much is this beef?
Pan-ya San, sono pan wa ikŭra desŭ ka?
Yao-ya San, kono jagaimo wa ikŭra desŭ ka?
Niku-ya San, sono buta-niku wa ikŭra desŭ ka?

Sono gyūniku wa ikkin ichi yen rokŭ jissen de gozaimasŭ ga kono buta-niku wa hachi jissen desŭ.
That beef is one yen, sixty sen a pound and this pork is eighty sen.
Sono jagaimo wa ni kin hichi sen de gozaimasŭ ga kono ninjin wa hĭto-taba go sen desŭ.
Kono kōhī wa san gin ichi yen de gozaimasŭ ga sono o-cha wa ikkin ni jū go sen kara jū yen made gozaimasŭ.

Sore de wa, kono gyūniku (w)o san gin kudasai.
Very well then, please give me three pounds of this beef.
Sore de wa, sono buta-niku (w)o rokkin kudasai.
Sore de wa, kono kōhī (w)o hakkin kudasai.
Sore de wa, sono o-kashi (w)o futa-hako kudasai.
Sore de wa, kono jagaimo (w)o jikkin kudasai.

Sore wa yo yen hachi jissen ni narimasŭ ne. Hai, sō de gozaimasŭ.
That comes to four yen, eighty sen, doesn't it? Yes, that's right.
Sore wa ni yen san jissen ni narimasŭ ne. Hai, sō de gozaimasŭ.
Sore wa ichi yen rokŭ jissen ni narimasŭ ne. Hai, sō de gozaimasŭ.
Sore wa hachi jū go sen ni narimasŭ ne. Hai, sō de gozaimasŭ.

Sōshĭte buta-niku wa iku kin sashiagemashō ka? Buta-niku wa irimasen.
And how many pounds of pork can I give you? I don't want (need) any pork.
Sōshĭte ninjin wa iku taba sashiagemashō ka? Ninjin wa irimasen.
Sōshĭte kōhī wa iku kin sashiagemashō ka? Kōhī wa irimasen.

Sōshĭte o-kashi wa iku hako sashiagemashō ka? O-kashi wa irimasen.
Sōshĭte gyūniku wa iku kin sashiagemashō ka? Gyūniku wa irimasen.
Tamago wa ikutsŭ irimasŭ ka? Tamago (w)o kokonotsŭ kudasai.
How many eggs do you need? Please give me nine eggs.
Suika wa ikutsŭ irimasŭ ka? Suika (w)o yottsŭ kudasai.
Isu wa ikutsŭ irimasŭ ka? Isu (w)o muttsŭ kudasai.
Tsukue wa ikutsŭ irimasŭ ka? Tsukue wo futatsu kudasai.
Anata no mise ni tamago wa arimasen ka? Iie, gozaimasŭ.
Don't you have eggs in your store? Yes, we do.
Anata no mise ni jagaimo wa arimasen ka? Iie, gozaimasŭ.
Anata no mise ni kōhī wa arimasen ka? Hai, gozaimasen.
Anata no mise ni buta-niku wa arimasen ka? Hai, gozaimasen.
Anata no mise ni ninjin wa arimasen ka? Iie, gozaimasŭ.
Kono tamago wa hĭtotsŭ san sen desŭ, shĭkashi kochira no ōkii no wa fŭtatsŭ hichi sen de gozaimasŭ.
These eggs are three sen a piece, but these big ones are seven sen for two.
Kono ninjin wa hĭto taba go sen desŭ, shĭkashi sochira no chiisai no wa yo taba jū go sen de gozaimasŭ.
Sochira no o-kashi wa hĭto hako wa go jissen desŭ, shĭkashi achira no shikakŭ no wa rokŭ jū go sen desŭ.
Dōzo, ichiban ii tamago (w)o ichi dāsŭ kudasai.
Please give me one dozen of the best eggs.
Dōzo ichiban ii tamago (w)o muttsŭ kudasai.
Dōzo ichiban ii jagaimo (w)o jū go kin kudasai.
Dōzo ichiban ii kōhī (w)o go kin kudasai.
Dōzo ichiban ii gyūniku (w)o ni kin kudasai.
Dōzo ichiban chiisai o-kashi (w)o mi hako kudasai.
Dōzo motto ōkii tamago (w)o kudasai.
Mina de ikŭra di narimasŭ ka? Mina de yo yen, ku jū ni sen ni narimasŭ.
How much does everything come to? Everything comes to four yen, ninety-two sen.
Mina de ikŭra ni narimasŭ ka? Mina de shi jū hichi sen ni narimasŭ.
Mina de ikŭra ni narimasŭ ka? Mina de hichi jū yen, hassen ni narimasŭ.
Mina de ikŭra ni narimasŭ ka? Mina de hachi jū ichi yen ni narimasŭ.
Hayakŭ yao-ya e ikimashō, mō ni ji jippun mae ni narimashĭta kara.
Let's go to the grocery store quickly, because it's already ten minutes of two.
Hayakŭ ikimashō, mō yo ji ni jippun mae ni narimashĭta kara.
Hayakŭ kaerimashō, mō jū ni ji jū go fun ni narimashĭta kara.
Hayakŭ araimashō, mō ku ji jū go fun mae ni narimashĭta kara.
Hayakŭ tabemashō, mō hachi ji ni jū rokŭ fun ni narimashĭta kara.

Kono ninjin wa ikŭra desŭ ka? Sore wa mi taba shi sen desŭ.
How much are these carrots? Those are four sen for three bunches.

Kono ninjin wa ikŭra desŭ ka? Sore wa hĭto taba jissen desŭ.
Kono ninjin wa ikŭra desŭ ka? Sono ninjin wa mi taba yon sen desŭ.
Kono suika wa ikŭra desŭ ka? Sore wa hĭtotsu shi jū go sen desŭ.
Kono ninjin wa ikŭra desŭ ka? Sore wa itsu taba ni jissen desŭ.
Kono ninjin wa ikŭra desŭ ka? Sore wa to taba shi jū go sen desŭ.
Sono ninjin wa ikŭra desŭ ka? Kono ninjin wa jū ni taba shi jissen desŭ.

Motto yasui jagaimo wa arimasen ka? Hai, kochira ni gozaimasŭ.
Don't you have any cheaper potatoes? Yes, here they are.

Motto ii o-kashi wa arimasen ka? Hai, sochira ni gozaimasŭ.
Motto ōkii tamago wa arimasen ka? Iie, achira ni gozaimasŭ.
Motto ii gyūniku wa arimasen ka? Iie, kochira ni gozaimasŭ.
Motto oishii suika wa arimasen ka? Hai, kochira ni gozaimasŭ.

Ōkii jagaimo ga yoroshiū gozaimasŭ ka? Chiisai no ga yoroshiū gozaimasŭ ka? Dochira (w)o o-tori ni narimasŭ ka?
Do you prefer big potatoes or do you prefer little ones? Which will you take?

Tamago ga yoroshiū gozaimasŭ ka? Niku ga yoroshiū gozaimasŭ ka? Dochira (w)o o-agari ni narimasŭ ka?
Marui hako ga yoroshiū gozaimasŭ ka? Shikaku no ga yoroshiū gozaimasŭ ka? Dochira (w)o motte o-ide ni narimasŭ ka?
Nippon go de tegami (w)o o-kaki ni narimasŭ ka? Eigo de tegami (w)o o-kaki ni narimasŭ ka? Dochira de o-kaki ni narimasŭ ka?
Gyūnyū ga yoroshiū gozaimasŭ ka? O-cha ga yoroshiū gozaimasŭ ka? Dochira (w)o o-agari ni narimasŭ ka?

O-cha (w)o o-agari ni narimashĭta ka?
Did you drink (partake of) the tea?

Niku (w)o o-agari ni narimashĭta ka?
Shikaku no hako (w)o motte o-ide ni narimashĭta ka?
Eigo de tegami (w)o o-kaki ni narimashĭta ka?
Ashĭta o-kaki ni narimasŭ ka?

Ōkii no ga sŭki desŭ ga amari takō gozaimasŭ kara, kochira (w)o moraimashō.
I like large ones, but since they are too expensive, I'll take these.

Chiisai no ga sŭki desŭ ga amari takō gozaimasŭ kara, sochira (w)o moraimashō.
Kochira no ga sŭki desŭ ga amari takō gozaimasŭ kara, achira (w)o moraimashō.
Gyūniku ga sŭki desŭ ga amari takō gozaimasŭ kara, buta-niku (w)o rokkin moraimashō.
O-kashi ga sŭki desŭ ga amari oishikŭ gozaimasen kara, suika (w)o moraimashō.

Kochira (w)o moraimashō.
I'll take this one.

Tamago (w)o muttsŭ moraimashō.
Tamago (w)o jū ni moraimashō.
Gyūniku (w)o go kin moraimashō.
Suika (w)o fŭtatsŭ moraimashō.
O-kashi (w)o to hako moraimashō.
Jagaimo (w)o go kin moraimashō.
Ninjin (w)o ya taba moraimashō.

Kono suika wa oishii desŭ ka? Hai, taihen oishiū gozaimasŭ.
Is this watermelon tasty? Yes, it's very good.

Kono niku wa oishii desŭ ka? Hai, taihen oishiū gozaimasŭ.
Sono o-kashi wa oishiū gozaimasŭ ka? Hai, taihen oishiū gozaimasŭ.
Ano buta-niku wa oishii desŭ ka? Hai, taihen oishii desŭ.
Sono sakana wa oishii desŭ ka? Iie, amari oishikŭ gozaimasen.

Hambun morau koto ga dekimasŭ ka? Hai, hambun de mo sambun no ichi de mo yoroshiū gozaimasŭ.
May I take a half? Yes, you may (take) either a half or a third.

Hambun no suika (w)o morau koto ga dekimasŭ ka? Hai, hambun no de mo shibun no san de mo yoroshiū gozaimasŭ.
Han gin morau koto ga dekimasŭ ka? Hai, ikkin de mo han gin de mo yoroshiū gozaimasŭ.

Hambun de takŭsan desŭ.
Half is enough.

Sore de takŭsan desŭ.
Go bun no san de takŭsan desŭ.
Hachi bun no go de takŭsan desŭ.
Fŭtatsŭ de takŭsan desŭ.
Rokkin de takŭsan desŭ.
Nana taba de takŭsan desŭ.

Pan-ya e itte, o-kashi (w)o kaimashō.
I shall go to the baker and buy some cake.

Niku-ya e itte, gyūniku (w)o kaimashō.
Uchi e kaette, tegami (w)o kakimashō.
Shashin-ya e itte, shashin (w)o totte moraimashō.
Hiruhan (w)o tabete, Nippon go no renshū (w)o shimashō.

Shimbun (w)o motte kite kara, anata wa dekakete mo ii n' desŭ.
After bringing (me) the newspaper, you may go out.

Pan-ya e itte kara, niku-ya e o-ide kudasai.
Uchi e kaette kara, tegami (w)o kaite kudasai.
Shashin-ya kara kaette kara, hiruhan (w)o o-agari ni natte mo ii n' desŭ.
Ano hon (w)o katte kara, uchi e kaette kudasai.

Pan-ya e itte iru aida ni,[80] Takahashi San to Nippon go de hanashĭte imashĭta.
While you went to the bakery, I was speaking in Japanese to Mr. Takahashi.

Anata ga gakkō ni iru aida ni, watakŭshi wa niku-ya e ikimashō.
Watakŭshi ga uchi ni iru aida ni, niku (w)o katte kite kudasai.
Ginza e o-ide ni natte iru aida ni, shashin-ya e mo o-ide kudasai.
Koko ni kakete iru aida ni, tegami (w)o kaite kudasai.

Pan-ya e iku mae ni, renshū (w)o shimashĭta.
Before I went to the bakery, I did the exercise.

Gakkō e iku mae ni, tegami (w)o kaite kudasai.
Uchi e kaeru mae ni, niku-ya e o-ide kudasai.
Shashin-ya e iku mae ni, te (w)o aratte kudasai.
Hiruhan (w)o o-agari ni naru mae ni, sŭkoshi Nippon go (w)o manande kudasai.
Shimbun (w)o motte kuru mae ni, dōzo kaimono ni o-ide kudasai.

Pan-ya e itte, o-kashi (w)o kaimashĭta.
I went to the bakery and bought some cake.

Niku-ya e itte, gyūniku (w)o kaimashĭta.
Uchi e kaette, tegami (w)o kakimashĭta.
Shashin-ya e itte, shashin (w)o totte moraimashĭta.
Hiruhan (w)o tabete, Nippon go no renshū (w)o shimashĭta.

Pan-ya e itte kara, niku-ya e ikimasŭ.
After going to the bakery, I'll go to the butcher shop.

Niku-ya e itte kara, yasai (w)o kaimasŭ.
Uchi e kaette kara, tegami (w)o kakimasŭ.
Shashin-ya e itte kara, kaimono ni ikimasŭ.
Hiruhan (w)o tabete kara, Nippon go no renshū (w)o shimasŭ.

Anata ga pan-ya e itte ita aida ni, Takahashi San to Nippon go de hanashimashĭta.
While you were at the bakery, I was speaking with Mr. Takahashi in Japanese.

Anata ga gakkō e itte ita aida ni, Nihon go no renshū (w)o shimashĭta.
Anata ga uchi ni ita aida ni, watakŭshi wa o-kashi (w)o kaimashĭta.
Ginza e o-ide ni natte ita aida ni, imōto San ga koko e o-ide ni narimashĭta.
Ano hĭto ga shimbun (w)o yonde ita aida ni, anata wa nani (w)o shimashĭta ka?

Dai Hachi K(w)a (Lesson VIII)

Pan-ya San, kono pan wa aikawarazu shichi sen desŭ ka?

Baker, is this bread still seven sen?

Iie, kono tsuki no hajime kara hachi sen ni narimashĭta.[69]

No, from the beginning of this month it became eight sen.

5 De wa, ni hon[64] kudasai.

Very well, please give me two loaves.

Anata no tonari no sakana-ya wa donna[73] mise desŭ ka?

What kind of shop is the fish store next door?

Asoko ni wa taisō ii sakana ga gozaimashō.

I think they have very good fish over there.

Kyō wa Kinyōbi desŭ kara, atarashii sakana 10 ga takŭsan aru sō desŭ.[65]

As to-day is Friday, I understand they have plenty of fresh fish.

Tsuide ni, pan-ya San, watakŭshi wa Beikokŭ-jin de gozaimasŭ kara, isshūkan no hi no namae (w)o yukkuri itte mite[66] kudasai.

By the way, baker, as I am an American, please say the names of the days of the week for me slowly.

15 Hai, kashĭkomarimashĭta. Nichiyōbi, Getsuyōbi, K(w)ayōbi, Suiyōbi, Mokuyōbi, Kinyōbi, Doyōbi[67] de gozaimasŭ.

Yes, with pleasure. They are Sunday, Monday, Tuesday, Wednesday, Thursday, Friday, Saturday.

Arigatō[43] gozaimashĭta. Mata asu mairimashō.

Thanks very much. I'll come again tomorrow.

At the Fish Store

20 Sakana-ya San, tonari no pan-ya San ga anata (w)o taihen homete imashĭta kara, koko e kimashĭta ga dōzo atarashii o-sakana (w)o go hiki[64] kudasai.

Fish man, as your next door baker was praising you so much, I came here, so please give me five fresh fish.

Sō de gozaimasŭ ka? Sore mo sono hazu de 25 gozaimashō.[68] Pan-ya wa watakŭshi no itoko de, Kōbe de[14] umarete, jū hachi ni naru made ano machi de ōkikŭ narimashĭta[69] ga ku nen hodo mae ni koko e mairimashĭta.

Is that so? That is quite natural. The baker is my cousin; he was born in Kobe and he was raised in that town until he became eighteen and he came here nine years ago.

De wa, Shōwa[70] jū nen ni Tōkiō e kimashĭta 30 ka?

Then, he came to Tokio the tenth year of *Showa?*

Hai, Shōwa jū nen no Nigatsŭ jū go nichi ni Tōkiō e kimashĭta.

Yes, he came the 15th of February, the tenth year of *Showa.*

Sore wa Seireki issen k(y)u hyakŭ san jū roku nen desŭ ne. Sate, kyō wa nan nichi 35 desŭ ka?

That's 1936 A. D., isn't it?[70] By the way, what is the date to-day?

Shōgatsŭ yōka desŭ. Okŭsan, soko[28] ni atarashii shake ga gozaimasŭ.

January 8th. Madam, there are some fresh salmon over there.

Sore de wa, kono shake (w)o roppiki[61] moraimashō.

Well then, I'll take six of these salmon.

40 Kesa ichi man no ebi ga tsukimashĭta ga mō rokŭ sembiki[61] urimashĭta.

This morning ten thousand shrimp came in (arrived) and we already sold six thousand.

48

Sō desŭ ka? Sono ebi wa ikŭra desŭ ka?
Hyappiki[61] hachi jū go sen de gozaimasŭ.
Anata no go-kazokŭ wa nan[73] nin[64] de
45 gozaimasŭ ka?
Kazokŭ wa otoko ga hĭtori[64] de, onna ga
fŭtari desŭ. Desŭ kara, san jū go roppiki
moraimashō.
Anata wa sashimi ga o-sŭki ja gozaimasen
50 ka?
Iie, amari sŭkimasen.
Koko ni ikita sakana ga gozaimasŭ. Ikkin
ni jū go sen desŭ ga makete jū go sen ni
shĭte okimasŭ.[81]
55 Jissen ni makete kudasai.
De wa, sō itashimashō.

Matsumoto Sama, nan ji made ni uchi e
kaera-nakereba narimasen ka?
Mō kaeru[26] jikan ga kimashĭta.
60 Kaeri[40] wa densha de nakŭte mo[57] ii deshō
ne.
Asoko ni[28] jinrikisha ga san dai[64] imasŭ.[71]
Kuruma-ya San, Motomachi sambyakŭ ni
jū go ban e tsurete itte kudasai.
65 Hai, kashĭkomarimashĭta.

Watakŭshi no uchi wa koko kara go
kemme[52] desŭ.
Kuruma-ya San, kuruma-chin wa ikŭra
desŭ ka?
70 Ichi yen ni jū go sen desŭ.

Is that right? How much are those shrimp?
Eighty-five sen per hundred.
How many people are there in your family?

My family consists of one man and two
women. Therefore, I'll take thirty-five or
thirty-six.
Don't you like *sashimi?* (slices of raw fish)

No, not very much.
Here are some live fish. They are twenty-
five sen a *kin*, but I'll reduce it to fifteen sen.

Please come down to ten sen.
Very well, I shall (do so).

Mrs. Matsumoto, by what time do you
have to be home?
It's already time to go home.
We don't have to go back by trolley car, do
we?
There are three rickshaws over there.
Rickshaw man, please take us to number
325 Motomachi St.
Yes, surely.

My house is the fifth from here.

Rickshaw man, how much is the rickshaw
fare?
One yen, twenty-five sen.

Exercises

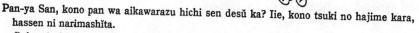

Pan-ya San, kono pan wa aikawarazu hichi sen desŭ ka? Iie, kono tsuki no hajime kara,
hassen ni narimashĭta.
Baker, is this bread still seven sen? Since the first of this month it has become eight sen.

Niku-ya San, kono niku wa aikawarazu ikkin, ichi yen desŭ ka? Iie, kono tsuki no hajime
kara, ichi yen go jissen ni narimashĭta.

Yao-ya San, kono tamago wa aikawarazu shi sen desŭ ka? Iie, kono tsuki no hajime kara,
go sen ni narimashĭta.

Sakana-ya San, sono sakana wa aikawarazu ikkin jū go sen desŭ ka? Iie, kono tsuki no
hajime kara, jū hichi sen ni narimashĭta.

Pan-ya San, kono pan wa aikawarazu hĭtotsŭ ni jissen desŭ ka? Iie, kono tsuki no hajime kara, ni jū go sen ni narimashĭta.

Pan (w)o ni hon kudasai.
Please give me two loaves of bread.

Pan (w)o ippon kudasai.
Fude (w)o sambon kudasai.
Empitsŭ (w)o shi hon kudasai.
Pen (w)o go hon kudasai.
Pan (w)o roppon kudasai.
Pan (w)o hachi hon kudasai.
Empitsŭ (w)o jippon kudasai.

Anata wa empitsŭ (w)o iku hon motte imasŭ ka? Empitsŭ (w)o jippon motte imasŭ.
How many pencils do you have? I have ten pencils.

Pen (w)o iku hon motte imasŭ ka? Pen (w)o go hon motte imasŭ.
Fude (w)o iku hon motte imasŭ ka? Sambon motte imasŭ.
Empitsŭ (w)o nambon motte imasŭ ka? Jippon motte imasŭ.

Kyō no remon pai wa oishii desŭ ga o-sŭki ja arimasen ka?
The lemon pie to-day is fine, so wouldn't you like some?

Kyō no shimbun wa koko ni arimasŭ ga mitakŭ arimasen ka?
Kinō no sakana wa oishikŭ arimasen deshĭta ga ano hĭto wa tabemasen deshĭta.
Ashĭta no shimbun (w)o matte imasŭ ga nan ji ni kimashō ka?
Kyō no o-kashi wa atarashii desŭ ga o-sŭki ja arimasen ka?

Kyō watakŭshi wa sakana-ya e ikimasŭ.
I am going to the fish store today.

Kinō watakŭshi wa niku-ya e ikimashĭta.
Ashĭta watakŭshi wa pan-ya e ikimashō.
Kyō watakŭshi wa sakana-ya e ikimasen.
Kinō watakŭshi wa niku-ya e ikimasen deshĭta.
Ashĭta watakŭshi wa pan-ya e ikimasen deshō.

Kinō watakŭshi wa Nihon go (w)o manabimashĭta.
I studied Japanese yesterday.

Kyō watakŭshi wa Nippon go (w)o manabimasŭ.
Ashĭta watakŭshi wa Nippon go (w)o manabimashō.
Kyō watakŭshi wa Nippon go (w)o manabimasen.
Kinō watakŭshi wa Nippon go (w)o manabimasen deshĭta.
Ashĭta watakŭshi wa Nippon go (w)o manabimasen deshō.

Konnichi no gogo watakŭshi wa kaera-nakereba narimasen.
I have to return this afternoon.

Kinō no asa jū ji ni wa watakŭshi wa kaera-nakereba narimasen deshĭta.

Ashĭta no ban hachi ji ni anata wa watakŭshi no uchi e ko-nakereba narimasen.

Kyō no gogo wa kaera-nakŭte mo ii n' desŭ.
I don't have to be back this afternoon.

Kinō no asa wa watakŭshi wa ika-nakŭte mo ii n' deshĭta.

Ashĭta no ban wa ano hĭto wa koko e ko-nakŭte mo ii deshō.

Anata no tonari no sakana-ya wa donna mise desŭ ka? Asoko ni wa taihen ii sakana ga gozaimashō.
What kind of store is the fish store next door? I think they have very good fish there.

Anata no tonari no hĭto wa donna hĭto desŭ ka? Taihen ii hĭto de gazaimashō.

Ano hĭto no tonari no niku-ya wa donna mise desŭ ka? Asoko ni wa taihen ii niku ga gozaimashō.

Watakŭshi no tonari no pan-ya wa donna mise desŭ ka? Asoko ni wa amari ii pan wa gozaimasen deshō.

Sono hon wa donna hon de gozaimasŭ ka? Kore wa taihen ii hon de gozaimasŭ.

Ano rikugun no skĭkan wa donna hĭto desŭ ka? Ano hĭto wa amari ii hĭto ja arimasen.

Atarashii sakana ga takŭsan aru sō desŭ.
They say they have a lot of fresh fish.

Pan wa hassen ni narimashĭta sō desŭ.

Koko de niku (w)o kau koto ga dekiru sō desŭ.

Ano mise ni tamago ga aru sō desŭ.

Ano hĭto wa Kyōto kara o-ide ni narimashĭta sō desŭ.

Kyō wa nan yōbi desŭ ka? Kyō wa Kinyōbi desŭ.
What day is to-day? To-day is Friday.

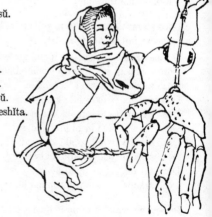

Kyō wa nan yōbi desŭ ka? Kyō wa Mokuyōbi desŭ.

Kyō wa nan yōbi desŭ ka? Kyō wa Getsuyōbi desŭ.

Ashĭta wa nan yōbi desŭ ka? Ashĭta wa Kayōbi desŭ.

Kinō wa nan yōbi deshĭta ka? Kinō wa Nichiyō[67] deshĭta.

Nichiyōbi wa isshūkan no hajime no hi desŭ.
Sunday is the first (beginning) day of the week.

Getsuyōbi wa isshūkan no ni bamme no hi desŭ.

Kore wa go hon me no empitsŭ desŭ.

Kore kara sam bamme no sakana ga hoshii.

Yo bamme no jinrikusha ni norimashō.

Koko kara jū nin me no hĭto ni hanashitai.

Kochira kara rokŭ dai me no hikōki (w)o miru koto ga dekimasŭ ka?

Tsugi no doyōbi ni dōzo mata o-ide kudasai. Doyōbi ni wa kuru koto ga dekimasen kara, tsugi no Getsuyōbi ni kimashō.
Please come again next Saturday. As I can't come on Saturday, I'll come next Monday.
Dōzo Nichiyōbi made ni watakŭshi ni kaite kudasai. Nichiyōbi made ni wa kaku koto ga dekimasen deshō kara, tsugi no Kayōbi made ni kakimashō.

Watakŭshi wa Beikokŭjin de gozaimasŭ kara, isshūkan no hi no namae (w)o yukkuri itte mite kudasai.
As I am an American, please say the names of the days of the week for me slowly.
Watakŭshi wa Beikokŭjin desŭ kara, anata no namae (w)o yukkuri itte mite kudasai.
Watakŭshi wa Beikokŭjin desŭ kara, yukkuri hanashĭte kudasai.
Watakŭshi wa wakarimasen deshĭta kara, dōzo sore (w)o mō ichido yukkuri itte kudasai.
Watakŭshi wa Beikokŭjin desŭ kara, ano pan-ya San no namae (w)o yukkuri itte mite kudasai.
Watakŭshi wa Nippon-jin ja arimasen, kono yasai no namae (w)o yukkuri itte mite kudasai.
Watakŭshi wa Beikokŭjin desŭ kara, ano mise-ya no namae (w)o yukkuri itte mite kudasai.

Tonari no pan-ya San ga anata (w)o taihen homete imashĭta kara, koko e kimashĭta.
As the baker next door praised you, I came here.
Tonari no hĭto ga anata (w)o taihen homete imashĭta kara, koko e kimashĭta.
Anata no tomodachi ga anata no koto (w)o hanashĭte imashĭta kara, koko e kimashĭta.
Matsumoto San ga anata (w)o taihen homete imashĭta kara, koko e kimashĭta.
Watakŭshi no Amerika-jin no tomodachi ga ano hĭto (w)o taihen homete imashĭta kara, asoko e mairimashĭta.

Dōzo atarashii sakana (w)o go hiki kudasai.
Please give me five fresh fish.
Dōzo atarashii shake (w)o ippiki kudasai.
Dōzo atarashii sakana (w)o sambiki kudasai.
Dōzo sakana (w)o shi hiki kudasai.
Dōzo sakana (w)o ni hiki kudasai.
Dōzo sakana (w)o roppiki kudasai.
Dōzo sakana (w)o hichi hiki kudasai.
Dōzo sakana (w)o happiki kudasai.
Dōzo sakana (w)o ku hiki kudasai.
Dōzo sakana (w)o jippiki kudasai.
Dōzo sakana (w)o san jū roppiki kudasai.

Pan-ya wa watakŭshi no itoko de, ku nen hodo mae ni koko e mairimashĭta.
The baker is my cousin and came here nine years ago.
Are wa watakŭshi no musŭko de, rokŭ nen hodo mae ni Nippon kara koko e mairimashĭta.

Are wa watakŭshi no musŭme de, hachi nen hodo mae ni Kōbe kara koko e mairimashĭta.

Ano sei no takai hĭto wa watakŭshi no otōsan de, yo nen hodo mae ni Beikokŭ kara, Nippon e mairimashĭta.

Ano onna no hĭto wa ano rikugun no shikan no okŭsan de, ni jū nen hodo mae ni Shina kara koko e o-ide ni narimashĭta.

Itsŭ Nippon e o-ide ni narimashĭta ka? Ichi nen hodo mae ni Amerika kara koko e mairimashĭta.

When did you come to Japan? I came here from America one year ago.

Itsŭ ano hĭto wa Amerika e o-ide ni narimashĭta ka? Ni nen hodo mae ni Amerika e ikimashĭta.

Itsŭ koko e o-ide ni narimashĭta ka? Mokuyōbi no gozen jū ji ni koko e kimashĭta.

Itsŭ ano hikōki wa koko e tsukimashĭta ka? Kinō gogo ku ji han ni tsukimashĭta.

Anata wa doko de umaremashĭta ka? Watakŭshi wa Amerika de umaremashĭta.

Where were you born? I was born in America.

Anata wa doko de umaremashĭta ka? Watakŭshi wa Nyū Yōkŭ de umaremashĭta.

Anata wa doko de umaremashĭta ka? Watakŭshi wa Nippon de umaremashĭta.

Ano hĭto wa doko de umaremashĭta ka? Ano hĭto wa Tōkiō de umaremashĭta.

Ano hĭtotachi wa doko de umaremashĭta ka? Takahashi San wa Kōbe de umarete, Matsumoto San wa Nagasaki de umaremashĭta.

Anata wa doko de ōkikŭ narimashĭta ka? Watakŭshi wa Nippon de ōkikŭ narimashĭta.

Where did you grow up? I was raised in Japan.

Anata wa doko de ōkikŭ narimashĭta ka? Watakŭshi wa Amerika de ōkikŭ narimashĭta.

Anata wa doko de ōkikŭ narimashĭta ka? Watakŭshi wa Shina de ōkikŭ narimashĭta.

Ano rikugun no shĭkan wa kono atari de ōkikŭ narimashĭta ka? Iie, ano shĭkan wa Kyōto de ōkikŭ narimashĭta.

Anata wa dono atari de ōkikŭ narimashĭta ka? Watakŭshi wa Tōkiō de ōkikŭ narimashĭta.

Itoko wa Shōwa gannen[113] no Nigatsŭ jū go nichi ni Tōkiō e kimashĭta.

My cousin came to Tokio February 15th, the first year of Showa.

Anata wa Shōwa ni jū ichi nen no Shōgatsŭ[114] muika[113] ni Nippon e kimashĭta ka?

Watakŭshi wa Shōwa ni nen no Shōgatsŭ ō-misoka[113] ni koko e tsukimashĭta.

Ano rikugun no shĭkan wa Shina kara Taishō[115] jū nen no Shigatsŭ yokka ni koko e kimashĭta.

Otōsan wa Ōsaka kara Meiji san jū nen Kugatsŭ[114] tsuitachi[113] ni koko e kimashĭta sō desŭ.

Kyō wa nan nichi desŭ ka? Shōgatsŭ yokka desŭ.

What is the date to-day? It's January 4th.

Kyō wa nan nichi desŭ ka? Jūgatsŭ tōka desŭ.

Kyō wa nan nichi desŭ ka? Hachigatsŭ hatsŭka[113] desŭ.

Ashĭta wa nan nichi desŭ ka? Hichigatsŭ itsŭka desŭ.

Kinō wa nan nichi deshĭta ka? Kinō wa Gogatsŭ tsuitachi deshĭta.

Kinō wa nan nichi deshĭta ka? Kinō wa Jūnigatsŭ ni jū ku nichi deshĭta.

Anata wa itsŭ koko e o-ide ni narimashĭta ka? Futsŭka hodo mae ni koko e kimashĭta.

When did you come here? I came here about two days ago.

Anata wa itsŭ asoko e o-ide ni narimashĭta ka? Nanuka hodo mae ni asoko e mairimashĭta.

Itsŭ ano hikōki wa koko e tsukimashō ka? Ima kara tōka gurai de tsuku sō desŭ.

Sore wa Seireki issen ku hyakŭ san jū rokŭ nen desŭ ne.

That's 1936 A. D., isn't it?

Kore wa Seireki issen ku hyakŭ shi jū rokŭ nen desŭ ne.

Anata wa Nippon e issen ku hyakŭ ni jū yo nen ni o-ide ni narimashĭta ka?

Soko ni atarashii shake ga gozaimasŭ. Sore de wa, kono shake (w)o roppiki moraimashō.

There are some fresh salmon. Very well, I'll take six of these salmon.

Koko ni atarashii ebi ga gozaimasŭ. Sore de wa, sono ebi (w)o ni jippiki moraimashō.

Asoko ni atarashii sakana ga gozaimasŭ. Sore de wa, ano sakana (w)o sambiki moraimashō.

Soko ni atarashii tamago ga gozaimasŭ. Sore de wa, kono tamago (w)o ichi dāsŭ moraimashō.

Asoko ni atarashii sakana ga gozaimasŭ. Sore de wa, ano sakana (w)o ni hiki moraimashō.

Kesa ichi man biki no ebi ga tsukimashĭta.

This morning ten thousand shrimp arrived.

Kesa ebi ga ichi man biki tsŭkimashĭta.

Kono gogo samman biki no ebi ga tsŭkimashĭta.

Kesa go man biki no ebi ga tsŭkimashĭta.

Komban ebi ga ku man biki tsŭkimashĭta.

Mō rokŭ sen biki urimashĭta.

I already sold six thousand.

Mō hachi sen biki urimashĭta.

Mō issen biki urimashĭta.

Tamago (w)o ni dāsŭ kaimashĭta.

Sono ebi wa ikŭra desŭ ka? Hyappiki ga hachi jū go sen de gozaimasŭ.

How much are those shrimp? Eighty five sen per hundred.

Kono ebi wa ikŭra desŭ ka? Sambyappiki ga ku jissen de gozaimasŭ.

Sono shake wa ikŭra desŭ ka? Ippiki ga ichi yen go jissen de gozaimasŭ.

Sono sakana wa ikŭra desŭ ka? Ni hiki ga ichi yen hichi jū go sen de gozaimasŭ.

Ano ebi wa ikŭra desŭ ka? Go hyappiki ga san yen de gozaimasŭ.

Anata no o-kazokŭ wa nan nin de gozaimasŭ ka? Watakŭshi no kazokŭ wa otoko ga hĭtori de, onna ga fŭtari desŭ.

How many people are there in your family? In my family there are two women and one man.

Anata no o-kazokŭ wa iku nin de gozaimasŭ ka? Watakŭshi no kazokŭ wa otoko ga go nin de, onna ga hichi nin desŭ.

Anata no o-kazokŭ wa iku nin de gozaimasŭ ka? Watakŭshi no kazokŭ ni wa jū nin no otoko ga gozaimasŭ.

Anata no o-kazokŭ wa iku nin de gozaimasŭ ka? Watakŭshi no kazokŭ wa onna san nin desŭ.

Ano shĭkan no kazokŭ wa nan nin de gozaimashō ka? Ano hĭto no kazokŭ wa otoko ga yo nin de, onna ga san nin de sō desŭ.

San jū go-roppiki moraimashō.
I'll take thirty-five or thirty-six.

Kashi (w)o hĭto hako moraimashō.
Kashi (w)o hĭto hako ka futa hako moraimashō.
Kashi (w)o futa hako moraimashō.
Kashi (w)o futa hako ka mi hako moraimashō.
Hĭto (w)o shi-go nin mimashĭta.
Mi hako no o-kashi (w)o moraimashō.
Mi hako ka yo hako no o-kashi (w)o moraimashō.
Shi-go nin no rikugun no shĭkan (w)o mimashĭta.

Anata wa sashimi ga o-sŭki de gozaimasŭ ka? Iie, amari sŭkimasen.
Do you like raw fish slices? No, I don't like (them) very much.

Sakana ga o-sŭki de gozaimasŭ ka? Hai, taihen sŭki desŭ.
O-kashi ga o-sŭki de gozaimasŭ ka? Iie, amari sŭkimasen.
Anata wa ebi ga o-sŭki ja arimasen ka? Hai, sŭki desŭ.

Koko ni ikita sakana ga gozaimasŭ.
Here are some live fish.

Ikita sakana wa ikaga de gozaimasŭ ka? Iie, ikita sakana wa kaitakŭ arimasen.
Anata wa ikita ebi ga hoshiū gozaimashĭta ka? Iie, ikita ebi wa hoshikŭ arimasen deshĭta.
Anata wa ikita shake ga hoshiū gozaimasŭ ka? Iie, ikita shake wa hoshikŭ gozaimasen.

Makete jū go sen ni shĭte okimasŭ.
I'll reduce it to fifteen sen.

Jissen ni shĭte okimasŭ.
Ni yen ni shĭte okimasŭ.
Go jū yen ni shĭte okimasŭ.
Go jissen ni shĭte okimasŭ.

Dōzo ano hako (w)o koko ni oite kudasai.
Please put that box here.

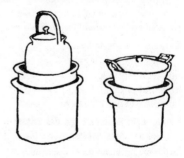

Dōzo sono tamago (w)o koko ni oite kudasai.
Dōzo ano shimbun (w)o asoko ni oite kudasai.
Dōzo sono empitsŭ (w)o soko ni oite kudasai.

Doko ni watakŭshi no zasshi (w)o okimashĭta ka?
Watakŭshi wa ano niku (w)o asoko ni okimashĭta.

Jissen ni makete kudasai. De wa, sō itashimashō.
Please come down to ten sen. All right, I'll do so.

Go jissen ni makete kudasai. Sō wa dekimasen.
Yo yen ni makete kudasai. De wa, sō itashimashō.
Hichi sen ni makete kudasai. De wa, sō itashimashō.
Ano sashimi (w)o jissen ni makete kudasai. Sō wa dekimasen.
Ano sakana-ya San wa kono sakana (w)o ku sen ni makete kudasaimashĭta.

Itsŭ kaera-nakereba narimasen ka? Ima kaera-nakereba narimasen.
When must you go back? I must go back now.

Itsŭ kaimono ni ika-nakereba narimasen ka? Ima ika-nakereba narimasen.
Itsŭ sakana (w)o kawa-nakereba narimasen ka? Ima kawa-nakereba narimasen.
Itsŭ ano tegami (w)o kaka-nakereba narimasen ka? Ima kaka-nakereba narimasen.
Itsŭ hiruhan (w)o o-agari ni nara-nakereba narimasen ka? Ima tabe-nakereba narimasen.

Kuruma ni notte, hayakŭ uchi e kaerimashō.
Let's ride and get back home quickly.

Jinrikisha ni notte, hayakŭ uchi e kaerimashō.
Jidōsha ni notte, hayakŭ sakana-ya e ikimashō.
Hikōki ni notte, hayakŭ Tōkiō e ikimashō.

Sonna ni isoga-nakŭte mo ii deshō.
You don't have to hurry so much.

Go ji han mae ni wa yūhan (w)o tabe-nakŭte mo ii n' desŭ.
Ima wa manaba-nakŭte mo ii n' desŭ.
Hanasa-nakŭte mo ii n' desŭ.
Yoma-nakŭte mo ii n' desŭ.
Mise e ika-nakŭte mo ii n' desŭ.
Jū ji mae ni wa ko-nakŭte mo ii n' desŭ.
Tegami wa kaka-nakŭte mo ii n' desŭ.
Jinrikisha ni nora-nakŭte mo ii n' desŭ.

Kuruma ni notte kudasai.
Please take-a rickshaw.

Jidōsha ni notte kudasai.
Hikōki ni notte kudasai.
Jinrikisha ni notte kudasai.

Asoko ni jinrikisha ga san dai arimasŭ.
There are three rickshaws over there.

Asoko ni jinrikisha ga ni dai arimasŭ.

Asoko ni yo dai no kuruma ga arimasŭ.

Asoko ni kuruma ga iku dai arimasŭ ka?

Asoko ni iku dai no hikōki ga arimasŭ ka?

Go dai arimasŭ.

Hikōki ga iku dai arimashĭta ka?

Ano machi ni wa ichi man dai arimashĭta.

Motomachi no sambyakŭ ni jū go ban e tsurete itte kudasai.

Please take me to 325 Motomachi St.

Ginza no shi hyakŭ go ban e tsurete itte kudasai.

Motomachi no ni hyakŭ go jū rokŭ ban e tsurete itte kudasai.

Hondōri no hyakŭ shi jū san ban e watakŭshi (w)o tsurete itte kudasai.

Kono tegami (w)o Motomachi no happyakŭ hichi jū ni ban e motte itte kudasai.

Watakŭshi no uchi wa koko kara go ken me desŭ.

My house is the fifth (one) from here.

Watakŭshi no tomadachi no o-taku wa asoko kara jikken me de gozaimasŭ.

Ni hon me no empitsŭ ga ano hĭto no desŭ.

Shi hiki me no sakana (w)o kudasai.

Rokŭ nin me no hĭto ni hanashitai desŭ.

Muttsŭ me no isu ni kakete kudasai.

Kuruma-chin wa ikŭra desŭ ka? Ichi yen ni jū go sen desŭ.

How much is the rickshaw fare? It's one yen, twenty-five sen.

Kuruma-chin wa ikŭra desŭ ka? Ni yen desŭ.

Koko kara Motomachi no ni hyakŭ ban made no kuruma-chin wa ikŭra desŭ ka? Ichi yen hichi jū go sen desŭ.

Koko kara anata no o-taku made no kuruma-chin wa ikŭra deshĭta ka? Go jissen deshĭta.

9
Dai K(y)u K(w)a (Lesson IX)

Watakŭshi wa depāto e kaimono ni iku tsŭmori[72] desŭ ga anata mo issho ni ikimasen ka?

I intend to go to a department store to go shopping, so don't you want to go with me?

Hai, go-issho ni mairimashō. Dono[73] depāto e yukimashō ka?

Yes, let's go together. To which department store will you go?

Takashima-ya e ika-nakereba narimasen shatsŭ ga shi-go[52] mai[64] irimasŭ[85] kara.

I have to go to Takashima's because I need four or five shirts.

Densha de ikimashō ka? Basŭ de ikimashō ka?

Shall we go by street-car, or shall we go by bus?

Sore wa densha no hō ga ii deshō.[59]

As for that (matter), a street-car is probably better.

Koko kara Takashima-ya made wa dono gŭrai arimasŭ ka?

About how far is it from here to Takashima's store?

Ichi ri kŭrai arimashō.[54] Ano junsa ni kiite mimashō. Shĭtsŭrei desŭ ga, watakŭshidomo wa Takashima-ya e yukitai n' desŭ ga Kyōbashi-yuki no densha ni doko de nottara[74] yoroshiŭ gozaimasŭ ka?

About one ri (2.44 miles). I think I'll ask that policeman. Pardon me, but as we want to go to Takashima's, where can we get the Kyobashi street-car?

Kono tsugi no kado kara, minami e magatte, ni chōme no kado de o-nori nasai.[32] Soshĭte doko de Kyōbashi-yuki e norikaetara ii ka[75] shashō ni o-kiki nasai.

From this next corner, turn south and take it on the second corner (from there). And ask the conductor where you transfer to the Kyobashi car.

Watakŭshidomo wa ima minami no hō e muite imasŭ ka?

Are we facing south now?

Iie, higashi no hō e muite imasŭ. Desŭ kara, migi no hō wa minami de, hidari no hō wa kita de, ushiro no hō wa nishi desŭ.

No, we are facing east. Therefore, south is to the right, the left side is north, and back (of you) is west.

Arigatō gozaimashĭta.

Thank you.

In the Street Car

Shashō San, Kyōbashi-yuki no densha ni wa doko de norikaetara yoroshiŭ gozaimasŭ ka?

Conductor, where should I transfer to the Kyobashi trolley?

Kono tsugi no teiryūjo de orite, Kyōbashi-yuki ni o-nori nasai. Soshĭte go-rokŭ chō yuku to[15] Takashima-ya ga massugu saki ni arimasŭ.

Get out at the next stop and take the Kyobashi car. And if you go five or six squares, Takashima's is straight ahead.

At the Department Store

Bantō San, shatsŭ wa doko ni arimasŭ ka?

Clerk, where are the shirts?

Shi kai nĭ gozaimasŭ kara, hidari no erebētā (w)o o-tori kudasai.[32]

They are on the fourth floor, so please take the elevator to the left.

Nani (w)o goran ni kakemashō[42] ka?
40 Dōzo waishatsŭ to shima no shatsŭ (w)o misete kudasai.
Dōzo kochira e o-ide kudasai. Kono wai-shatsŭ wa taihen kiji ga yō gozaimashĭte, o-nedan mo sahodo takakŭ arimasen; ichi mai san yen go jissen de gozaimasŭ. Ikaga
45 de gozaimashō ka?
Chotto sore[11] (w)o misete kudasai. Kono shatsŭ wa kanari ii yō[65] desŭ ne; karā no ōkisa[43] ga jū go de, sode no nagasa ga ni shaku hassun no (w)o san mai morau[54] koto ga
50 dekimasŭ ka?
Hai, kashĭkomarimashĭta. Anata no uchi e todokemashō ka matawa motte o-kaeri ni narimasŭ ka?
Okutte morattara,[76] itsŭ watakŭshi no uchi
55 e tsukimashō ka? Taku wa Kanda no itchōme desŭ ga . . .
Tabun ni-san nichi no uchi ni wa tsukimashō.

Sore de wa dōzo okutte kudasai.
Dōzo anata no o-namae to banchi (w)o
60 oshiete kudasai.
Watakŭshi no namae wa Sŭmisŭ de, Kanda no itchōme no jū yo ban ni sunde imasŭ.

What would you care to see?
Please show me some white and some striped shirts.
Please come this way. These white shirts are very good quality, and the price is not so high either; three yen, fifty sen apiece. What do you think (about them)?

Please let me see them a moment. These shirts really seem quite good; may I take three of fifteen size collar and two *shaku* (one *shaku* = .994 foot) eight *sun* (one *sun* = 1.2 inch) sleeve length?
Yes, certainly. Shall we deliver them to your home, or do you want to take them with you?
If I have them sent, when will they arrive at my house? My home is in Kanda, First Street . . .
They will probably arrive inside of two or three days.
In that case, please send (them).
Please give me your name and address.

My name is Smith and I live in Kanda (section), number fourteen, First Street.

Exercises

Watakŭshi wa depāto e kaimono ni iku tsumori desŭ.

I intend to go to a department store to go shopping.

Anata wa kyō kembutsu ni o-ide ni naru tsumori de gozaimasŭ ka?

Watakŭshi wa uchi e kaette, tegami (w)o kaku tsumori desŭ.

Go ji han ni yūhan (w)o taberu tsumori desŭ.

Anata wa imōto San (w)o tsurete iku tsumori de gozaimasŭ ka?

Ano hĭto wa shatsu (w)o ni mai kau tsumori deshō.

Anata mo issho ni ikimasen ka?

Aren't you going along too?

Ano hĭto mo issho ni ikitai sō desŭ.

Ano onna no hĭto mo issho ni kitai sō deshĭta.

Watakŭshi mo issho ni ikitai desŭ.

Ano hĭtotachi mo issho ni kitai sō desŭ.

Issho ni mairimashō.
I'll go with you.

Watakŭshi no tomodachi wa anata to issho ni ikimashō.
Anata wa watakŭshi to issho ni o-ide ni narimasŭ ka?
Watakŭshi wa issho ni ikimashō.
Matsumoto San wa anata to issho ni ikimashō.
Watakŭshidomo wa anata to issho ni mairimashō.

Dono depāto e ikimashō ka?
To which department store shall we go?

Dono densha ni norimashō ka?
Dono mise e ikimashō ka?
Dono pan-ya e ikimashō ka?
Dono shatsu (w)o kaimashō ka?
Dono hon ga yoroshiŭ gozaimasŭ ka?
Dono shĭkan ni hanashitō gozaimasŭ ka?

Dochira no depāto e ikimashō ka?
To which (of two) department stores shall we go?

Dochira no densha ni norimashō ka?
Dochira no mise e ikimashō ka?
Dochira no pan-ya e ikimashō ka?
Dochira no shatsu (w)o kaimashō ka?
Dochira no hon ga yoroshiŭ gozaimasŭ ka?
Dochira no shĭkan ni hanashitō gozaimasŭ ka?

Takashima-ya e ika-nakereba narimasen.
I must go to Takashima's.

Anata wa Kyōbashi-yŭki no densha ni nora-nakereba narimasen.
Anata wa ano hon (w)o yoma-nakereba narimasen.
Watakŭshi wa ima kaera-nakereba narimasen.
Junsa ni kika-nakereba narimasen.

Shatsu ga shi-go mai irimasŭ.
I need (want) four or five shirts.

Rokŭ mai no shatsu ga irimasŭ.
Kami ga san-yo mai irimasŭ.
Shimbun ga ni mai irimasŭ.
Jidōsha ga ichi-ni dai irimasŭ.
Hĭto ga jū nin irimasŭ.

Densha de ikimashō ka? Basŭ de ikimashō ka?
Shall we go by bus or by street car?
Jinrikĭsha de ikimashō ka? Densha de ikimashō ka?
Jinrikĭsha de ikimashō ka? Basŭ de ikimashō ka?
Hikōki de ikimashō ka? Jidōsha de ikimashō ka?
Anata wa jinrikĭsha de o-ide ni narimashĭta ka? Jidōsha de o-ide ni narimashĭta ka?

Densha no hō ga ii deshō.
A trolley will be better.
Densha de iku hō ga ii desŭ.
Ima kaeru hō ga ii deshō.
Tegami (w)o kaku hō ga ii desŭ.
Nippon go de hanasu hō ga ii desŭ.
O-cha (w)o nomu hō ga ii desŭ.
Dekakeru hō ga ii desŭ.
Kono shatsu no hō ga ii desŭ.
Migi no hō e iku no ga ii deshō.

Koko kara Takashima-ya made wa dono gurai arimasŭ ka? Ichi ri gurai deshō.
How far is it from here to Takashima's? It's about one ri. (2.44 *miles, i.e.,* 3.927 *kilometers*)
Koko kara pan-ya made wa dono gurai arimasŭ ka? Jū go rokŭ chō deshō.
Koko kara niku-ya made wa dono gurai arimasŭ ka? Hatchō gurai deshō.
Koko kara densha no teiryūjo made wa dono gurai arimasŭ ka? San chō hodo deshō.
Koko kara Kanda made wa dono gurai arimasŭ ka? San jitchō gurai deshō.
Koko kara Yokohama made wa dono gurai arimasŭ ka? Jū ri gurai deshō.
Nagasaki kara Kōbe made wa dono gurai arimasŭ ka? Hyakŭ go jū ri gurai deshō.

Ano junsa ni kiite mimashō.
I think I'll ask that policemen.
Ano rikugun no shĭkan ni kiite mimashō.
Pan-ya San ni kiite mimashō.
Ano hĭto wa watakŭshi ni kikimashĭta.
Dōzo ano bantō ni kiite mite kudasai.
Tegami (w)o kaite mimashō.
Densha ni notte mimashō.

Shĭtsŭrei desŭ ga, Kyōbashi-yuki no densha ni wa doko de nottara yoroshiŭ gozaimasŭ ka?
Pardon me, but where do I take the Kyobashi trolley car?
Shĭtsŭrei desŭ ga, Kōbe-yuki no hikōki ni wa doko de nottara yoroshiŭ gozaimasŭ ka?
Shĭtsŭrei desŭ ga, Kanda-yuki no densha ni wa koko de nottara yoroshiŭ gozaimasŭ ka?
Shĭtsŭrei desŭ ga, Motomachi-yuki no basŭ ni wa doko de nottara yoroshiŭ gozaimasŭ ka?

Hachi ji han made ni kaettara yoroshiū gozaimasŭ ka?
If I come back by eight thirty, is it all right?

Ashĭta no gogo made ni shitara yoroshiū gozaimasŭ ka?
Motomachi to Sanchōme no kado de oritara yoroshiū gozaimasŭ ka?

Hachi ji ni kaettara, tomodachi wa watakŭshi no kaeru no (w)o matte imashĭta.
When I returned at eight o'clock, my friend was waiting for me.

Takashima-ya e ittara, shatsu wa arimasen deshĭta.
Motomachi to Sanchōme no kado de oritara, tomodachi wa imasen deshĭta.

Kono tsugi no kado kara, migi e magatte, san chōme no kado de o-nori nasai.
At this next corner, turn to the right and take (it) on the corner of Third Street.

Kono ni chōme no kado kara, hidari e magatte, san chōme ni arimasŭ.
Kono tsugi no kado kara, kita e magatte, go chōme ni Takashima-ya ga arimasŭ.
Motomachi to, ni chōme no kado kara, higashi e magatte ku chō hodo o-ide nasai.

Massugu saki e o-ide nasai.
Go straight on.

Nichō hodo massugu saki e itte, sore kara, migi e magari nasai.
San chō hodo massugu saki e itte, sore kara, hidari e magari nasai.
Kono tsugi no kado kara, kita e magatte, shi chō hodo massugu saki e o-ide nasai.

Minami e magari nasai.
Turn to the South.

Kita e magatte kudasai.
Higashi e magari nasai.
Higashi e o-magari kudasai.
Nishi e o-magari nasai.

Ni chōme no kado de o-nori nasai.
Take (it) at the corner of Second Street.

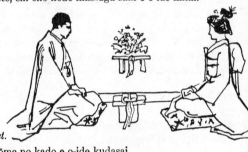

Dōzo rokŭ ji ni Bentendōri* no san chōme no kado e o-ide kudasai.
Ju hatchōme no kado de ori nasai.
Ni jū go chōme no kado de jinrikĭsha ni nottara yoroshiū gozaimashō ka?
Kono tegami (w)o Motomachi no shi chōme no hyakŭ ban e motte itte kudasai.

Doko de Kyōbashi-yuki e norikaetara ii ka shashō ni o-kiki nasai.
Ask the conductor where you transfer to the Kyobashi car.

Doko de Kanda-yuki e norikaetara yoroshiū gozaimasŭ ka?
Koko kara Tōkiō made wa dono gurai arimasŭ ka ano hĭto ni kiite mi nasai.
Takashima-ya made wa dono gurai kakarimashō ka ano kuruma-ya ni kiite mi nasai.

Ano tegami (w)o kaki nasaimashĭta ka?
Did you write that letter?

Ano hon (w)o o-yomi nasaimashĭta ka?

Mai nichi hiruhan ni wa nani (w)o o-agari nasaimasŭ ka?

Takashima-ya no depāto de nani ka o-kai nasaimashĭta ka?

Watakŭshidomo wa ima minami no hō e muite imasŭ ka?
Are we now facing South?

Hai, wakŭshidomo wa minami no hō e muite imasŭ.

Watakŭshi wa ima dochira no hō ni muite imasŭ ka?

Anata wa ima kita ni muite irasshaimasŭ.

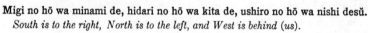

Migi no hō wa minami de, hidari no hō wa kita de, ushiro no hō wa nishi desŭ.
South is to the right, North is to the left, and West is behind (us).

Hidari no hō wa kita de, migi no hō wa minami de, ushiro no hō wa nishi desŭ.

Migi no bō wa higashi de, hidari no hō wa nishi de, ushiro no hō wa minami desŭ.

Migi no hō wa nishi de, hidari no hō wa higashi de, ushiro no hō wa kita desŭ.

Tōkiō wa dochira no hō ni arimasŭ ka?
What direction is Tokio?

Tōkiō wa higashi no hō ni arimasŭ.

Kōbe wa nishi no hō ni arimasŭ.

Nagasaki wa nishi no hō ni arimasŭ.

Hokkaidō wa kita no hō ni arimasŭ.

Kyōbashi-yuki no densha ni wa doko de norikaetara yoroshiū gozaimasŭ ka?
Where do I transfer to the Kyobashi car?

Kanda-yuki no basŭ ni wa doko de norikaetara yoroshiū gozaimasŭ ka?

Motomachi-yuki no densha ni wa doko de norikaetara yoroshiū gozaimasŭ ka?

Shinagawa-yuki no densha ni wa doko de norikaetara yoroshiū gozaimasŭ ka?

Kyōbashi e yuku ni wa densha (w)o norikae-nakereba narimasen ka?
Do I have to change trolleys to go to Kyobashi?

Hai, Kyōbashi e yuku ni wa norikae-nakereba narimasen.

Iie, Kyōbashi e yuku ni wa norikae-nakŭte mo yoroshiū gozaimasŭ.

Shinagawa e yuku ni wa densha (w)o norikae-nakereba narimasen.

Kono tsugi no teiryūjo de orite, Kyōbashi-yuki ni o-nori nasai.
Get out at the next stop and take the Kyobashi car.

Koko kara notte, go chōme no teiryūjo de orite, Kanda-yuki ni o-nori nasai.

Kono tsugi no teiryūjo de orite, Kyōbashi-yuki ni nottara ii deshō ka?

Motomachi e iku ni wa doko no teiryūjo de oritara ii deshō ka?

Jitchōme no teiryūjo de oritara ii deshō.

Kono tsugi no teiryūjo de ori nasai.
Get out at the next stop.

Kono tsugi no teiryūjo de orite kudasai.
Kono tsugi no teiryūjo de o-kudari* kudasai.

Watakŭshi wa Motomachi e ikitai n' desŭ ga Motomachi e kitara, dōzo shirasete* kudasai.
I want to go to Motomachi Street so when we come to Motomachi, please let me know.

Tomodachi wa Bentendōri e ikitai sō desu kara, Bentendōri e kitara dōzo shirasete agete kudasai.

Bantō San, shatsu wa doko ni arimasŭ ka? Shikai ni gozaimasŭ kara, hidari no erebētā (w)o o-tori kudasai.
Clerk, where are the shirts? Since they're on the fourth floor, take the elevator to the left.

Bantō San, waishatsu wa doko ni arimasŭ ka? San gai ni gozaimasŭ kara, migi no erebētā (w)o o-tori nasai.
Bantō San, shima no shatsu wa doko ni arimasŭ ka? Hakkai ni gozaimasŭ kåra, asoko no erebētā (w)o totte kudasai.

Nani (w)o goran ni kakemashō ka? Dōzo waishatsu to shima no shatsu (w)o misete kudasai.
What do you wish to see? Please show (me) some white shirts and some striped shirts.

Nani (w)o goran ni kakemashō ka? Dōzo karā to shatsu (w)o misete kudasai.
Nani (w)o goran ni kakemashō ka? Dōzo o-kashi (w)o misete kudasai.
Nani (w)o goran ni kakemashō ka? Dōzo tsukue (w)o misete kudasai.

Dōzo kochira e o-ide kudasai.
Please come here.

Dōzo sochira e o-ide kudasai.
Dōzo achira e o-ide kudasai.
Anata wa dochira no hō e o-ide ni narimashĭta ka?
Watakŭshi wa Ginza e itte[37] kimashĭta.
Watakŭshi wa achira e itte kimashĭta.
Ano rikugun no shikan wa dochira e ikimashĭta ka?
Achira e ikimashĭta.

Kono waishatsu·wa taihen kiji ga yō gozaimashĭte, nedan mo sahodo takakŭ arimasen.
These white shirts seem like very good material, and the price is not so high either.

Sono shima no shatsu wa taihen kiji ga ii yō desŭ ga nedan wa sŭkoshi takai yō desŭ.
Kono waishatsu wa taihen kiji ga ii desŭ ga nedan wa amari takakŭ arimasen.
Sono shatsu wa amari kiji ga yō gozaimasen kara, taihen yasui desŭ.

Ichi mai san yen go jissen de gozaimasŭ. Ikaga de gozaimashō ka?
They are three yen, fifty sen a piece. What do you think?

Karā wa ni hon ichi yen de gozaimasŭ. Ikaga de gozaimashō ka?

Ano kami wa hyakŭ mai jissen de gozaimasŭ. Ikaga de gozaimashō ka?
Ano sakana wa ippiki ichi yen de gozaimasŭ. Ikaga de gozaimashō ka?
Kono jidōsha wa ichi dai sen yen de gozaimasŭ. Ikaga de gozaimashō ka?

Chotto sore (w)o misete kudasai.
  Let me see it a bit (a moment).
Chotto kochira e o-ide kudasai.
Chotto o-machi kudasai.
Chotto sore (w)o koko e motte kite kudasai.
Imōto wa chotto kaimono ni ikimashĭta.

Kono shatsu wa kanari ii yō desu.
  These shirts seem quite good.
Ano depāto wa kanari ōkii yō desu.
Kono shatsu wa watakŭshi ni wa sŭkoshi chiisai yō desu.
Kono sashimi wa atarashii yō desu.
Ano hĭto wa taihen genki na yō desu.
Ano hĭtotachi wa Nippon go de hanashĭte iru yō desu.

Karā no ōkisa ga jū go desu.
  The size of the collar is fifteen.
Sono shatsu no ōkisa wa ikutsŭ desu ka?
Shatsu no ōkisa wa jū rokŭ han desu.
Anata no sei no takasa wa dono gurai arimasŭ ka?
Kono waishatsu no ōkisa wa jū go desu. Sono shima no shatsu no ōkisa wa jū shi han desŭ.

Sode no nagasa wa ni shaku hassun desu.
  The length of the sleeves is two shaku, eight sun. (1 sun = 1.2 inch) (1 shakŭ = .994 foot)
Sono kami no nagasa wa jissun desu.
Kono shatsu no sode no nagasa wa iku sun desu ka?
Ano tsukue no nagasa wa nan zun desu ka?
Kono empitsu no nagasa wa jissun desu.

Anata no sei no takasa wa ikura arimasŭ ka?
  What is your height?
Watakŭshi no sei no takasa wa shi shaku ku sun desu.
Ano rikugun no shĭkan no sei no takasa wa rokŭ shaku desu.
Tomodachi no sei no takasa wa go shaku san zun desu.

Sam mai morau koto ga dekimasŭ ka?
  May I take three?
Yo mai morau koto ga dekimasŭ ka?
Go mai utte moraitai n' desu.

Fude (w)o sambon morau koto ga dekimasŭ ka?
Sakana (w)o sam biki utte morau koto ga dekimasŭ ka?
Gyūniku (w)o san gin morau koto ga dekimasŭ ka?

Anata no uchi e todokemashō ka?
 Shall we deliver them to your home?
Tomodachi no uchi e todokemashō ka?
Anata no uchi e okurimashō ka?
Itsu anata no mise e todokemashō ka?
Tsugi no Mokuyōbi made ni watakŭshi no uchi e todokete kudasai.
Ashĭta no asa made ni watakŭshi no uchi e todokeru koto ga dekimasŭ ka?

Motte o-kaeri ni narimasŭ ka?
 Do you want to take (it) with you?
Iie, motte kaeritakŭ arimasen kara, dōzo todokete kudasai.
Ano hon wa amari ōkii deshĭta kara, motte kaerimasen deshĭta.
Ano shimbun (w)o motte kaette mo yoroshiū gozaimasŭ ka?
Amari takŭsan no tamago (w)o kaimashĭta kara, motte kaeritakŭ arimasen.

Okutte morattara, itsu watakŭshi no uchi e tsukimashō ka?
 If I have (them) sent, when will they arrive?
Ku ji ni dekaketara, itsu asoko e tsukimashō ka?
Todokete morattara, itsu Matsumoto San no mise e tsukimashō ka?
Tomodachi wa suiyōbi ni Tōkiō e tsukimashĭta.
Itsu Kōbe e o-tsuki ni narimashĭta ka?

Taku wa Kanda no itchōme desŭ ga . . .
 My house is in the Kanda district, First Street and . . .
Anata no o-taku wa dochira de gozaimasŭ ka?
Taku wa Kyōbashi no san chōme desŭ ga . . .
Taku wa Kanda no ni chōme no jū hichi ban desŭ ga . . .
Matsumoto San no o-taku wa doko desŭ ka?
Ano hĭto no taku wa Kyōbashi no Motomachi no hyaku hachi jū ku ban desŭ.

Tabun ni-san nichi no uchi ni wa tsukimashō.
 Perhaps they will arrive inside of two or three days.
Tabun shi-go nichi no uchi ni wa dekakemashō.
Tabun ichi nichi fŭtsŭka no uchi ni wa todokeru koto ga dekimashō.
Tabun go-rokŭ nen no uchi ni wa Beikokŭ e kaeru koto ga dekimashō.
Tabun san-shi ka[114] getsŭ no uchi ni wa anata ni okurimashō.

Dōzo anata no namae to banchi (w)o oshiete kudasai.
 Please give (show) me your name and address.
Dōzo anata no shatsu no ōkisa (w)o oshiete kudasai.

Dōzo shatsu no sode no nagasa (w)o oshiete kudasai.

Dōzo anata no otōsan no namae to banchi (w)o oshiete kudasai.

Dōzo ano rikugun no shĭkan no namae to banchi (w)o oshiete kudasai.

Watakŭshi no namae wa Sumisŭ de, Kanda no itchōme no jū yo ban ni sunde imasŭ.
My name is Smith and I live in Kanda, number 14 First Street.

Watakŭshi no okāsan no namae wa Takahashi de, Kyōbashi no ni jitchōme no jū go ban ni sunde imasŭ.

Ano rikugun no shĭkan no namae wa Matsumoto de, Kanda no jū go chōme no jū ban ni sunde imashĭta.

Watakŭshi no musŭko no namae wa Jones de, Ginza no san chōme no jū rokŭ ban ni sunde imasŭ.

10

Dai Jikk(w)a (Lesson X)

Kuroi kutsu (w)o issokŭ misete kudasai.
Hai, kashĭkomarimashĭta. Ōkisa wa ikutsŭ[73] de gozaimasŭ ka?
Tashika muttsŭ desŭ.

5 Sayō de gozaimasŭ ka? De wa, kore (w)o haite[77] mite kudasai.
Kore wa sŭkoshi hiro-sugiru[78] kara, kono onaji ōkisa de, mō[47] sŭkoshi semai no (w)o misete kudasai.

10 O-ki-no-dokŭ sama desŭ ga, ainikŭ kira-shĭte orimasŭ ga koko ni cha-iro to tobi-iro no ii no ga gozaimasŭ.
De wa, shĭkata ga arimasen kara, sono cha-iro no (w)o moraimashō.[76] Dōzo, tsu-
15 tsunde kudasai, motte kaerimasŭ kara.
Hai, arigatō gozaimasŭ. Soshĭte, kore wa anata no o-tsuri de gozaimasŭ.
Kono tsugi no heya de bōshi (w)o utte imasŭ ne.
20 Hai kakari no mono (w)o o-yobi itashimasŭ kara, dōzo o-hairi kudasai.

O-kyakŭ Sama, donna bōshi ga o-nozomi de gozaimasŭ ka?
Ā, kuro[43] no nakaore-bōshi to shiro to kuro
25 no goban no toriuchi-bōshi (w)o misete kudasai. Mō aki desŭ kara, mugiwara-bōshi wa sŭteru tsŭmori desŭ. Uriko San, tsuide ni, Nippon go de shiki no namae (w)o itte mite kudasai.
30 Hai, haru, natsu, aki, fuyu to iimasŭ.[15]

Kono nakaore-bōshi wā hakurai de gozai-masu, kara o-nedan wa ni jū yen de gozai-masu.
Soshĭte kono toriuchi-bōshi wa san yen de
35 gozaimasŭ.
Sō desŭ ka?
Ryōhō tomo o-tori ni narimasŭ ka?
Iie, nakaore-bōshi dake [79] moraimashō.
Maido arigatō gozaimasŭ.
40 Watakŭshi wa kaeru mae[80] ni tokei (w)o naoshĭte moratte,[76] yōfuku (w)o itchaku chūmon shĭte[50] okitai[81] desŭ ga kamaimasen ka?
Hai,[82] yoroshiŭ gozaimasŭ tomo.

Please show me a pair of black shoes.
Yes, with pleasure. What is your size?

Six, if I remember correctly.
Is that right? Well, then, please try these on.

As these are a little too wide, please let me see some a little narrower in this same size.

I am very sorry, but they are out of stock, but here are some good tan and brown ones.

Well then, since it can't be helped, I'll take those tan ones. Please wrap (them) up be-cause I'll take (them) with me.
Yes, thanks very much. And here is your change.
They sell hats in this next room, don't they?
Yes, I'll call the person in charge, so please go in.

Sir, (customer) what kind of hat do you wish?
Oh, please show me a black felt hat and a black and white checked cap. As it is already autumn, I intend to throw away my straw hat. Saleslady, by the way, please tell me the names of the four seasons in Japanese.

Yes, they are called spring, summer, au-tumn and winter.

As this hat is imported, the price is twenty yen.

And this cap is three yen.

Is that so?
Will you take both?
No, I'll take only the hat.
Thank you very much.
Before I go home, I want to have my watch repaired and order a suit made if you don't mind.

Yes, of course, it's all right.

68

At the Tailor's

45 Watakŭshi wa fuku (w)o koshiraete moraitai desŭ ga . . .	I want to have a suit made.
Sayō de gozaimasŭ ka? Mihon wa koko ni takŭsan gozaimasŭ kara, dōzo goran kudasai.	Is that so? As there are a lot of samples here, please look (them over).
50 Cha-iro no wa hade-sugiru to[15] omoimasŭ kara, kono kon no kiji no hō ga hoshii desŭ ga ikŭra kakarimasŭ ka?	As I think that the tan one is too loud, I want this dark blue material, so how much does it cost?
Kinu no ura (w)o tsukemasŭ to,[15] mitsu-gumi ga rokŭ jū yen de gozaimasŭ. Hoka no yori 55 yokŭ o-niai to omoimasŭ.	If we put in (attach) a silk lining, the suit is sixty yen. I think it looks better than the others on you.
Ja, sore de koshiraete kudasai.	All right, please make (one) up from that.
Kashĭkomarimashĭta. Shĭtsŭrei desŭ ga, uwagi to chokki to zubon no sumpō (w)o ō-tori itashimashō. Raishū made ni wa kari-60 nui ga dekimasŭ[54] kara . . .[29]	Gladly. Excuse me, but I'll take the measurements of the coat, vest, and trousers. By next week the preliminary sewing will be done, so . . .
Sore wa kekkō desŭ. Uchikin (w)o okimashō ka?	That's splendid. Shall I put down (something) on account?
Arigatō gozaimasŭ ga, o-kane wa dekiagarimashĭta toki[80] de yoroshiŭ gozaimasŭ.	Thank you, but it will be all right (to pay) the money when it is finished.
65 Ja, shĭta e orite, kutsushĭta ya[83] zubonshĭta (w)o kaimashō.	All right, let's go down (to the first floor) and buy some socks and drawers.

Exercises

Uriko San, kutsu wa doko ni arimasŭ ka?

Saleslady, where are the shoes?

Bantō San, shatsu wa doko ni arimasŭ ka?

Bantō San, bōshi wa doko ni arimasŭ ka?

Uriko San, yōfuku wa doko ni arimasŭ ka?

Uriko San, karā wa doko ni arimasŭ ka?

Kutsu wa sangai no omote no hō ni gozaimasŭ.

Shoes are on the third floor front.

Shatsu wa ni kai no ura no hō ni gozaimasŭ.

Bōshi wa shi kai ni gozaimasŭ.

Yōfuku wa go kai no omote no hō ni gozaimasŭ.

O-kashi wa kono sangai no ura no hō ni gozaimasŭ.

Zubonshĭta wa shĭta* ni gozaimasŭ.

Kuroi kutsu (w)o issokŭ misete kudasai.

Please show me a pair of black shoes.

Cha-iro no kutsu (w)o ni sokŭ kaitai n' desŭ.

Tobi-iro no kutsu (w)o jissokŭ kaitai n' desŭ.

Hakurai no kutsu (w)o shi sokŭ kaitai n' desŭ.
Tobi-iro no nakaore-bōshi (w)o fŭtatsŭ kaitai n' desŭ.
Shiroi kutsushĭta (w)o jū ni sokŭ kaitai n'desŭ.

Ōkisa wa ikutsŭ de gozaimasŭ ka? Tashika muttsŭ desŭ.
What is your size? If I remember correctly, six.

Kutsu no ōkisa wa ikutsŭ de gozaimasŭ ka? Tashika nanatsŭ han desŭ.
Nakaore-bōshi no ōkisa wa ikutsŭ de gozaimasŭ ka? Tashika muttsŭ han desŭ.
Shatsu no ōkisa wa ikutsŭ de gozaimasŭ ka? Tashika jū rokŭ desŭ.
Ano toriuchi-bōshi no ōkisa wa ikutsŭ desŭ ka? Itsutsŭ han de gozaimasŭ.

Kore (w)o haite mite kudasai.
Please try these on.

Ōkii hō (w)o haite mite kudasai.
Chiisai hō (w)o haite mitai desŭ.
Mō sŭkoshi hiroi hō (w)o haite mite kudasai.
Iie, semai hō (w)o haite mitai desŭ.

Kono jidōsha (w)o mawashĭte mite kudasai.
Please try to drive this automobile.

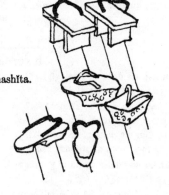

Eigo (w)o hanashĭte mite kudasai.
Sono sakana (w)o tabete mite kudasai.
Sore (w)o shĭte mite kudasai.
Nippon go (w)o hanashĭte mitai desŭ.
Kinō watakŭshi wa tegami (w)o kaite mimashĭta.

Kore wa hiro-sugimasŭ.
These are too wide.

Sore wa sema-sugimasŭ.
Are wa ōki-sugimasŭ.
Kore wa chiisa-sugimasŭ.
Kore wa taka-sugimasŭ.
Sore wa hiku-sugimasŭ.
Sore wa yasu-sugimasŭ.
Ano niku-ya wa koko kara tō-sugimasŭ.

Kono onaji ōkisa de, mō sŭkoshi semai no (w)o misete kudasai.
Please let me see a little narrower one in this same size.

Ano onaji ōkisa de, mō sŭkoshi hiroi no (w)o misete kudasai.
Kono onaji ōkisa de, mō sŭkoshi yasui no (w)o misete kudasai.
Ōkisa wa jū go de, motto ii no (w)o misete kudasai.
Kono atari de, mō sŭkoshi chikai tokoro e ikitai n' desŭ.

Kore wa onaji nedan desŭ.
This is the same price.

Ano hĭtotachi wa onaji hi ni umaremashĭta.
Onaji hĭto ni hanashimashĭta.
Onaji koto desŭ.
Ano hĭto wa watakŭshi to onaji toki ni koko e kimashĭta.

Hoka no bōshi ga arimasŭ ka?
Do you have another hat (different one)?

Hoka no hĭto ni hanashitai n' desŭ.
Hoka no kutsu wa irimasen.
Hoka no hon wa hoshikŭ arimasen.
Hoka no empitsŭ (w)o kudasai.
Hoka no mono (w)o goran ni kakemashō ka?

O-ki-no-doku Sama desŭ ga ainikŭ kirashĭte orimasŭ.
I'm very sorry, but unfortunately we are all sold out.

O-ki-no-doku Sama desŭ ga ainikŭ watakŭshi wa isoide orimasŭ.
O-ki-no-doku Sama desŭ ga ainikŭ watakŭshi wa dekake-nakereba narimasen.
O-ki-no-doku Sama desŭ ga ainikŭ ima watakŭshi no kanai wa kaimono ni itte orimasŭ.

Watakŭshi wa tegami (w)o haite orimasŭ.
I am writing a letter.

Watakŭshi wa asahan (w)o tabete orimasŭ.
Anata wa kembutsu ni itte orimashĭta ka?
Anata wa renshū (w)o manande orimashĭta ka?

Koko ni cha-iro to tobi-iro no ii no ga gozaimasŭ.
Here are some good tan and brown ones.

Koko ni atarashii ii sakana ga gozaimasŭ.
Koko ni kuroi ii kutsu ga gozaimasŭ.
Soko ni cha-iro no ii kiji ga gozaimasŭ.
Asoko ni chiisai ii o-kashi ga gozaimasŭ.

Shĭkata ga arimasen kara, sono tobi-iro no (w)o moraimashō.
Since it can't be helped, I'll take those brown ones.

Shĭkata ga arimasen kara, ano kuroi no (w)o moraimashō.
Shĭkata ga arimasen kara, ano takai no (w)o moraimashō.
Shĭkata ga arimasen kara, uchi e kaerimashō.
Shĭkata ga arimasen kara, hayakŭ jinrikisha ni norimashō.
Shĭkata ga arimasen kara, imōto (w)o tsurete ikimashō.

Dōzo tsutsunde kudasai, motte kaerimasŭ kara.
Please wrap (them *or* it), *because I want to take* (them *or* it) *with me.*

Dōzo uchi e todokete kudasai, motte kaerimasen kara.

Dōzo okutte kudasai, motte ikimasen kara.

Dōzo tsutsunde kudasai, motte kaera-nakereba narimasen kara.

Kore wa anata no o-tsuri de gozaimasŭ.
Here is your change.

Watakŭshi no tsuri wa doko ni arimasŭ ka?

Tsuri (w)o kudasai.

Anata wa tsuri (w)o ikŭra moraimashĭta ka?

Anata ni o-tsuri (w)o sashiagemashĭta ka?

Anata ni wa go yen no o-tsuri ga arimasŭ ka?

Kono tsugi no heya de, bōshi (w)o utte imasŭ ne.
In this next room they sell hats, don't they?

Kono heya de shatsu (w)o utte imasŭ ne.

Sono tsugi no heya de, muŗiwara-bōshi (w)o utte imasŭ ne.

Kono tsugi no heya de, toriuchi-bōshi (w)o utte imashĭta ne.

Ano tsugi no heya de, nani (w)o utte imasŭ ka?

Ano heya de wa nani mo utte imasen.

Kono tsugi no heya de, yōfuku (w)o koshiraete imasŭ ne.

Kakari no mono (w)o o-yobi itashimasŭ.
I'll call the person in charge.

Kakari no hĭto (w)o yonde kudasai.

Kakari no hĭto ni hanashitai desŭ.

Kakari no bantō ni hanasu koto ga dekimasen deshĭta.

"Motte o-kaeri ni narimasŭ ka?" to kakari no hĭto ga kikimashĭta.

"Iie, dōzo todokete kudasai," to kakari no hĭto ni iimashĭta.

Dōzo o-hairi kudasai.
Please enter.

Dōzo kono tsugi no heya e haitte kudasai.

Dōzo o-tsutsunde kudasai.

Dōzo ano kami (w)o sŭtete kudasai.

Dōzo kono kutsu (w)o haite kudasai.

Donna bōshi ga o-nozomi de gozaimasŭ ka? Kuro no nakaore-bōshi to toriuchi-bōshi (w)o misete kudasai.
What kind of hat do you desire? Please show me a black felt hat and a cap.

Donna shatsu ga o-nozomi de gozaimasŭ ka? Waishatsŭ to shima no shatsu (w)o misete kudasai.

Donna yōfuku ga o-nozomi de gozaimasŭ ka? Kon no zubon (w)o misete kudasai.

Donna kutsu ga o-nozomi de gozaimasŭ ka? Kuro no kutsu to cha-iro no (w)o misete kudasai.

Donna uwagi ga o-nozomi de gozaimasŭ ka? Goban no uwagi (w)o misete kudasai.

Donna chokki ga o-nozomi de gozaimasŭ ka? Shima no chokki (w)o misete kudasai.

Mō aki desŭ kara, mugiwara-bōshi wa sŭteru tsumori desŭ.
   As it is already autumn, I intend to throw away my straw hat.

Mō natsu desŭ kara, nakaore-bōshi (w)o kaitakŭ arimasen.

Mō bōshi-ya e itte kimashĭta.

Mō hiruhan (w)o o-agari ni narimashĭta ka?

Mō fuyu desŭ kara, kono shiroi kutsu wa kau tsumori ja arimasen.

Ano kami (w)o sŭtete kudasai.
   Please throw that paper away.

Ano shimbun (w)o sŭte nasai.

Ano sakana wa atarashikŭ arimasen kara, sŭtete kudasai.

Nippon go de shiki no namae (w)o itte mite kudasai.
   Please say for me the names of the seasons in Japanese.

Ano hon no namae (w)o itte mite kudasai.

Anata no namae (w)o yukkuri itte mite kudasai.

Watakŭshi wa Beikoku-jin desŭ kara, yokŭ wakarimasen deshĭta ga anata no namae (w)o katakana de kaite mite kudasai.

Ano mise no namae (w)o itte mite kudasai.

Hai, haru, natsu, aki, fuyu to iimasŭ.
   Yes, they are called spring, summer, autumn, winter.

Hai, kono hon no namae wa "Nippon go Renshū" to iimasŭ.

Anata no namae wa nan to iimasŭ ka?

Watakŭshi no namae wa Takahashi to iimasŭ.

Ano hĭto no namae wa nan to iimasŭ ka?

Ano hĭto no namae wa Matsumoto San to iimasŭ.

Ano mise no namae wa Takashima-ya to iimasŭ.

Kono nakaore-bōshi wa hakurai de gozaimasŭ kara, o-nedan wa ni jū yen de gozaimasŭ.
   As this felt hat is imported, the price is twenty yen.

Kono yōfuku wa hakurai ja arimasen kara, o-nedan wa go jū yen de gozaimasŭ.

Anata no nakaore-bōshi wa hakurai desŭ ka? Iie, hakurai ja arimasen.

Kore wa hakurai no mihon desŭ ka? Hai, sō de gozaimasŭ. Desŭ kara, o-nedan wa hichi jū yen de gozaimasŭ.

Watakŭshi no nakaore-bōshi wa hakurai deshĭta kara, nedan wa ku yen deshĭta.

Ryōhō tomo o-tori ni narimasŭ ka? Iie, nakaore-bōshi dake moraimashō.
Will you take both of them? No, I'll only take the felt hat.

Ryōhō tomo o-tori ni narimasŭ ka? Iie, toriuchi-bōshi dake moraimashō.

Ryōhō no empitsŭ ga hoshii desŭ ka? Iie, empitsŭ wa ippon dake hoshii desŭ.

Ryōhō tomo o-nozomi de gozaimasŭ ka? Iie, ryōhō tomo wa hoshikŭ arimasen.

Ryō-nin tomo anata no o-tomodachi desŭ ka? Iie, hĭtori dake ga watakŭshi no tomodachi desŭ.

Ryōhō tomo sŭkimasen.
I don't like both of them.

Ryōhō wa irimasen.

Ryōhō tomo sŭki desŭ.

Ryōhō wa moraimasen.

Mata ashĭta dōzo o-negai itashimasŭ.
I'll ask you a favor again tomorrow.

Mata ashĭta no asa dōzo o-negai itashimasŭ.

Ashĭta no gogo o-negai itashimasŭ.

Ashĭta no ban o-negai itashimasŭ.

Yōfuku (w)o itchaku chūmon shĭte okitai.
I want to order a suit of clothes.

Yōfuku (w)o san chaku go-chūmon shĭte kudasaimasŭ ka?

Iie, ni chaku dake chūmon shĭte okitai desŭ.

Ano Beikokŭ-jin ni wa yōfuku ga jitchaku aru sō desŭ.

Anata wa atarashii yōfuku (w)o kaimashĭta ne.

Niku (w)o ni kin chūmon shĭte okimasŭ.

Dōzo hon-ya e itte, atarashii hon (w)o chūmon shĭte oite kudasai.

Chūmon shĭte okimasŭ ga kamaimasen ka?
I'll place an order, if you don't mind.

Ano ko (w)o tsurete itte mo kamaimasen ka? Hai,[82] kamaimasen.

Ima tabete mo kamaimasen ka? Hai, kamaimasen.

Sŭkoshi wa matte mo kamaimasen ka? Hai, kamaimasen.

O-saki e gomen kudasai.
Excuse my going first.

Gomen kudasai.

Gomen nasai.

Yokŭ irasshaimashĭta.
You are welcome.

Watakushi wa Nippon go (w)o yokŭ hanasu koto ga dekimasen.

Ano hĭto wa Eigo (w)o yokŭ yomu koto ga dekimasen yō desŭ.

Anata wa hikōki de tobu koto ga dekimasŭ ka?

Ano hĭtotachi wa mina Nippon go (w)o yokŭ kaku koto ga dekimasŭ ka?

Ano onna no ko* wa renshū (w)o yokŭ shĭte imashĭta.

Ano otoko no ko wa yokŭ yomimashĭta.

Watakŭshi wa yōfuku (w)o itchaku koshiraete moraitai desŭ.
I want to have a suit of clothes made.

Kutsu (w)o naoshĭte moraitai desŭ.

Tokei (w)o naoshĭte moraitai desŭ.

Kono jidōsha (w)o naoshĭte kudasai.

Watakŭshi wa shatsu (w)o ichi mai koshiraete moraimashĭta.

Ano hĭto wa kirei na yōfuku (w)o koshiraete moraimashĭta.

Kutsu (w)o koshiraete kudasai.

Kono kami wa nani iro desŭ ka? Shiro desŭ.
What color is this paper? It is white.

Kono empitsŭ wa nani iro desŭ ka? Tobi-iro desŭ.

Kono yōfuku wa nani iro desŭ ka? Cha-iro desŭ.

Kono zubon wa nani iro desŭ ka? Kon desŭ.

Kono chokki wa shiro to kuro no goban desŭ.

Kono uwagi wa nani iro desŭ ka? Kuro desŭ.

Dōzo goran kudasai.
Please take a look.

Watakŭshi wa mihon (w)o mimashĭta.

Ano hĭto wa mihon (w)o mimashĭta.

Watakŭshidomo wa nakaore-bōshi (w)o mite imashĭta.

Anata wa mihon (w)o goran nasaimashĭta ka?

Anata wa toriuchi-bōshi (w)o goran ni narimashĭta ka?

Nani ka goran ni kakemashō ka?

Cha-iro no wa hade-sugiru to omoimasŭ.
I think that the tan one is too showy.

Cha-iro no wa hade-sugiru to iimashĭta.

Cha-iro no wa hade sugiru to omoimashĭta.

Tobi-iro no wa hade-sugiru to Uriko San ga iimashĭta.

Ano hĭto wa Takashima-ya e ikimashĭta to anata no okŭsan ga iimashĭta.

Anata wa go ji han ni kaeru koto ga dekimasŭ ka? to ano hĭto ga kikimashĭta.

Hade-sugiru to omoimasŭ.
I think it's too loud.

Sore wa taka-sugimasŭ.

Sore wa hiro-sugiru to omoimasŭ.

Kore wa sema-sugimasŭ.
Sore wa naga-sugiru to omoimasŭ.

Kono kon no kiji no hō ga hoshii desŭ.
I want this dark blue one.
Kono jōtō na kiji no hō ga hoshii desŭ.
Kono kuroi hō ga hoshii desŭ.
Ano kinu no hō ga hoshii desŭ.
Sono waishatsŭ no hō ga hoshii desŭ.
Ano yasui hō ga hoshii.

Kinu no ura (w)o tsukemasŭ to mitsu-gumi no yōfuku ga rokŭ jū yen de gozaimasŭ.
If I attach a silk lining, the three parts of the suit will be sixty yen.
Anata ga sono kutsu (w)o kaimasŭ to, watakŭshi wa kono kutsu (w)o kaimashō.
Anata ga Nippon go no renshū (w)o yokŭ shimasŭ to, Nippon go de hanasu koto ga deki-mashō.
Watakŭshi ga tegami (w)o kakimasŭ to, tomodachi wa Matsumoto San e motte itte kuda-saimashō.

Hoka no yori jōtō na kiji de, anata ni wa yokŭ o-niai to omoimasŭ.
This is finer quality than the others and I think it becomes you very much.
Anata wa sei ga takai kara, kono shima no kiji wa anata ni wa yokŭ o-niai to omoimasŭ.
Mō natsŭ desŭ kara, shiroi kutsu no hō ga kuroi kutsu yori o-niai to omoimasŭ.
Cha-iro no hō ga kuro no kiji yori o-niai to omoimasŭ.

Sumpō (w)o o-tori itashimashō.
I'll take your measurements.
Ano bantō San wa anata no sumpō (w)o torimashĭta.
Ano bantō San wa watakŭshi no sumpō (w)o torimashĭta.
Watakŭshi no sumpō (w)o totte kudasai.
Watakŭshi no uwagi no sumpō (w)o totte kudasai.
Watakŭshi no zubon no sumpō (w)o totte kudasai.
Watakŭshi no chokki no sumpō (w)o totte kudasai.
Kono zubon wa sŭkoshi naga-sugiru to omoimasŭ.

Raishū made ni wa kari-nui ga dekiagarimasŭ.
By next week the preliminary sewing will be finished.
Raigetsŭ made ni koshiraeru koto ga dekimasŭ ka?
Rainen made ni Amerika e kaeru koto ga dekimasŭ.
Rai-haru made ni wa kono hon ga dekiagarimashō.
Rainen no fuyu made ni wa kono atarashii jidōsha wa dekiagarimashō.
Raishū no getsuyōbi made ni wa anata no shatsu wa dekiagarimashō.

Kari-nui wa itsŭ dekiagarimashō ka?

Rainen no Sangatsŭ made ni wa watakŭshi no tomodachi wa koko e kuru tsumori desŭ to
  kaite kimashĭta.

Kōhī (w)o o-agari ni narimasŭ ka? Iya, mō kekkō.
  Will you have some coffee? No, this is plenty.

Aikawarazu genki desŭ. Sore wa kekkō desŭ.

Sore wa kekkō desŭ.

Uchikin (w)o okimashō ka?
  Shall I put down a deposit.

Iie, uchikin wa irimasen.

Iie, uchikin wa nakŭte mo yoroshiū gozaimasŭ.

Uchikin (w)o oka-nakereba narimasen ka?

Uchikin (w)o o-negai itashimasŭ.

O-kane wa dekiagarimashĭta toki de yoroshiū gozaimasŭ.
  It's all right to give the money when it is finished.

Anata ga Nippon e itta toki ni wa doko (w)o kembutsŭ shimashĭta ka?

Watakŭshi ga Takashima-ya e itta toki ni, kuroi kutsu wa arimasen deshĭta.

Tōkiō ni ita toki ni Takashima-ya e kaimono ni ikimashĭta.

Itsŭ kono tokei wa dekiagarimasŭ ka?
  When will this watch be finished?

Itsŭ kono kutsu wa dekiagarimasŭ ka?

Itsŭ kono yōfuku wa dekiagarimasŭ ka?

Itsŭ kono zubon wa dekiagarimasŭ ka?

Itsŭ kari-nui wa dekiagarimasŭ ka?

11

Dai Jū Ikk(w)a (Lesson XI)

Hanako San, anata ga hanashĭte ita[18] hĭto[84] wa dare desŭ ka?
Sentaku-ya de gozaimasŭ.
Senshū okutta sentaku mono (w)o motte
5 kimashĭta ne?
Hai, motte mairimashĭta.
De wa, ni kai ni aru yogorete iru sentaku mono[84] (w)o watashĭte[86] kudasai.
Hai, kashĭkomarimashĭta.
10 Sentaku-ya ni karā ni nori (w)o tsukete, shatsu ni wa nori (w)o tsuke-nai yō ni[65] hanashĭte kudasai. Soshĭte sentaku mono wa itsŭ dekiru[54] ka kiite kudasai.

Hanako, who is that man to whom you were speaking?
He is the laundry man.
He brought the laundry that we sent last week, didn't he?
Yes, he brought (it).
Then, please give him the soiled wash which is on the second floor.
Yes, I shall.
Please tell the laundry man to starch the collars and not to put starch in the shirts. And please ask (him) when the wash will be done.

Sŭmisŭ San, kesa anata to issho ni aruite ita
15 gunjintachi[4] wa donatagata[73] de gozaimasŭ ka?
Eikoku no suihei to Fŭransŭ no heishi de gozaimasŭ.
O-naka ga sŭkimashĭta ga, doko ka[23] de
20 oishii yūhan (w)o tabeyō[54] ja arimasen ka?
Watakŭshi wa dai sansei desu. Doko no ryōriya ga ichiban ii deshō ka?
Nihon shokŭ wa ikaga desŭ ka?
Hai, keredomo unagi-meshi wa chūmon shi-
25 nai de kudasai.[32]
Sore de wa watakŭshi ga takŭsan no yūmei no hĭto ga yokŭ yuku ryōriya[84] e tsurete itte agemashō.[86] Komban wa yokochō no Kagetsŭ e yukimashō.
30 Sore wa taihen ii kangae desŭ ne. Kagetsŭ wa tomodachi ga watakŭshi ni tegami de hanashĭta ryōriya[84] deshō.
Sono o-tegami ni wa nan to[15] kaite arimashita ka?
35 Zehi ichi-dŏ K(w)agetsŭ e itte tabete goran to kaite arimashĭta. Kono aida Beikokŭ kara watakŭshi ni kozutsumi (w)o okutte kureta hĭto[84] wa ano kata[11] desŭ.
Sŏ desŭ ka? Sā, ima kara ryōriya e ikimashō.

Mr. Smith, who are those military men who were walking with you this morning?
They are an English sailor and a French soldier.
I am very hungry, so shall we not eat a good dinner somewhere?
I agree with you absolutely. Which restaurant do you think is the best?
What do you say to Japanese food?
Yes, but please don't order eels and rice.

Well then, I shall take you to a restaurant where a great many famous people often go. To-night let's go to the (little) side street restaurant (called) *Kagetsu*.
That's really a very good idea. *Kagetsu* is the restaurant which my friend spoke to me about in (his) letter.
What did it say (was written) in that letter.

It said that I should be sure to try the *Kagetsu* restaurant once. He is the person who recently sent me the package from America.
Is that right? Come now, let's go to the restaurant right now.

In the Restaurant

40 Komban wa.
Yokŭ irasshaimashĭta.[18] Komban wa nani
(w)o sashiagemashō ka?
Dōzo sŭkiyaki (w)o fŭtari mae[64] negaimasŭ.
Hajime ni, tōfu no suimono (w)o motte
45 kite kudasai. Soshĭte, tomodachi wa hashi
(w)o tsukau koto ga deki-nai kara, nikusashi to hōchō to saji (w)o wasure-nai de
kudasai.
Hai, de, o-sake wa ikaga desŭ ka?

50 Ā, nodo ga kawaite imasŭ[31] kara, bīru (w)o
ni hon[64] moraimashō. Soshĭte budōshu mo
ippon[61] negaimasŭ.
O-kyakŭ Sama, koko e niku to yasai (w)o
motte mairimashĭta.
55 Sŭmisŭ San, ototoi Komatsŭ no ryōriya de
tabeta niku wa dame deshĭta ga koko no[10]
niku wa kanari yawarakai yō desŭ ne.

Hai, o-naka ga ippai ni narimashĭta.[69]
Tabako wa ikaga desŭ ka?
60 Hai, arigatō. Hamaki (w)o motte imasŭ.[31]
Kyūji San, mizu (w)o mō[87] ni hai motte kite
kudasai, soshĭte kanjō mo. . .
Hai, sugu motte mairimasŭ.
Ja, kore wa jū yen satsŭ da[26] kara, kore de
65 kanjō (w)o haratte kudasai. O-tsuri wa
anata e no kokorozashi desŭ yo.[88]

Good evening.
Welcome! What can we do for you this eve-
ning?
We'll take two portions of *sukiyaki* please.
First, please bring us some bean-curd soup.
And, since my friend doesn't know how to
use chopsticks, please don't forget a fork,
knife, and spoon.

Yes, and, how about something to drink?
(some liquor).
Oh, as I'm thirsty, I'll take two bottles of
beer. And also one bottle of wine.

Sir, here are (I brought) the meat and vegetables.
Mr. Smith, that meat we ate the day before
yesterday in the Komatsu restaurant was
no good, but this meat seems quite tender,
doesn't it?
Yes, I am completely filled up.
How about a smoke?
Yes, thanks, I have a cigar.
Waitress, please give us two more glasses of
water and also the bill. . .
Yes, I'll bring them at once.
Well now, here is a ten yen note, so please
pay the bill with it. The change is a tip for
you.

Exercises

Anata ga hanashĭte ita hĭto wa dare desŭ ka? Sentaku-ya de gozaimasŭ.
Who is that man to whom you were speaking? He is the laundry-man.

Anata ga hanashĭte iru hĭto wa dare desŭ ka? Kutsu-ya San de gozaimasŭ.
Anata ga hanashitai hĭto wa dare desŭ ka? Yao-ya desŭ.
Ano kata ga yonde iru hon wa donna hon desŭ ka? Nippon go no hon desŭ.
Ano onna no kata ga nutte iru mono wa nani desŭ ka? Chokki desŭ.
Anata ga mite iru mono wa nani desŭ ka? Empitsu desŭ.
Ano kata ga yonde iru shimbun no namae wa nan desŭ ka? Nichi-Nichi to iimasŭ.
Ano shimbun (w)o yonde iru hĭto no namae wa nan to iimasŭ ka? Matsumoto San to iimasŭ.

Kare[104] ga itta koto (w)o watakŭshi ni hanashĭte kudasai.
Please tell me what he said.

Matsumoto San ga kaita koto (w)o watakŭshi ni hanashĭte kudasai.
Ano hĭto ga shĭta koto (w)o watakŭshi ni hanashĭte kudasai.
Ano hĭtotachi ga mita koto (w)o ano shĭkan ni hanashimashĭta.
Watakŭshi ga tabeta koto (w)o anata ni hanashimashō.

Senshū okutta sentaku mono (w)o kudasai.
Please give me the laundry we sent last week.

Sengetsŭ no zasshi (w)o kudasai.
Senshū no shimbun (w)o sŭtete kudasai.
Watakŭshi ga sengetsŭ okutta tegami wa tsukimasen deshĭta ka?
Sengetsŭ koshiraeta hikōki ga mitai n' desŭ.
Senshū koko e kita shĭkan wa watakŭshi no itoko desŭ.

Nikai ni aru yogorete iru sentaku mono (w)o watashĭte kudasai.
Please give him the soiled wash that is on the second floor (upstairs).

Shĭta ni aru kozutsumi (w)o Takahashi San no o-taku e motte itte kudasai.
Motomachi ni aru ryōriya e ikimashō ka?
Sangai ni sunde iru hĭto no namae wa nan to iimasŭ ka?
Ano shi kai ni aru shimbun (w)o sŭtete kudasai.
Ano shĭta ni iru kata ni hanashĭte kudasai.

Karā ni wa nori (w)o tsukete kudasai.
Please put starch on the collars.

Karā ni wa nori (w)o tsuke-nai de kudasai.
Shatsu ni wa nori (w)o tsuke-nai de kudasai.
Shatsu ni wa nori (w)o tsukete kudasai.
Uwagi ni wa kinu no ura (w)o tsukete kudasai.
Uwagi ni wa kinu no ura (w)o tsuke-nai de kudasai.

Shatsu ni wa nori (w)o tsuke-nai yō ni itte kudasai.
Please tell him not to starch the shirts.

Shatsu ni wa nori (w)o tsukeru yō ni hanashĭte kudasai.
Dōzo watakŭshi no yōfuku (w)o ashĭta no jū ji made ni motte kuru yō ni itte kudasai.
Watakŭshi wa kyō uchi ni imasen kara, dōzo ano kozutsumi wa todokete kure-nai yō ni itte kudasai.
Dōzo Takahashi San ni raishū no Kinyōbi no ban koko e kuru yō ni kaite kudasai.
Dōzo Hanako San ni hachi ji ni kaeru yō ni itte kudasai.
Ano otoko no ko ni kyō ko-nai yō ni itte kudasai.

Sentaku mono wa itsŭ dekiru ka kiite kudasai.
Please ask him when the laundry will be ready.

Watakŭshi no musŭme ni itsŭ dekakeru ka kiite kudasai.
Watakŭshi no kanai ni itsŭ kaeru ka kiite kudasai.
Yōfuku-ya San ni yōfuku ga itsŭ dekiagaru ka kiite kudasai.
Ano suihei no namae (w)o Matsumoto San ni kiite kudasai.

Hai, kikimashō.
Yes, I'll ask.

Hai, sō itashimashō.
Hai, sō shimashō.
Hai, sō hanashimashō.
Hai, sō iimashō.

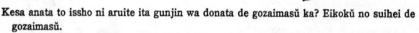

Kesa anata to issho ni aruite ita gunjin wa donata de gozaimasŭ ka? Eikokŭ no suihei de gozaimasŭ.
Who is that military man that you were walking with this morning? He is an English sailor.

Kinō depāto e anata ga tsurete itta otoko no ko wa dare deshĭta ka? Matsumoto San no musŭko deshĭta.
Watakŭshi ga kinō issho ni aruite ita onna no kata wa Takahashi San de gozaimashĭta.
Anata to Nippon go de hanashĭte ita hĭto wa dare desŭ ka? Matsumoto San to iimasŭ.
Anata ga kinō kaita tegami wa doko ni okimashĭta ka? Ni kai ni arimasŭ.

O-naka ga sŭkimashĭta.
(I am) hungry.

Watakŭshi wa o-naka ga sŭkimashĭta.
Anata wa o-naka ga sŭkimashĭta ka?
Anata mo o-naka ga sŭkimashĭta ka?
Ano hĭto wa o-naka ga suita deshō ka?

Doko ka de oishii yŭhan (w)o tabeyō ja arimasen ka?
Shall we not eat a good dinner somewhere?

Itsŭ ka oishii yūhan (w)o tabemashō ka?
Doko ka e ĭtte yukkuri hanashimashō ka?
Itsŭ ka watakŭshi no uchi e o-ide ni narimasen ka?
Doko ka de yōshokŭ (w)o tabeyō ja arimasen ka?

Bĭru (w)o issho ni nomō ja arimasen ka? Iie, hiruhan (w)o tabeyō to omoimasŭ.
Won't you drink a beer with me? No, I think I shall eat lunch.

Jū ji no basŭ ni norō to omoimasŭ.
Hayakŭ gakkō e ikō to omoimasŭ.

Zubonshĭta (w)o kaō to omoimasŭ.
Ashĭta tegami (w)o kakō to omotte imasŭ.

Watakŭshi wa dai sansei desŭ.
I heartily agree with you.

Anata wa watakŭshi ni sansei shimasŭ ka?
Iie, watakŭshi wa sansei shimasen.
Watakŭshi wa ano hĭto ni sansei shimasŭ.
Ano kata wa Takahashi San ni.sansei shimasen deshĭta.
Takahashi San to Matsumoto San wa sansei shimasen deshō.

Doko no ryōriya ga ichiban ii deshō ka?
Which restaurant do you think is the best?

Doko no depāto ga ichiban ii deshō ka?
Doko no sakana-ya e itte kimashĭta ka?
Doko no shatsu-ya ni ii shima no shatsu ga arimasŭ ka?
Doko no kutsu-ya e ikitō gozaimasŭ ka?

Yōshokŭ wa ikaga desŭ ka?
How about some western food (European or American)?

Nihon shokŭ wa ikaga desŭ ka?
Shina-meshi wa ikaga desŭ ka?

Unagi-meshi wa chūmon shi-nai de kudasai.
Please do not order eels and rice.

Takai mise e tsurete ika-nai de kudasai.
Watakŭshi no tegami (w)o ake-nai de kudasai.
Ano gunjin ni wa hanasa-nai de kudasai.
Ima nani mo kaka-nai de kudasai.
Asahan (w)o ima tabe-nai de kudasai.
Dōzo imōto·wa tsurete ko-nai de kudasai.
Jū ni ji made wa ko-nai de kudasai.

Watakŭshi ga takŭsan no yūmei na hĭto ga yokŭ iku ryōriya e tsurete itte agemashō.
I'll take you to a restaurant where many famous people often go.

Watakŭshi no tomodachi ga yokŭ iku ryōriya e tsurete itte agemashō.
Takahashi San ga watakŭshi ni kaita tegami (w)o misete agemashō.
Watakŭshi ga okāsan ga kaimono ni yokŭ iku depāto e tsurete itte agemashō.
Ikita sakana (w)o utte iru sakana-ya e tsurete itte kudasai.

Watakŭshidomo no yokŭ yomu zasshi (w)o agemashō.
I shall give you a magazine which we often read.

Anata no sŭki na hon (w)o agemashō.
Ano hĭto ga motte kita shatsu (w)o agemashō.

Kinō katta empitsu (w)o agemashō.
Senshū hanashǐta hǐto ni ano kozutsumi (w)o agemashǐta.
Sono hon (w)o kudasaimasǔ ka?
Hai, kono hon (w)o agemashō.
Watakǔshi ga kaita hon (w)o sashiagemasǔ.

Nichi-Nichi shimbun (w)o yokǔ yomimasǔ ka? Hai, yokǔ yomimasǔ.
Do you often read the Nichi-Nichi newspaper? Yes, often.

Ano ryōriya e yokǔ o-ide ni narimasǔ ka? Iie, amari mairimasen.
Takashima-ya e anata no otōsan wa kaimono ni yokǔ ikimasǔ ka? Iie, amari ikimasen.
Yūhan ni wa bīru (w)o yokǔ nomimasǔ ka? Hai, yokǔ nomimasǔ.
Sashimi (w)o yokǔ o-agari ni narimasǔ ka? Iie, amari tabemasen.

Nichi-Nichi (w)o yonda koto ga arimasǔ ka? Iie, yonda koto wa arimasen.
Have you ever read Nichi-Nichi? No, I have never read (it).

Ano ryōriya e itta koto ga arimasǔ ka? Iie, itta koto wa arimasen.
Takashima-ya e anata no otōsan wa kaimono ni itta koto ga arimasǔ ka? Hai, itta koto ga
arimashō.
Yūhan ni wa sashimi (w)o tabeta koto ga arimasǔ ka? Iie, tabeta koto wa arimasen.

Nichi-Nichi (w)o itsǔ mo yomimasǔ ka? Iie, itsǔ mo wa yomimasen.
Do you always read Nichi-Nichi? No, not always.

Ano ryōriya e itsǔ mo o-ide ni narimasǔ ka? Iie, itsǔ mo wa mairimasen.
Anata no otōsan wa Takashima-ya e kaimono ni itsu mo ikimasǔ ka? Iie, itsǔ mo wa iki-
masen.
Yūhan ni wa bīru (w)o itsǔ mo nomimasǔ ka? Hai, itsǔ mo nomimasǔ.
Hashi (w)o itsǔ mo tsukaimasǔ ka? Iie, itsǔ mo wa tsukaimasen.

Komban wa Kagetsǔ e ikimashō.
Let's go to the Kagetsu restaurant to-night.

Komban wa Komatsǔ e ikimashō.
Komban wa Matsumoto San no o-taku e ikimashō.
Kyō no gogo wa Takashima-ya e ikimashō.
Kesa anata ga hanashǐte ita tokoro e ikimashō.
Senshū watakǔshidomo ga itta ryōriya e mō ichido ikimashō.

Sore wa taihen ii kangae desǔ.
That's a very good idea.

Anata no kangae wa taihen yō gozaimasǔ.
Ano kata no kangae wa amari yokǔ arimasen.
Ano onna no kata no kangae wa taihen ii yō deshǐta.
Watakǔshi no kangae wa taihen ii deshǐta to Matsumoto San ga iimashǐta

Kagetsŭ wa tomodachi ga watakŭshi ni tegami de hanashĭta ryōriya deshō.
Kagetsu must be the restaurant which my friend wrote me about.

Takashima-ya wa Matsumoto San ga watakŭshi ni tegami de hanashĭta depāto deshō.
Sore wa tomodachi ga watakŭshi ni okutte kureta kozutsumi desŭ.
Are wa watakŭshi ga zasshi (w)o katta hon-ya* desŭ.
Kore wa imōto ga itte ita gakkō desŭ.

Sono tegami ni wa nan to kaite arimashĭta ka?
What was written in that letter?

Kono tegami ni wa nan to kaite arimasŭ ka?
Kono kozutsumi ni wa dare no namae ga kaite arimashĭta ka?
Sono kozutsumi no naka* ni wa nani ga haitte imasŭ ka?
Kono kami ni wa nan to kaite arimasŭ ka?
Kono hon ni wa donna koto ga kaite arimashĭta ka?

Kitto ichi-do Kagetsŭ e itte tabete goran to kaite arimashĭta.
He wrote that I should certainly try eating at the Kagetsu once.

Kitto ichi-do Kōbe e kembutsŭ ni itte goran to kaite arimashĭta.
Kitto ichi-do Nippon shokŭ (w)o tabete goran to kaite arimashĭta.
Ichi-do sashimi (w)o tabete goran kudasai.
Ichi-do unagi-meshi (w)o tabete goran kudasai.
Watakŭshidomo wa Kagetsŭ e itte, Nihon shokŭ (w)o tabete mimashĭta to tomodachi ni
   kakimashĭta.

Kono aida Beikokŭ kara watakŭshi ni kozutsumi (w)o okutte kureta hĭto wa ano kata desŭ.
He is the man who recently sent me the package from America.

Watakŭshi ga kinō yonde ita hon wa kore desŭ.
Kinō Takashima-ya de katta shatsu (w)o misete kudasai.
Senshū watakŭshi ga nonda hamaki wa dame deshĭta.
Kesa kaita tegami wa doko ni arimasŭ ka?

Kyūji wa watakŭshi ni hashi (w)o motte kite kuremashĭta.
The waiter kindly brought me the chopsticks.

Ano hĭto wa tegami (w)o kaite kuremasen deshĭta.
Ano hĭto wa mainichi watakŭshi ni Eigo (w)o oshiete* kuremasŭ.
Takahashi San wa watakŭshi ni kono hon (w)o kuremashĭta.
Matsumoto San wa watakŭshi ni kono hon (w)o kudasaimashĭta.

Dōzo sŭkiyaki (w)o futarimae negaimasŭ.
I should like to have two portions of sukiyaki.

Dōzo sŭkiyaki (w)o hitorimae negaimasŭ.
Dōzo tempura (w)o san nin mae negaimasŭ.

Dōzo sŭkiyaki (w)o yo nin mae negaimasŭ.

Dōzo tempura (w)o go nin mae negaimasŭ.

Hajime ni, tōfu no suimono (w)o motte kite kudasai.

First of all, please bring us some bean soup.

Hajime ni, sŭkiyaki (w)o hitorimae motte kite kudasai.

Hajime ni, sentaku-ya e itte kudasai.

Hajime ni, te (w)o aratte kudasai.

Hajime ni, Takashima-ya e ikimashō.

Tomodachi wa hashi (w)o tsukau koto ga dekimasen.

My friend doesn't know how to use chopsticks.

Watakŭshi wa hashi (w)o tsukau koto ga dekimasen.

Anata wa hashi (w)o tsukau koto ga dekimasŭ ka?

Amerika-jin wa fude (w)o yokŭ tsukau koto ga dekimasen.

Nippon-jin wa mina hashi (w)o tsukaimasŭ.

Nikusashi to hōchō to saji (w)o wasure-nai de kudasai.

Please don't forget a fork, knife, and spoon.

Niku to yasai (w)o wasure-nai de kudasai.

Watakŭshi wa hon (w)o wasuremashĭta.

Wasure-nai de kaite kudasai.

Takashima-ya e itte shatsu (w)o wasure-nai de katte kite kudasai.

Kyūji wa watakŭshidomo ni tamago (w)o motte kuru koto (w)o wasurete imashĭta.

O-sake wa ikaga desŭ ka? Bīru (w)o ni hon moraimashō.

How about something to drink? I'll take two bottles of beer.

O-sake wa ikaga desŭ ka? Bīru (w)o sambon moraimashō.

O-sake wa ikaga desŭ ka? Hai, Fŭransŭ no budōshu (w)o ni hon moraimashō.

O-sake wa ikaga desŭ ka? Sake (w)o ippon moraimashō.

O-sake wa ikaga desŭ ka? Bīru (w)o ippon moraimashō.

O-sake wa ikaga desŭ ka? Hai, arigatō gozaimasŭ ga mizu dake moraimashō.

Watakŭshi wa nodo ga kawakimashĭta.

I am thirsty.

Anata wa nodo ga kawakimashĭta ka?

Ano hĭto wa nodo ga kawakimashĭta sō desŭ.

Nodo ga kawaite ita kara, bīru (w)o shi hon nomimashĭta.

Dōzo tabe-hajimete kudasai.

Please begin eating.

Dōzo nomi-hajimete kudasai.

Dōzo kaki-hajimete kudasai.

Dōzo hanashi-hajimete kudasai.

Ototoi Komatsŭ no ryōriya de tabeta niku wa dame deshĭta ga koko no niku wa kanari yawarakai yō desŭ ne.

The meat we ate the day before yesterday in the Komatsu restaurant was no good, but this meat seems quite tender.

Ototoi Kagetsŭ no ryōriya de nonda budōshu wa dame deshĭta ga koko no budōshu wa kanari oishii yō desŭ ne.

Sengetsŭ Takashima-ya de katta shatsu wa dame deshĭta ga koko no shatsu wa ii yō desŭ ne.

Kinō Yokohama de nonda kōhī va dame deshĭta ga koko no kōhī wa kanari oishii yō desŭ ne.

Ano ototoi naoshĭte moratta tokei wa dame desŭ ga anata no tokei wa ii yō desŭ ne.

Kono niku wa yawarakakŭ arimasen.

O-naka ga ippai ni narimashĭta.
I am completely filled.

Watakŭshi wa o-naka ga ippai ni narimashĭta.
Anata wa o-naka ga ippai ni narimashĭta ka?
Ano hĭto wa o-naka ga ippai ni narimashĭta sō desŭ.

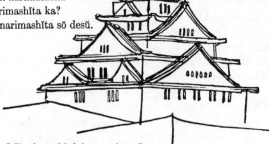

Kurokŭ narimashĭta.
It became black.

Shirokŭ narimashĭta.
Takakŭ narimashĭta.
Yasukŭ narimashĭta.
Ōkikŭ narimashĭta.

Maki-tabako* (w)o nomimasŭ ka? Iie, hamaki dake nomimasŭ.
Do you smoke cigarettes? No, I smoke only cigars.

Maki-tabako (w)o nomimasŭ ka? Iie, kiseru* dake de suimasŭ.*
Tomodachi wa hamaki ga o-sŭki desŭ ka? Taihen sŭki da sō desŭ.
Hamaki wa nomimasen. Maki-tabako dake nomimasŭ.
Hamaki wa nomimasen kara, dōzo maki-tabako (w)o kudasai.
Hamaki (w)o hito hako kaitai desŭ.
Anata ni wa matchi* ga arimasŭ ka?
Matchi (w)o futa hako moraimashō.

Mizu (w)o ni hai motte kite kudasai.
Please bring us two glasses of water.

Mizu (w)o ippai motte kite kudasai.
Bīru (w)o ippai motte kite kudasai.
Bīru (w)o mō ippai motte kite kudasai.
Budōshu (w)o mō sambai motte kite kudasai.

Bīru (w)o ippon motte kite kudasai.
Please bring a bottle of beer.

Budōshu (w)o sambon motte kite kudasai.
O-sake (w)o roppon motte kite kudasai.
O-sake (w)o shi hon motte kite kudasai.

Kanjō (w)o kudasai.
Please give me the check.

Kyūji wa kanjō (w)o motte kimashǐta.
Kanjō wa ikǔra desǔ ka?
Kanjō wa ni yen go jissen de gozaimasǔ.
Watakǔshi ga kanjō (w)o haraimashō.
Iie, watakǔshi ga haraitai desǔ.
Kutsu ni go yen haraimashǐta.

Kore wa go yen satsǔ desǔ.
This is a five yen note.

Watakǔshi wa anata ni go yen satsǔ (w)o watashimasen deshǐta ka?
Sore wa taihen ii hamaki da to omoimasǔ.
Ano yōfuki wa taihen jōtō na kiji da to bantō ga iimashǐta.
Kyō wa Nichiyōbi da kara, gakkō e ikimasen.
Tomodachi no tegami ni Kagetsǔ wa ichiban ii ryōriya da to kaite arimasǔ.

O-tsuri wa anata e no kokorozashi desǔ yo.
The change is for you!

Kyūji e no kokorozashi wa ichi yen de takǔsan desǔ ka?
Sore de takǔsan deshō.
Kore wa tomodachi kara anata e no tegami desǔ.
Takǔsan tabe-nai to, sugu o-naka ga sǔkimasǔ yo.
Kono kogane* (w)o go yen satsǔ ni kaete kudasai.
Kono sakana wa dame desǔ kara, tabete wa ikemasen yo.

12 Dai Jū Ni K(w)a (Lesson XII)

Shĭtsŭrei desŭ ga, kono machi de dono yado-ya ga ichiban ii ka go-zonji desŭ ka?

Amari yokŭ wa shirimasen ga moshi anata ga seiyō fū no hoteru ga o-sŭki nareba,[89]
5 Gŭrando Hoteru ga ichiban atarashĭkŭte, ōkiū gozaimasŭ. Moshi anata ga seiyō fū no yado-ya (w)o o-konomi de[39] nakereba,[89] Amanoya to iu[15] furui ii yado-ya ga gozaimasŭ.

10 Amanoya wa koko kara tōi desŭ ka?

Takŭshĭ de o-ide ni nareba, asoko ni mieru[90] tatemono[84] ga Amanoya de gozaimasŭ kara, hichi fun gurai de mairemashō.[90]

Arigatō gozaimashĭta.

I beg your pardon, but do you know which hotel in this town is the best?

I don't know very well, but if you like a western style hotel, Grand Hotel is the newest and the largest. If you don't want a western style hotel, the Amano is a good old inn.

Is the Amano far from here?

If you go by taxi, since the Amano is the building you can see over there, one can go in about seven minutes time.

Thank you very much.

At the Hotel

15 Bantō San, heya ga arimasŭ ka?

Hai, zashiki ga hĭtoma to shinshitsŭ ga gozaimasŭ. Sangai[61] ga yoroshiū gozaimasŭ ka? Shi kai ga yoroshiū gozaimasŭ ka?

Hā, sangai no hō (w)o negaimasŭ, shĭkashi
20 shizuka na heya ga hoshii desŭ kara, michi ni mukatte i-[56]nai heya (w)o kudasai.

Hai, kashĭkomarimashĭta.

Ima o-me ni kakemasŭ kara, soshĭte uwazōri wa kochira ni gozaimasŭ kara, dōzo kutsu
25 (w)o kore ni hakikaete o-agari kudasai.

Kono heya wa taihen kokoromochi no ii heya desŭ ne. Zembu no heya wa niwa ni men shĭte[50] imasŭ shi, soshĭte takŭsan no hana ya ki ga me no shĭta ni[14] miemasŭ.

30 Goran no tōri, kono heya wa jun Nihon fū de gozaimasŭ kara, shindai wa gozaimasen,[49] keredomo o-furo to benjo wa kono tsugi no heya ni gozaimasŭ.

Arigatō gozaimasŭ. Kore wa taisō ōkikŭte,[43]
35 akaru-sō[65] no heya desŭ ga ikŭra desŭ ka?

Hĭtoban jū yen desŭ ga isshūkan nara, go jū yen de, hĭto tsuki ga hyakŭ hichi jū go yen de gozaimasŭ. Dono gurai o-tomari no tsŭmori[72] desŭ ka?

40 Isshūkan kurai o-jama[38] ni narimashō. Jochū ni watakŭshi no nimotsu (w)o motte kite kureru[32] yō ni itte kudasai.

Clerk, do you have any rooms?

Yes, there is a living room and a bedroom. Do you prefer the third or the fourth floor?

Oh, I see. I should like the third floor, but as I want a quiet room, please give me a room that doesn't face the road (street).

Yes, gladly.

Since I'll show it to you now, and as here are some slippers, please change your shoes to these and go up.

This room is a very pleasant room, isn't it? The whole room faces the garden and besides one can see lots of flowers and trees, and such things under his eyes.

As you see, since this room is genuine Japanese style, there is no bed, but the bath and toilet are in this next room.

Thank you. This is a very large and bright looking room. How much is it?

It's ten yen per night, but if (you take it) for one week, it's fifty yen; by the month it's one hundred seventy-five yen. About how long do you intend to stay?

I'll stay about a week. Please tell the maid to kindly bring my luggage.

Daidokoro wa mada aite[91] imasŭ ka?
O-ki-no-dokŭ sama desŭ ga, ima wa mō
45 shimatte[91] imasŭ.
De wa, watakŭshi wa kanari tsukarete
imasŭ ga, sugu furo ga toremashō[90] ka?
Hai, moshi o-tsukare nareba, sekken ya
tenugui wa furoba ni gozaimasŭ ga yukata
50 wa ima jochū ga motte agarimasŭ[37] kara,
o-kikae ni natte,[44] o-furo (w)o o-tori kudasai.
Okŭsan, o-yu[38] no o-kagen wa ikaga[73] de
gozaimasŭ ka?
Ā, sŭkoshi atsu-sugiru yō da[65] kara, tsu-
55 metai mizu (w)o tashĭte kudasai.

Is the kitchen still open?
I'm very sorry but, it's already closed now.
Well then, I'm quite tired, so can I take a
bath right now?
Yes, if you are tired, soap and towels are in
the bathroom and, as the maid will bring up
a bathrobe, please change and take (your)
bath.
Madam, how is the temperature of the hot
water?
Oh, it seems a little too hot, so please add
some cold water.

Exercises

Kono machi de dono yado-ya ga ichiban ii n' desŭ ka? Yokŭ shirimasen.
Which is the best hotel in this town? I really don't know.

Kono machi de dono yado-ya ga ichiban atarashii n' desŭ ka? Yokŭ shirimasen.
Kono atari de dono ryōriya ga ichiban ii n' desŭ ka? Zonjimasen.
Bentendōri de dono yado-ya ga ichiban ii n' desŭ ka? Shirimasen.
Kagetsŭ to Komatsŭ de wa dochira ga ii n' desŭ ka?
Watakushi wa Beikoku-jin desŭ kara, sonna koto wa shirimasen.
Kono machi de dono shatsu-ya ga ichiban ii n' desŭ ka?

Go-zonji desŭ ka? Iie, shirimasen.
Do you know? No, I don't know.

Anata wa tomodachi ga Nippon e kono aida kimashĭta koto (w)o shĭtte imasŭ ka? Iie,
shirimasen.
Anata ga Nippon go ga dekiru to wa shirimasen deshĭta.
Anata wa Matsumoto San (w)o go-zonji desŭ ka? Iie, ano kata (w)o shĭtte imasen.
Ano onna no kata wa ano Beikokŭ no heishi (w)o go-zonji deshō ka? Iie, go-zonji de nai
deshō.

Seiyōfū no hoteru de gozaimasŭ ka? Nihon-fū no yado-ya ga o-sŭki de gozaimasŭ ka?
Do you want a western-style hotel or would you like a Japanese-style inn?

Seiyōfū no ryōriya ga o-sŭki desŭ ka? Nippon-fū no ryōriya de gozaimasŭ ka?
Ryōri wa Nippon-fū ni shĭte kudasai.
Hakurai no kiji no hō ga o-sŭki desŭ ka? Nippon no kiji no hō ga o-sŭki desŭ ka?
Yōfukŭ de gozaimasŭ ka? Kimono ga o-sŭki de gozaimasŭ ka?
Nihon-fū no tatemono ga o-sŭki desŭ ka? Seiyōfu no tatemono ga o-sŭki desŭ ka?

Moshi anata ga seiyōfū no hoteru ga o-sŭki nareba, Gŭrando Hoteru ga ichiban atarashĭkŭte ōkiū gozaimasŭ.
If you would like a western style hotel, Grand Hotel is the newest and the largest.

Moshi anata ga Nihon-fū no yado-ya (w)o o-konomi nareba, Amanoya ga gozaimasŭ.

Moshi anata ga takŭsan o-agari ni nara-nakereba sugu o-naka ga sŭkimashō.

Moshi anata ga tegami (w)o o-kaki ni nara-nai nareba, deru koto wa dekimasen deshō.

Moshi anata ga sore (w)o katakana de kaite kudasaimasureba, watakŭshi wa wakarimashō.

Moshi sore ga dekiagarimasureba, motte kite kudasai.

Moshi anata ga o-ide ni naru koto ga o-sŭki nareba, dōzo o-ide kudasai.

Moshi watakŭshi ga sono tegami (w)o kakeba, anata wa Takahashi San e motte ikimashō ka?

Moshi watakŭshi ga kono tegami (w)o kaka-nakereba, tomodachi wa koko e kyō kimashō.

Moshi anata ga Nippon no hikōki (w)o goran ni nareba, watakŭshi ni sō itte kudasai.

Moshi anata ga Takahashi San (w)o goran ni nara-nakereba, hayakŭ kaette kudasai.

Moshi ano kata ga kaimono ni ikeba, watakŭshi wa ano hĭto to issho ni ikimashō.

Watakŭshi no kanai ga kyō depāto de shatsŭ (w)o kaeba, watakŭshi wa dekake-nakŭte mo ii deshō.

Moshi watakŭshi no otōsan wa kutsushĭta (w)o kawa-nakereba, watakŭshi wa Takahima-ya e ika-nakereba narimasen.

Gŭrando Hoteru ga ichiban atarashĭkŭte, ōkii tatemono de gozaimasŭ.
Grand Hotel is the newest and it is a big building.

Kono kutsu wa shirokŭte kirei desŭ.

Ano hana wa, tobi-iro de, chiisai desŭ.

Ano ōkikŭte atarashii tatemono wa Gŭrando Hoteru desŭ.

Watakŭshi no bōshi wa chiisakŭte kuroi n' desŭ.

Moshi anata ga seiyōfū no yado-ya o-konomi de nakereba, Amanoya ga gozaimasŭ.
If you don't want a western style hotel, there is the Amanoya.

Moshi anata ga Nihon shokŭ ga o-konomi de gozaimasureba, Komatsŭ no ryōriya ga gozaimasŭ.

Moshi anata no Nippon no tomodachi ga Shina-meshi (w)o o-konomi de nakereba, Kagetsŭ wa Nippon-fū no ryōriya desŭ.

Moshi anata ga ima haraitaku nakereba, uchikin dake de mo yoroshiū gozaimasŭ.

Moshi anata ga ashĭta kitaku nakereba, dōzo watakŭshi ni sō itte kudasai.

Amanoya to iu furui ii yado-ya ga gozaimasŭ.
There is a good old inn called Amanoya.

Kono tatemono ga Takashima-ya to iu depāto desŭ.

Ima asoko de hanashĭte iru hĭto wa Tanaka San to iu kata desŭ.

Kore wa nan to iu yasai desŭ ka?

Sore wa ninjin to iu yasai desŭ.

Takahashi San to iu kata wa doko ni imasŭ ka?

Anata ga depāto e ittara, Matsumoto to iu bantō ni watakŭshi no shatsu no koto (w)o kiite kudasai.

Amanoya wa koko kara tōi desŭ ka? Moshi takŭshĭ de oide nareba, hichi fun kan gurai de mairemashō.

Is the Amanoya far from here? If you go by taxi, you can go in about seven minutes.

Kagetsŭ wa koko kara tōi desŭ ka? Moshi jinrikĭsha de o-ide ni nareba, jippun kan gurai de ikemashō.

Takashima-ya wa Komatsŭ kara tōi desŭ ka? Moshi anata ga aruite o-ide ni nareba, jū go fun kan gurai de ikemashō.

Anata wa Nippon go ga kakemasŭ ka? Hai, keredomo katakana dake sŭkoshi kakemasŭ.

Can you write Japanese? Yes, but I can only write a little in katakana.

Anata wa Fŭransŭ go ga yomemasŭ ka? Iie, sŭkoshi mo yomemasen.

Watakŭshi wa Nippon go wa hanasemasen.

Ima dekakeru koto ga dekimasŭ ka?

Watakŭshi wa ano budōshu wa nomemasen deshĭta.

Takashima-ya de shima no shatsŭ ga kaemashō ka? Tabun kaemashō.

Asoko ni mieru tatemono wa gakkō desŭ.

Heya ga arimasŭ ka? Hai, zashiki ga hĭto ma to shinshitsŭ ga gozaimasŭ.

Do you have any rooms? Yes, there is a parlor and a bedroom.

Heya ga aite* imasŭ ka? Ni kai ni ii heya ga fŭta ma gozaimasŭ.

Shinshitsŭ ga iku ma irimasŭ ka? Shinshitsu ga mi ma hoshii desŭ.

Zashiki to shinshitsŭ (w)o o-nozomi de gozaimasŭ ka?

Iie, shinshitsŭ dake hoshii desŭ.

Shinshitsŭ (w)o hito ma misete kudasai.

Nan gai ga o-sŭki desŭ ka? Shĭta (w)o negaimasŭ.

Which floor do you like? I would like the first floor.

Nan gai ga o-sŭki desŭ ka? Ni kai (w)o negaimasŭ.

Nan gai ga o-sŭki desŭ ka? Go kai ga sŭki desŭ.

Nan gai ga o-sŭki desŭ ka? Rokkai ga sŭki desŭ.

Nan gai ga o-sŭki desŭ ka? Hachi kai ga sŭki desŭ.

Ano tatemono ni wa nan gai arimasŭ ka?

How many floors are there in that building?

Ano tatemono ni wa hachi kai arimasŭ.

Watakŭshi no jimusho wa san gai desŭ.

Amanoya ni wa shi kai arimasŭ.

Ano tatemono no takasa wa dono gurai arimasŭ ka?

Hyakŭ go jisshakŭ gurai deshō.

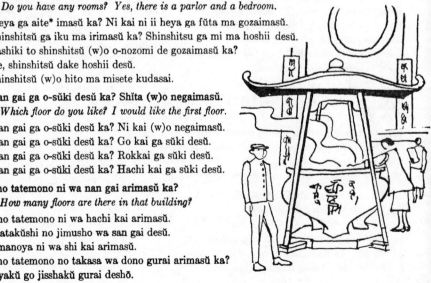

Shizuka na heya ga hoshii desŭ.
I want a quiet room.

Motto ōkii heya ga hoshii desŭ.
Kono yado-ya de ichiban ōkii heya ga hoshii desŭ.
Motto chiisai heya ga hoshii desŭ.
Motto akarui heya ga hoshii desŭ.

Michi ni mukatte i-nai heya (w)o kudasai.
Please give me a room which does not face the street.

Michi ni mukatte iru heya (w)o kudasai.
Niwa ni mukatte iru heya (w)o kudasai.
Watakŭshi ga Tōkiō ni ita toki ni wa, ano tatemono ni mukatte iru heya ni sunde imashĭta.
Michi ni mukatte i-nai heya (w)o bantō ni negaimashĭta.

Heya (w)o ima o-me ni kakemashō.
I'll show you the room now.

Watakŭshi no katta hon (w)o ima o-me ni kakemashō.
Watakŭshidomo no niwa (w)o ima o-me ni kakemashō.
Watakŭshi no atarashii yōfuku (w)o ima o-me ni kakemashō.
Okāsan kara moratta tokei (w)o ima o-me ni kakemashō.

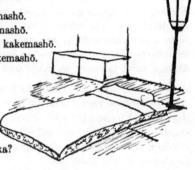

Dōzo kutsu (w)o kore ni hakikaete kudasai.
Please change your shoes to these.

Kono atarashiį zubon ni hakikaete kudasai.
Kono cha-iro no kutsu ni hakikaete kudasai.
Kono uwazōri ni hakikaete kudasai.
Anata wa kesa kutsushĭta (w)o hakikaemashĭta ka?
Kono yukata ni kikaete kudasai.
Dōzo kono yōfuku ni kikaete kudasai.

Kyō wa kokoromochi ga ii desŭ ka? Hai, taihen ii kokoromochi desŭ.
Are you feeling fine to-day? Yes, I feel very fine.

Kore wa taihen kokoromochi no ii heya desŭ.
Kore wa amari kokoromochi no ii shinshitsu ja arimasen.
Kinō wa kokoromochi ga yokŭ nai deshĭta.
Ano hĭto wa kokoromochi ga ii to itte imashĭta.

Zembu no mado wa niwa ni men shĭte imasŭ.
The whole window faces the garden.

Zembu no mado wa michi ni men shĭte imasen.
Fŭtatsu no mado dake niwa ni men shĭte imasŭ.
Zembu no heya wa higashi ni men shĭte imasen.
Zembu no tenugui wa yogorete imasŭ.

Takŭsan no hana ga me no shĭta ni miemasŭ.
You can see a lot of flowers under your eyes.

Takahashi San no niwa ni takŭsan no ki ga miemasŭ.
Asoko ni ōki na tatemono ga miemasŭ.
Densha no mado kara takŭsan no hĭto ga miemasŭ.
Heya no mado kara michi ga me no shĭta ni miemasŭ.

Go-zonji no tōri, kono ryōriya wa jun Nippon-fū de gozaimasŭ kara, saji ya hōchō ya nikusashi wa amari tsukaimasen.
As you know, since this restaurant is pure Japanese style, they don't use spoons or knives or forks very much.

Goran no tōri, kono yado-ya wa jun Nippon-fū de gozaimasŭ kara, shindai wa gozaimasen.
Goran no tōri, kono heya wa jun Nippon-fū de gozaimasŭ kara, isu wa gozaimasen.
Goran no tōri, kono ryōriya wa jun Nippon-fū de gozaimasŭ kara, hashi (w)o tsukaimasŭ.
Go-zonji no tōri, kono hoteru wa jun seiyōfū de gozaimasŭ kara, heya ni wa mina shindai ga arimasŭ.

O-furo to benjo wa kono tsugi no heya ni gozaimasŭ kara, dōzo go-zuii ni o-negai itashimasŭ.
As the bathroom and toilet are in this next room, feel free to do as you please.

O-furo wa migi no hō ni gozaimasŭ kara, dōzo go-zuii ni o-negai itashimasŭ.
O-cha wa koko ni oite mairimasŭ kara, dōzo go-zuii ni o-negai itashimasŭ.
Shimbun wa koko ni gozaimasŭ kara, go-zuii ni goran kudasai.
O-kashi wa koko e motte mairimashĭta kara, go-zuii ni o-negai itashimasŭ.

Kore wa taisō ōkikŭte akaru-sō na heya desŭ.
This is a very big room and it seems light.

Sore wa taisō ōkikŭte oishii-sō na o-kashi desŭ.
Kore wa taisō kirei de ōii heya desŭ.
Kore wa akarukŭte kirei na shinshitsŭ desŭ.
Kono shima wa hade desŭ kara, tomodachi ga sŭki-sō na shatsŭ desŭ.

Hĭtoban jū yen desŭ ga isshūkan nara, go jū yen de gozaimasŭ.
It is ten yen for one night, but it is fifty yen per week.

Hĭtoban jū yen desŭ ga fŭtaban nara, jū go yen de gozaimasŭ.
Isshūkan go jū yen desŭ ga ni shūkan nara, hachi jū go yen de gozaimasŭ.
Kono jidōsha chin wa ichi jikan ni yen desŭ ga ni jikan nara, san yen go jissen desŭ.
Kono jidōsha wa ichi nichi ni jū yen desŭ ga fŭtsŭka nara, san jū go yen de, han nichi wa jū go yen de gozaimasŭ.
Kono heya wa hĭto tsuki hyakŭ yen desŭ ga ichi nen nara, sen yen de gozaimasŭ.

Dono gŭrai o-tomari no tsŭmori desŭ ka? Isshūkan gŭrai o-jama ni narimashō.
How long do you intend to stay? I'll probably stay about one week.

Dono gŭrai o-tomari no tsŭmori desŭ ka? Ni shūkan gŭrai o-jama ni narimashō.

Dono gŭrai o-tomari deshĭta ka? Watakŭshi wa Amanoya ni fŭta tsuki no aida o-jama ni natte imashĭta.

Ano kata wa dono gŭrai koko ni tomatte imashĭta ka? Ano kata wa Gŭrando Hoteru ni mi tsuki no aida tomatte imashĭta.

Ano kata wa Amanoya ni yokka no aida tomatte imasŭ.

Dono gŭrai Tōkiō ni o-sumi ni natte imasŭ ka? Watakŭshi wa Tōkiō ni ku nen kan sunde imasŭ.

Jochū ni watakŭshi no nimotsŭ (w)o motte kite kureru yō ni itte kudasai.
Please tell the maid to kindly bring me my baggage.

Jochū ni watakŭshi no nimotsŭ (w)o heya e motte itte kureru yō ni itte kudasai.

Jinrikĭsha-ya ni kono kozutsumi (w)o Takahashi San no o-taku e motte itte kureru yō ni itte kudasai.

Jochū ni watakŭshi no heya e mizu (w)o ippai motte kuru yō ni itte kudasai.

Jochū ni kono yogoreta sentaku mono (w)o sentaku-ya ni watasu yō ni itte kudasai.

Jochū ni watakŭshi no heya e kuru yō ni itte kudasai.

Tomodachi ga kitara, watakŭshi no heya e kuru yō ni itte kudasai.

Daidokoró wa mada aite imasŭ ka? Iie, ima wa mō shimatte imasŭ.
Is the kitchen still open? No, it's already closed (now).

Mado wa mada aite imasŭ ka? Iie, ima wa mō shimatte imasŭ.

Matsumoto San wa mada anata no uchi ni imasŭ ka? Iie, mō kaerimashĭta.

Anata wa Nihon go (w)o mada manande imasŭ ka? Iie, ima wa manande imasen.

Tomodachi wa mada* kimasen ka? Hai, mada kimasen.

Anata wa mada hiruhan (w)o tabemasen ka? Hai, mada tabemasen.

Moshi o-arai ni narimasureba, sekken ya tenugui wa kochira ni gozaimasŭ.
If you are going to wash, here are towels and soap and so forth.

Moshi o-naka ga o-sŭki nareba, gohan* (w)o agemashō.

Moshi musŭko San ga o-konomi de nakereba, shĭkata ga gozaimasen.

Moshi nodo ga o-kawaki nareba, mizu (w)o sashiagemashō.

Moshi anata ga tegami (w)o kaki nareba, kami to pén (w)o motte mairimashō.

Moshi anata ga yōfuku (w)o kaitai nareba, hoka no yōfuku-ya e ikimashō.

Sekken to tenugui (w)o motte kite kudasai.

Jochū ni sekken to tenugui (w)o motte kuru yō ni itte kudasai.

Sekken (w)o hĭto hako moraitai desŭ.

Kono uwagi (w)o kite kudasai.
Please put on this coat.

Kono shatsŭ (w)o kite kudasai.

Kono yōfukŭ (w)o kite kudasai.
Cha-iro no yōfukŭ (w)o kite, dekakemashĭta.
Yukata ni o-kikae kudasai.
Kono kuroi kutsu (w)o haite kudasai.
Sono kutsushĭta (w)o hakitakŭ arimasen.

Bōshi (w)o kaburi nasai.
   Put on your hat.
Ano nakaore-bōshi (w)o kabutte kudasai.
Sono toriuchi-bōshi wa kabura-nai de kudasai.
Kono kuroi nakaore-bōshi (w)o o-kaburi kudasai.

Kutsŭ (w)o nuide kudasai.
   Please take off your shoes.
Anata no yōfuku (w)o nuide kudasai.
Ano hĭto wa bōshi (w)o nugitakŭ nai to iimashĭta.
Yogoreta kutsushĭta (w)o nugitai desŭ.

Danna Sama, o-yu no o-kagen wa ikaga de gozaimasŭ ka? Sŭkoshi atsu-sugimasŭ.
   Sir, how is the temperature of the water? It's a little too hot.
Kono heya wa atsu-suigimasŭ.
Kono mizu wa amari tsumetakŭ arimasen kara, motto tsumetai no (w)o motte kite kudasai.
Kono o-cha wa sŭkoshi tsumetakŭ narimashĭta.

San ni go (w)o tasu to, hachi ni narimasŭ.
   If you add five to three, it becomes eight. (Five and three are eight.)
Rokŭ ni shi (w)o tasu to, ikutsŭ ni narimasŭ ka? Jū ni narimasŭ.
Jū san ni go (w)o tasu to, jū ku ni narimasŭ ka? Iie, sō ja arimasen. Jū hachi ni narimasŭ.

Sŭkoshi o-nagashi itashimashō ka? Iya, sore ni wa oyobimasen.
   Shall I perform the bath service for you? No, don't bother about that.
Sŭkoshi o-machi itashimashō ka? Iya, sore ni wa oyobimasen.
Asahan (w)o anata no heya e motte agarimashō ka? Iya, sore ni wa oyobimasen.
Mizu (w)o motte mairimashō ka? Iya, sore ni wa oyobimasen.
Matsumoto San no o-taku made o-okuri itashimashō ka? Iya, sore ni wa oyobimasen.

13

Dai Jū San K(w)a (Lesson XIII)

Ano kusuri no bin wa kowasaremashĭta[92] ka? Doko ni arimasŭ ka?

Shindai no soba ni aru hazu[68] desŭ.

Konna[28] tsukue no hashi ni oite wa abunai desŭ.

Denwachō ga mitsukarimasen[92] ga dō[73] sareta[92] n' deshō ka?

Sō de gozaimasŭ ka? De wa, tonari no denwachō (w)o karite mairimashō[37] ka?

Dōzo ane San ni o-isha San e denwa (w)o kakesasete[93] kudasai. Watakŭshi wa sakuban hĭtoban-jŭ[94] neraremasen[92] deshĭta.

Was that medicine bottle broken? Where is it?

It should be beside the bed.

Putting it on the edge of the table like this is dangerous.

I can't find the phone book so what happened to it?

Is that so? Then, shall I go borrow the neighbor's phone book?

Please have my elder sister phone the doctor. I couldn't sleep last night the whole night through.

At the Telephone

Moshi. Moshi. Motomachi no sen roppyakŭ san jū yo ban e.

Motomachi no sen roppyakŭ san jū yo ban desŭ ka?

Hai, sō desŭ.

Ainiku anata no bangō wa fusagatte imasŭ kara, sŭkoshi o-machi kudasai. Ima o-de ni narimashĭta[40] kara, ryōkin (w)o irete, o-hanashi kudasai.

Hai, arigatō. Ima iremasŭ yo![88]

Hello. Hello. (Give me) Motomachi 1634.

Motomachi 1634?

Yes, that's right.

Unfortunately, as your line is busy now, please wait a little. Since I have the connection through now, please put in the money (phone charge) and (go ahead and talk).

Yes, thanks. I'm putting it in now. (Here it goes.)

Moshi. Moshi.

Moshi. Moshi. Anata wa Takagi San no o-taku desŭ ka?

Hai, sō de gozaimasŭ.

Watakŭshi wa Yamada de gozaimasŭ ga, o-isha San wa o-ide de gozaimasŭ ka?

Hai, irasshaimasŭ.

Chotto watakŭshi ni hanasasete[93] kudasai.

O-isha San, Yamada San kara o-denwa de gozaimasŭ.

Moshi. Moshi. Anata wa Yamada San desŭ ka? Watakŭshi wa Takagi desŭ ga nani ka yōji ga arimasŭ ka?

Hai, Takagi San, imōto no byōki no yōsu ga sŭkoshi warui yō de, mō ichi-do go-shinsatsŭ (w)o o-negai shĭtai n' desŭ[55] ga anata no go-tsugō wa ikaga de gozaimasŭ ka?

Hello. Hello.

Hello. Hello. Is this Dr. (Mr.) Takagi's residence?

Yes, it is.

I am Miss Yamada. Is the doctor in?

Yes, he is.

Please let me speak (to him).

Doctor, Miss Yamada is calling on the phone.

Hello. Hello. Are you Miss Yamada? I am Dr. Takagi. Is there something I can do for you? (Do you have any business with me?)

Yes, Dr. Takagi, (the condition of) my sister's illness seems a little worse and we would like you to examine her once more, so how would it suit your convenience?

96

40 Ja, sugu itte mite agemashō.[86]
O-machi shĭte orimasŭ. Sayōnara.

Very well, I'll try to come at once.
We'll be waiting for you. Goodbye.

Hanako San, dō iu[73] ambai desŭ ka?
Hai, Takagi San, sakuban wa taihen na
zutsū ga shĭte,[50] neraremasen[92] deshĭta no
45 de,[29] kesa wa nedoko kara okiraremasen.[92]
Ane San ni ano kusuri (w)o nomasaremashĭta[93] ga mada kibun wa yokŭ arimasen.
Mune ya kata ya ude ya karada-jū[94] ga
itande, komatte orimasŭ.
50 Dono hen ga ichiban itai n' desŭ ka[75] misete
kudasai.
Kono hen desŭ ga dōzo amari sawara-nai
de kudasai.[32]
Chotto kuchi (w)o akete, shĭta (w)o dashĭte
55 kudasai. Ima netsŭ (w)o hakatte mimashō.
Sore kara, dōzo sŭkoshi migi no hō e yoko ni
natte, fukakŭ[28] iki (w)o sutte kudasai.
Kondo wa iki (w)o haki-dashĭte[27] kudasai.
Anata wa kaze (w)o hiite ita no ni,[95] sŭkoshi
60 muri (w)o shĭta to miete, haien ni natta yō
ni omowaremasŭ.[92] Kŭsuri (w)o agemasŭ
kara, ni jikan-goto ni hĭto saji-zutsŭ[53] nonde
kudasai. Sō sureba, shi-go nichi no uchi ni
wa naorimashō.

Miss Hanako, how are you getting along?
Well, Dr. Takagi, last night I had a bad
headache and because I couldn't sleep, this
morning I can't get out of bed. My elder
sister made me drink that medicine, but I
don't feel well yet. My chest, shoulder, arm,
and my whole body hurts and I am suffering.

Please show me where it hurts the most.

It's this part, so please don't touch it much.

Please open your mouth a moment and put
out your tongue. Now I'm going to take
your temperature. After that, please turn
on your right side and take a deep breath.
This time please breathe out.
Although you got a cold, it seems you took
little care and it looks as if it has become the
grippe. I'll give you some medicine, so
please take (drink) one teaspoonful every
two hours. If you do that, inside of four or
five days you will get better.

Exercises

Ano kusuri no bin wa kowasaremashĭta ka?
Was that medicine bottle broken?

Ano isu wa dare ni kowasaremashĭta ka?
Watakŭshi no musŭko ni sore wa kowasaremashĭta.
Watakŭshidomo no denwa wa kowasaremashĭta kara dōzo naoshĭte moratte kudasai.
Ano otoko no ko wa imōto ni kashi (w)o taberarete komatte imasŭ.
Ano otoko no ko wa tabako (w)o nonde iru no (w)o otōsan ni miraremashĭta.
Watakŭshi nó tokei wa dare ka ni toraremashĭta.
Jochū wa shujin ni yobaremashĭta.

Shindai no soba ni aru hazu desŭ.
It should be beside the bed.

Tsukue no soba ni aru hazu desŭ.
Tsukue no shĭta ni aru hazu desŭ.

Tsukue no ue ni aru hazu desŭ.
Hako no naka ni aru hazu desŭ.
Furoba ni aru hazu desŭ.
Sono tsukue (w)o shindai no soba ni oka-nai de kudasai.
Tsukue no ue ni oite kudasai.
Tsukue no shĭta ni oka-nai de kudasai.
Empitsu wa anata no mae ni arimasŭ; anata no ushiro ni wa arimasen.

Kyō koko e kuru hazu no tomodachi wa mada kite imasen.
My friend who is supposed to come today has not come yet.

Ashĭta anata ga iku hazu no tokoro wa doko desŭ ka?
Tomodachi wa shitte iru hazu desŭ ga wasureta to iimashĭta.
Tanaka San wa watakŭshi no uchi e gogo ichi ji ni tsuku hazu deshĭta.

Konna tsukue no hashi ni oite wa abunai desŭ.
Putting it like this on the edge of the table is dangerous.

Konna mado no soba ni oite wa abunai desŭ.
Sonna mado no chikakŭ e iku to, abunai desŭ.
Ano jidōsha wa amari furui kara, abunai desŭ.
Sonna takai tokoro kara tonde wa abunai desŭ.

Denwachō ga mitsukarimasen deshĭta ga dō sareta n' deshō ka?
I can't find the telephone book. What was done with it?

Kutsu ga mitsukarimasen ga dō sareta n' deshō ka?
Watakŭshi no bōshi ga mitsukarimasen ga dō sareta n' deshō ka?
Tomodachi ga mitsukarimasen.
Tsugi no heya de ano kata no chokki (w)o mitsukemashĭta.*
O-kashi (w)o tabete ita ko wa okāsan ni mitsukeraremashĭta.
Konna koto wa dare ni saremashĭta ka?
Ano warui ko ni saremashĭta.

Tonari no denwachō (w)o karite mairimashō ka?
Shall I go borrow the neighbor's phone book?

Tomodachi kara hon (w)o karite kite agemashō ka?
Watakŭshi wa empitsŭ ga mitsukarimasen ga anata no (w)o karite mo ii n' desŭ ka? Hai, tsukatte mo ii n' desŭ.
Ane San kara kami (w)o karite kimashĭta.
Otōsan kara o-kane (w)o karite kudasai.

Dōzo ane San ni o-isha San e denwa (w)o kakesasete kudasai.
Please have my elder sister phone the doctor.

Dōzo Takahashi San ni ano tegami (w)o kakasete kudasai.
Watakŭshi wa Hanako San ni kono shatsŭ (w)o kawasasemashĭta.

Dōzo jochū ni koko e kosasete kudasai.

Tsugi no Suiyōbi ni sentaku-ya ni sentaku mono (w)o motte kosasete kudasai.

Jochū ni kaimono ni ikasemashō.

Dōzo Takagi San e denwa (w)o kakete kudasai.

Tomodachi e denwa (w)o kaketai desŭ. Ima anata no o-denwa (w)o tsukatte mo yoroshiū gozaimasŭ ka?

Chotto denwa (w)o watakŭshi ni kakesasete kudasai.

Watakushi wa sakuban hĭtoban-jū neraremasen deshĭta.
I could not go to sleep the whole night last night.

Watakushi wa ichi nichi-jū deraremasen deshĭta.

Dōzo koko ni nete kudasai; shinsatsŭ (w)o itashimasŭ kara.

Dōzo tatte kudasai; shinsatsŭ (w)o itashimasŭ kara.

Mai ban yokŭ neraremasen.

Anata wa sakuban yokŭ neraremashĭta ka?

Ano sashimi wa taberaremasen deshĭta.

Ano kutsu wa sema-sugiru kara, hakemasen.

Ano yōfuku wa hade-sugiru kara, kiraremasen.

Moshi! Moshi! Motomachi no sen roppyakŭ san jū yo ban e. Motomachi no sen roppyakŭ san jū yo ban desŭ ka?
Hello! Hello! Give me Motomachi 1634. Motomachi 1634?

Moshi! Moshi! Kyōbashi no go hyakŭ rei rokŭ ban e. Kyōbashi no go hyakŭ rokŭ ban desŭ ka?

Moshi! Moshi! Honjō no sen ni hyakŭ jū ichi ban e. Honjō no sen ni hyakŭ jū ichi ban desŭ ka?

Dōzo Takagi San e denwa (w)o kakete kudasai. Bangō wa Kanda no ni hyakŭ jū rokŭ ban desŭ kara, sugu kuru yō ni hanashĭte kudasai.

Ainikŭ anata no bangō wa ima fusagatte imasŭ, sŭkoshi o-machi kudasai.
Sorry, the line is busy now, please wait a minute.

Anata no denwa no bangō wa nan ban desŭ ka?

Watakŭshi no denwa no bangō wa Motomachi ni hyakŭ yo ban desŭ. Dōzo ashĭta no ban rokŭ ji ni watakŭshi ni denwa (w)o kakete kudasai.

Benjo wa ima fusagatte imasŭ.

Ainikŭ zembu no heya wa ima fusagatte imasŭ; dōzo ashĭta no asa kite mite kudasai.

Watakŭshi wa jū ji ni deru tsumori desŭ.
I intend to leave at ten o'clock.

O-ki-no dokŭ Sama desŭ ga, imōto wa kusuri (w)o kai ni dete imasŭ.

Kono tsugi no basŭ wa nan ji ni demasŭ ka?

Kinō anata wa uchi (w)o nan ji ni demashĭta ka?

Ryōkin (w)o irete kudasai.
Please put in the (charge) money.

Ano hako ni kane (w)o irete kudasai.
Doko e watakŭshi no tegami (w)o iremashĭta ka? Tsukue no ue ni okimashĭta.
Ryōkin (w)o iremashō.

Chotto watakŭshi ni hanasasete kudasai.
Please let me speak (to him) a moment.

Ano tegami (w)o ano kata ni kakase-nai de kudasai.
Ano mise no nedan wa taka-sugiru kara, jochū ni ano mise de wa kawase-nai de kudasai.
Ano ko ni Nippon shokŭ (w)o tabesasete kudasai.
Ano kata ga anata ni hanashĭta koto (w)o kikasete kudasai.

O-isha San, Yamada San kara o–denwa de gozaimasŭ.
Doctor, Mr. Yamada is on the phone.

Takahashi San, Matsumoto San kara o–denwa de gozaimasŭ.
Anata wa donata de gozaimasŭ ka? Watakŭshi wa Takagi desŭ. Sŭkoshi o-machi kudasai.
Sugu o-yobi itashimasŭ kara. Yamada San, Takagi San kara o–denwa de gozaimasŭ.
Chotto gomen kudasai. Buraun San, Sŭmisŭ San kara o–denwa de gozaimasŭ. Arigatō gozai-
masŭ. Sugu mairimasŭ.
Denwa wa donata kara desŭ ka?
Tomodachi kara denwa ga kakarimashĭta.
Dare ka kara denwa ga kakarimashĭta ka?

Nani ka yōji ga arimasŭ ka?
Do you have any business with me?

Watakŭshi wa kyō takŭsan yōji ga arimasŭ kara, o-ki-no-dokŭ desŭ ga anata no uchi e iku
koto ga dekimasen.
Donna yōji de machi e ikitai n' desŭ ka?
Kesa wa nani mo yōji ga arimasen kara, yukkuri hanashĭte irasshatte kudasai.
Ashĭta nani mo yōji ga nakereba, issho ni kembutsŭ ni ikimashō ka?

Imōto no byōki no yōsu ga sŭkoshi warui yō desŭ.
The condition of my sister's illness seems a little bad.

Anata no okŭsan no byōki no yōsu wa ikaga de gozaimasŭ ka?
Anata wa itsŭ kara byōki ni o-nari nasaremashĭta ka?
Isha ni mite moratte imasŭ kara, byōki no yōsu wa sŭkoshi ii yō desŭ.
Anata no tomodachi no byōki no yōsu wa ikaga de gozaimasŭ ka?
Takahashi San no musuko San wa byōki da sō desŭ.

Go-shinsatsŭ (w)o o-negai shĭtai n' desŭ.

I want to ask you for an examination.

Go-shinsatsu (w)o o-negai itashimashĭta.

Watakŭshi no byōki no yōsu ga warui yō deshĭta kara, o-isha San ni shinsatsŭ (w)o negai-mashĭta.

Anata ga byōki nara, Takagi San ni shinsatsŭ (w)o shĭte morattara ii deshō.

O-ki-no-dokŭ Sama desŭ ga kono gogo made wa shinsatsŭ (w)o shĭte ageru koto ga deki-masen.

Anata no go-tsugō wa ikaga de gozaimashō ka?

How does that suit your convenience?

Anata no go-tsugō wa nan ji ga ichiban ii deshō ka?

Kyō Takagi San wa tsugō ga deki-nakatta kara, hoka no isha (w)o yoba-nakereba nari-masen deshĭta.

Watakŭshi no tsugō wa amari yokŭ arimasen.

Anata wa komban tsugō ga yō goraimasŭ ka? Iie, tsugō ga warui desu.

Anata no go-tsugō wa komban ii deshō ka?

Komban wa hima* desu ka? Iie, hima ja arimasen.

Dekiru dake hayakŭ o-ide kudasai.

Please come as soon as possible.

Hachi ji made ni itte mite agemashō.

Kono gogo mite morau koto ga dekimasŭ ka?

Tomodachi ga byōki ni narimashĭta kara, sugu itte mite agemashĭta.

Anata wa dono isha ni mite moratte imasŭ ka?

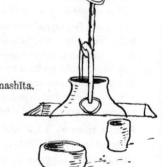

O-machi shĭte orimasŭ.

We will wait for you.

Mada o-ide ni narimasen kara, o-machi shĭte imasŭ.

Matsumoto San (w)o matte imasŭ.

Uchi e kaera-nakereba narimasen deshĭta kara, o-machi suru koto ga dekimasen deshĭta.

Mada tomodachi ga koko e tsukimasen kara, mō matsŭ koto wa dekimasen.

Dō iu ambai desŭ ka?

How is your condition?

Karada no ambai wa ikaga desŭ ka?

O-cha wa ambai yokŭ demashĭta ka?

Ano kata wa dō iu hĭto desŭ ka? Taihen ii hĭto desŭ.

Sore wa dō iu hanashi desŭ ka? Gakkō no hanashi desŭ.

Sakuban wa taihen zutsū ga shimashĭta.
Last night I had a bad headache.

Ima wa taihen zutsū ga shĭte imasŭ.
Kinō taihen zutsū ga shimashĭta ga ima wa yokŭ narimashĭta.
Anata wa warui kaze (w)o hikimashĭta ne?
Sŭkoshi zutsū ga shimasŭ.
Sŭkoshi kaze (w)o hikimashĭta.
Sengetsŭ haien ni narimashĭta.
Anata wa haien ni natta koto ga arimasŭ ka?

Sakuban nemuremasen deshĭta no de, kesa wa nedoko kara okiraremasen.
Because I could not sleep last night, this morning I can not get up out of bed.

Sakuban nemuraremasen deshĭta no de, ima wa mada kibun ga warui desŭ.
Sakuban nemuremasen deshĭta no de, kesa wa taihen tsukarete imasŭ.
Sakuban neraremasen deshĭta no de, kusuri (w)o nomimashĭta.
Sakuban nani mo taberaremasen deshĭta no de, kesa wa sŭkoshi o-naka ga sŭkimashĭta.
Sakuban byōki ni narimashĭta kara, tegami wa kakemasen deshĭta.
Sakuban tomodachi ga uchi ni imasen deshĭta kara, karite kuru koto wa dekimasen deshĭta.

Ane San ni ano kusuri (w)o nomasaremashĭta.
I was made to drink that medicine by my sister.

Dōzo mizu (w)o ippai nomasete kudasai.
Imōto ni tamago (w)o tabesasemashĭta.
Ano ko ni ano nedoko ni nesasemashĭta.
Ano warui otoko no ko wa watakŭshi no musŭko ni tabako (w)o nomasemashĭta.
Musŭme ni anata e komban hachi ji ni denwa (w)o kakesasemasŭ.
Watakŭshi no netsŭ (w)o hakarasete kudasai.
Okāsan ni tamago (w)o tabesaremashĭta.

Kyō wa kibŭn wa ikaga desŭ ka?
How do you feel to-day?

Chikai uchi ni kibun ga yokŭ narimasŭ.
Go-kibun ga warui sō desŭ ne.
Sore (w)o suru kibun ni naremasen.

Mune ya kata ya ude ga itai n' de, komatte imasŭ.
My chest and shoulder and arm and all hurt me and I am suffering (a great deal).

Mune ga itai n' desŭ.
Kata ga itai n'de, komatte imasŭ.
Anata no ude wa itai n' desŭ ka?
Ano hĭto wa ude ga itakŭte komatte iru sō desŭ.
Watakŭshi no me ga itai n' desŭ.
Watakŭshi no o-naka ga itai n' desŭ.

Dono hen ga ichiban itai n' desŭ ka?
Which part hurts the most?

Kono hen ga ichiban itai n' desŭ ka?
Mune no kono hen ga ichiban itai n' desŭ.
Ude-jū ga itai n' de, komatte imasŭ.
Te ga itakŭte, komatte imasŭ.

Watakŭshi no kusuri (w)o mitsuketa tokoro wa doko desŭ ka misasete kudasai.
Please let me see the place where you found my medicine.

Watakŭshi ni anata no tokei (w)o misasete kudasai.
Watakŭshi ni budōshu (w)o nomasete kudasai.
Musŭko ni gyūnyū (w)o nomasemashĭta.
Ano ko ni nedoko kara okisasete kudasai.

Dōzo kore nĭ atara-nai de kudasai.
Please don't touch this.

Migi no te ga itai n' desŭ kara, atara-nai de kudasai.
Ano tsukue no ue ni aru bin ni atara-nai de kudasai.
Kore wa taihen abunai mono desŭ kara, atara-nai de kudasai.
Kono kŭsuri ni wa ano ko ni atarase-nai de kudasai.

Kuchi (w)o akete, shĭta (w)o dashĭte kudasai.
Please open your mouth and put out your tongue.

Nimotsŭ (w)o akete, kutsu (w)o dashĭte kudasai.
Ano to (w)o akete, tsugi no heya e haitte mite kudasai.
Mata-nakereba narimasen deshĭta kara, hon (w)o akete, sŭkoshi yonde imashĭta.
Nimotsŭ (w)o mina ake-nakereba, are wa mitsukarimasen deshō.
Ano hako kara wa mina dashĭte kudasai.
Shĭta (w)o misete kudasai.

Netsŭ (w)o hakatte mimashō.
I'll take your temperature. (I'll measure the fever.)

Dōzo netsŭ (w)o hakatte mite kudasai.
Kono heya no ōkisa (w)o hakatte kudasai.
Mado no hirosa (w)o hakattara san jakŭ* ni sun arimashĭta.
Isha wa anata ni netsŭ ga aru to iimashĭta ka?

Utsumuki ni nete kudasai.
Please lie face downward.

Agomuki* ni nete kudasai.
Hidari no hō e yoko ni natte kudasai.
Migi no hō e yoko ni natte kudasai.
Mŏ sŭkoshi migi e yotte* kudasai.

Dōzo koshi (w)o magete* kudasai.
Dōzo okite kudasai.
Dōzo nete kudasai.
Dōzo kochira e mukete* kudasai.
Dōzo migi no hō (w)o goran nasai.

Iki (w)o shi-nai de ite kudasai.
Please don't breathe.

Fŭkakŭ iki (w)o suu koto ga dekimasen, amari o-naka ga itai n' desŭ kara.
Ano hĭto wa mada kokyū* (w)o shĭte imasŭ ka? Iie, shinimashĭta.*
Ano hĭtotachi wa byōki deshĭta kara, fŭkakŭ iki (w)o suu koto ga dekimasen.
Asoko mizu ga fŭkai desŭ kara, haitte wa ikemasen.
Mizu no fŭkasa wa dono gŭrai desŭ ka? Jisshakŭ gŭrai deshō. Desŭ kara, amari fŭkakŭ
arimasen.

Iki (w)o haki-dashĭte kudasai.
Please breathe out.

Ano ko wa kesa tabeta gohan (w)o haki-dashimashĭta.
Nonda kŭsuri wa haki-dasa-nai de kudasai.
Watakŭshi wa iki (w)o suru koto ga dekimasen.
Amari isoida kara, iki ga hayakŭ* narimashĭta.

Kaze (w)o hiite ita no ni, sŭkoshi muri (w)o shĭta to miemashĭta.
Although you had a cold, I think you exerted yourself a little too much.

Nippon go ga wakarimasŭ no ni, wakarimasen to iimashĭta.
Nihon-shokŭ ga taihen sŭki desŭ no ni, byōki desŭ kara, taberu koto ga dekimasen.
Takashima-ya koko chikai desŭ no ni, nəze asoko e ikimasen deshĭta ka?
Anata wa kaze (w)o hikimashĭta ka? Hai, sŭkoshi muri (w)o shĭte, omoi kaze (w)o hiki-
mashĭta.
Muri (w)o shi-nai de kudasai.
Sonna muri na koto itte wa ikemasen.
Hayakŭ kuru to itta no ni, mada kite imasen.

Haien ni natta yō ni omowaremasŭ.
I think that it has become pneumonia.

Kaze (w)o hiita yō ni omowaremasŭ.
Moshi anata ga muri (w)o shi-nakereba, haien ni nara-nakatta deshō.
Tomodachi ga haien ni natta to kikimashĭta.
Ano hĭto wa haien wa sugu yokŭ naru to omowaremasŭ ka?

Ni jikan goto ni, hĭto saji-zutsŭ nonde kudasai.
Please take one teaspoonful every two hours.

Yo jikan goto ni, fŭta saji-zutsŭ nonde kudasai.

Ichi jikan goto ni, mizu (w)o ippai-zutsŭ nonde kudasai.

Ni shukan goto ni, watakŭshi ni tegami (w)o kaite kudasai.

San jikan goto ni, mi saji no kŭsuri (w)o koppu hambun no mizu ni irete nonde kudasai.

Shi-go nichi no uchi ni wa naorimashō.

You will probably recover inside of four or five days.

Ni-san nichi no uchi ni wa naorimashō.

Taihen byōki deshĭta ga ikka getsŭ[114] no uchi ni yokŭ narimashĭta.

Sō shi-nakereba, naorimasen deshō.

Sono kŭsuri (w)o noma-nakereba, naora-nai deshō.

Ni-san ka getsŭ no uchi ni wa naorimashō to omowaremasŭ.

Hĭto tsuki ka fŭta tsuki no uchi ni wa naorimashō to omoimasŭ.

14 Dai Jū Shi K(w)a (Lesson XIV)

At the Bank

O-hayō[43] gozaimasŭ.	Good morning.
Kyō no Amerika no kawase no nedan wa ikŭra desŭ ka?	What is the American rate of exchange to-day?
Ichi doru wa ni yen, ni jū go sen desŭ.	One dollar is two yen, twenty-five sen.
5 Kono kogitte wa genkin ni kaete morau koto ga dekimasŭ ka?	Can you cash this check for me?
Anata wa kono ginkō de torihiki shĭte imasŭ ka?	Do you have an account with this bank?
Hai, torihiki shĭte imasŭ.	Yes, I have.
10 Sore de wa, kono kogitte ni uragaki (w)o shĭte kudasai.	Very well then, please endorse this check.
Hai, itashimashō.	Yes, I shall.
Kore wa anata no o-kane desŭ kara, o-tori kudasai.	Here is your money. (As this is your money, please take it).
15 Tsuide ni, kono ni jū yen satsŭ (w)o ichi yen satsŭ to chiisai ginka ni kaete kudasai-masen[32] ka?	By the way, won't you please give me one yen bills and some small change for this twenty yen bill?
O-yasui koto desŭ.	It's no trouble at all.
Watakŭshi wa kono go jū yen (w)o chokin 20 shĭte okitai n' desŭ ga. . .	I should like to deposit this fifty yen. . .
Sō desŭ ka? Sore de wa, dōzo koko kara sambamme no mado e itte, azukete kudasai.	You do? Very well then, please go to the third window from here and deposit it.
Arigatō gozaimashĭta.	Thank you.

Mā, Kimura San, shĭbarakŭ deshĭta ne. 25 Sono go wa ikaga desŭ ka?	My heavens! Mr. Kimura, it's been a long time (since I've seen you). How have you been since then?
Arigatō. Botsŭ-botsŭ[4] yatte imasŭ.	So, so, thanks.
Dochira e desŭ ka?	Where are you bound for?
Watakŭshi wa ima koko de sŭkoshi kane (w)o dashimashĭta. Kore kara, yūbin-kyokŭ 30 e itte, Bŭrajiru ni iru ototo e yūbin kawase de kane (w)o okutte yarō[37] to[15] omotte iru tokoro[31] desŭ.	I just now drew out a little money here. Right now I'm going to the post-office, for I intend to send a postal money order to my younger brother in Brazil.
Anata no ototo San wa Minami Amerika de nani (w)o shĭte irasshaimasŭ[31] ka?	What is your younger brother doing in South America?
35 Ototo no shokugyō wa denki no gishi de, ima ni-san[70] getsŭ Bŭrajiru ni imasŭ[96] ga raigetsŭ kara[45] Arŭzenchin e tennin sareru[92] sō desŭ.[65]	My younger brother's occupation is (that of) electrical engineer and he has been in Brazil now two or three months and I hear he is being transferred to Argentina next month.

106

Sore wa taihen omoshiro-sō[65] na o-shigoto
40 desŭ ne.
Watakŭshi no musŭko mo daigakŭ (w)o
deru to[15] Minami-Amerika e yukitai to itte
imasŭ.
De wa, ima kara issho ni yūbin-kyokŭ made
45 yukimashō ka? Kozutsumi (w)o okuri-dashi,
tegami (w)o kakĭtome ni shĭte, hagaki ya
kitte mo shi-go mai kaitai desŭ kara.

That certainly seems like very interesting
work.
My son too says that he would like to go to
South America when he is graduated from
the university.
Well, shall we go to the post-office together
now? I want to mail a package, register a
letter and buy four or five post cards and
stamps.

At the Post-Office

Kono Kōbe-yuki no[84] tegami wa sŭkoshi
omo-sugiru to omoimasŭ ga kitte wa ikŭra
50 hara-nakereba narimasen[57] ka?
Hai, hakatte mite agemashō.
Hikōyūbin ka sokutatsŭ de okuritai n' desŭ
ka?
Iie, futsū de yoroshiū gozaimasŭ.
55 De wa, rokŭ sen no kitte (w)o hatte kudasai.

Kono kozutsumi (w)o Nagasaki e okuritai
ga ikŭra kakarimashō ka?
Naka ni[14] wa nani ga haitte imasŭ ka?
Hon ga ni satsŭ haitte imasŭ. Soshĭte dōzo
60 jū yen no hoken (w)o kakete[42] kudasai.
Mina de[22] ni jū go sen ni narimasŭ.[69]
Dōzo o-negai itashimasŭ.
Sā, ima kara denshin-kyokŭ e itte, dempō
(w)o uchimashĭtara,[74] kyō no yōji wa sunde
65 shimaimasŭ.[97]

I think this letter for Kobe is a little too
heavy, so how much postage (stamps) must
I put on it?
Very well, I'll weigh it for you.
Do you want to send it airmail or special de-
livery?
No, regular (mail) will be all right.
Well then, please put on (stick on) a six-sen
stamp.
I want to send this package to Nagasaki, so
how much will it cost?
What's inside?
It contains two books. And please insure it
for ten yen.
It comes to twenty-five sen all together.
Please take care of it for me.
Well, now I'm going to the telegraph-office
and when I send a telegram, to-day's busi-
ness will be completely finished.

Exercises

O-hayō gozaimasŭ.
  Good morning.
Dōzo asu no asa hayakŭ kite kudasai.
Ima ika-nakŭte mo ii deshō; mada hayai desŭ kara.
Kesa hayakŭ okimashĭta ka?
Taihen tsukarete imasŭ kara, hayakŭ dekaketakŭ arimasen.
Hayakŭ gakkō e ikimashō.

Kyō no Amerika no kawase no nedan wa ikŭra desŭ ka? Ichi doru wa ni yen ni jū go sen desŭ.

What is the American rate of exchange to-day? One dollar is (worth) two yen, twenty-five sen.

Kyō no Eikokŭ no kawase no nedan wa ikŭra desŭ ka? Ichi pondo wa ni jū yen shi sen desŭ.

Kyō no Fŭransŭ no kawase no nedan wa ikŭra desŭ ka? Ichi fŭrankŭ wa hachi jū go sen desŭ.

Kyō no Shina no kawase no nedan wa ikŭra desŭ ka? Yokŭ wakarimasen.

Kinō no Amerika no kawase no nedan wa ikŭra deshĭta ka? Kinō ichi doru wa ni yen go jissen deshĭta.

Asu no Amerika no kawase no nedan wa ikŭra deshō ka? Dō omoimasŭ ka? Sŭkoshi agaru deshō.

Kono kogitte wa genkin ni kaete morau koto ga dekimasŭ ka?

Can you cash this check for me?

Dōzo kono kogitte (w)o genkin ni kaete kudasai.

Ainikŭ genkin wa arimasen.

Kono kogitte (w)o kaeru koto ga dekimasŭ ka?

Chiisai ginka wa arimasen ga kono jū yen satsŭ de kamaimasen ka?

Watakŭshi no tomodachi no kogitte (w)o genkin ni kaete morau koto ga dekimasŭ ka?

Anata wa kono ginkō de torihiki shĭte imasŭ ka? Hai, torihiki shĭte imasŭ.

Do you have dealings (an account) with this bank? Yes, I do.

Anata wa Yokohama Shōkin* Ginkō de torihiki shĭte imasŭ ka? Iie, Dai Ichi* Ginkō to torihiki shĭte imasŭ.

Watakŭshi wa kono ginkō to torihiki shĭtai desŭ.

Anata wa chokin dake shitai n' desŭ ka? Kogitte wa tsukaimasen ka?

Takahashi San wa Yokohama Shōkin Ginkō de torihiki shĭte imasŭ ka? Go-zonji desŭ ka?

Watakŭshi no chokin wa ikŭra arimasŭ ka?

Kono kogitte ni uragaki (w)o shĭte kudasai.

Please endorse this check.

Shĭtsŭrei desŭ ga anata wa kono kogitte ni uragaki (w)o suru koto (w)o wasurete imasŭ.

Kono kawase ni uragaki ga arimasen kara, genkin ni kaeru koto ga dekimasen.

Matsumoto San ni kono kogitte ni uragaki (w)o shĭte kureru yō ni itte kudasai.

Kono kogitte no uragaki wa yomemasen.

Kore wa anata no uketori desŭ kara, o-tori kudasai.

This is your receipt so please take it.

Kore wa anata no o-tsuri desŭ kara, o-tori kudasai.

Sore wa anata no kogitte desŭ kara, o-tori kudasai.

Kore wa anata no ni jū go yen satsŭ desŭ kara, o-tori kudasai.

Kore wa watakŭshi no kane desŭ kara, tora-nai de kudasai.

Kono jū yen satsŭ (w)o ichi yen satsŭ ni kaete kudasai.
Please change this ten yen bill into one yen bills.

Kono ichi yen satsŭ (w)o ginka ni kaete kudasaimasen ka?
Kono ni jū yen satsŭ (w)o go yen satsŭ ni kaete kudasai.
Kono go jū yen satsŭ (w)o jū yen satsŭ ni kaete kudasai.
Kono hyakŭ yen satsŭ (w)o go jū yen satsŭ ni kaete kudasaimasen ka?
Kono jū doru satsŭ (w)o Nippon no kane ni kaete kudasai.

Chiisai ginka ga arimasŭ ka?
Do you have any small change?

Chiisai ginka (w)o motte imasen kara, dōzo kono satsŭ (w)o ginka ni kaete kudasaimasen ka?
Ainikŭ satsŭ ga arimasen kara, anata ni chiisai ginka (w)o age-nakereba narimasen ga kamaimasen ka?
Dōzo chiisai ginka (w)o kure-nai de kudasai.
Watakŭshi wa chiisai ginka ga arimasen deshĭta kara, bantō ni jū yen satsŭ (w)o kaete kudasai to negaimashĭta.

Kono hon wa taihen yomi-yasui desŭ.
This book is easy to read.

Nihon go wa hanashi-yasukŭ arimasen.
Eigo mo hanashi-yasukŭ arimasen.
Katakana wa kanari kaki-yasui desŭ.
Kono renshū wa shi-yasukŭ arimasen.

Watakŭshi wa kono go jū yen (w)o chokin shĭte okitai n' desŭ.
I want to deposit this fifty yen.

Anata wa kane (w)o chokin shĭtai n' desŭ ka matawa kane (w)o dashitai n' desŭ ka?
Kono hichi jū yen no kogitte (w)o chokin shĭte okitai n' desŭ.
Yokohama Shōkin Ginkō ni otōsan ga okutte kita yūbin kawase (w)o chokin shĭte kudasai.
Kesa otōto wa ginkō ni hyakŭ yen chokin shimashĭta.

Dōzo koko kara sambamme no mado e itte, azukete kudasai.
Please go to the third window from here and deposit (it).

Dōzo hidari e ni bamme no mado e itte, azukete kudasai.
Dōzo migi e yo bamme no mado e itte, azukete kudasai.
Kono hachi jū yen (w)o azuketai n' desŭ.
Migi no sambamme no to (w)o akete kudasai.

Mā, Kimura San, shĭbarakŭ deshĭta ne. Sono go wa ikaga desŭ ka?
Why, Mr. Kimura, it's been a long time (since I last saw you). How have you been since then?

Matsumoto San, anata no okŭsan ni wa shĭbarakŭ o-me ni kakarimasen ga ikaga de gozai-masŭ ka?

Takahashi San, shĭbarakŭ o-me ni kakarimasen deshĭta ne. Sono go wa ikaga desŭ ka?
Tanaka San kara shĭbarakŭ tegami (w)o moraimasen ga naze deshō ka?
Anata ni wa shĭbarakŭ o-me ni kakarimasen deshĭta ga sono go wa dō desŭ ka?

Keiki* wa dō desŭ ka? Mā, botsŭ botsŭ yatte imasŭ.
How's business? Oh, so, so (Coming along slowly).

Botsŭ botsŭ aruite kudasai.
Botsŭ botsŭ yonde kudasai.
Botsŭ botsŭ hanashĭte kudasai.
Kyūji ni ikŭra kokorozashi (w)o yarimashō ka?
Ichi yen yattara ii deshō ka?
Shimbun-ya ni kane (w)o yarimashĭta.

Dochira e desŭ ka?
Where are you going? (Where to?)
Dochira kara desŭ ka? Ginkō kara kimashĭta.
Ima kara dochira e desŭ ka? Ginkō made.
Kinō wa dochira e deshĭta ka? Nyū Yōku e ikimashĭta.
Dochira made desŭ ka? Yūbinkyokŭ made.

Watakŭshi wa ima koko de sŭkoshi kane (w)o dashimashĭta.
I just now drew a little money out here.

Anata wa ikŭra dashitai n' desŭ ka?
Watakŭshi wa ni jū go yen dashitai n' desŭ.
Ima ginkō e itte, sŭkoshi kane (w)o dashĭte, kono kogitte (w)o chokin shĭte oku tsumori desŭ.
Anata wa ginkō e itte, ikŭra dashimashĭta ka?
Anata wa hon (w)o dashĭte, sŭkoshi yonde kudasai.
Anata no atarashii yōfuku (w)o dashĭte, misete kudasai.
Ano hako kara empitsŭ (w)o dashĭte kudasai.

Bŭrajiru ni iru ototo e yūbin kawase (w)o okuritai.
I want to send a postal money order to my brother in Brazil.

Arŭzenchin ni iru otōsan e yūbin kawase (w)o okuritai.
Yūbin kawase (w)o ikŭra kaitai desŭ ka?
Ni hyakŭ yen no yūbin kawase (w)o kaitai desŭ.
Kono yūbin kawase (w)o kaete kuremasen ka?

Yūbin kawase de kane (w)o okutte yarō to omoimasŭ.
I think I'll send the money by postal money order.

Kono tegami (w)o dasō to omoimasŭ.
Ima dekakeyō to omoimasŭ.
Kono gogo daigakŭ e ikō to omoimasŭ.

Watakŭshi wa o-isha san (w)o yobō to omoimasŭ.
Ashĭta no asa rokŭ ji ni okiyō to omoimasŭ.

Kyūji ni ichi yen no kokorozashi (w)o yatte kudasai.
Please give one yen tip to the waitress.

Kono chiisai ginka (w)o jochū ni yatte mo ii n' desŭ ka?
Tomodachi ni tabako (w)o yarimashĭta.
Kyūji ni ikŭra kokorozashi (w)o yarimashō ka?
Ane wa imōto ni kashi (w)o yatta sō desŭ.

Kane (w)o okutte yarō to omotte iru tokoro desŭ.
I am about to send him some money.

Gohan (w)o tabeyō to shĭte iru tokoro desŭ.
Bīru (w)o nomō to omotte iru tokoro desŭ.
Watakŭshi wa sakana-ya e ikō to shĭte iru tokoro desŭ.
Watakŭshi ga tsuita toki ni wa tomodachi ga dekakeyō to shĭte iru tokoro deshĭta.

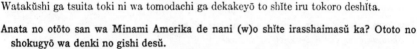

Anata no otōto san wa Minami Amerika de nani (w)o shĭte irasshaimasŭ ka? Ototo no shokugyō wa denki no gishi desŭ.
What does your brother do in South America? My brother is an electrical engineer.

Anata wa koko de nani (w)o shĭte irasshaimasŭ ka? Watakŭshi no shokugyō wa junsa desŭ.
Anata no shokugyō wa nani desŭ ka? Watakŭshi wa bantō desŭ.
Ano Matsumoto San to iu hĭto no shokugyō wa nan desŭ ka? Go-zonji desŭ ka?
Yōfukŭ-ya darō to omoimasŭ.
Anata wa ano ryōriya de nani (w)o shĭte imasŭ ka? Kyūji (w)o shĭte imasŭ.

Denki (w)o keshĭte kudasai.
Please put out the electric light.

Denki (w)o tsukete kudasai.
Anata no mise de denki no tokei (w)o utte imasŭ ka?
Ano tatemono ni denki ga tsuite imasŭ ka?
Kono taku ni wa denki no gishi ga sunde imasŭ.

Ni-san ka getsŭ Bŭrajiru ni imasŭ ga raigetsŭ kara, Arŭzenchin e tennin sareru sō desŭ.
He has been in Brazil for two or three months and next month I hear he is being transferred to Argentina.

Anata no musŭko san wa dono gurai Beikokŭ ni irasshaimasŭ ka? Go ka nen Kĭta-Amerika ni imasŭ ga rainen kara, Minami-Amerika e tennin sareru sō desŭ.
Anata wa dono gurai koko ni irasshaimasŭ ka? Shi shūkan koko ni imasŭ ga ni-san nichi shitara, Kyōto e iku tsumori desŭ.
Ano Bŭrajiru no kata wa doko e tennin saremashĭta ka? Go-zonji desŭ ka? Shina e tennin saremashĭta sō desŭ.

Sore wa taihen omoshiro-sō na shigoto desŭ ne.
That must really be an interesting kind of work.
Tōkiō wa taihen omoshiroi machi desŭ ne.
Sore wa omoshiro-sō na hon desŭ ne.
Takahashi San wa omoshiro-sō na hĭto desŭ ne.
Sono shigoto wa amari omoshirokŭ arimasen deshĭta.
Sore wa omoshiroi koto desŭ ne.
Anata no shigoto wa nani desŭ ka? Denki no gishi desŭ.

Watakŭshi no musŭko wa daigakŭ (w)o deru to, Minami-Amerika e ikitai to itte imasŭ.
My son says that he wants to go to South America when he is graduated from the university.
Anata wa daigakŭ (w)o deru to, donna shokuygō (w)o mochitai desŭ ka?
Anata wa daigakŭ (w)o demashĭta ka? Hai, san nen mae ni daigakŭ (w)o demashĭta.
Anata wa itsŭ daigakŭ (w)o demasŭ ka? Ni nen no uchi ni deru tsŭmori desŭ.
Ano onna no kata wa daigakŭ (w)o demashĭta ka? Go-zonji desŭ ka? Iie, mada demasen deshō.

Ima kara issho ni yūbin-kyokŭ made yukimashō ka?
Shall we go to the post-office together now?
Ima kara issho ni ginkō made yukimashō ka?
Ima kara issho ni ryōriya made yukimashō ka?
Ima kara issho ni yado-ya made yukimashō ka?
Ima kara issho ni gakkō made yukimashō ka?
Ima kara issho ni densha no teiryūjo made yukimashō ka?
Ima kara issho ni depāto made yukimashō ka?

Kozutsumi (w)o okuri-dashitai n' desŭ.
I want to send off a package.
Itsŭ ano kozutsumi (w)o okuri-dashimashĭta ka?
Anata ni ototoi okurimashĭta.
Itsŭ watakŭshi ni ano kozutsumi (w)o okutte kuremasŭ ka?
Ashĭta okuri-dashimashō.
Kono kozutsumi wa omo-sugiru kara, hikōyūbin de okuru koto wa dekimasen.

Tegami (w)o kakitome ni shĭtai n' desŭ.
I want to register a letter.
Kono tegami (w)o kakitome in shĭte morattara, ikŭra desŭ ka?
Dōzo jochū ni tegami (w)o kakitome ni shĭte dasu yō ni itte kudasai.
Dōzo sono tegami (w)o kakitome ni shĭte kudasai.
Anata no tegami wa kakitome de kimashĭta ka?

Hagaki (w)o rokŭ mai kudasai.
Please give me six post cards.
Ano kesa moratta hagaki wa dare kara kimashĭta ka?

Jū mai no hagaki (w)o kaitai n' desŭ.

Anata wa Kyōto e tsuitara, watakŭshi ni hagaki (w)o ichi mai okutte kudasaimasen ka?

Yūbin-kyokŭ e itte, hagaki (w)o jū ni mai katte kite kudasai.

Kono tegami (w)o kado no yūbin-bako ni irete kudasai.
Please put this letter in the mail box on the corner.

Koko kara ichiban chikai yūbin-bako wa doko ni arimasŭ ka?

Kono kozutsumi wa yūbin-bako ni hairimasen.

Watakŭshi no tegami (w)o kono yūbin-bako ni iretara, yoroshiū gozaimasŭ ka?

Dōzo kono tegami (w)o dashĭte kudasai.
Please post this letter.

Ima ano hagaki wa dasa-nai de kudasai. Watakŭshi ga dekakeru toki ni sore (w)o yūbin-bako ni iremashō.

Watakŭshi wa kinō yūbin-kyokŭ e ika-nakereba narimasen deshĭta kara, ano tegami (w)o dashimashĭta.

Kitte (w)o shi-go mai kaitai n' desŭ.
I want to buy four or five stamps.

Dōzo yūbin-kyokŭ e itte, jū mai no kitte (w)o katte kite kudasai.

San sen no kitte (w)o jū ni mai kaitai n' desŭ.

Dōzo kitte (w)o rokŭ mai kudasai.

Watakŭshidomo wa kitte ga nai kara, dōzo yūbin-kyokŭ e ittara, kitte (w)o hichi-hachi mai katte kite kudasai.

Kono Kōbe-yuki no tegami wa sŭkoshi omo-sugiru to omoimasŭ.
I think this letter for Kobe is a little too heavy.

Kono Amerika-yuki no kozutsumi wa omo-sugiru to omoimasŭ.

Kono nimotsŭ wa omo-sugiru kara, motte ika-nakereba narimasen.

Kono Tōkiō-yuki no kozutsumi wa omo-sugiru to omoimasŭ kara, hikōyūbin de okutte wa ikemasen.

Kono hako wa omoi desŭ kara, yūbin de okuru koto ga dekimasen.

Kitte wa ikŭra hara-nakereba narimasen ka?
How much (in) stamps must I paste on?

Kono tegami wa Nagasaki e okuritai desŭ ga kitte wa ikŭra hara-nakereba narimasen ka?

Kono tegami wa hikōyūbin de dashitai desŭ ga kitte wa ikŭra hara-nakereba narimasen ka?

Kono tegami wa sokŭtatsŭ de okuritai desŭ ga go jissen no kitte (w)o hattara, ii n' desŭ ka?

Kono kozutsumi wa Kyōto e okuritai nara, hichi jū go sen no kitte (w)o hara-nakereba narimasen.

Hakatte mite agemashō.
I'll weigh it for you.

Dōzo kono kozutsumi (w)o hakatte mite kudasai.

Hakatte mitara, nagasa ga shi shakŭ arimashĭta.

Hakatte mitara, omosa ga ni kin arimashĭta.

Hikōyūbin ka sokutatcŭ de okuritai n' desŭ ka? Iie, futsū de yoroshiū gozaimasŭ.

Do you want to send it airmail or special delivery? No, ordinary is all right.

Futsū yūbin de yoroshiū gozaimasŭ ka? Iie, sokutatsŭ de okuritai n' desŭ.

Kyō o-taku ni wa sokutatsŭ no tegami ga kimashĭta ka? Iie, hikōyūbin no tegami ga kimashĭta.

Dōzo kono tegami (w)o hikōyūbin ka sokutatsŭ de dashĭte kudasai.

Konnen* no atsusa wa futsū ja arimasen.

Rokŭ sen no kitte (w)o hatte kudasai.

Please paste on a six sen stamp.

Jissen no kitte (w)o hatte kudasai.

Kono kozutsumi (w)o Nagasaki made Yokohama kara okuru ni wa go jissen no kitte de takŭsan deshō ka?

Dōzo shi sen no kitte (w)o go mai kudasai.

Kono kozutsumi (w)o Nagasaki e okuritai n' desŭ ga ikŭra kakarimashō ka?

I want to send this package to Nagasaki. How much will it cost?

Kono kozutsumi (w)o Beikokŭ e okuritai n' desŭ ga ikŭra kakarimashō ka?

Kono tegami (w)o Fŭransŭ e okuritai n' desŭ ga ikŭra kakarimashō ka?

Kono tegami wa sokutatsŭ de Hokkaidō e okuritai n' desŭ ga ikŭra kakarimashō ka?

Kono tegami (w)o hikōyūbin de okuttara, itsŭ Kōbe e tsukimashō ka?

Ano hikidashi no naka ni wa nani ga haitte imasŭ ka? Hon ga ni satsŭ haitte imasŭ.

What is inside that drawer? Two books.

Ano hako no naka ni wa nani ga haitte imasŭ ka? Nani mo haitte imasen.

Takŭsan no mono ga haitte imasŭ ka? O-kashi dake haitte imasŭ.

Ano hikidashi no naka ni wa nani ga haitte imasŭ ka? Kami ga haitte imasŭ.

Ano kozutsumi no naka ni wa nani ga haitte imasŭ ka? Zasshi ga jissatsŭ haitte imasŭ.

Asoko ni hon ga iku satsŭ arimasŭ ka? Go satsŭ arimasŭ.

Anata wa hoken ni haitte imasŭ ka?

Are you insured?

Anata wa hoken ni hairitai desŭ ka?

Anata no o-taku ni wa hoken ga ikŭra tsukete arimasŭ.

Dōzo kono kozutsumi ni hyakŭ yen no hoken (w)o kakete kudasai.

Anata no okosan ni wa hoken ga tsuite imasŭ ka?

Mina de ni jū go sen ni narimasŭ.

It all comes to twenty-five sen.

Mina de ikŭra ni narimasŭ ka?

Mina de san jissen ni narimasŭ.

Mina de ikŭra deshĭta ka?
Mina de yo yen ni narimashĭta.
Ano hĭtotachi wa mina kekkon shĭte imasŭ.
Dōzo o-negai itashimasŭ.
Please take charge of it. (Please, I ask you).
Anata wa dare ni o-hanashi shĭtai n' desŭ ka? Suzuki San ni o-negai shĭtai n' desŭ.
Dōzo Takahashi San ni koko de hĭtoban o-tomari ni naru yō ni negatte kudasai.
Ashĭta wa hayakŭ kuru yō ni negaimasŭ.
Kore (w)o motte kite kudasai to negaimashĭta.
Ima kara denshin-kyokŭ e itte, dempō (w)o utsu tsumori desŭ.
Now I'm going to the telegraph office and I intend to send a telegram.
Watakŭshi wa kono dempō (w)o Tōkiō e uchitai desŭ ga ikŭra desŭ ka?
Dōzo watakŭshi ni dempō de shirasete kudasai.
Dōzo kono dempō (w)o sokutatsŭ de utte kudasai.
Anata ga sono dempō (w)o futsū de uttara, motto yasui deshō.
Ano warui hĭto wa junsa ni utaremashĭta.*
Anata wa doko (w)o utaremashĭta ka?
Watakŭshi wa mune (w)o utaremashĭta.
Kyō no yōji wa sunde shimaimashĭta.
To-day's business is all finished.

Kyō no shigoto wa sumimashĭta.
Watakŭshi wa kashi (w)o tabete shimaimashĭta.
O-sumi ni nattara, sŭkoshi hanashi ga aru n' desŭ ga
Hiruhan wa sumimashĭta ka?
Shĭte shimatta koto wa shĭkata ga arimasen.
Yōji ga nakereba, denshin-kyokŭ e issho ni ikimasen ka?
Ainikŭ desŭ ga, kyō wa yōji ga gozaimasŭ kara.
Nani ka watakŭshi ni yōji ga arimasen ka? Arigatō gozaimasŭ ga, nani mo arimasen.
Watakŭshi ni donna yōji ga gozaimasŭ ka? Machi e ittara, zasshi (w)o katte kite kudasai.
Yōji ga atte, Kyōto e itte imasŭ.
Sono hon wa yonde shimaimashĭta.
I finished reading that book.
Kore de shigoto (w)o shimatte kudasai.
Anata wa nan ji ni sono shigoto (w)o shimaimasŭ ka? Jū ji ni shimau tsumori desŭ.
Sakŭban no renshū (w)o kaite shimaimashĭta ka? Hai, mina kaite shimaimashĭta.
Tomodachi wa Tōkiō e itte shimaimashĭta.
Dare ga kono bīru (w)o nonde shimaimashĭta ka? Shirimasen.

15

Dai Jū Go K(w)a (Lesson XV)

At the Barber's

Toko-ya San, kono tsugi no kĭsha (w)o toritai kara, isoide kami (w)o katte, hige (w)o sotte kudasai. Amari mijkakŭ²⁸ karanai de kudasai.

Barber, as I want to take this next train, please quickly give me a haircut and a shave. Please don't cut it too short.

At the Information Window

5 Kono tsugi no Nagasaki-yuki wa nan ji ni demasŭ ka?

What time does the next (train) to Nagasaki leave?

Jū ji go fun desŭ.

At ten-five.

Sore wa kyūkō desŭ ka? Tokkyū desŭ ka?

Is that an express train or a limited?

Tokkyū desŭ.

It's a limited.

10 Tokkyū wa jū ichi ji han ni tachimasŭ.

The limited leaves at eleven-thirty.

Sore wa nan ji ni Nagasaki e³³ tsukimasŭ ka?

What time does it arrive at Nagasaki?

Myōgo-jitsŭ no asa no hachi ji han ni tsukimasŭ.

It arrives the day after tomorrow at eight-thirty in the morning.

15 Tokkyū ni wa Kanda eki kara noremasŭ⁹⁰ ka?

Can I take the limited at the Kanda station?

Iie, tokkyū wa Kanda eki ni wa tomarimasen.⁹¹

No, the limited doesn't stop at Kanda station.

Sore de wa, kyūkō kata-michi no kĭsha chin

Well then, how much is the express train fare one way?

20 wa ikŭra desŭ ka?

Ni jū go yen desŭ.

It's twenty-five yen.

Ōfuku wa ikŭra desŭ ka?

How much is a round-trip?

Yon⁵² jū go yen desŭ.

It's forty-five yen.

At the Ticket Window

Nagasaki e kyūkō ni tō kata-michi ichi mai⁶⁴
25 kudasai.

Please give me one second-class one-way express ticket to Nagasaki.

Shindai ken mo desŭ ka?

Do you also want a berth ticket?

Hai, dōzo negaimasŭ.

Yes, please.

Shindai wa ue⁴³ shika⁷⁹ nokotte imasen. Shĭta wa mina urikiremashĭta ga. . .

There are only upper berths left. The lowers were all sold out.

30 Shĭkata ga nai kara, ue (w)o moraimashō.

Since it can't be helped, I'll take an upper.

Ryōhō de²² san jū hachi yen ni narimasŭ.

Both together come to thirty-eight yen.

Akabō San, kono ōkii kaban (w)o chikki ni shĭte⁵⁰ kudasai. Chiisai hō⁴⁷ no wa kĭsha no naka e mochikonde kudasai. Shindai no
35 bangō wa san gō⁵² sha no ni ban desŭ kara.

Porter, please check this big suitcase. Please carry the little one into the train. The berth number is number two in the third train.

116

Hai, kashikomarimashĭta.
Kippu (w)o o-kashi kudasai, torankŭ (w)o
azukete kimasŭ[37] kara.

Yes, very well, sir.
Please lend me (your) ticket and I'll check
the trunk.

In the Train

Shĭtsŭrei desŭ ga, anata mo Nagasaki e
40 o-ide ni narimasŭ ka?
Hai, sō desŭ.
Anata wa Beikokŭ no kata no yō ni[65] miukemasŭ ga, itsŭ kochira e o-koshi ni narimashĭta[40] ka?
45 Hai, ni shūkan mae ni[80] Yokohama e tsukimashĭta.
Kono-goro no zeikan no tori-atsukai wa dō
desŭ ka?
Kanari yasashikatta[43] to omoimasŭ. Ryoken
50 wa motte ita shi,[44] nimotsŭ wa mina[43]
watakŭshi jishin no fŭrugi ya hitsuyō na
mono bakari[79] de, zeikin (w)o harau-beki[68]
mono wa nakatta[43] kara, amari muzukashikŭ
arimasen deshĭta.
55 Sore wa kekkō deshĭta ne. Umi no ue wa dō
deshĭta ka?
Fune wa ōkii deshĭta. Tenki mo taihen
yokatta[43] kara, amari yowazu ni[98] mairimashĭta. Watakŭshi no shindai wa ichiban
60 ue no kampan ni arimashĭta no de, sŭkoshi
osorete imashĭta ga, arai nami ni[99] wa awazu
ni[98] Yokohama e tsukimashĭta.
Kono-goro no funa-chin wa takakŭ natte iru
sō ja arimasen ka?
65 Hai, sŭkoshi wa takakŭ natta sō desŭ ga
taishĭta koto wa arimasen.

Pardon me, but are you also going to Nagasaki?
Yes, that's right.
You look like an American. When did you
come over here?

Yes, I arrived at Yokohama two weeks ago.

How is the treatment at the customs these
days?
I think it was quite easy. I had a passport
and the baggage was just my own old clothes
and useful articles, and as I didn't have to
pay any duty, it wasn't very difficult.

That's really splendid. How was the crossing? (How was it over the ocean?)
The ship was large. As the weather was very
good also, I arrived without getting very
seasick. Since my berth was on the top deck,
I was a little frightened, but we arrived at
Yokohama without meeting any rough
waves.
I hear that the ship fare now-a-days has
become high, hasn't it?
Yes, they say it has become a little high, but
it isn't (so) very much.

Exercises

Toko-ya San, kono tsugi no kĭsha (w)o toritai kara, isoide kami (w)o katte kudasai.
Barber, as I want to take this next train, please give me a haircut quickly.

Toko-ya San, chotto kami (w)o katte kudasai.
Kami wa kara-nai de kudasai.
Watakŭshi wa kami (w)o katte moraitai n' desŭ ga, ii toko-ya ga kono kinjo ni arimasŭ ka?
Isoide aruite kudasai.

Isoide motte kite kudasai.
Kĭsha wa jū ji ni demasŭ kara, isoide yukimashō.

Kuchi-hige wa sora-nai de kudasai.
Please don't shave off my mustache.
Ano hige no nai hĭto wa suihei de, ano nagai hige no aru hĭto wa shĭkan desŭ.
Hige (w)o sotte moraitai n' desŭ.
Tomodachi wa ano toko-ya san ni hige (w)o sorasemashĭta.
Anata wa watakŭshi no toko-ya ni soraseru hō ga ii deshō.
Kesa wa hige (w)o sorazu ni gakkō e ikimashĭta.

Amari mijikakŭ kara-nai de kudasai.
Please don't cut it too short.
Kono zubon wa mijikai desŭ ga, sore wa nagai desŭ.
Ano tegami wa amari nagakŭ kaka-nai de kudasai.
Ano tegami wa amari mijakakŭ kaka-nai de kudasai.
Kanai wa kami (w)o mijikakŭ katte imasŭ.
Kono sode wa ni sun mijikai desŭ.
Kono-goro wa hi ga mijikakŭ natte kimashĭta.
Kono uwagi (w)o san zun* mijikakŭ shĭte kudasai.

Kono tsugi no Nagasaki-yuki wa nan ji ni demasŭ ka? Jū ji go fun desŭ.
When does the next train for Nagasaki leave? At ten five.
Kono tsugi no Kōbe -yuki wa nan ji ni demasŭ ka? Go ji han ni demasŭ.
Kono tsugi no Tōkiō kara kuru kĭsha wa nan ji ni tsukimasŭ ka? Gogo yo ji desŭ.
Kono tsugi no Yokohama-yuki (w)o toritai desŭ ga nan ji ni demasŭ ka? Komban no hachi ji desŭ.
Kĭsha ga botsŭ-botsŭ to* dekakemashĭta.
A! Kĭsha ga dete shimaimashĭta.
Nan ji no kĭsha de oide desŭ ka?
Kĭsha wa jippun okuremashĭta.*
Kĭsha wa jippun hayarimashĭta.*

Sore wa kyūkō desŭ ka? Tokkyū desŭ ka?
Is that the express train or the limited?
Kyūkō wa nan ji ni demasŭ ka? Tokkyū wa nan ji ni demasŭ ka?
Tokkyū wa ku ji de, kyūkō wa ku ji han ni demasŭ.

Nagasaki e no kyūkō wa jū ji ni tatte, tokkyū wa jū ji han ni tachimasŭ.

Tōkiō kara Nagasaki e wa Kōbe made tokkyū de itte, Kōbe de kyūkō ni norikaemasŭ.

Ōsaka kara no tokkyū wa Tōkiō e go ji han ni tsŭkimasŭ, sōshĭte kyūkō wa go ji ni tsuki-masŭ.

Sore wa nan ji ni Nagasaki e tsŭkimasŭ ka? Myōgo nichi* no asa no hachi ji han ni tsŭki-masŭ.

What time does it arrive at Nagasaki? It arrives the day after tomorrow at eight thirty in the morning.

Kyūkō wa nan ji ni Kōbe e tsŭkimasŭ ka? Myōgo-nichi no gogo no san ji jū go fun mae ni tsŭkimasŭ.

Myōgo-nichi nan ji ni Nagasaki (w)o deru tsŭmori desŭ ka? Myōgo-nichi no ban no hichi ji ni Tōkiō no tokkyū (w)o toru tsŭmori desŭ.

Nagasaki e nan ji no kĭsha de tatsu tsŭmori desŭ ka? Yo ji no kĭsha de tatsu tsŭmori desŭ.

Anata no kĭsha wa nan ji ni Nagasaki e tsŭkimashĭta ka? Kĭnō no asa no ku ji ni tsŭki-mashĭta.

Anata wa kinō nan ji no kĭsha de Tōkiō (w)o demashĭta ka? Kinō gogo ni ji no kĭsha de demashĭta.

Tokkyū ni wa kono teishaba* de noremasŭ ka? Iie, tokkyū wa kono teishaba de wa tomari-masen.

Can one take the limited at this station? No, the limited doesn't stop at this station.

Kyūkō ni wa Shinagawa eki kara noremasŭ ka? Iie, kyūkō wa Shinagawa eki de wa tomari-masen.

Hachi ji no Nagasaki-yuki ni wa Kanda eki kara noremasŭ ka? Hai, koko de tomarimasŭ.

Moshi anata ga Ōsaka e ikitai nareba, Kanda eki kara tokkyū de ittara, ii deshō.

Watakŭshi wa Yokohama e itte, Gŭrando Hoteru de hĭtoban tomarimashĭta.

Kyūkō kata-michi no kĭsha-chin wa ikŭra desŭ ka? Ni jū go yen desŭ.

How much is the express train fare one way? Twenty-five yen.

Tokkyū ō-fuku no kĭsha chin wa ikŭra desŭ ka? Shi jū yen desŭ.

Tōkiō kara Nagasaki made kata-michi no kĭsha chin wa ikŭra desŭ ka? San jū yen desŭ.

Shashō San, densha chin wa ikŭra desŭ ka? Go sen desŭ.

Dōzo kata-michi no kippu (w)o ichi mai kudasai.

Ōfuku wa ikŭra desŭ ka? Yon jū go yen desŭ.

How much is the round trip? Forty-five yen.

Ōfuku no kippu (w)o kattara, motto yasui desŭ ka? Hai, ōfuku no kippu (w)o kattara, motto yasui deshō.

Tōkiō kara Kōbe made no ōfuku kippu wa ikŭra desŭ ka? San jū go yen desŭ.

Hiroshima made no ōfuku kippu wa ikŭra desŭ ka? San yen desŭ.

Kata-michi nara, ni jū shi sen de; ōfuku nara, shi jissen desŭ.

Aruite itte kuru to san jikan kakarimasŭ ga jidōsha de ōfuku shitara, nan jikan karaki-mashō ka?

Kono fune wa San Fŭranshisŭko e ōfuku shimasŭ ka?

Ni mai no kata-michi kippu yori wa ōfuku kippu no hō ga yasui desŭ.

Nagasaki e kyūkō ni tō kata-michi ichi mai kudasai.

Please give me one second-class one way express ticket to Nagasaki.

Shizuoka e tokkyū ittō ōfuku ni mai kudasai.

Okayama e kyūkō ni tō kata-michi sammai kudasai.

Kyōto e tokkyū ni tō ōfuku yo mai kudasai.

Dōzo Kanda eki e itte, Maebashi-yuki no futsū ni tō kata-michi no kippu (w)o jū mai katte kite kudasai.

Ano kĭsha ni wa shindaisha* ga tsuite imasŭ ka?

Does that train have a sleeping car?

Nagasaki made no shindai ken wa ikŭra desŭ ka? Ue wa jū yen de, shĭta wa hichi yen desŭ.

Ue no shindai (w)o negaimasŭ.

Shĭta no shindai (w)o negaimasŭ.

Shindai wa ue shĭka nokotte imasen.

There are only upper berths left.

Tabako wa nokotte imasŭ ka? Tabako wa hĭto hako shĭka nokotte imasen.

Nippon go (w)o manabi-hajimete kara ichi nen ni shĭka narimasen.

Go yen shĭka nokotte imasen.

Ano kata wa tomodachi (w)o hĭtori shĭka tsŭrete kimasen deshĭta.

Nippon go no hon (w)o ni satsŭ shika yoma-nai to iimashĭta.

Eigo shĭka hanashimasen.

Ainikŭ shĭta no shindai wa mina urikiremashĭta. Shĭkata ga nai kara, ue (w)o moraimashō

Sorry, the lowers were all sold out. Since it can't be helped, I'll take an upper.

Ainikŭ kyō kuroi kutsushĭta wa mina urikiremashĭta. Shĭkata ga nai kara, shiroi no (w)o moraimashō.

Ainikŭ kyō niku wa mina urikiremashĭta. Shĭkata ga nai kara, hoka no tokoro e ikimashō.

Ainikŭ suika wa mina urikiremashĭta. Shĭkata ga nai kara, hoka no yao-ya e itte mimashō.

Ainikŭ ittō no kippu wa mina urikiremashĭta ga. . . Shĭkata ga nai kara, hoka no kĭsha (w)o torimashō.

Ryōhō de san jū hachi yen ni narimasŭ.
Both together they come to thirty-eight yen.
Shindai dake wa jū yen desŭ.
Kĭsha no kippu dake wa yon jū yen desŭ.
Mina de shi jū yen ni narimasŭ.
Kutsŭ to bōshi to ryōhō ni, san jū go yen haraimashĭta.

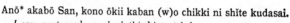

Anō* akabō San, kono ōkii kaban (w)o chikki ni shĭte kudasai.
I say, porter, please check this big satchel.
Anō, akabō San, kono nimotsŭ (w)o chikki ni shĭte kudasai.
Anō, akabō San, watakŭshi no kaban (w)o totte, kĭsha no naka e motte itte kudasai.
Anō, akabō San, watakŭshidomo no kaban wa azukete arimasŭ kara, kono kippu (w)o motte itte, totte kite kudasai.
Akabō San, kono ōkii kaban wa omo-sugiru kara, dōzo chikki ni shĭte kudasai.
Chikki ni suru ni wa kane ga ikŭra kakarimasŭ ka? Sore wa tada* desŭ.

Chiisai hō no wa kĭsha no naka e mochikonde kudasai.
Please put this little one inside the car.
Kĭsha no naka e watakŭshi no nimotsŭ (w)o motte itte kudasai.
Watakŭshi no kozutsumi (w)o toko-ya e motte itte kudasai.
Kono ōkii kaban wa kĭsha no naka e mochikonde kudasai.
Kono torankŭ mo ni gō sha e mochikonde kudasai.

Shindai no bangō wa san gō sha no ni ban desŭ.
The berth number is number two in the third train.
Anata no shindai no bangō wa nan gō sha no desŭ ka? Shi gō sha no jū ni bamme desŭ.
Takahashi San no shindai wa nan ban desŭ ka? Go gō sha no samban desŭ.
Anata no denwa no bangō wa Motomachi no roppyakŭ shi jū ban desŭ ne?
Shinshitsŭ no bangō wa ni bamme no kampan no san jū ban desŭ.
Anata no o-taku no bangō wa Ginza no sen shi hyakŭ ban desŭ ne?

Kippu (w)o o-kashi kudasai.
Please lend me your ticket.
Ano hon (w)o yonde shimattara, dōzo watakŭshi ni kashĭte kudasai.
Anata ga pen (w)o tsukatte i-nai nara, chotto watakŭshi ni kashĭte kudasai.
Kane (w)o kashĭte kudasai to negaimashĭta, keredomo kashĭte kuremasen deshĭta.

Ni jū yen tsugi no Doyōbi made watakŭshi ni kashĭte kuremasen ka? to tomodachi ga iimashĭta.
Ano hĭto ni kane (w)o kasa-nai de kudasai.

Torankŭ (w)o azukete kimasŭ.
I'll check your trunk.

Watakŭshi no kippu wa koko ni arimasŭ kara, torankŭ to kaban (w)o azukete kite kudasai.
Watakŭshi no yōfuku (w)o koko ni azukete mo ii n' desŭ ka?
Watakŭshi no torankŭ wa Matsumoto San nò taku ni azukete okimashĭta.
Ima kara yao-ya e itte kimasŭ.

Shĭtsŭrei desŭ ga, anata mo Nagasaki e o-ide ni narimasŭ ka? Hai, sō desŭ.
Excuse me, but are you also going to Nagasaki?

Shĭtsŭrei desŭ ga, anata mo Kōbe e o-ide ni narimasŭ ka? Hai, sō desŭ.
Shĭtsŭrei desŭ ga, anata mo kono kĭsha ni norimasŭ ka? Iie, norimasen.
Shĭtsŭrei desŭ ga, anata mo Tōkiō kara kimashĭta ka? Hai, sō desŭ.
Shĭtsŭrei desŭ ga, anata mo kono fune de Beikokŭ e o-ide ni narimasŭ ka? Iie, watakŭshi wa kono tsugi no "Taiyō Maru" *de iku tsumori desŭ.

Anata wa Beikokŭ no kata no yō ni miukemasŭ.
You look like an American.

Anata wa Nippon-jin no kata no yō ni miukemasŭ.
Anata no tomodachi wa Fŭransŭ-jin no kata no yō ni wa miemasen.
Takahashi San wa Nippon-jin no kata no yō ni miukemasŭ ga, Beikokŭ-jin da sō desŭ.
Anata wa Eikokŭ-jin no yō ni miukemasŭ ga, sō de gozaimasŭ ka?

Itsŭ kochira e o-koshi ni narimashĭta ka? Ni shūkan mae ni Yokohama e tsukimashĭta.
When did you cross over here? I arrived at Yokohama two weeks ago.

Anata wa umi (w)o o-koshi ni natta koto ga arimasŭ ka? Iie, arimasen.
Itsŭ Amerika e o-koshi ni narimashĭta ka? Mikka mae ni San Fŭranshisŭko e tsukimashĭta.
Itsŭ Eikokŭ e o-koshi ni narimashĭta ka? Shi ka getsŭ mae ni mairimashĭta.
Itsŭ otōto San wa Minami Amerika e o-koshi ni narimashĭta ka? Jū nen mae ni ikimashĭta.

Kono-goro no zeikan no tori-atsukai wa dō desŭ ka?
How is the treatment now-a-days at the customs?

Kono-goro no kawase no nedan wa dō desŭ ka? Sŭkoshi takakŭ narimashĭta.
Ane San no kono-goro no byōki no yōsu wa dō desŭ ka? Arigatō. Sŭkoshi ii hō desŭ.
Ano yado-ya no tori-atsukai wa ii desŭ ka? Kanari ii sō desŭ.
Ano jidōsha wa taihen tori-atsukai-yasui desŭ.

Kanari yasashikatta to omoimasŭ.
I think it was very easy.

Kanari muzukashikatta to omoimasŭ.

Kanari omokatta to omoimasŭ.

Kanari omoshirokatta to omoimasŭ.

Taihen oishikatta to omoimasŭ.

Kono renshū wa taihen yasashii to omoimasŭ ka?

Eigo wa Nippon go yori yasashii to omoimasŭ.

Watakŭshi wa Fŭransŭ go wa Eigo gurai yasashii to omoimasŭ ga musŭko wa Fŭransŭ go wa Eigo hodo yasashikŭ nai to omou to iimashĭta.

Ryoken wa motte ita shi nimotsŭ wa watakŭshi jishin no furugi deshĭta.
I had a passport and besides my baggage was (just) my old clothes.

Anata ni wa ryoken ga arimasŭ ka?

Ainikŭ desŭ ga watakŭshi wa ryoken (w)o motte kimasen deshĭta.

Anata jishin de shĭte kudasai.

Watakŭshi ni wa furugi shika arimasen kara, anata to issho ni iku koto wa dekimasen.

Anata wa furugi (w)o uritai n' desŭ ka?

Doko ni furugi-ya ga arimasŭ ka?

Kyō wa tenki wa ii shi o-kane wa takŭsan motte imasŭ kara, kaimono ni ikimasen ka?

Watakŭshi wa taihen tsukarete imasŭ shi kanai mo byōki desŭ kara, hayakŭ toko ni narimasŭ

Kono tegami wa anata jishin ga kakimashĭta ka?

Zeikin (w)o harau beki mono wa arimasen.
There is no duty that I should pay.

Anata no kaku beki tegami wa dare e desŭ ka?

Anata no morau beki kane wa ikŭra desŭ ka?

Watakŭshi no hanasu beki koto wa nani desŭ ka?

Watakŭshi no su* beki koto wa nan desŭ ka?

Nihon go wa taihen muzukashii desŭ.
The Japanese language is very difficult.

Fŭransŭ go wa amari muzukashikŭ arimasen.

Kono renshū wa watakŭshi ni muzukashi-sugimasŭ.

Ano hito wa taihen muzukashii kata desŭ.

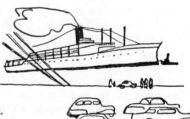

Kono hon wa yomi-nikui desŭ.
This book is hard to read.

Kono kusuri wa nomi-nikui desŭ.

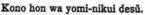

Nippon go wa kaki-nikui desŭ.
Sono shĭgoto wa shi-nikui desŭ ka?
Kono-goro tabako wa kai-nikui desŭ.

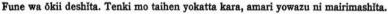

Umi no ue wa dō deshĭta ka?
How was the crosssing?
Tenki wa dō deshĭta ka?
Fune no ue wa dō deshĭta ka?
Zeikan no tori-atsukai wa dō deshĭta ka?
Umi (w)o o-koshi ni narimashĭta ka? Iie, koshimasen deshĭta.
Hikōki de umi no ue (w)o tonda koto ga arimasŭ ka? Hai, arimasŭ.

Fune wa ōkii deshĭta. Tenki mo taihen yokatta kara, amari yowazu ni mairimashĭta.
The ship was large. As the weather was fine too, I came over without getting very seasick.
Fune wa chiisai deshĭta. Tenki mo taihen warukatta kara, yoimashĭta.
Ano Nihon no fune no namae wa nan to iimasŭ ka? Taiyō Maru* to iimasŭ.
Fune ni yotta koto ga arimasŭ ka? Iie, arimasen.
Ano hĭto wa taihen sake ni yotte imasŭ.
Ano hĭto wa itsu mo[106] yotte imasŭ ka?
Tōkiō no natsŭ wa ii desŭ ka? Iie, sŭkoshi atsui desŭ.

Watakŭshi no shinshitsŭ wa ichiban ue no kampan ni arimashĭta no de, sŭkoshi osorete imashĭta.
Because my state-room was on the top deck I was a little frightened.
Watakŭshi no shinshitsŭ wa ichiban shĭta no kampan ni arimashĭta no de, sŭkoshi osorete imashĭta.
Anata no shinshitsŭ wa dono kampan ni arimasŭ ka? Ni bamme no kampan ni arimasŭ.
Anata no shinshitsŭ no bango wa nani desŭ ka? Sambamme no kampan no sambyakŭ san jū yo ban desŭ.
Kono-goro funa-chin ga takakŭ natte iru kara, rainen made wa Beikokŭ e iku tsŭmori ja arimasen.
Ano ko wa neru koto (w)o osoremasŭ.
Anata wa nani mo osoreru koto ga arimasen.
Ano ko wa junsa (w)o osoremasŭ ka? Hai, taihen osorete imasŭ.

Arai nami ni wa awazu ni Yokohama e tsukimashĭta.
We arrived at Yokohama without meeting any rough waves.
Kinō Takashima-ya e itta toki ni, Matsumoto San ni aimashĭta.
Anata ga shirasete kureta kata ni wa awazu ni kaerimashĭta.
Kesa wa tegami (w)o kakazu ni dekakemashĭta.

Yūhan (w)o tabezu ni koko e kimashĭta ka?

Denwa (w)o kakezu ni ko[116]-nai de kudasai.

Umi no ue wa dō deshĭta ka? Nami wa amari arakŭ arimasen deshĭta.

Anata wa tomodachi ni doko de au hazu desŭ ka?

Funa-chin wa takakŭ natte iru sō ja arimasen ka? Hai, sŭkoshi wa takakŭ natta sō desŭ ga taishĭta koto wa arimasen.

I hear the ship fare has gone up, hasn't it? Yes, they say it's gone up a little, but it's nothing much.

Densha-chin wa yasukŭ natte iru sō ja arimasen ka? Iie, amari yasukŭ natte imasen.

Kĭsha-chin wa yasukŭ narimashĭta ka? Iie, kisha-chin wa sŭkoshi takakŭ natta sō desŭ ga taishĭta koto wa arimasen.

Anata no okusama wa byōki da sō desŭ ga ikaga desŭ ka? Arigatō, sŭkoshi kaze (w)o hiite imasŭ ga taishĭta koto wa arimasen.

16 Dai Jū Rokk(w)a (Lesson XVI)

Ueda San, ii tenki desŭ kara, sampo (w)o shi nagara,[80] Nippon no koto ni tsuite[100] o-hanashi shĭte kudasaimasen ka?

Miss Ueda, since it's good weather, while we're taking a walk, won't you please speak about Japan?

Hai, Nippon wa Taiheiyō ni aru Ajiya no
5 shimaguni de, sono[13] menseki wa Amerika no Tekisasŭ shū to hotondo onaji[*7] de arimasŭ ga, jinkō wa kare-kore hichi sen go hyakŭ man nin desŭ.

Yes, Japan is an island country of Asia in the Pacific Ocean, and it's area is approximately the same as that of the American state of Texas; the population is about seventy-five million.

Kita no hō wa, Nippon-Kai (w)o koseba,[89]
10 Shiberiya kara tsuzuite Roshya no hongokŭ e[33] hairimasŭ.

To the north, crossing the Sea of Japan, continuing on from Siberia, one enters the Russian mainland.

Nippon-Kai no nishi ni wa, Chōsen hantō ga ari,[44] minami wa Taiwan kara Shina ni men shĭte, Nan-yō e, higashi wa Taiheiyō
15 de arimasŭ.

The Korean peninsula is to the west of the Japan Sea and to the south from Formosa it faces China and toward the South Seas and to the east is the Pacific Ocean.

Kuni wa yottsŭ no shima de naritatte imasŭ: sono uchi Honshū wa mannaka[101] de, minami ni wa Shikokŭ to Kyūshū ga ari, kita ni wa Hokkaidō ga arimasŭ.

The country consists of four islands: among them Honshu is the middle one, to the south are Shikoku and Kyushu, and Hokkaido is to the north.

---

20 Nippon wa sampu to shi jū sangen ni wakatte imasŭ. Sampu wa Tōkiō fu, Kyōto fu, Ōsaka fu no koto desŭ. Nippon no shufu wa Tōkiō de, Honshū ni arimasŭ.

Japan is divided into three metropolitan districts* and forty-three prefectures: The three districts are the Tokio district, Kyoto district, and the Osaka district. The capital of Japan is Tokio, and it is in Honshu.

Tōkiō ni tsuide,[100] ōkii tokai wa Ōsaka,
25 Kyōto, Kōbe, Yokohama, nado de arimasŭ. Tokai ni wa kanari ōkii tatemono ga arimasŭ ga jishin no tame ni[29] amari takai tatemono wa tateraremasen.

Following Tokio the large cities are Osaka, Kyoto, Kobe, Yokohama, etc. In the cities there are quite large buildings, but because of earthquakes very high buildings can not be built.

Nihon ni wa takŭsan no takai yama ya kawa
30 ga arimasŭ ga mottomo[47] yūmei na no[55] wa Fuji-san desŭ.[102] Kawa de nadakai no wa Shinano-gawa de, mizuumi de wa Biwa-ko desŭ.

In Japan there are many high mountains and rivers; the most famous one is Fujiyama. Of the rivers the Shinano river is a well-known one; of the lakes, Lake Biwa is (well-known).

Omo na sambutsŭ toshĭte[100] wa kiito ga
35 sekai ni shirarete imasŭ.

Silk is known throughout the world as its principal product.

Shūkyō wa shu-to-shĭte Bukkyō to Kĭrisŭto-kyō to Shintō nado de arimasŭ.

The religions are chiefly Buddhism, Christianity, Shinto, and so forth.

Nihon no kyōiku seido wa Ō-Bei no to yokŭ nite, taihen shimpo shĭte imasŭ.

The Japanese system of education is similar to that of the Occident (Europe and America) and is very advanced.

⁴⁰ Chotto o-machi kudasai. Kyōiku seido to iu¹⁵ kotoba wa dō iu⁷³ imi desŭ ka?
Sore wa Eigo de *educational system* no¹³ imi desŭ.
Arigatō. Sore de yokŭ wakarimashĭta.
⁴⁵ Jinjō shō-gakkō kara, kōtō shō-gakkō, chū-gakkō, kōtō gakkō, daigaku ni itaru made¹⁰⁰ yokŭ kambi shĭte imasŭ.

Please wait a moment. What is the meaning of the word *kyōiku seido?*
That means educational system in English.
Thank you. Now I understand.
It is complete from elementary school, higher primary school, middle (high) school, college, up to the university.

Kokumin wa taihen kimben desŭ ga iro-iro no undō mo konomimasŭ: bēsŭ-bōru, ⁵⁰ tenisŭ, suiei, sumō, jūdō, nado ga omo na mono desŭ ga shōsū no hĭto wa gorŭfŭ (w)o shĭte asonde iru-rashii¹⁰³ desŭ. Tō kokŭ ni wa keshiki no yoi tokoro ga takŭsan⁴³ aru no de, gaikokŭ kara tasū no hĭto ga kem-⁵⁵ butsŭ ni kimasŭ.

The people are very industrious, but they like all kinds of sports also: baseball, tennis, swimming, wrestling, judo, etc. are the principal ones but it seems a small number play golf. To this (the said) country, because of its many scenic places, come large numbers of people from foreign countries to go sightseeing.

---

* There are now only two *fu*, as Tokio has been recently designated a *to* (miyako).

Exercises

Sampo (w)o shi nagara, Nippon no koto ni tsuite o-hanashi shĭte kudasaimasen ka?
While we are taking a walk, won't you speak about Japanese things?

Watakŭshi wa sampo ga taihen sŭki desŭ.
Anata wa sampo (w)o shĭtai n' desŭ ka?
Anata wa Nippon no koto ni tsuite no hon (w)o yomimashĭta ka?
Ano hĭto wa Shina no koto ni tsuite hanashimashĭta.
Anata wa ryōri no koto ni tsuite shitte imasŭ ka?
Anata wa Nippon no rikugun no koto ni tsuite shitte imasŭ ka?
Tabe nagara, hanashimashō.
Aruki nagara, tabako (w)o nomu koto wa konomimasen.

Nippon wa Taiheiyō ni aru Ajiya no shimaguni desŭ.
Japan is an island country of Asia in the Pacific Ocean.

Eikokŭ wa Taiseiyō ni aru Yōroppa no shimaguni desŭ.
Chōsen wa Taiheiyō ni aru hantō desŭ.
Taiwan wa Taiheiyō ni aru shima desŭ.
Taiheiyo wa sekai de ichiban ōkii umi desŭ ka?
Shina wa Ajiya ni arimasŭ.

Sono menseki wa Amerika no Tekisasŭ shū to hotondo onaji de arimasŭ ga jinkō wa kare kore hichi sen go hyakŭ man nin desŭ.

It's area is approximately the same as that of the American state of Texas and the population is about seventy million.

Amerika no menseki wa dono gurai desŭ ka?

Nippon no menseki to Kariforuniya* no menseki to wa dochira ga ōkii desŭ ka?

Anata wa doko kara kimashĭta ka? Watakŭshi wa Penshirubania* shū kara kimashĭta.

Watakŭshi no sei wa anata to hotondo onaji desŭ.

Nippon-jin to Shina-jin to wa hotondo onaji mono (w)o tabemasŭ ka?

Amerika no jinkō wa dono gurai arimasŭ ka? Ichi oku* san zen man nin gurai arimasŭ.

Tōkiō no jinkō wa sekai de sambamme da sō desŭ.

Ima wa kare-kore jū ji desŭ.

Watakŭshi wa kare-kore ni jikan manabimashĭta.

Kĭta no hō wa Nippon-Kai (w)o koseba, Shiberiya kara tsuzuite, Roshya no hongokŭ e hairimasŭ.

To the north, crossing the Sea of Japan and continuing on from Siberia, one enters the Russian mainland.

Ano hĭto wa ni jikan hanashi-tsuzukemashĭta.

Yomi-tsuzukete kudasai.

Ano hĭto wa mata shigoto (w)o tsuzukemashĭta.

Tomodachi wa hongokŭ e kaerimashĭta.

Nippon-Kai no nishi ni wa, Chōsen hantō ga ari, minami wa Taiwan kara Shina ni men shĭte, Nan-yō e, higashi wa Taiheiyō de arimasŭ.

The Korean peninsula is to the west and to the south from Formosa it faces China and to the east to the South Seas and the Pacific Ocean.

Beikokŭ no nishi wa Taiheiyō de, higashi wa Taiseiyō, kita ni wa Kanada ga ari, minami wa Mekĭshĭko ni men shĭte imasŭ.

Eikokŭ no nishi wa Taiseiyō de, higashi wa, kaikyō* (w)o koseba, Berŭgi ni hairi, minami wa Fŭransŭ ni men shĭte, kĭta wa tōkŭ Noruwē (w)o mite imasŭ.

Fŭransŭ no minami wa doko no kuni desŭ ka?

Nishi ni wa donna kuni ga arimasŭ ka?

Eikokŭ wa shimaguni desŭ ka? Hantō desŭ ka?

Nan-yō to iu imi wa nan desŭ ka? Taiwan no minami no hō ni aru Taiheiyō (w)o Nan-yō to iimasŭ.

Nanyō wa Taiwan kara minami no hō e Ōsŭtorariya* made no umi (w)o Nan-yō to iimasŭ.

Nan-yō ni wa ni-san zen no shima ga arimasŭ.

Kuni wa yottsŭ no shima de naritatte imasŭ: sono uchi Honshū wa mannaka de, minami ni wa Shĭkokŭ to Kyūshū ga ari, kĭta ni wa Hokkaidō ga arimasŭ.

The country consists of four islands: among them Honshu is the middle one, to the south are Shikoku and Kyushu, and Hokkaido is to the north.

Beikokŭ wa shi jū hachi shū de naritatte imasŭ.

Kono machi no mannaka ni aru ōkii tatemono wa nan desŭ ka?

Tomodachi ga michi no mannaka (w)o aruite imasŭ.

Kono kuni wa sŭki desŭ ka?

Ano kuni (w)o dō omoimasŭ ka?

Nippon wa ni fu to shi jū sangen ni wakatte imasŭ.

Japan is divided into two metropolitan districts and forty-three prefectures.

Amerika wa shi jū hachi shū to Hawai, Arasŭka ni wakatte imasŭ.

Fu to iu no wa nani no imi desŭ ka? Fu wa ōkii machi no imi desŭ.

Nippon no shufu wa Tōkiō de, Honshū ni arimasŭ.

The capital of Japan is Tokio and it is in Honshu.

Fŭransŭ no shufu wa Parī de, Yōroppa* ni arimasŭ.

Beikokŭ no shufu wa Washinton de, Kĭta Amerika ni arimasŭ.

Itarī no shufu wa Rōma de, Yōroppa ni arimasŭ.

Chōsen no shufu wa Keijō de, Ajiya ni arimasŭ.

Taiwan no shufu wa Kiirun de, Ajiya no shimaguni de arimasŭ.

Eikokŭ no shufu wa Rondon de, Yōroppa ni arimasŭ.

Roshya no shufu wa Mosukō de, Doitsŭ* no shufu wa Berurin desŭ.

Tōkiō ni tsuite, ōkii tokai wa Ōsaka, Kyōto, Kōbe, Yokohama, nado de arimasŭ.

Following Tokio, the large cities are Osaka, Kyoto, Kobe, Yokohama, etc.

Nyū Yōkŭ ni tsuite, ōkii tokai wa Shikago, San Fŭranshisŭko, Hiraderuhiya, Bosŭton nado de arimasŭ.

Rondon* ni tsuite, ōkii tokai wa doko desŭ ka?

Rio de Janeiro ni tsuite, ōkii tokai wa Saun* Pauro, desŭ ka?

Buenosu Airesu* ni tsuite, ōkii tokai wa Rosario desŭ ka?

Tokai ni wa kanari ōkii tatemono ga arimasŭ ga jishin no tame ni amari takai tatemono wa tateraremasen.

In the cities there are quite large buildings, but because of earthquakes, very high buildings are not built.

Kono machi ni wa ōkikŭte takai tatemono ga arimasŭ ne.

Kesa jishin ga arimashĭta.

Warui mizu (w)o nonda tame ni, byōki in narimashĭta.

Ano hĭto wa isha ni naru tame ni manande imasŭ.

Ano tatemono wa jishin no tame ni kowaremashĭta.

Ōkii jishin no toki ni wa takeyabu* e nigekomimasŭ.*

Nihon ni wa takŭsan no takai yama ya kawa ga arimasŭ ga mottomo yūmei na no wa Fuji San desŭ.

In Japan there are many high mountains and rivers; the most famous one is Fujiyama.

Kono machi de mottomo yūmei na hĭto wa dare desŭ ka?

Beikokŭ ni wa takŭsan no takai yama ya kawa ga arimasŭ ga mottomo yūmei na no wa Rokki-zan ya Mishishippi-gawa desŭ.

Tōkiō no soba ni yūmei na Sumida-gawa ga arimasŭ.

Fuji San no takasa wa kare-kore san mairu arimasŭ.

Fuji San kara yūmei na Asama-yama ga miemasŭ.

Asama-yama wa funkazan* no hĭtotsŭ desŭ.

Kawa de nadakai no wa Shinano-gawa de, mizuumi de wa Biwa-ko desŭ.

Of the rivers, the Shinano river is a well-known one and of the lakes, Lake Biwa is (famous).

Amerika de yūmei na mizuumi wa nan to iimasŭ ka? Mishigan-ko ya Huron-ko deshō.

Kyōto to Ōsaka no chikakŭ ni arimasŭ.

Natsŭ wa takŭsan no hĭto ga kono mizuumi de asobimasŭ.*

Nippon-jin wa mizuumi de amari oyogimasen* ga umi ya kawa de yokŭ oyogimasŭ.

Omo na sambutsŭ toshĭte wa kiito ga sekai ni shirarete imasŭ.

Silk is known throughout the world as its chief product.

Kono machi no omo na sambutsŭ wa nan desŭ ka? Kono machi de wa o-cha ga takŭsan dekimasŭ.*

Nippon-jin toshĭte wa kome ga mottomo hitsuyō na mono desŭ.

Nihon no o-cha mo sekai ni yokŭ shirarete imasŭ.

Roshya no rikugun wa sekai de ichiban ōkii sō desŭ.

Shūkyō wa shu-to-shĭte Bukkyō to Kĭrisŭto-kyō to Shintō nado de arimasŭ.

The religions are chiefly Buddhism, Christianity, Shinto, and so forth.

Amerika no shūkyō wa shu-to-shĭte Shinkyō to Kyūkyō to Yudaya-kyō nado de arimasŭ.

Anata no shūkyō wa nan desŭ ka? Watakŭshi no shūkyō wa Kĭrisŭto-kyō desŭ.

Kamakura no daibutsŭ* wa Nihon de mottomo yūmei desŭ.

O-miya* de yūmei na no wa Meiji-jingū* desŭ.

Nihon no kyōiku seido wa Ō-Bei no to yokŭ nite, taihen shimpo shĭte imasŭ.

The Japanese system of education is like that of Europe and America and it has progressed a great deal.

Nihon no kekkon seido wa Ō-Bei no to yokŭ nite imasen, taihen chigatte* imasŭ.

Ano ko wa okāsan ni yokŭ nite imasŭ.

Ano tatemono wa watakŭshi no gakkō ni yokŭ nite imasŭ.

Amerika no denki wa taihen shimpo shǐte imasǔ.
Ajiya de Nippon no kyōiku seido ga ichiban shimpo shǐte imasǔ.

Chotto o-machi kudasai. Kyōiku seido to iu kotoba wa dō iu imi desǔ ka? Sore wa Eigo de educational system no imi desǔ.
Pardon me. What is the meaning of the word "kyoiku seido"? In English that means "educational system."
Chotto o-machi kudasai. O-miya wa Eigo de nani no imi desǔ ka? Sore wa Eigo de *shrine* no imi desǔ.
Chotto o-machi kudasai. Daibutsǔ to iu kotoba wa dō iu imi desǔ ka? Sore wa Eigo de *statue of Buddha* no imi desǔ.
Chotto o-machi kudasai. Kaji to iu kotoba wa Fǔransǔ-go de nan to iimasǔ ka? Sore wa Fǔransǔ-go de *feu* to iimasǔ.
Chotto o-machi kudasai. Kekkon seido to iu kotoba wa dō iu imi desǔ ka? Sore wa *marriage customs* no imi desǔ.

Arigatō. Sore de yokǔ wakarimashǐta.
Thanks. That makes it very clear.
Shǐtsǔrei desǔ ga sore de mo* mada wakarimasen.
Sore de yokǔ wakarimashǐta ka?
Sore de wa watakǔshi wa ima kara uchi e kaerimashō.
Dono kotoba no imi ga wakarimasen ka? Chigaimasǔ to iu kotoba no imi ga wakarimasen deshǐta.

Jinjō shō-gakkō kara, kōtō shō-gakkō, chū-gakkō, kōtō gakkō, daigaku ni itaru made yokǔ kambi shǐte imasǔ.
It is complete from elementary school, higher primary school, middle school, high school, up to the university.
Nippon-jin wa mina shō-gakkō (w)o de-nakereba narimasen; chū-gakkō ya kōtō gakkō e wa itte mo ika-nakǔte mo ii n' desǔ.
Anata wa kōtō gakkō (w)o demashǐta ka? Hai, demashǐta.
Rainen daigaku (w)o deru hazu desǔ.
Kono jimusho* no naka wa mina yokǔ kambi shǐte imasǔ.

Kokumin wa taihen kimben desǔ ga iro-iro no undō mo konomimasǔ.
The people are very industrious, but they like all kinds of sports also.
Amerika no kokumin wa kimben desǔ ga bēsǔ-bōru, ya fūto-bōru nado (w)o konomimasǔ.
Donna undō ga sǔki desǔ ka? Watakǔshi wa tenisǔ no hō ga ichiban sǔki desǔ.
Ano hǐto wa taihen kimben desǔ ga musǔko san wa amari kimben ja arimasen.
Suiei wa taihen yoi undō desǔ.

Besŭ-bōru, tenisŭ, suiei, sumō, jūdō, nado ga omo na mono desŭ.
Baseball, tennis, swimming, wrestling, judo, etc. are the principal ones.

Anata wa tenisŭ (w)o shĭte asobimasŭ ka? Iie, tenisŭ wa shimasen ga suiei ga sŭki desŭ.

Sumō wa mita koto ga arimasen ga jūdō wa mita koto ga arimasŭ.

Kono-goro wa rikugun de takŭsan no heishi ga jūdō (w)o naratte* iru sō desŭ.

Raishū jūdō no shiai* ni tsurete itte kudasai.

Shōsŭ no hĭto wa gorŭfŭ (w)o shĭte asonde iru-rashii desŭ.
A small number of people, I think, play golf.

Kyō wa ii tenki ni naru-rashii desŭ.

Shujin-rashii hĭto ga ima densha ni norimashĭta.

Ano hĭto wa takŭsan sake (w)o nonda-rashii desŭ.

Tomodachi wa taihen tsukarete iru-rashii desŭ.

Anata wa Nihon-jin-rashikŭ Nihon go (w)o hanasemasen ka?

Kono kuni ni wa keshiki no yoi tokoro ga takŭsan aru no de, gaikokŭ kara tasū no hĭto ga kembutsŭ ni kimasŭ.
To this country, because of its many fine scenic places, come large numbers of people from foreign countries to go sightseeing.

Doko ka[106] keshiki no yoi tokoro e itte mitai desŭ.

Nikkō no keshiki (w)o mita koto ga arimasŭ ka?

Gaikokŭ-jin ga takŭsan Nikkō e kembutsŭ ni kuru sō desŭ.

Anata wa nani ka gaikokŭ go ga hanasemasŭ ka?

Hai, Sŭpein* go to Horutogarŭ* go ga sŭkoshi dekimasŭ.

GRAMMAR

The Roman numerals and Arabic numerals in parentheses refer to lessons and lines respectively.

PRONUNCIATION

ROMANIZATION

Japanese is Romanized in this text to facilitate the development of a knowledge of the spoken language. The Japanese, however, do not usually write with the Roman letters, but with Chinese characters and two syllabaries (see page 215).

The system of Romanization or **romaji** which is employed here is the one used by practically all text books, scholarly works, dictionaries, and newspapers and magazines in English. While it lacks the virtue of simplifying morphological detail, it makes up for this lack by simplifying the acquisition of correct pronunciation.

The following table lists the differences between the system most widely used and that promulgated in the Japanese Government decree of 1937, which is essentially that of the phonemic transcription used by some writers.

Hepburn System	Japanese Government	Hepburn System	Japanese Government
cha	tya	jo	zyo
chi	ti	ju	zyu
cho	tyo	sha	sya
chu	tyu	shi	si
fu	hu	sho	syo
ja	zya	shu	syu
ji	zi	tsu	tu

LONG VOWELS AND CONSONANTS

A long vowel such as ā, ō, ū, etc., or a vowel followed by a nasal in the same syllable must be held twice as long as a vowel without the line over it, such as a, o, u, etc. A short ĭ or ŭ is a whispered vowel and may often not be heard at all. Doubled consonants likewise are held twice as long as single ones. In English this occurs only when two words, the first of which ends in, and the second of which begins with the same consonant, are pronounced in the same breath, e. g., pen(k)nife, good day. The **pp** of **roppiki** (VIII, 38) *six 'animals'*, for example, sounds like the *pp* in *cap-pistol*. Long **ch** is written **tch**, e. g., **itchaku** (X, 41) *one 'suit'*. It is often important to distinguish long vowels and consonants from others as a difference in meaning results therefrom. For instance, **tofu** means *a city* or *town*, **tōfu** (XI, 44) *bean-curds* and **tōfū** *the east wind;* **motto** (VI, 36) means *more* and **moto** *beginning, origin*.

SYLLABIFICATION

A syllable consists of a vowel alone, or of a vowel preceded by a consonant. A long vowel counts as two syllables, and a final n counts as a separate syllable. Each of two contiguous vowels makes a separate syllable and each of the vowels retains the same sound it has when not in combination with another vowel. For instance, **ikura** (VII, 37) divided into syllables is **i-ku-ra** and **naoshite** (X, 41) **na-o-shi-te**. However, **au** may sometimes be pronounced **ō**; e. g., **morau** (VII, 60).

PITCH ACCENT

Japanese has very little stress accent and care must be taken to pronounce each syllable with the same degree of loudness or force. The accent marks over the words in the vocabulary indicate that the syllables over which the marks appear are distinguished from the unaccented syllables by a higher musical pitch, and not by stress.

An accented syllable is pronounced in a tone about a musical third higher than an unaccented syllable. When a word has a number of consecutive accented syllables the last accented syllable has a light stress accent as well as a pitch accent. It will be noticed that the polite verbal ending **másŭ** generally has the accent on the syllable **ma**, but this higher tone is heard only if the final **u** is pronounced or if a word with level pitch follows. A pitch accent on the last syllable of a word is noticeable only when followed by a word beginning with an unaccented syllable. Note that the negative form **masén** has the accent on the **e**.

A word having no accent mark in the Japanese-English Dictionary, p. 219 (except those marked with an asterisk, the pitch of which has not been ascertained) is pronounced on a level pitch, and when followed by postpositions, the postposition is accented; e. g., **hashi nó** *of the edge*, but in **hashí no** *of the bridge* **hashí** keeps its accent and **no** is pronounced on level pitch. Compare **háshi nó** *of the chopstick*.

Long vowels usually have a drop in pitch, and the second of two consecutive vowels is usually lower than the first. Where the second of two consecutive vowels is accented, both vowels are on the same pitch, but are both lower than a following accented syllable. It is also important to note that in any word all the syllables which precede the accented syllable, except the first syllable, are pronounced in the same pitch as the accented syllable.

It will be noted that in true adjectives (see section 43) the pitch accent is usually on the syllable before the **i** ending, but that in the adverbial form and consequently in the tense forms and in the gerund (which are based on the adverbial form) the accent is thrown back one syllable, e. g., **nagái, nágaku, nágakatta, nágakŭte**. There is also a similar shift in accent in the past and gerundial forms of verbs of the first class ending in **eru**, e. g., **tabéru, tábeta, tábete**.

It must be remembered that various dialects of Japanese often place the accent in a different manner from the Tokio speech.

The Dictionary of this book (see page 219) for the most part gives the pitch marked by Kaku Jimbo and Chisato Tsunefuka in their "Kokugo Hatsuon Akusento Jiten" and represents the Tokio pitch only.

PHRASING

Within a sentence a pause may usually be made after a postposition or after the second of two consecutive postpositions.

PRONUNCIATION OF ROMAJI

LETTERS	APPROXIMATE SOUND AND EXPLANATION	EXAMPLE
a	like the *a* in father, but shorter and not drawled	arigatō (I, 3)
b	like *b* in English	ban (I, 36)

LETTERS	APPROXIMATE SOUND AND EXPLANATION	EXAMPLE
ch	like *ch* in *church*, but with the tongue back of the upper teeth instead of the upper gum	chiisai (VI, 36)
d	like *d* in *day*, but with the tongue touching the upper teeth instead of gum	dare (II, 23)
e	like *e* in m*e*t; the postposition **e** is often **ye** after **n**.	ebi (VIII, 42)
f	like *h* in *h*oot, but with the lips close together. This sound is made by the breath escaping between the upper and lower lip and not between the teeth and the lower lip as is English *f*. It appears before **u** only, for **h** is used before other vowels.	fune (XV, 57)
g	1. at the beginning of a word like *g* in *g*o 2. in the middle of a word, or in the postposition **ga** like the *ng* in ri*ng* (Tokio pronunciation)	gozen (VII, 23) agari (VI, 54) ga (XIII, 6)
h	1. Before **a, e,** and **o** like *h* in *h*op 2. before **i** like *h* in *h*eap (or it is usually pronounced like German *ch* in *ich*); i. e. the tongue is in position for *y* as in *y*ellow, but *h* is pronounced instead. It sounds about half way between *h* and *sh*.	hai (I, 19), hen (XIII, 50) hon (I, 9) hikui (VI, 47)
i	1. like the *i* in mach*i*ne 2. between two voiceless consonants and sometimes elsewhere **i** is voiceless; i. e. whispered or not pronounced at all. This **i** is usually marked short; i. e., Ĭ in the text. 3. (i) may be pronounced or not.	ikaga (I, 2) deshĭta (III, 16) nan(i) (I, 16)
j	like the *j* in *j*eer, but with the tongue behind the upper teeth instead of the upper gum	Jirō (II, 5)
k	like *k* in English	kane (X, 63)
m	like *m* in *m*other	manabimasen (I, 43)
n	1. at the beginning of a word or syllable like the *n* in *n*eat, but with the tip of the tongue touching the upper teeth instead of the upper gum 2. at the end of a phrase or sentence or before **k** or **g** like the *ng* in si*ng*, or sometimes like *n* in ti*n*, but held longer.	namae (VIII, 13) Nippon-kai (XVI, 9) arimasen (VI, 29)
o	like the *o* in n*o*rth, but pronounced sharply, not drawled or diphthongized	ano (II, 12)
p	like p in English	Nippon (I, 37)

LETTERS	APPROXIMATE SOUND AND EXPLANATION	EXAMPLE
r	made by a quick flapping of the tip of the tongue, lightly touching the gums behind the upper teeth. somewhat like the pronunciation of *r* as a *d* by some English people who seem to say *veddy* for *very*. closer to English *l* than to English *r*. neither the trilled nor uvular *r*, but one light tap of the tongue.	kore (I, 18)
s	always voiceless like the *s* in *s*ympathy, but with the tip of the tongue touching the back of the upper teeth, not the upper gum	sayonara (I, 48)
sh	like the *sh* in *sh*ip, but with the tongue tip back of the upper teeth instead of the upper gum	shimbun (I, 33)
t	like the *t* in English, but with the tongue tip touching the back of the upper teeth instead of the gum	tomodachi (III, 24)
ts	a combination of t and s without any intervening sound. like *ts* in ge*ts*.	tsukue (I, 30)
u	1. between the sound of *u* in r*u*le and the *u* in p*u*sh. not drawled or diphthongized	mawasu (IV, 31)
	2. between two voiceless consonants and sometimes elsewhere u is voiceless, i. e. whispered or is not pronounced at all. This u has been marked short in the text, i. e., ŭ.	sŭkoshi (VII, 16) desŭ (I, 5)
w	like *w* in *w*atch. the w of the postposition (w)o is not usually heard except after a word ending in n. It is therefore placed in parenthesis as are all letters which may or may not be pronounced.	watakŭshi (II, 6) (w)o (I, 35) ikk(w)a (I, 0) K(w)ayōbi (VIII, 16)
y	like the *y* in *y*ellow, never like the *y* in b*y*.	yomimasŭ (I, 33) byōki (XIII, 36) ryōriya (XI, 27)
z	like the *z* in *z*inc, but with the tongue tip touching the back of the upper teeth instead of the gum. also pronounced by some people like *ds* in fa*ds*	zasshi (I, 46)

ka

1. ka after the verb makes a declarative sentence interrogative. No change in the declaratives word order is made.

Nani desu ka? (I, 12)	*What is it?*
Mai ban nani wo shimasu ka? (I, 36)	*What do you do every evening?*
Watakushi no zasshi wo mimashita ka? (III, 19)	*Did you see my magazine?*

For other interrogative and indefinite uses of **ka,** see sections **23** and **24.**

ARTICLES

2. There is neither a definite nor indefinite article in Japanese. The demonstrative adjectives (see section 10) sometimes correspond to the definite article and the numeral **ichi** corresponds on occasion to the indefinite article (see section 52).

wa AND wo

3. Wa and wo are postpositions. **Wa** usually indicates that the preceding word or phrase is the logical subject of the sentence and **wo** that the preceding word or phrase is the object of the verb. **Wa** may be translated by the expression *as for*, but **wo** has no English equivalent (see section **20**). In a negative sentence **wa** usually follows the object or the predicate nominative.

Kore wa fude desu ka? (I, 18)	*As-for this, is it a brush?*, i. e., *Is this a writing brush?*
Koko kara Ōsaka e wa Kōbe e iku yori tōi desu ka? (VI, 30)	*From here as-for to Osaka, is it farther to go than to Kobe?*, i. e., *Is Osaka farther from here than Kobe?*
Mai asa nani wo shimasu ka? (I, 32)	*What do you do every morning?*
Mai asa shimbun wo yomimasu (I, 33)	*I read the newspaper every morning.*
Hikōki wa kaitaku arimasen (IV, 26)	*I don't want to buy a plane.*

PLURALS

4. Nouns and pronouns do not usually change their form in the plural. **Kore wa hon desu ka?** (I, 20) may mean *Is this a book?* or *Are these books?* Similarly, **Hai, hon desu** (I, 21) may mean either *Yes, this is a book* or *Yes, these are books.* The meaning is usually made clear by the context.

The suffixes **tachi, tomo** (**domo**), **ra,** and **kata** (**gata**) are sometimes added to nouns or pronouns to make plurals, e. g., **hitotachi** (III, 44) *men*, **watakushidomo** (II, 31) *we*, **anatagata** (II, 16), *you* (*plural*), **gunjintachi** (XI, 15) *military men*, **donatagata** (XI, 15) *who* (*plural*) (see section **11**).

> Tachi is sometimes added to nouns denoting living things; tomo (sonant form domo) meaning companion, **kata** (sonant form gata), and -ra usually apply to persons. **Kata** means *side*, tomo means *and others like me*, so that as Samson says (HGJ, p. 87), "The Japanese noun denotes a true universal like 'man' in 'man is mortal' which includes both 'a man' and 'men.' The suffix domo expresses the idea of a group or class rather than of number . . . "Tomodachi friend, although composed of tomo plus dachi, i. e., the sonant form of tachi, has no plural significance." (HGJ, p. 86).

Botsu-botsu (XIV, 26) means *drop by drop.* **Botsu** means *a point, a dot, a spot.* Duplication sometimes indicates plurality or one thing after the other, e. g., **nichi-nichi** *day after day, days;* **tokidoki** *from time to time, times;* **kuniguni** *country after country, various provinces;* **yamayama** *mountain after mountain, mountains.*

ga

5. In affirmative sentences **ga** is used in place of **wa** (see section 3), in order to emphasize the subject, e. g., **Kore ga hon desu ka?** (I, 26) *Is this a book?* and *this* is emphasized in English. It means *is this one* in contradistinction to *that one a book?* However, **Kore wa hon desu ka?** (I, 20) means *Is this a book?* and *book* is emphasized. It means *is this a book?*

in contradistinction to any other object. It may be said that **wa** emphasizes the predicate and **ga** the subject (see sections 20 and 85).

At the end of a clause or sentence **ga** means *but, and,* or *so.* It is also employed without much meaning, much as is English *so* . . . Compare the similar use of **kara** (section 29).

Oishiku arimasen ga dōzo o-agari kudasai (VI, 54)	*They are not very good, but please have some.*
Shitsurei desu ga . . . (X, 57)	*pardon me, but . . .*
Iku tsumori desu ga anata mo issho ni ikimasen ka? (IX, 1)	*I intend to go, so won't you go also?*
Taku wa Kanda no itchōme desu ga . . . (IX, 55)	*My home is on First Street in the Kanda district so . . .*

ja

6. Ja, a contraction of **de wa,** is generally used after a noun form or pronoun subject of the verb *to be* in the negative.

Iie, hon ja arimasen (I, 27)	*No, it is not a book.*
Sō ja arimasen (I, 29)	*It's not that.*
Takahashi Jirō ja arimasen (II, 6)	*I am not Jiro Takahashi.*
Sashimi ga o-suki ja gozaimasen ka? (VIII, 49)	*Don't you like sashimi?*

When the subject is not emphasized, **wa** is omitted.

O-konomi de nakereba (XII, 7)	*If you don't care for*

VERBS

7. Verbs are placed at the end of a sentence or phrase. They do not by their form indicate either person or number.

Mai asa hon wo yomimasu ka? (I, 38)	*Do you read books every morning?*
Mai asa shimbun wo yomimasu (I, 33)	*Every morning I read the newspaper.*
Ano otoko no hito wa dare desu ka? (II, 14)	*Who is he?*
Hon desu (I, 9)	*It is a book.*
Kami to fude desu (I, 17)	*They are paper and a brush.*

The polite present form of the verb is made by the addition of the suffix **masu** to the continuative stem (see section 27). This polite form is used to express an action which is habitually performed. However, there are certain exceptions to this rule (see section 31).

Mai asa nani wo shimasu ka? (I, 32)	*What do you do every morning?*
Mai ban Nippon go wo manabimasu (I, 37)	*I study Japanese every night.*

The compounded form of the verb in -**masu** is usually employed only in final verbs. In dependent clauses the simple form (see sections 18, 26, and 54), appears more often.

motte kite kureru yō ni itte kudasai (XII, 41)	*please tell her to kindly bring*
atsu-sugiru yō da kara (XII, 54)	*because it is too hot*
kaze wo hiite ita no ni (XIII, 59)	*although you caught cold*
okutte yarō to omotte iru tokoro desu (XIV, 31)	*I think that I shall send*

However, note **dekiagarimashita toki de** (X, 63) *when it is finished*

For the present tense used as future (see section 96).

NEGATIVE OF masu

8. The negative of the **masu** ending is **masen**. Thus **arimasen** is the negative of **arimasu**, the latter a more formal way of expressing the verb *to be* than **desu**. **Desu**, a contracted form of **de arimasu**, has no negative form, and thus **arimasen** must be used.

Hon ja arimasen; shimbun desu, (I, 27)	*It is not a book; it is a newspaper.*
kakimasu (I, 35)	*write, writes*
kakimasen (I, 45)	*do not write, does not write*
yomimasu (I, 33)	*read, reads*
yomimasen (I, 46)	*do not read, does not read*

NAMES

9. The family name is stated first and then the given name. However, western names are given according to western custom. Girls' given names of not more than two syllables end in **ko**, *child;* compare **Ano ko wa** (VII, 18) *That child* and **okosan** (*o-ko-san*) (VI, 42) *children.*

Anata wa Rōi Sumisu desu	*You are Roy Smith.*

It is not customary to use the title **San** or **Sama** *Mister, Miss, Mrs.* when speaking of one's self.

San may be used after a given name, e. g., **Hanako San** (VI, 49) *Hana-ko*

Takahashi Jirō San desu (II, 15)	*He is Mr. Jiro Takahashi.*
Watakushi wa Matsumoto desu (II, 9)	*I am (Mr.) Matsumoto.*
Anata wa Takahashi Jirō San desu ka? (II, 5)	*Are you Mr. Jiro Takahashi?*

DEMONSTRATIVE ADJECTIVES AND PRONOUNS

10. **Kono** means *this*, **sono** *that* (near the person spoken to or in reference to something which has been previously mentioned), and **ano** *that* (distant from both the speaker and the person addressed or referring to something not recently mentioned. These are adjectives. The corresponding demonstrative pronouns are **kore, sore,** and **are**.

kono onna no hito (II, 28)	*this woman*
sono otoko no hito (II, 26)	*that man*
sono o-tegami (XI, 33)	*that letter* (you just mentioned)
ano onna no hito (II, 12)	*that woman over there*
Kore wa dare no empitsu desu ka? (II, 23)	*Whose pencil is this (one)?*
Sore wa watakushi no empitsu desu (II, 24)	*That (near you) is my pencil.*
Are wa anata no shimbun desu ka? (II, 27)	*Is that (over there) your newspaper?*

The forms **kochira** *this place, here*, **sochira** *that place, there (near you)*, and **achira** *over there, that place (distant from you)* as well as **koko, soko,** and **asoko** (*with corresponding meanings*) are often used as demonstratives (see section 105).

Kochira wo moraimashō (VII, 57)	*I'll take these.*
Sochira wa hitotsu san sen desu (VII, 43)	*Those are three sen apiece.*
achira no ōkii no (VII, 44)	*those big ones*
koko no niku (XI, 56)	*this meat*

Compare **dochira** and **doko** *which* (section 73).

PERSONAL PRONOUNS

11. The personal pronouns are usually omitted both as subject and object when the context makes the reference clear. Honorific forms make it clear that the first person is not meant

and the second or third person is thereby implied. Similarly, humble expressions indicate that the action is performed by the first person (see section **38**).

Hiruhan ni nani wo tabemasu ka? (III, 5)	*What do you eat for lunch?*
Hiruhan ni wa sakana to gohan wo tabe-masu (III, 6)	*I eat fish and rice for lunch.*
Sono cha-iro no wo moraimashō (X, 13)	*I'll take those brown ones.*
Ryōhō tomo o-tori ni narimasu ka? (X, 37)	*Will you take both?*

Onna no hito or onna no kata *she* and otoko no hito or otoko no kata *he* are necessary only when one wishes to distinguish the sex of the third person (onna means *female* and otoko means *male*). Otherwise ano hito, sono hito, kono hito *that person, this person* will suffice. Ano ko, sono ko, kono ko *he or she* refer to children; otoko no ko *boy* and onna no ko *girl* may also be used in this way; e. g., ano otoko no ko *he*.

ano hito (III, 35)	*he*
ano kata (XI, 38)	*he*
ano otoko no hito (II, 14)	*he*
ano onna no hito (II, 12)	*she*
ano ko (VII, 18)	*she*

Kono hito or kono kata indicate that the person referred to is near the speaker, sono hito, sono kata that he or she is near the person addressed, and ano hito, ano kata that he or she is distant from the person addressed (see section **10**). In these phrases kata is some-what more polite than hito. The same distinctions exist in the plural with hitotachi people, e. g., ano hitotachi (II, 19) *they*, ano otoko no hitotachi (II, 20) *they (men)* and ano onna no hitotachi (II, 21) *they (women)*.

A contracted form watashi is also used by women for the first person singular. Its plural is watashidomo (VI, 45) *we*. Anata *you* has a plural anatagata which is used when speaking to more than one person, e. g., Anata wa Nippon-jin desu ka? (II, 10) *Are you Japanese?* Ana-tagata wa Amerika-jin desu ka? (II, 16) *Are you Americans?*

It as subject or object may be expressed by the demonstrative pronoun (see section **10**).

Sore wa ... *educational system* no imi desu (XVI, 42)	*It means educational system.*
Sore wo misete kudasai	*Please let me see it.*

See section **104**.

THE POSTPOSITION mo

12. Mo means *also, besides* when used with an affirmative verb. When used with a negative verb, it may mean *either*. When mo is used, neither wa nor wo is employed (see section **19**).

Anata mo Amerika-jin desu (II, 18)	*You also are an American.*
Anata mo issho ni ikimasen ka? (IX, 2)	*Aren't you going also?*
Budōshu mo ippon negaimasu (XI, 51)	*I'd like a bottle of wine also.*
O-nedan mo sahodo takaku arimasen (IX, 43)	*The price is not so high either.*
Anata no tomodachi mo yomimasen deshita ka? (III, 24)	*Didn't your friend read them either?*

POSSESSIVE CASE

13. Possessives are made by placing the postposition no after the possessor much as English places 's. Possessive adjectives and pronouns are made in this way from all the personal pronouns (see section **11**).

Sore wa Takahashi San no desu ka? (II, 37)   *Are those Mr. Takahashi's?*

Sore wa watakushi no empitsu desu (II, 24)   *That is my pencil.*

Watakushi no ja arimasen (II, 28)   *It is not mine.*

Kono onna no hito no shimbun desu (II, 28)   *It is her newspaper.*

The demonstrative sono may be used for the possessive *its*, e. g., sono menseki (XVI, 5) *its size*.

It is important to realize that no has other functions than that of indicating the possessive case and therefore Sansom's remarks will be found helpful: "no may be defined as a genitive particle, but its employment can be better understood if it is regarded as establishing an attributive rather than a possessive partitive relation between two words." (HGJ, p. 225.) See sections 43 and 55.

THE POSTPOSITION ni

14. Ni is used to indicate the locative and also the temporal relationships (with ji, gatsu, nen and the days of the week). These relationships are usually expressed in English with the prepositions *at* or *in*.

Nyū Yōku ni sunde imashita (V, 44)   *lived in New York*

Kono kinjo ni niku-ya ga arimasu ka? (VII, 27)   *Is there a butcher shop in this neighborhood?*

Burajiru ni imasu (XIV, 36)   *has been in Brazil*

Nan ji ni demasu ka? (XV, 5)   *What time does it leave?*

Nigatsu jū go nichi ni (VIII,31)   *on the fifteenth of February*

ni jikan-goto ni (XIII, 62)   *every two hours*

However, the postposition de (see section 22), expresses the locative when the verb is one of action rather than of a state of being.

Kono tsugi no heya de bōshi wo utte imasu ne (X, 18)   *In this next room they sell hats, don't they?*

Kono ginkō de torihiki shite imasu ka? (XIV, 7)   *Do you have an account with this bank?*

Kōbe de umarete (VIII, 26)   *being born in Kobe*

hichi fun kan gurai de (XII, 13)   *in about seven minutes*

The postposition ni or de is generally employed with locative adverbs except with the verb desu or any of its forms.

asoko ni (XII, 11)   *there*

shita ni (XII, 19)   *under*

soba ni (XIII, 3)   *beside*

doko ni (XIII, 2)   *where*

doko de (IX, 16)   *where*

naka ni (XIV, 58)   *inside*

If the verb on which the locative depends is one of motion, the postposition used is e, e. g., Kisha no naka e mochikonde kudasai (XV, 33) *Please carry it into the station* (see section 33).

Ni also expresses (*in order*) *to, into,* or *for;* e. g., kaimono ni iku tsumori desu (IX, 1) *intend to go shopping;* kore ni hakikaete . . . kudasai (XII, 25) *please change into these.* A verb, object of *in order to* may be translated by the continuative form of the verb (see section 27), followed by ni, e. g., Nagasaki e kinu wo kai ni ikimashita *He went to Nagasaki in order to buy silk.*

Ni indicates the indirect object of the verb. It may not be omitted as it is sometimes in English.

Dare ni ano tegami wo watashimashita ka? (III, 28)	*To whom did you hand that letter?*
Tomodachi ni ano tegami wo watashimashita (III, 30)	*I gave that letter to my friend.*
Shashō ni o-kiki nasai (IX, 21)	*Ask the conductor.*
Jochū ni . . . itte kudasai (XII, 41)	*Please tell (to) the maid.*

THE POSTPOSITION to

15. To is used to mean *and*, connecting nouns and pronouns. It is not used after the last noun or pronoun in a series, and is never used to express *and* connecting clauses (see section 83).

Hamu to tamago wo tabemasu (III, 3)	*I eat ham and eggs.*
Waishatsu to shima no shatsu wo misete kudasai (IX, 39)	*Please show me some white shirts and some striped shirts.*
Koko ni cha-iro to tobi-iro no ii no ga gozaimasu (X, 11)	*Here are some good tan and brown ones.*

After the present form of the verb at the end of a dependent clause to means *when, whenever,* or *if,* and it usually expresses a habitual occurrence. In this case, if the final verb is past, the dependent verb is construed as referring to past time also.

go-roku chō yuku to (IX, 32)	*when one goes* or *if one goes*
Kinu no ura wo tsukemasu to, mitsu-gumi ga roku jū yen de gozaimasu (X, 53)	*If we put in a silk lining, the suit will be sixty yen.*
daigaku wo deru to (XIV, 41)	*when he is graduated from the university*

To is also equivalent to the conjunction *that.*

Kagetsu e itte, tabete goran to kaite arimashita (XI, 35)	*It said (it was written) that I should go to the Kagetsu restaurant and try it.*
Muri wo shita to miete (XIII, 60)	*it appears that you abused yourself and*
Kane wo okutte yarō to omotte iru tokoro desu (XIV, 31)	*I think that I shall send money.*
Yukitai to itte imasu (XIV, 42)	*He says that he wants to go.*

To iimasu or to mōshimasu accordingly means *said that, said as, is called.*

Haru, natsu, aki, fuyu to iimasu (X, 30)	*They are said as Spring, Summer, Autumn, Winter,* i. e. *they are called Spring, Summer, etc.*
Amanoya to iu . . . yado-ya (XII, 8)	*an inn said as Amanoya,* i. e. *an inn called Amanoya.*
Anata no namae wa nan to iimasu ka?	*Your name, what is it said as?,* i. e. *What is your name?*
Buraun to mōshimasu (VI, 5)	*I am called Brown.*

To iu is often used simply to connect a subordinate clause with the noun it modifies.

Kyōiku-seido to iu kotoba (XVI, 40)	*the word which is called kyōiku-seido,* i. e. *the word kyōiku-seido*

TWO POSTPOSITIONS

16. Two postpositions often govern the same noun. Each postposition then has the same function that it has when used singly.

Watakushi ni wa kakimasen deshita (III, 37)	*As-for to me, he didn't write* i. e., *He didn't write to me.*
Ni shaku hassun no wo san mai morau koto ga dekimasu ka? (IX, 48)	*May I take three two shaku, eight sun ones?*

17. Gohan is cooked rice. Uncooked rice is **kome.**

18. The verb form ending in **masu** is made past by changing masu to mashi and adding **ta.** The past of desu is **deshita** and when the latter is added to the negative form of the verb in -masen (see section 8), the polite past tense in the negative is formed.

Nani wo tabemashita ka? (III, 11)	*What did you eat?*
Zasshi wo mimashita ka? (III, 19)	*Did you see the magazine?*
Hon wo yomimashita ka? (III, 21)	*Did you read the book?*
Nani mo tabemasen deshita (III, 15)	*I didn't eat anything.*
Kakimasen deshita (III, 37)	*He didn't write.*

The past ending is **ta** and this is added to the continuative stem of verbs (see section **27**). When verbs of the second class add **ta** to the continuative stem, the verb undergoes the same phonetic changes which take place when **te,** the gerundial ending (see section **30**), is added. Thus the simple past tense may be formed by changing the **te** of the gerund to **ta,** e. g., **tabeta** (XI, 56), **ita** (XI, 14), **okutta** (XI, 4), **hanashita** (XI, 32) are past forms of **taberu, iru, okuru,** and **hanasu** respectively.

Attributively or in dependent clauses, the simple past is used more often than the form in -mashita.

The past form is often used attributively to modify a noun, e. g., **ikita sakana** (VIII, 52) *live fish* (ikiru is the verb *live, be alive*), **dekiagarimashita toki de** (X, 63) *the completed time,* i. e. *when it is finished.*

The past form sometimes corresponds to a present in English, e. g., **yoku irasshaimashita** (XI, 41) *you are welcome,* **arigatō gozaimashita** (VIII, 18) *it was kind,* i. e. *you are very kind,* and **o-naka ga sukimashita** (XI, 19) *stomach became empty,* i. e., *I am hungry.* These forms would seem to correspond to a perfect.

> The colloquial suffix **ta** comes from **tari** which was originally **te** plus **ari,** and tari does not of itself constitute a past tense, but it does to some extent correspond with a perfect tense and did not function as a preterit; vid. HGJ, pp. 178, 179.

19. The postposition **mo** is used after interrogative pronouns (see section **73**), to form the negative of indefinite pronouns. The verb with which they are used must be negative for these pronouns to have a negative sense. e. g., **Nani mo shitaku arimasen** (IV, 13) *I don't want to do anything,* **Dare mo imasen** *Nobody is in.* See the formation of indefinite pronouns (section **23**).

20. With a negative verb the use of **wa** instead of **wo** emphasizes the object (see sections **3** and **5**).

Anata no zasshi wa mimasen deshita (III, 20)	*I didn't see your magazine.*
Ano otoko no hitotachi ni wa okurimasen deshita (III, 46)	*I didn't send them to them.*

DESIRE

21. The desiderative form of the verb may be made by removing the ending **masu** and adding **tai** to the continuative stem of the verb (see section **27**). The suffix **tai** is an adjective (see section **43**) and therefore has a negative form **taku** which is used to form the negative desiderative. Both positive and negative desideratives may be followed by the verb **to be**. In such a case, the positive may be followed or not by **'n**, a contracted form of **mono** *thing.*

hanashitai (IV, 3)	*want to speak*
hanashitaku (IV, 5)	*don't want to speak*
okuritai (XIV, 56)	*want to send*
kaitai desu (XIV, 47)	*want to buy*
kaitaku arimasen (IV, 26)	*don't want to buy*
toritai (XV, 2)	*want to take*

Hoshii or **nozomi** *want, desire* followed or not by the verb *to be* expresses wish for a *thing.* The thing desired is followed by **ga** in the affirmative and **wa** in the negative (see section **20**). Hoshii is an adjective and therefore its negative is **hoshiku**.

Shizuka na heya ga hoshii desu (XII, 20)	*I want a quiet room.*
Bōshi ga o-nozomi de gozaimasu ka? (X, 22)	*Do you wish a hat?*

THE POSTPOSITION de

22. The postposition **de** expresses the instrumental case, i. e. the means by which something is accomplished, and may be translated **by** or **with**.

hikōki de (IV, 27)	*by means of an airplane*
kore de (XI, 64)	*by means of this*, i. e. *with this*
Basu de ikimashō ka? (IX, 8)	*Shall we go by bus?*
densha de (VIII, 60)	*by street car*
sokutatsu de (XIV, 52)	*by special delivery*

De often corresponds to English **in**, e. g., **Nihon go de hanashitai desu ka?** (IV, 3) *Do you want to speak in Japanese?* **tegami de hanashita ryōriya** (XI, 31) *the restaurant spoken about in the letter.* With **naru** *become* it has the meaning *for* in expressions like **Mina de ni jū go sen ni narimasu** (XIV, 61) *It comes to twenty-five sen for all* and **Ryōhō de san jū hachi yen ni narimasu** (XV, 31) *It's thirty-eight yen for both.*

INDEFINITE PRONOUNS AND ADVERBS

23. The postposition **ka** placed after an interrogative pronoun forms an indefinite pronoun; e. g., **nani ka** (IV, 14) *anything, something,* **nani ka yōji** (XIII, 34) *some business or other,* **doko ka** (XI, 34) *somewhere, anywhere,* **dare ka** *somebody.* (See sections **1, 19, 73,** and **106**.)

CORRELATIVES

24. *Either . . . or* correlating nouns, pronouns, or adjectives is expressed by the postpositions **de mo** placed after each noun, pronoun, or adjective. *Neither . . . nor* is expressed in like fashion by **mo . . . mo** with the verb in the negative. *Either* alone is **de mo** with a negative verb.

kōhī de mo, o-cha de mo (IV, 18)	*either coffee or tea*
Amari ōkiku mo chiisaku mo gozaimasen (VI, 41)	*It's neither too big nor too small.*
hambun de mo, sambun no ichi de mo (VII, 61)	*either a half or a third*

Sō de mo gozaimasen (VI, 35)   *It isn't that either*, i. e. *Not at all.*

Alternative questions are made by the juxtaposition of two independent questions with or without a conjunction.

Densha de ikimashō ka? Basu de ikimashō   *Shall we go by trolley or by bus?*
ka? (IX, 8)

Sangai ga yoroshiū gozaimasu ka? Shi kai   *Do you prefer the third floor or the fourth*
ga yoroshiū gozaimasu ka? (XII, 17)   *floor.*

Anata no uchi e todokemashō ka matawa   *Shall we deliver it to your home or do you*
motte o-kaeri ni narimasu ka? (IX, 51)   *want to take it with you?*

CAPABILITY

25. The attributive form of the verb (see section 26) modifying **koto** *thing* used as subject of the verb **dekiru** *is possible* expresses capability. In the affirmative the postposition **ga** is always employed after **koto**. The negatives and the past tense of this expression are formed in the usual manner (see section 8 and 18). Compare the potential, section 90.

tobu koto ga dekimasu (IV, 28)   *flying thing is possible*, i. e. *can fly*

Yomu koto ga dekimasen (IV, 41)   *the reading thing is not possible; Reading*
                                                 is not possible, i. e., *(I) can't read.*

Taberu koto ga dekimashita ka? (IV, 34)   *was eating possible?*, i. e., *Could you eat?*

tsukau koto ga deki-nai kara (XI, 46)   *because he can't use*

CONCLUSIVE FORM OF THE VERB

26. In the present-day colloquial, the attributive and the predicative or conclusive form of the verb are the same (see HGJ, p. 92 for development).

Most Japanese dictionaries and grammars in Roman letters give verbs in the conclusive form, and for this reason this form is sometimes referred to as an infinitive. Its functions, however, do not correspond to our infinitive, for it is used as a present tense. In contradistinction to the polite present (see section 7) it may be called the simple present.

There are two classes of verbs in Japanese. To class I belong those verbs whose conclusive form ends in **ru** preceded by a syllable ending in **e** or **i**, e. g., **taberu** (IV, 34) *eat*, **kazoeru** (VII, 1) *count*, **miru** *see*, **dekiru** (XI, 13) *be possible, be ready*, **iru** (XI, 7) *be*. There are very few verbs of the first class ending in **iru**, so that most verbs ending in **ru** preceded by any vowel other than **e** belong to the second class.

To class II belong verbs whose conclusive form has the last syllable ending in **bu, gu, ku, mu, nu, ru, su, tsu,** or a vowel plus **u**. If a verb ends in **ru** preceded by **a, o,** or **u,** or sometimes when preceded by two vowels, it belongs in class II. The following are verbs of class II: **tobu** (IV, 28) *fly;* **isogu** (IV, 45) *hurry;* **kaku** *write,* **yomu** (IV, 41) *read,* **shinu** *die,* **suwaru** (IV, 47) *sit;* **mawasu** (IV, 31) *drive;* **tatsu** (IV, 44) *stand,* **kau** (IV, 29) *buy,* **iu** (XVI, 41) *say.*

An exception to the latter rule may be noted in **kaeru** *change* which belongs to class I, while **kaeru** *return, come back* belongs to class II. Thus the gerundial form of **kaeru** *change* is **kaete** with one *t* and its continuative stem is **kae** (see **hakikaete** (XII, 25) and **kikae** (XII, 51), while the gerundial form of **kaeru** (VII, 15) *return* is **kaette** with two *t's* and **kaeri** (IX, 52) is its continuative stem. (See sections 27, 30, 116, and 117.)

There are two irregular verbs in Japanese, **suru** (IV, 43) *do* and **kuru** *come.*

The simple present form is more often used than the polite form as an attributive or in dependent clauses. The verb **desu** has the simple present form **da** or **de aru.** The simple negative present is made by adding **nai** to the negative form (see sections 56 and 57).

sukoshi hiro-sugiru kara (X, 7)	*because it's a little too wide*
Itsu dekiru ka kiite kudasai (XI, 13)	*please ask when it will be ready*
tsukau koto ga deki-nai kara (XI, 46)	*because he can't use*
jū yen satsu da kara (XI, 64)	*since it's a ten yen bill*
atsu-sugiru yō da kara (XII, 54)	*as it seems too hot*
yogorete iru sentaku mono (XI, 7)	*the soiled laundry*

CONTINUATIVE FORM OF THE VERB

27. By removing the ending **ru** of the conclusive form (see section **26**) of verbs of class I, we obtain the continuative stem of those verbs. Verbs of the second class change the final u of the conclusive form to i to form their continuative stem. Two phonetic changes take place when i is added to verbs of class II: verbs ending in tsu drop the su and the t is palatalized, giving the continuative ending **chi** while verbs ending in su have their continuative ending **si** palatalized to **shi**. The continuative stem of the irregular verbs **kuru** and **suru** are **ki** and **shi** respectively.

The continuative form of **desu** is **de**, and the r of gozaru, nasaru, kudasaru, and irassharu usually disappears in the colloquial giving a continuative stem **gozai-**, **nasai-**, **kudasai-**, and **irasshai-** respectively.

The continuative stem is so called because it is the form to which suffixes or other verbs are added, e. g., **hakikaete** (XII, 25) *change (shoes, socks, etc.)* is composed of **haku** *put on* (*shoes, socks, etc.*) and **kaeru** *change*, **norikaetara** *if transfer* is made up of **noru** *ride* and **kaeru** *change* while **uriko** (X, 27) *salesgirl, salesman* is composed of **uru** *sell* and **ko** *child* (see section **9**). When the suffix **masu** is added to the continuative stem, we obtain the polite present form of the verb. When we add **tai**, we obtain the desiderative form.

Another continuative use of this form may be seen in section **44**. The continuative stem and the noun form are identical (see section **40**).

Compound verbs sometimes have a different meaning than would be derived from the two parts. The verb **dasu** (XIII, 54) *put out* is sometimes used with the continuative stem of verbs to mean *begin to;* however in **okuri-dashi** (XIV, 45) *to send off* and **haki-dashite** (XIII, 58) *throw out, expel* **dasu** adds little to the meaning of the verb.

ADVERBS

28. Adverbs generally precede the verbs or adjectives they modify.

sugu motte mairimasu (XI, 63)	*I'll bring immediately*
yoku yuku (XI, 27)	*often go*
kanari yawarakai (XI, 57)	*quite tender*

However an adverb often precedes a noun subject or object.

Fukaku iki wo sutte kudasai (XIII, 57)	*Please breathe deep.*
Hayaku yao-ya e yukimashō (VII, 48)	*Let's go quickly to the grocery store.*
taihen kiji ga yō gozaimashite (IX, 42)	*the material seems very good and*

An adjective modifying a verb is used in the adverbial form (see section **43**).

| Mijikaku kara-nai de kudasai (XV, 3) | *Please don't cut it short.* |

Adverbs of place usually take the locative particle ni (see section **14**), but adverbs of time or quantity take no postposition except for emphasis.

Ima tegami wo kakitai desu ka? (IV, 20)	*Do you want to write a letter now?*
Ima wa nani mo suru koto ga dekimasen (IV, 43)	*I can't do anything now.*
Sukoshi o-machi kudasai (XIII, 19)	*Please wait a little.*

Sukoshi wa dekimasu (IV, 38)	*I can a little.*
Kesa ichi man no ebi ga tsukimashita (VIII, 40)	*This morning ten thousand shrimp arrived.*
Kesa wa nedoko kara okiraremasen (XIII, 45)	*I can't get out of bed this morning.*

The adverbs of place koko (VIII, 66) *here,* soko (VIII, 36), *there* (near the person addressed), and asoko (VIII, 62) *over there* (distant from the person addressed) and the forms kochira, sochira, and achira correspond to the related demonstratives (see section 10).

Konna ni *in this manner,* sonna ni *in that manner,* anna ni *in that manner* all correspond to *such, in such a way,* and they differ from each other as do the corresponding demonstratives.

Most adverbs as Sansom says "are either adverbial phrases or other parts of speech functioning as adverbs. Such a word as ima *now* is a noun by origin (ma--space) . . ." (HGJ, p. 290) Nouns are sometimes made to function as adverbs by the addition of the postpositions ni or to; e. g., hajime ni (XI, 44) *first of all;* verbs in the gerundial form may function as adverbs; e. g., hajimete (VI, 12) *for the first time,* isoide (XV, 2) *quickly,* adverbial forms of hajimeru *begin* and isogu *hurry* respectively. Adjectives by the addition of ku to the stem may become adverbs; e. g., hayai *fast, quick* forms hayaku (VII, 48) *quickly.*

BECAUSE

29. Kara *because* always *follows* the explanation. Note that kara after the gerundial form of the verb does not mean *because* (see section 80).

tatsu koto ga dekimasen kara (IV, 44)	*because I can't stand*
isogimasu kara (IV, 21)	*because I'm in a hurry*
Nippon-go wo yomu koto ga dekimasen kara (IV, 41)	*because I can't read Japanese.*

Kara is often used as is English *so* at the end of a thought. Many times kara has no meaning whatever and is used simply to wind up a sentence; compare the same function of ga, section 5.

kusuri wo agemasu kara (XIII, 61)	*I'll give you some medicine and . . .*

No de is used to mean *because.*

neraremasen deshita no de (XIII, 44)	*because I couldn't sleep*
ichiban ue no kampan ni arimashita no de (XV, 59)	*because it was on the top deck*
keshiki no yoi tokoro ga takusan aru no de (XVI, 53)	*because it has many fine scenic places*

Because of, on account of, for the sake of is expressed by *no tame ni;* e. g., jishin no tame ni (XVI, 27) *on account of earthquakes.*

GERUNDIAL FORM OF THE VERB

30. The gerundial form of the verb is formed by the addition of the suffix **te** (for development see HGJ, p. 175 et seq.) to the continuative stem of the verb (see section 27), e. g., tabete (V, 1) *eating,* mite (V, 3) *seeing,* irete (XIII, 20) *inserting.* These are all verbs of class I, as may be seen by their conclusive forms which are taberu, miru, and ireru respectively.

When te is added to verbs of class II, certain sound changes take place; viz. the final i of the continuative stem is dropped and a resulting final k vocalizes to i, e. g., the verb

kaku *write* (conclusive form) is **kaki** in its continuative form and dropping the **i**, we have the base, and to the base **te** is added. Thus the hypothetical form **kakte** gives us, by the vocalization of the **k**, the gerundial form **kaite** (V, 13) *writing*. If the final consonant of the base is **g** (the voiced form of **k**) it also vocalizes, but after having voiced the **t** of the gerundial ending **te** to **de**; e. g., **isogu** (IV, 45) is **isogi** in its continuative form, and dropping the **i** and obtaining the base, we have **isog-**. When we add **te**, however, we get the gerundial form **isoide** (V, 47) *hurrying*.

Verbs whose bases end in **n**, **m**, or **b** likewise voice the **t** of **te** to **d**, e. g., **shinu** *die*, **shini** (continuative form), **shin-** (base), **shinde** (gerundial form) *dying;* **yomu** (IV, 41) *read;* **yom** plus **te** gives **yonde** (V, 22) *reading;* **tobu** (IV, 28) *fly:* **tob** plus **te** gives **tonde** (VII, 9) *flying, skipping.* In the case of **bt** becoming **nd** and **mt** becoming **nd**, note that besides voicing the **t**, both the **b** and the **m** have become accommodated (i. e. partially assimilated) to the following dental. That is, they have become the *dental* nasal **n**.

If the base of the verb ends in **ch** or **r**, these sounds are assimilated to the following **t** of **te**, e. g., **tatsu** (IV, 44) *stand:* **tach-** plus **te** gives **tatte** (V, 5) *standing;* **suwaru** (IV, 47) *squat:* **suwar-** plus **te** gives **suwatte** (V, 30) *squatting.*

Verbs whose base ends in a vowel simply double the **t** of the **te** ending, e. g., **arau** *wash:* **ara-** plus **te** gives **aratte** (V, 34) *washing;* **suu** *suck:* **su-** plus **te** gives **sutte** (XIII, 57) *sucking.*

It should be noted that the gerundial form of **iku** *go* is spelled irregularly **itte** *going*, and it should not be confused with **itte** *saying* which is from **iu.**

The honorific form of **iku** *go*, **kuru** *come*, and **iru** *be* is **ide** and it is preceded by the honorific prefix **o.**

Kochira e o-ide kudasai (IX, 41)	*Please come this way.*
Nagasaki e o-ide ni narimasu ka? (XV, 39)	*Are you going to Nagasaki?*
O-isha San wa o-ide de gozaimasu ka? (XIII, 28)	*Is the doctor at home?*

The -**te** form is often employed as a noun, and thus the name gerundial although not completely accurate, seems adequate.

Tsukue no hashi ni oite wa abunai desu (XIII, 4)	*Putting it on the edge of the table is dangerous.*

The uses of the -**te** form as Sansom says (HGJ, p. 175) "can all be explained as conjunctive uses" (see sections **37** and **44**).

See sections **116** and **117.**

PROGRESSIVE FORM OF THE VERB

31. The progressive tenses are made by the gerundial form of the verb (see section **30**) plus the verb **iru** (its honorific form, **irassharu**) or **oru** meaning *be* (see section **71**). When **iru** and **oru** are in the present tense, the verb is in the present progressive; when **iru** or **oru** are past, the verb is past progressive.

The progressive tenses only partially correspond to those in English. The simple present or polite present (see section **7**) is used for customary action, but the progressive must be used in Japanese when the action of the verb is continuing.

Nani wo shite imasu ka? (V, 8)	*What are you doing?*
Nani mo shite imasen (V, 9)	*I am not doing anything.*
Nani wo shite irasshaimasu ka? (XIV, 34)	*What is he doing?*
Nani wo motte imasu ka? (V, 10)	*What do you have?*
Empitsu wo motte imasu (V, 11)	*I have a pencil.*
Nani go wo yonde imashita ka? (V, 19)	*What language were you reading?*

Ryoken wa motte ita (XV, 49)	*I had a passport*
kirashite orimasu (X, 10)	*out of stock*
Yottsu no shima de naritatte imasu (XVI, 16)	*It consists of four islands.*
Nani ga haitte imasu ka? (XIV, 58)	*What is inside?*

The progressive is often used to express a resultant state or condition and corresponds to a perfect tense in English. This is generally true with the verb **iku** *go* so that **itte imasu** (VI, 27) means *have gone, went.*

yogorete iru sentaku mono (XI, 7)	*the laundry which has been soiled*
yukitai to itte imasu (XIV, 42)	*he has said that he wants to go*
Nodo ga kawaite imasu (XI, 50)	*throat has become dry,* i. e. *I am thirsty.*
shimpo shite imasu (XVI, 39)	*has progressed*
kambi shite imasu (XVI, 47)	*has been perfected*

The negative progressive is formed by the gerund followed by the negative of **iru, oru,** etc. Iru is a verb of the first class so that its continuative stem is **i.**

| Nani mo kaite imasen deshita (V, 14) | *I wasn't writing anything.* |
| michi ni mukatte i-nai heya (XII, 20) | *a room not facing the street* |

The verb **shiru** *know* is used in the progressive in the affirmative, e. g., **shitte imasu ka?** *do you know* but not in the progressive when negative, e. g., **shirimasen** (XII, 3) *don't know.*

The word **tokoro** *place* by extension has come to mean *situation* or *time* and therefore also *when* or *while.* Sometimes it means *the thing that* or *that which.* The attributive form of the progressive often modifies **tokoro desu** which seems simply to give expression to the certainty of the statement. Compare **no desu** (section **55**).

| okutte yarō to omotte iru tokoro desu (XIV, 31) | *I am at the intending-to-send point, i. e., I intend to send* |

See section **117.**

PLEASE

32. A polite request is made by the addition of **kudasai** *condescend* to the gerundial form of the verb (see section **30**). Kudasai is an imperative form of **kudasaru.** Dōzo *please* may also be used.

Hanashite kudasai (V, 6)	*Please speak.*
Yonde kudasai (V, 17)	*Please read.*
Jissen ni makete kudasai (VIII, 55)	*Please reduce it to ten sen.*
Dōzo tatte kudasai (V, 5)	*Please stand up.*

The gerundial form may be used with **nasai,** but as **nasai** is the imperative of **nasaru** *do,* such an expression corresponds more to a command than to a polite request. However, if either **nasai** or **kudasai** is used with the noun form of the verb (see section **40**), the latter preceded by the honorific prefix **o,** a very polite request is made.

O-kiki nasai (IX, 21)	*Please ask.*
O-nori nasai (IX, 19)	*Please get on.*
Erebētā wo o-tori kudasai (IX, 36)	*Please take the elevator.*
Dōzo o-hairi kudasai (X, 21)	*Please enter.*

The verb **kureru** *give, let have* (see section **86**) is used for *please* also, but it is not so polite as **kudasaru.** It is often used to avoid repetition of the latter verb, e. g., **motte kite kureru yō ni itte kudasai** (XII, 41) *please tell (her) to please bring.*

A polite request not to do something is formed by the negative stem of the verb (see section **56**) plus **nai de kudasai.**

Chūmon shi-nai de kudasai (XI, 24)	*Please do not order.*
Sawara-nai de kudasai (XIII, 52)	*Please don't touch.*
Wasure-nai de kudasai (XI, 47)	*Please don't forget.*

The gerund and **kudasaimasen ka?** express *won't you please*, e. g., **chiisai ginka ni kaete kudasaimasen ka?** (XIV, 16) *won't you please change?*

THE POSTPOSITION e

33. The postposition **e** indicates motion toward, and may be translated by *to*. The postposition **ni** (see section **14**) indicates a more stationary relationship and corresponds more frequently to *at* or *in*. However, with verbs of motion **e** sometimes corresponds to *at* or *in*.

minami e magatte (IX, 18)	*turning to the south*
Koko e niku to yasai wo motte mairima-shita (XI, 53)	*I brought here meat and vegetables.*
O-isha San e denwa wo kakesasete kudasai (XIII, 10)	*Please have her phone to the doctor.*
Nan ji ni Nagasaki e tsukimasu ka? (XV, 11)	*What time does it arrive at Nagasaki?*
hongoku e hairimasu (XVI, 10)	*one enters (in) the mainland*

wakaru

34. **Wakaru** is the intransitive form of **wakeru** *divide, distinguish, classify* (see section **91**) and does not take an object. **Wakaru** means *to be clear* and therefore **Watakushi ni wa wakarimasen deshita** (V, 18) means *It was not clear to me.*

PERMISSION

35. To ask permission the gerundial form of the verb (see section **30**) is followed by **mo** *even, if* and the phrase **ii desu ka?** or **ii n' desu ka?** *is it good? is it all right?* In this expression **n'** is a contracted form of **mono** thing. Naturally in granting permission **ka** is omitted.

Aratte mo ii n' desu ka? (V, 33)	*Is it all right if I wash;* i. e., *May I wash?*
Haitte mo ii n' desu ka? (V, 40)	*May I enter?*
Akete mo ii n' desu (V, 28)	*You may open it.*

PROHIBITION

36. Prohibition is expressed by the gerundial form of the verb (see section **30**) followed by **wa ikemasen** (see section **20**). **Ikemasen,** a potential form of **iku** (see section **90**) means *cannot go*, so that **haitte wa ikemasen** (V, 41) means *as for entering, it doesn't go*, i. e. *you must not enter*. **Narimasen** may replace **ikemasen** in these expressions.

USE OF COME AND GO WITH THE GERUNDIAL FORM OF THE VERB

37. **Motte kuru** *come having* means *bring*. The conclusive form of **motte** is **motsu** *have, possess*. The expression **motte kite kudasai** (V, 12) is literally *condescend to come having*. **Motte iku** *go having* means *take* and the phrase **motte itte kudasai** (V, 15) literally means *condescend to go having*.

Bringing or taking a person is expressed in a like manner with **tsurete,** the gerundial form of **tsureru** *accompany*. **Tomodachi wo tsurete kite kudasai** (V, 37) means *Please come accompanying your friend*, i. e. *please bring your friend* and **Watakushi wo benjo e tsurete itte kudasai** (V, 35) means *Please go accompanying me to the lavatory*, i. e. *Please take me to the lavatory* (W.C.).

The conclusive form of tsuite is **tsuku** *follow.* **Tsuite itte** (V, 38) means *go following* while **tsuite kite** (V, 39) means *come following.* Therefore, *Please follow me* is **Tsuite kite kudasai** (V, 39) and *Please follow him* is **Tsuite itte kudasai.**

The verbs **kuru** and **iku** may be replaced by humble or honorific forms with the same meanings (see section 38), e. g., **motte kimashita** (XI, 4) *he brought* and **motte mairimashita** (XI, 54) *I brought.*

The verb **agaru** *go up* replaces **kuru** and **iku** to mean *bring up* or *take up,* e. g., **jochū ga motte agarimasu** (XII, 50) *the maid will bring up* while **kaeru** replaces **kuru** and **iku** to mean *bring home* or *take home,* e. g., **motte o-kaeri ni narimasu ka?** (IX, 52) *Will you return having it?* i. e., *Will you take it with you?* and **motte kaerimasu kara** (X, 15) *because I am taking it home.*

In speaking of an errand, one does not say go and do something, but do something and come back, e. g., **toranku wo azukete kimasu.** (XV, 37) *I'll check the trunk and come,* i. e., *I'll go and check the trunk.*

Japanese is more explicit than English in the expression **okutte yarō** (XIV, 31) *I shall send and give* which expresses the fact that the money is not only sent, but also given.

HONORIFICS

38. The prefixes **go** or **o** are used with nouns or adjectives to indicate respect. Thus a personal or possessive pronoun is often unnecessary. **Go-shujin** means *honorable master,* thus, *your master,* and **o-taku** means *honorable house,* thus, *your house.* The honorific prefixes are used with the things of the third person, but they are not employed to indicate the things of the first person. In fact, certain humble words or expressions are sometimes employed to indicate one's own things or one's own actions. Thus **kanai** (VI, 10) means *my wife,* but **okusama** (VI, 20) means *your wife* or *his wife;* **musuko** (VI, 44) means *my son,* but **musuko San** means *your son;* **ototo** (XIV, 35) *my younger brother* but **otōto San** (XIV, 33) *your younger brother.** The prefix **go** is usually used with words of Chinese origin and **o** with native words, but this is not always the case.

o-kazoku (VIII, 44)	*your family*
o-namae (IX, 59)	*your name*
o-tegami (XI, 33)	*your letter*
o-furo (XII, 51)	*your bath*
o-shigoto (XIV, 39)	*his work*
go issho ni (IX, 4)	*with you*
kazoku (VIII, 46)	*my family*
namae (IX, 61)	*my name*
tegami (XI, 31)	*my letter*
furo (XII, 47)	*my bath*

The honorific prefix is used (especially by women) with nouns or adjectives having no relation to the person addressed simply to show respect, e. g., **o-nedan** (IX, 43) *the price;* **o-isha** (XIII, 10) *the doctor;* **go-shinsatsu** (XIII, 37) *medical examination;* **o-yasui** (VII, 54) *cheap;* **o-kagen** (XII, 52) *temperature.*

* The following list of nouns denoting family relationships will be found useful: *aunt* **oba**; *elder brother* **ani**; *brother-in-law* (elder sister's husband) **ane-muko**; (younger sister's husband) **imōto-muko**; (one's wife's brother) **sai no ani** or **sai no otōto**; *daughter* **musume**; **ojōsan**; *daughter-in-law* **yome**; *father:* (my) **chichi**; (your or my) **otōsan**; *father-in-law* **yōfu**; *grandfather* **sofu**; *grandmother* **obāsan**; *grandson* **mago**; *granddaughter* **mago-musume**; *mother* (my) **haha**; (your or my) **okāsan**; *mother-in-law* **yōbo**; *nephew* **oi**; *niece* **mei**; *sister-in-law* (elder) **giri no ane**; (younger) **giri no imōto**; (wife of one's elder brother) **ani-yome**; *son* **musuko**; *son-in-law* **muko**; *uncle* **oji.**

It is the custom to speak derogatorily concerning one's own things and therefore in offering something to eat, the lady says **Amari oishiku arimasen** (VI, 41) *It's not very good.* The prefix **o** is generally used and without honorific significance with certain nouns, viz., **o-cha** (III, 9) *tea*, **o-yu** (XII, 52) *hot water*, **o-naka** (XI, 58) *stomach.*

Sansom (HGJ, p. 118) explains the origin of the prefix **o** as a combination of **mi** *august* and **ō** *great* with sound changes.

Both the verb **gozaru** and the verb **irassharu** are more polite forms of *be* than **desu** or **arimasu**, and refer to the being of the second or third person. **Gozaru**, however, is used also by the first person in speaking to women or superiors in order to indicate respect. Women usually use the verb **gozaru** and it may be said that their language is generally more polite than that of men, e. g., **Sō de gozaimasu ka?** (VI, 20) *Is that so?* and **Ima dochira ni irasshaimasu ka?** (VI, 21) *Where is she now?* **Irassharu** is also an honorific form for **iku** and **kuru.**

Even certain pronouns and adverbs are considered more polite than others. For instance, **donata** (VI, 3) is more polite than **dare** (II, 8) for *who* and **dochira** (VI, 21) more polite than **doko** (IV, 9) for *where.*

Verbs are usually made honorific by prefixing **o** to their noun form (see section **40**), but there are also special honorific and humble verbs and expressions, e. g., **o-tomari no tsumori desu** (XII, 38) *you intend to stay* and **o-jama ni narimashō** (XII, 40) *I shall be a disturbance;* i. e., *I shall stay.* The honorific form **goran** is used for *see* instead of **miru,** e. g., **Nani wo goran ni kakemashō ka?** (IX, 38) *What do you wish to see?*

For some common verbs there are humble, plain, and honorific forms, e. g., for *go* or *come* these are **mairu, iku, o-ide ni naru** respectively, for *do* **itasu, suru,** and **nasaru** respectively. (see section **109**).

Because of the existence of these distinct forms a pronoun subject is not usually expressed.

Sansom says (HGJ, p. 80): "It is important to remember that, in Japanese, sentences can easily be constructed where, owing to the existence of special honorific locutions, the personal pronoun can be omitted without ambiguity. It may indeed be stated that a typical Japanese sentence does not include a personal pronoun, and where one is used it generally has an emphatic value. Thus:

irasshaimasu ka	*are you going.*
mairimasu	*I am going*

The use of honorific or humble verbs dispenses with the need for a pronoun, and if pronouns are used, . . . the sentence is better translated in an emphatic way . . ."

THE POSTPOSITION **de**

39. The postposition **de** is used after a noun or pronoun predicate of the verbs **aru** or **gozaru** *be.* It is the first syllable of the copula **desu** (a contraction of **de arimasu**). When **gozaru** or **aru** in the negative are preceded by nouns or by predicate adjectives which are not true, the **de wa** or **ja** (a contracted form of **de wa**) is used.

Donata de gozaimasu ka? (VI, 3)	*Who are you?*
Hachi jū go sen de gozaimasu (VIII, 43)	*It is eighty-five sen.*
Shikaku ja arimasen (VI, 51)	*It is not square.*

THE NOUN FORM OF THE VERB

40. The continuative stem is used as a noun, e. g., **Kaeri wa densha de nakute mo, ii deshō ne.** (VIII, 60) *The-return if not by trolley, it's all right, isn't it?*, i. e., *We don't have to go back by trolley, do we?*

A polite form of the verb is made by prefixing **o** to the noun form of the verb and adding the verb *do, be* or *become* (**ni naru**) to the latter. **Iku** *go,* **kuru** *come* and **iru** *be* have the irregular polite form **o-ide** (see section **32**).

O-yobi itashimasu (VI, 6)	*honorable-calling I do*, i. e., *I'll call*
O-matase itashimashita (VI, 8)	*honorable-causing to wait I did. I made you wait*, i. e., *I'm sorry I made you wait.*
Bōshi ga o-nozomi de gozaimasu ka? (X, 22)	*Is wishing a hat?*, i. e., *Do you wish a hat?*
Sashimi ga o-suki ja gozaimasen ka? (VIII, 49)	*Don't you like sashimi?*
O-isha San wa o-ide de gozaimasu ka? (XIII, 28)	*Is the doctor in?*
O-hanashi shite kudasaimasen ka? (XVI, 3)	*won't you please do speaking?*, i. e., *Won't you please talk?*
Ryōhō tomo o-tori ni narimasu ka? (X, 37)	*Will you take both?*
Nagasaki e o-ide ni narimasu ka? (XV, 39)	*Are you going to Nagasaki?*
Itsu o-koshi ni narimashita ka? (XV, 43)	*When did you cross over?*
O-de ni narimashita (XIII, 19)	*It went out; It went through*, i. e., *The connection is made.*

The verb **negau** means *request* and the expression **o-negai itashimasu** *honorable-request I do;* i. e., *I beg you* is variously used, e. g., **Dōzo yoroshiku o-negai itashimasu** (VI, 13) means *Please (think) well (of me) I do beg; I beg you think well of me,* i. e., *I am pleased to meet you.*

agaru

41. Agaru means *to rise, come up, go up* and by extension *be offered.* The first occurrence of Dōzo o-agari kudasai (VI, 9) means *Please come up,* i. e., *Please come in;* the second (VI, 54) means *Please (accept) the going up (to offer you),* i. e., *Please be offered.* The antonym of agaru is kudaru *come down* to which kudasaru *condescend* is related. Note that agaru means *go up* in Hakikaete o-agari kudasai (XII, 25) *Please change and go up.*

kakaru AND kakeru

42. Kakaru and kakeru *hang* (see section 91) are used in many Japanese idioms. The expression Hajimete o-me ni kakarimasu (VI, 12) literally means *For the first time I hang on your honorable eyes,* i. e., *I'm glad to meet you.* The expressions Ima o-me ni kakemasu (XII, 23) *Now I'll hang it on your eyes,* i. e., *Now I'll show it to you;* Jū yen no hoken wo kakete kudasai. (XIV, 60) *Please hang ten yen insurance on it,* i. e., *Please insure it for ten yen;* Nani wo goran ni kakemashō ka? (IX, 38) *What can I show you?* all show idiomatic uses of these verbs.

Kakaru means *require* in expressions referring to time or price, e. g., Dono kurai kakarimashō ka? (VII, 34) *About how much will it require?*, i. e., *How long will it take?* and Ikura kakarimasu ka? *How much does it cost?* Note the meaning of *hanging, dependent* in the expression kakari no mono (X, 20) *the person in charge.*

ADJECTIVES

43. True adjectives end in **ai, ii, oi** or **ui** and modify a noun directly.

chiisai ginka (XIV, 16)	*small silver*
okii uchi (VI, 36)	*big house*
kuroi kutsu (IX, 1)	*black shoes*
marui hako (VI, 53)	*round box*

Other adjectives, which were originally nouns, or nouns used adjectively require **no** or **na** before a following noun which they modify. **Na** is from **naru** *be, become;* for **no** (see section 13).

Amerika no shikan (VI, 17)	*American officer*
o-kashi no hako (VI, 49)	*candy box*
tsugi no heya (X, 18)	*next room*
roku sen no kitte (XIV, 55)	*six sen stamp*
kirei na o-taku (VI, 33)	*beauty is home; a home where beauty is,* i. e., *beautiful home.*
shizuka na heya (XII, 20)	*quietness is room; a room where quietness is,* i. e., *a quiet room*
omo na sambutsu (XVI, 34)	*chief product*

The stem (the part remaining when the adjectival ending **i** is removed) of true adjectives may be used with **no** to modify nouns, e. g., **shiro to kuro no goban** (X, 24) *black and white check.*

When true adjectives are used not attributively, as in the above examples, but predicatively with all verbs except **desu** and **gozaru** in the affirmative, they have a special adverbial form which is made by changing the final **i** to **ku.** The predicate form of adjectives which are not true is the same as their attributive form.

tōku arimasen (VI, 29)	*is not far*
ōkiku gozaimasen (VI, 41)	*is not big*
chiisaku gozaimasen (VI, 41)	*is not small*
hikuku arimasen (VI, 48)	*is not short*
takaku natte iru (XV, 63)	*has become expensive*
ōkiku narimashita (VIII, 27)	*became big*
shikaku ja arimasen (VI, 51)	*is not square*

Predicate adjectives with **desu** are used in the attributive or noun (stem) form, but with the verb **gozaru** *be,* true adjectives have a special form. This is formed by changing the endings **ai** and **oi** to **ō, ii** to **iū** and **ui** to **ū.**

tōi desu (VI, 28)	*is far*
takō gozaimasu (VII, 56)	*is high*
tō gozaimasu (VII, 32)	*is far*
oishiū gozaimasu (VII, 59)	*is tasty*
hikū gozaimasu	*is short*

The expression **o-hayō gozaimasu** (XIV, 1) *good morning* is literally *it is early* (**hayai** meaning *quick, fast, early;* cf. **hayaku** (VII, 48) *quickly*). **Arigatō** (XIV, 26) is composed of **aru** *be* and **katai** *difficult.* The literal meaning of *thank you* is (*kindness*) *is difficult* (*to find*).

The forms ending in ai, ii, oi, or ui originally had a **k** before the **i.** **Ki** was the attributive ending and **ku,** the conjunctive or adverbial form. By a process of sound change, the **k** vocalized in the attributive form..The 'adverbial' form changed, but later reverted, except in several dialects, to the **ku** form. With the verb gozaru, however, the contracted forms persist in the standard colloquial. See HGJ, p. 109.

Most adjectives in **-i** may be used predicatively in the present tense without the verb *be,* e. **g.**, **Doko de norikaetara ii ka?** (IX, 29) *Where if I change is it good?,* i. e., *Where should I change?* **Dono yado-ya ga ichiban ii ka?** (XII, 1) *Which inn is the best?*

True adjectives may be made past by eliding the final **u** of the adverbial form and affixing the verb **aru** in the simple past tense. Other adjectives must be followed by the verb *be* when used predicatively, and the verb *be* may be varied in tense. **Nai,** the negative of **aru,** is an adjective and has a past **nakatta.**

yasashii *easy, simple* (attributive form); yasashiku (adverbial form) yasashikatta (XV 49) *was easy*

yoi *good* (attributive form); yoku (adverbial form); yokatta (XV, 58) *was good.*

nakatta (XV, 53)   *was not*

As this process gives a suffix karu with a past form katta and a gerund katte added to the base of adjectives (and because of a morphological similarity of verbs and adjectives) there are grammarians who speak of the conjugation of the adjective in Japanese (see sections 107 and 108).

When adjectives are used before other adjectives, they often add te to the adverbial form. Compare the continuative use of te with verbs (section 44).

atarashikute ōkiū gozaimasu (XII, 5)   *is new and big*
Ōkikute akaru-sō na heya desu (XII, 34)   *It is a large bright room.*

True adjectives used attributively, however, can be coördinated merely by juxtaposition, while others require no or na.

furui ii yado-ya (XII, 8)   *good old inn*
kirei na ii heya   *pretty room*

Adjectives of quantity and position sometimes follow the noun they modify just as do numeral auxiliaries (see section 64).

yoi tokoro ga takusan (XVI, 53)   *many good places*
nimotsu wa mina (XV, 50)   *all the baggage*
shindai wa ue (XV, 28)   *upper berth*

Abstract nouns may be made from adjectives by affixing sa to the stem, e. g., ōkii (VI, 36) *large,* ōkisa (IX, 48) *size,* nagai (VI, 57) *long,* nagasa (IX, 48) *length.*

For pronouns formed from adjectives (see section 55).

COÖRDINATION AND SUBORDINATION

44. The continuative stem of the verb (see section 27) or the gerundial form (see section 30) are often used to form compound sentences. When so used, they have no tense or mood in themselves and derive their tense or mood from that of the final verb upon which they depend.

Rikugun no shikan de, Nyū Yōku kara   *He is an army officer and comes from New*
o-ide ni narimashita (VI, 17)   *York.*

Kōbe de umarete (VIII, 26)   *being born in Kobe, i. e., was born in Kobe*
                                               and

(Watakushi no) tokei wo naoshite moratte   *I want to have my watch fixed and . . .*
okitai (X, 40)

kekkon shite (VI, 45)   *he is married and . . .*
Pan-ya e itte (VII, 64)   *Let's go to the bakery and . . .*
makete (VIII, 53)   *I'll reduce it and . . .*
nishi ni wa Chōsen hantō ga ari (XVI, 12)   *to the west is the Korean peninsula and . . .*

The te form of the verb or the continuative stem often indicate that the action of that verb occurs prior to the action of the final verb, and then signify *after.* Sometimes they indicate a causal relationship between the gerund or continuative and the final verb, and then mean *because.*

O-kikae ni natte, o-furo wo o-tori kudasai.   *After changing, please take a bath, i. e.,*
(XII, 51)   *Please change and take a bath.*

kozutsumi wo okuri-dashi (XIV, 45)   *after sending off a package*

Soshite or shi *and* may be used to connect clauses, e. g., Ryoken wa motte ita shi nimotsu... (XV, 49) *I had a passport and the baggage* . . .

kara

45. The postposition **kara** indicates motion away from. It is used both locatively and temporally and may be translated by *from*. **Ima kara** means *from now on* and refers to the future.

Nyū Yōku kara (VI, 18)	*from New York*
koko kara (VI, 28)	*from here*
raigetsu kara (XIV, 37)	*from next month on*
Ima kara, kaimono ni ikimashō (VII, 12)	*Let's go shopping from now;* i. e., Let's go shopping now.
Ima kara ryōriya e ikimashō (XI, 39)	*Let's go to the restaurant now.*

Compare **Ima haitte wa ikemasen** (V, 41) *You mustn't come in now* and also **Ima dochira ni irasshaimasu ka?** (VI, 21) *Where is she now?*

ACCOMPANIMENT

46. *Together with* signifying accompaniment is expressed by the phrase **to issho ni** *together, at* (see section 15). To is omitted when the person accompanied is not expressed or when the person accompanied is governed by another postposition.

Watashidomo to issho ni sunde imasu (VI, 45)	*He lives with us.*
Anata to issho ni aruite ita gunjintachi (XI, 14)	*the military men who were walking with you*
Go-issho ni mairimashō. (IX, 4)	*I'll go with you.*
Anata mo issho ni ikimasen ka? (IX, 2)	*Don't you also want to go along?*

COMPARISON OF ADJECTIVES AND ADVERBS

47. The comparative is often formed by placing **motto** *more* before adjectives or adverbs and **mō** before adverbs of quantity. The superlative is made by placing **ichiban** (literally *number one,* i. e., *first*) or **mottomo** before the adjective.

motto ōkii uchi (VI, 36)	*a bigger house*
ichiban ōkii (VI, 38)	*the largest house*
ichiban ii tamago (VII, 46)	*the best eggs*
ichiban itai (XIII, 50)	*most painful*
mottomo yūmei (XVI, 30)	*most famous*
mō sukoshi semai (X, 8)	*little narrower*

Hō *side, direction* is often used with the adjective to express the comparative, e. g., **chiisai hō no** (XV, 33) *the small side one,* i. e., *the smaller one* (see section 59).

Than after the comparative is expressed by **yori** in which case the adjective may be used in its positive form, e. g., **Kōbe e iku yori tōi desu ka?** (VI, 30) *Than to go to Kobe, is it far? Is it farther than Kobe?* In the negative **hodo** *extent* is used instead of **yori**, e. g., **Kōbe e yuku hodo tōku arimasen** (VI, 32) *The-going extent to Kobe is-not far; It is not far to the extent of going to Kobe,* i. e., *It is not so far as Kobe.* **Musume hodo hikuku arimasen** (VI, 48) *He is not short to the extent of the girl,* i. e., *He is not so short as the girl.*

The comparison of equality may be expressed by **to onaji** *the same as,* e. g., **sono menseki wa Tekisasu-shū to onaji de arimasu** (XVI, 5) *It's size is the same as the state of Texas.*

THE PARTICLE ne

48. The particle **ne** at the end of sentences adds the thought *isn't that so?* Sometimes it serves to intensify the thought of the sentence and corresponds somewhat to *really*. Other times it is added simply out of politeness, for it takes away from the positiveness of the sentence.

Kirei na o-taku ni sunde imasu ne (VI, 33)	*You really live in a beautiful house.*
ichiban ōkii desu ne (VI, 38)	*this is the largest, isn't it?*
Kono tsugi no heya de bōshi wo utte imasu ne (X, 18)	*They sell hats in this next room, don't they?*

THERE IS, THERE ARE, POSSESSION

49. The subject of *there is* or *there are* is governed by the postposition **ga** in the affirmative and **wa** in the negative, e. g., **Niku-ya ga arimasu ka?** (VII, 27) *Is there a butcher store?* **shindai wa gozaimasen** (XII, 31) *There is no bed.* See section **71.**

Aru and gozaru are often used to indicate possession, in which case the possessor, if expressed, becomes the indirect object, e. g., **Anata ni wa okosan ga arimasu ka?** (VI, 42) *To you are there any children?*, i. e., *Do you have any children?* **Musume ga gozaimasu** (VI, 44) *There is a daughter*, i. e., *I have a daughter.*

USE OF suru

50. The verbs **suru, nasaru** or **itasu** meaning *do* added to a noun convert that noun into a verb. The noun in some cases is used without any postposition; in others with the postposition **wo**, and in still others, it is governed by **ni**, e. g., **kekkon suru** *do marriage*, i. e., *(to) marry;* see **kekkon shite** (VI, 45) *being married.*

Shitsurei shimashita (VI, 58)	*I did rudeness. I was rude*, i. e., *I'm sorry.*
taihen nagai wo shite (VI, 57)	*doing very long*, i. e., **staying a long time**
chūmon shite (X, 42)	*do an order*, i. e., *to order*
men shite imasu (XII, 27)	*is doing face*, i. e., *is facing*
torihiki shite (XIV, 7)	*doing dealings*, i. e., *dealing*
chokin shite (XIV, 19)	*doing deposit*, i. e., *depositing*
tennin sareru (XIV, 37)	*is done a transfer*, i. e., *is transferred, will be transferred*
uragaki wo shite kudasai. (XIV, 10)	*please do indorsement*, i. e., *please endorse.*
muri wo shita (XIII, 60)	*did abuse*, i. e., *abused*
sampo wo shi (XVI, 1)	*do a walk*, i. e., *walk*
gorufu wo shite (XVI, 51)	*do golfing, (to) golf*, i. e., *play golf*
kakitome ni shite (XIV, 46)	*doing a registration*, i. e., *(to) register*
chikki ni shite kudasai (XV, 32)	*please do checking*, i. e., *please check*

Suru is used with nouns referring to our senses or feelings meaning *have, get, be, become*. The noun of feeling is then governed by the postposition **ga**, e. g., **zutsū ga shite** (XIII, 44) *I had a headache and . . .* Suru has a similar meaning in the expressions **soshite** (sō shite) *and (being so)* and **sō sureba** (XIII, 63) *if it is so.*

THE POSTPOSITION made

51. Made *up to, until, by* indicates motion up to a point either temporal or spatial.

yo ji han made ni (VII, 24)	*by four-thirty*
niku-ya made (VII, 34)	*as far as the butcher shop*
jū hachi ni naru made (VIII, 26)	*until he became eighteen*

NUMERALS

52. There are two sets of numbers: those derived from the Chinese, **ichi, ni, san,** etc. and those of native origin, **hitotsu, futatsu, mittsu,** etc. The Japanese numbers are, with few exceptions, not used beyond *ten.* It may be said that, in general, the numbers which are of Chinese derivation are used to modify words of Chinese origin, while those of native origin are used to modify native words, e. g., **ikkin** (VII, 39) *one kin,* **ichi yen** (VII, 39) *one yen,* but **Sochira wa hitotsu** (VII, 43) *one of those (eggs),* **yottsu no shima** (XVI, 16) *four islands.*

The suffix **tsu** of the numbers of native origin is omitted when the numeral precedes the noun it modifies, e. g., **hito-taba** (VII, 51) *one bunch.*

Yo *four* is often used with nouns of time, place, or those referring to people to avoid using **shi** which is homophonous with **shi** *death* (see HGJ, p. 83), e. g., **gogo no yo ji han** (VII, 24) *four thirty P. M.;* **itchōme no jū yo ban** (IX, 62) *number fourteen, First Street.* However see **shikai** (IX, 36) *fourth floor.* Shi and shichi are often replaced by **yo** (**yon**) and **nana** respectively, as their similarity in sound might lead to confusion, e. g., **yon jū go yen** (XV, 23) *forty-five yen.* However, **yo** is always used with **yen** and **shi** or **yon** with **sen.**

Hichi and **shichi, kyu** and **ku** (VIII, 28) are variant forms. The native numbers may be spelled with one **t**, e. g., **yotsu, mutsu, yatsu.**

The numbers above ten are constructed by using **jū** *ten* as a base. A number placed before **jū** multiplies it, while a number placed after it is added to it.

san jitchōme (VII, 29)	*thirtieth street*
roku jissen (VII, 39)	*sixty sen*
jū issai (VII, 19)	*eleven years old*
san jū go (VII, 53)	*thirty-five*

Counting above **sen** *a thousand* is done by means of **man** *ten thousand* and thus **ni man** *two ten-thousands* is *twenty thousand,* **jū man** *one hundred thousand,* and **hyaku man** *one hundred ten-thousands* is *a million.* There is, however, a special word **oku** *one hundred million.* It is also important to note that numbers above one thousand are not stated in hundreds as they sometimes are in English, e. g., **sen roppyaku san jū yo ban** (XIII, 13) *number one thousand six hundred thirty-four* (not *sixteen hundred and thirty-four*).

Two or three, four or five, etc. are expressed by juxtaposition of the numerals, e. g., **shi-go** (IX, 7) *four or five;* **go-roku** (IX, 32) *five or six;* **ni-san nichi** (IX, 57) *two or three days.* In consecutive numbers above ten used in this way, **jū** is omitted in the second number, e. g., **ni˙jū go-roku** *twenty-five or twenty-six.*

Fractions are expressed by means of the word **bun** *part,* thus: **sambun no ichi** (VII, 61) *of three parts—one,* i. e., *one of three parts,* i. e., *one third;* **shibun no san** *of four parts—three,* i. e., *three-fourths.* However, note the word **hambun** (VII, 61) *half* (see **han,** VII, 24) and **bun** *part.*

Ordinal numbers are formed by adding **bamme** (**ban** *number* and **me** *eye, division, mark on a scale* (see HGJ, p. 84) to the cardinals. Again, the numeral may be preceded by **dai** *order, succession* or followed by **gō** *mark.* However, when a numeral auxiliary (see section **64**) is used with an ordinal number, **ban** is omitted and **me** follows the auxiliary. The postposition **no** is used between the ordinal and a following noun in accordance with section **43.**

san bamme no mado (XIV, 22)	*third window*
koko kara san jitchōme no tokoro (VII, 29)	*a place the thirtieth street from here*
Dai ikkwa (I, 0)	*first lesson*
go ken me (VIII, 66)	*fifth house*
ni chōme no kado (IX, 19)	*second street corner*
san gō sha (XV, 35)	*third vehicle*

The ordinal idea is often expressed merely by juxtaposition, e. g., **shi kai** (IX, 36) *fourth floor* (see section 70).
See section 110.

THE SUFFIX zutsu

53. Zutsu is a suffix meaning *each, by, per.*

tō-zutsu tonde (VII, 9)	*skipping (flying over) ten each,* i. e., *by tens*
jikan goto ni hito saji-zutsu (XIII, 62)	*one teaspoonful per every two hours*

FUTURE

54. The so-called 'future' tense is actually a present tense which expresses probability or conjecture. It may denote either an action which is probably taking place in the present or one which will be performed in the future. The 'future' tense is used also to express the imperative *let us.*

> "It has been pointed out that the Japanese verb in its simple forms is neutral as to time. In the earlier stages of the language time-relations do not appear to have been expressed with precision, but a number of suffixes which originally denoted other aspects, such as certainty, probability, etc., may now be looked upon as having developed a tense-significance." (HGJ, pp. 318–319.)

This 'future' form is made by the addition of **yō** to the negative stem (see section **56**) of verbs of the first class, and **u** to the negative stem of those of the second class. However, when **u** is added to the **a** of the stem of second class verbs, the combination **au** contracts to **ō** (compare the pronunciation of **morau** as **morō** (VII, 60). Masu and desu have the irregular 'future' forms **-mashō** and **deshō** (XI, 32) respectively (see sections 116 and 117).

tabeyō (XI, 20)	*will eat*
yarō (XIV, 31)	*will give*
ii deshō (VII, 21)	*it is probably better*
Ikaga de gozaimashō ka? (IX, 44)	*What do you think about them?*
Ichi ri gurai arimashō (IX, 13)	*It probably is about one ri. I think it's about one ri.*
kakarimashō (VII, 36)	*it probably takes*
Kochira wo moraimashō (VII, 57)	*I'll take this.*
Nan ji ni dekakemashō ka? (VII, 31)	*What time shall we leave?*
Yao-ya e yukimashō (VII, 48)	*Let's go to the grocery.*
Kashi wo kaimashō (VII, 64)	*Let's buy some cake.*

The present is often used to express a future action (see section 96).

The present tense or the attributive form of the verb with **tsumori** (see section 72) is used to express the future action of the second person, e. g., **Anata wa nan ji ni dekakemasu ka?** or **Anata wa nan ji ni dekakeru tsumori desu ka?** *What time will you leave?* or *What time do you intend to leave?*

THE POSTPOSITION no

55. No (perhaps a contracted form of **mono** *thing*) often serves to make a noun of a verb, e. g., **kaeru no** (VII, 15) *the return.* It may also serve to make a pronoun of an adjective.

ōkii no (VII, 44)	*the big ones*
mō sukoshi semai no (X, 8)	*little narrower ones*
cha-iro no (X, 14)	*tan ones*
yūmei na no (XVI, 30)	*famous one*

The expression **no desu** or its contracted form, **n' desu,** at the end of a sentence merely serves to round out the thought and make it specific rather than general. **No desu** means *it is a thing*, i. e., *it is a fact that.*

Dō sareta n' deshō ka? (XIII, 6)　　　　*I wonder what was done with it. What could have happened to it?*

Go-shinsatsu wo o-negai shitai n' desu　*I want to request your examination,* i. e.,
(XIII, 37)　　　　　　　　　　　　　　　　　*I want to ask you for an examination.*

NEGATIVE STEM OF VERBS

56. The negative stem of verbs of the first class is identical with their continuative forms (see section **27**). It may be formed by adding **i** to the base of **iru** verbs and **e** to the base of **eru** verbs. The base of verbs of the first class is obtained by removing the **iru** or **eru** ending of the conclusive form. The negative stem of the verb **iru** *be*, **i** (XII, 21) is therefore quite regular. Verbs of the second class add **a** to the base (i. e., the conclusive form with the **u** removed). Verbs ending in **tsu** drop the **su** and thus their base ends in **t**, e. g., **matsu** *wait* is seen in its negative form in **mata-nakereba** (VII, 15) *if not wait.* Verbs whose base ends in a vowel add a **w** which prevents hiatus, thus **kau** forms **kawa-nakereba** (VII, 26) *if not buy*, **au** forms **awa(zu)** (XV, 61) *not meet*, and **you** forms **yowa(zu)** (XV, 58) *not being seasick.*

dekake-nakereba (VII, 33)	*if not leave*
wasure-nai (XI, 47)	*not forget*
kaera-nakereba (VII, 25)	*if not return*
tsurete ika-nai (VII, 20)	*not accompanying*
sawara-nai (XIII, 52)	*not touch*
hara-nakereba (XIV, 50)	*if not paste*

Kuru *come* has an irregular negative stem **ko** or **ki**, while the irregular negative stem of **suru** *do* is either **shi** or **se**. **Aru** *be* has no corresponding negative form; the adjective **nai** *is not* serves as its negative, e. g., **Shikata ga nai** (XV, 30) *There is no help for it.* (See sections **57** and **116**.)

OBLIGATION

57. The negative stem of the verb followed by **nakereba narimasen, nakute wa narimasen,** (or by **nakereba ikemasen** for the second or third persons only) expresses the idea of *have to, be obliged to,* or *must.* **Nakereba** is the conditional form of **nai** and means *if it is not* (see sections **56** and **89**). **Narimasen** is from **naru** *become* and therefore **Mata-nakereba narimasen** (VII, 15) literally means *if not wait, not become; if I don't wait, nothing will become,* i. e., *I must wait, I have to wait.*

Kaera-nakereba narimasen ka? (VIII, 58)　*Do you have to go home?*
Ika-nakereba narimasen (IX, 6)　　　　　　*I must go.*
hara-nakereba narimasen ka? (XIV, 50)　　*must I paste?*

Nai and its past **nakatta,** used after the negative stem of the verb, form a present and past negative which are not so polite as the **masen** and **masen deshita** endings (see section **8**). The affirmative forms which correspond to them in lack of politeness are the conclusive and the simple past respectively (see sections **26** and **18**).

To express the fact that there is no obligation or necessity **nakute mo ii desu** may be used following the negative stem of the verb when the latter is expressed.

Ika-nakute mo ii desu　　　　　　　　　*Even not going, it's all right,* i. e., *You don't have to go.*

Kaeri wa densha de nakute mo ii deshō ne   *We don't have to go back by trolley, do we?*
(VIII, 60)

AGE

58. In asking a person's age, the expression **Anata wa ikutsu desu ka?** *As for you, how many are you?* is used, and the answer corresponds in form to the English. However with ages under ten the numeral auxiliary referring to years of age, **sai,** must be used with the numbers of Chinese origin, or else the numbers of native origin, i. e., **hitotsu, futatsu,** etc. are employed. Above ten, the numbers of Chinese origin are used with or without **sai.** The word **hatachi,** however, is used for *twenty years old.*

    Ano ko wa iku sai desu ka? (VII, 18)   *How old is she?*
    Jū issai desu (VII, 19)   *She is eleven.*

PREFERENCE

59. To express the idea that something is better than another or that it is better to do one thing rather than another, the word **hō** *side* is used modified by a noun or pronoun in the one case, and by the simple present of the verb or its corresponding negative form in the other. The expressions **yoroshiū gozaimasu** and **ii desu** mean *it is good.* Sometimes **hō** is not required and then an object preferred is governed by the postposition **ga.**

    Densha no hō ga ii deshō (IX, 10)   *A trolley car is probably better,* i. e., *A trolley car would be preferable.*
    Tsurete ika-nai hō ga ii deshō (VII, 20)   *It would be better not to take her along.*
    Sangai ga yoroshiū gozaimasu ka? (XII, 17)   *Do you prefer the third floor?*
    Futsū de yoroshiū gozaimasu (XIV, 54)   *Ordinary (mail) is all right,* i. e., *I prefer ordinary (mail).*

-ya

60. The suffix **ya** indicates the store where a thing is sold or the keeper of that store as well. In addressing the shopkeeper, however, **San** is added.

    niku (VII, 26) *meat;* **niku-ya** (VII, 34) *butcher shop;* **niku-ya San** (VII, 37) *butcher*
    Takashima-ya (IX, 11)   *Takashima's*
    sentaku-ya (XI, 3)   *laundry man*

PHONETIC CHANGES

61. Some numbers change their form when followed by nouns beginning with certain sounds:
    (a) **ichi** *one.* The final **i** is dropped when followed by a noun beginning with **ch,** and the resulting long **ch** is spelled **tch.** The final **i** is dropped, and the **ch** assimilates to an initial **k, s, sh,** or **t** of a following word which **ichi** modifies. The lengthening of **sh** is indicated by an **s** before the **sh.** The **ch** also assimilates to a following **f** or **h** after the initial **f** or **h** is changed to **p.**

> P or ph was probably the original sound of f or h.
> Sansom says "the modern pronunciations are ha, hi, fu, he, ho. There is very good evidence to show that the early forms of these syllables were not aspirate plus vowel, but labial plus vowel, which might be represented approximately by pa, pi, pu, pe, po or better perhaps by pha, phi, phu, phe, pho" (HGJ, p. 47). Sansom also calls attention to the modern pronunciation of f as a labial and to the fact that the voiced forms of ha, hi, fu, he, and ho are ba, bi, bu, be, bo (HGJ, 1. c.).

itchaku (X, 41)   *one suit*
ikkin (VII, 39)   *one kin*

issai (VII, 19)	*one year of age*
isshūkan (VIII, 12)	*one week*
itteki	*one drop*
ippon (XI, 52)	*one bottle*

(b) **hachi** may become **ha** just as **ichi** becomes **i**, and then the same changes take place in the initial consonant of the following word.

hatchaku	*eight suits*
hakkin	*eight kin*
hassai	*eight years old*
hasshūkan	*eight weeks*
hatteki	*eight drops*
happon	*eight bottles*

The uncontracted forms of the above examples with **hachi** are also used, e. g., compare **hassun** (IX, 49) *eight sun* and **hachi sen** (VIII, 3) *eight sen*.

(c) **jū** *ten* becomes **ji** just as **ichi** becomes **i**, and the same changes take place in the initial consonant of the following word, e. g., **jitchōme** (VII, 29) *tenth block*, **jippun** (VII, 49) *ten minutes*, **jissen** (VII, 39) *ten sen*.

(d) **roku** *six* and **hyaku** *hundred*. The final u is dropped before a word which they modify beginning with **k**, and also before those with initial **f** or **h**. The **f** or **h** becomes **p** and the **k** of roku or hyaku assimilates to it, e. g., **rokkin** (VII, 53) *six* kin; **roppiki** (VIII, 38) *six animals;* **hyappiki** (VIII, 43) *one hundred animals*.

(e) **san** *three,* **sen** *one thousand,* and **han** *half* change **n** to **m** before a word which they modify beginning with **b** or **m** and before those with initial **f** or **h**. The **f** or **h** is used in its original form, i. e., **p** (see (a) supra). The change of the dental nasal to the labial nasal before a labial is known as nasal accomodation, a partial assimilation. It should be noted that the nasal usually voices the following **p** to **b** (an exception is **sampun** *three minutes*).

sambun (VII, 61)	*three parts, third*
sambyaku (VIII, 63)	*three hundred*
sambamme (XIV, 22)	*third*
sembiki (VIII, 41)	*one thousand animals*
hambun (VII, 63)	*one half*

The nasal voices a following **k** to **g**, **s** to **z**, and **sh** to **j**, e. g., **sangai** (XII, 19) *third floor,* **san-zen** *three thousand,* **san-jaku** *three shaku.*

When words are joined to form compounds, an initial voiceless stop of the second element will often become voiced; e. g., **daidokoro** (XII, 42) *kitchen* from **dai** and **tokoro** *place;* **nadakai** (XVI, 31) *famous* from **na** *name* and **takai** *high;* **uragaki** (XIV, 10) *endorsement* from **ura** *back* and **kaki** *writing;* **Iwo Jima** *Iwo Island* from **Iwo** and **shima** *island.*

The form of a word with a voiced initial stop is referred to as its sonant form, e. g., **dokoro** is the sonant-form of **tokoro** (see section 112).

THE SUFFIX kan

62. **Ji** is used in referring to a point of time, i. e., the hour of the day, but the suffix **kan** *interval, period, duration* must be added in speaking of a number of hours or when speaking of a certain time. **Kan** is also added to **shū** *week* with the same meaning.

Nan ji desu ka? (VII, 22)	*What time is it?*
kaeru jikan (VIII, 59)	*time to return*
raishū	*next week*
ni shūkan	*two weeks' duration*

TIME

63. In telling time, the expression **gozen** *the forenoon* and **gogo** *afternoon* followed by **no** indicate *A. M.* and *P. M.* respectively. The number of the hour is followed by **ji** *hour*. The minutes after or before are then stated followed by **fun** *minute* (fun in combination with certain numbers becomes **pun** (see section 61). **Mae** *before* is used to indicate the minutes to the hour and **sugi** *past, after* may be used to indicate the minutes after the hour. Sugi, however, may be omitted.

Gozen jū ichi ji desu (VII, 23)	*It is eleven A. M.*
gogo no yo ji han made ni (VII, 24)	*by four-thirty P. M.*
ni ji jippun mae (VII, 49)	*ten minutes to two*
ni ji jippun sugi	*ten minutes after two*
ni ji jippun	*ten minutes after two*

NUMERAL AUXILIARIES

64. In English the words *pieces, head, drops,* and *loaves* in the phrases *ten pieces of chalk, three head of cattle, four drops of water* and *five loaves of bread* correspond somewhat to the Japanese numeral auxiliaries. Just as *ten chalks, three cattle, four waters, five breads* sound strange, so do Japanese nouns and numerals used without an auxiliary (where one exists) or used with the wrong numeral auxiliary. However, the numeral auxiliaries are unlike the above-mentioned English words in that they do not single out smaller divisions of the noun, but rather indicate that the noun belongs to a certain larger group of objects. For this reason they are sometimes called classifiers. Thus, **hon** is used for long narrow objects, and loaves of bread, bottles, pens or pencils come in this category.

(Pan wo) ni hon kudasai (VIII, 5)	*Bread two loaves please give;* i. e., *Please give me two loaves of bread.*
Bīru wo ni hon moraimashō (XI, 50)	*I'll take two bottles of beer.*
Empitsu wo ni hon kudasai	*Please give me two pencils.*

The numeral auxiliary takes no postposition, but the noun which it classifies does. The numeral auxiliary may follow the noun or precede it. If it precedes, it is connected to the noun by the postposition **no** (see section 43).

Besides **hon** some frequently used numeral auxiliaries are:

dai (VIII, 62)	*for vehicles*
hiki (VIII, 23)	*for animals*
ma (hitoma) (XII, 16)	*for rooms*
mae (XI, 43)	*for portions*
mai (IX, 49)	*for flat things such as paper, clothes, blankets, etc.*
nin (VIII, 44)	*for people*
satsu (XIV, 59)	*for books, magazines, etc.*

All of the above auxiliaries are of Chinese origin except **ma** and **mae**. The numerals of native origin, **hitotsu, futatsu,** etc. (see section 52) are used before numeral auxiliaries of native origin or with nouns having no special auxiliary, while those of Chinese origin, **ichi, ni, san,** etc. are generally used before auxiliaries of Chinese origin.

The number may be used with the numeral auxiliary without the noun that the latter classifies. As the ending **tsu** of the native numbers is a numeral auxiliary itself, meaning *piece,* it is not used before an auxiliary.

sakana wo go hiki (VIII, 23)	*five fish*

go hiki no sakana wo	*five fish* (used as above)
jinrikusha ga san dai (VIII, 62)	*three jinrikshaws*
kitte mo shi-go mai (XIV, 47)	*also four or five stamps*
shatsu ga shi-go mai irimasu (IX, 7)	*I need four or five shirts*
hon ga ni satsu (XIV, 59)	*two books*
ichi man no ebi (VIII, 40)	*ten thousand shrimp*
Ichi mai san yen go jissen de gozaimasu (IX, 43)	*They are three yen, fifty sen each* (*shirt*).
kata-michi ichi mai (XV, 24)	*one one-way ticket*
zashiki ga hito-ma (XII, 16)	*one room*
hito-tsuki (XII, 37)	*one month*

Note, however, **hitoban** (XII, 36) *one night*

One, two and *four* referring to people, however, are expressed by **hitori, futari** and **yottari** respectively, and not by the numeral and **nin**.

Kazoku wa otoko ga hitori de, onna ga futari desu (VIII, 46)	*As for* (*my*) *family, men one person is and women, two persons are,* i. e., *My family consists of one man and two women.*
Suki-yaki wo futari mae negaimasu (XI, 43)	*We should like two portions of sukiyaki.*

See section **111.**

sŏ AND yŏ

65. **Sŏ desu** following a verb in the conclusive form or simple past means *so they say* or *so I hear.* Sŏ desu following a verb in the continuative form expresses likelihood or possibility.

Tennin sareru sŏ desu (XIV, 37)	*I hear he has been transferred.*
Sakana ga takusan aru sŏ desu (VIII, 9)	*I hear they have a lot of fish.*
Takaku natta sŏ desu (XV, 65)	*They say it has gone up in price.*
Tenki wa yoku nari sŏ desu	*It looks as if it will be good weather.*

Sŏ added to the stem of an adjective (see section **43**) gives the meaning of *appearance.*

akaru-sŏ na heya (XII, 35)	*a bright-looking room*
omoshiro-sŏ na o-shigoto (XIV; 39)	*sort of interesting work*

Yŏ means *manner* or *appearance.* When followed by the verb *be* (desu, da, gozaimasu, etc.), the phrase means *it seems, it appears.*

Kanari ii yŏ desu ne (IX, 47)	*It really seems quite good.*
Yawarakai yŏ desu ne (XI, 57)	*It really seems tender.*
atsu-sugiru yŏ da kara (XII, 54)	*as it appears a little too hot*
yŏsu ga sukoshi warui yŏ de . . . (XIII, 37)	*the condition appears a little worse and . . .*

Yŏ ni means *in the manner of, so as, so that, in order to* and it is used in clauses of purpose or manner. It is therefore used in asking a person to tell someone to do something.

Beikoku ņo kata no yŏ ni miukemasu (XV, 42)	*You look in the manner of an American,* i. e., *You look like an American.*
Haien ni natta yŏ ni omowaremasu (XIII, 60)	*I think that it became pneumonia. I think you got pneumonia.*
Shatsu ni wa nori wo tsuke-nai yŏ ni hana-shite kudasai (XI, 11)	*Please tell* (*to him*) *so that* (*he*) *not put starch in the shirts,* i. e., *Please tell him not to put starch in the shirts.*
Jochū ni watakushi no nimotsu wo motte kite kureru yŏ ni itte kudasai (XII, 41)	*Please tell the maid to kindly bring my baggage.*

miru

66. The verb **miru** or its honorific form **goran** used after the gerundial form of a verb has the meaning *try*. It is often used simply to soften the abruptness of a command.

Ano junsa ni kiite mimashō (IX, 13)	*I'll try asking that policeman.*
yukkuri itte mite kudasai (VIII, 13)	*Please say slowly . . .*
Kore wo haite mite kudasai (X, 6)	*Please put these on.*
Kagetsu e itte, tabete goran to kaite arimashita (XI, 35)	*Go to the Kagetsu restaurant and try eating —thus was written,* i. e., *He wrote me to try eating at the Kagetsu restaurant.*
Sugu itte mite agemashō (XIII, 40)	*I'll try to come soon.*
Netsu wo hakatte mimashō (XIII, 55)	*I'll try taking your temperature (fever).*
Hakatte mite agemashō (XIV, 51)	*I'll try weighing it.*

DAYS OF THE WEEK

67. The days of the week are named after the elements; viz., sun day, moon day, fire day, water day, wood day, metal day, and earth day, e. g., **Nichiyōbi, Getsuyōbi, Kayōbi,** etc. (VIII, 15). Bi is the sonant form (see section 61) of **hi** *day* and may be omitted as **yō** also signifies *day*, i. e., **Nichiyō** *Sunday,* **Getsuyō** *Monday,* etc. (see section 113).

SHOULD

68. **Hazu** means *should, expect, ought,* and implies obligation, e. g., **Shindai no soba ni aru hazu desu** (XIII, 3) *It should be beside the bed.* **Sore mo sono hazu de gozaimashō** (VIII, 24) *That's to be expected.* is an idiom.

Beki may be used independently or after **hazu** with similar meanings, e. g., **harau beki mono wa nakatta** (XV, 52) *should pay thing there was not,* i. e., *There was nothing to be paid.*

naru

69. A noun preceding the verb **naru** *become, be* takes the postposition **ni.** Other parts of speech take no postposition.

Hachi sen ni narimashita (VIII, 3)	*It became eight sen. It went up to eight sen.*
O-naka ga ippai ni narimashita (XI, 58)	*My insides became all filled up,* i. e., *I am all filled up.* (ippai is a contraction of ichi and hai (see section 61); hai is a noun.)
Ni jū go sen ni narimasu (XIV, 61)	*It comes to twenty-five sen.*
ōkiku narimashita (VIII, 27)	*became big,* i. e., *grew up*
takaku natte iru (XV, 63)	*is high*

DATES

70. In dates the Japanese year period is mentioned first, then the number of the year followed by the month and day. A new Japanese year period begins when a new emperor ascends the throne. The present era, **Shōwa,** began in 1926. The cardinal (not ordinal) numbers precede **nen** *year* and **nichi** *day.* The months of the year are named numerically, e. g., **Nigatsu** (VIII, 31) *second month,* i. e., *February.* However, **Shōgatsu** or **Ichigatsu** may be used for *January.*

The days of the month from the second to the tenth are formed with the numbers of native origin and **ka,** a native numeral auxiliary meaning *days.* Above ten, the Chinese numerals are used with **nichi.**

ichi nichi		muika	*sixth*
or	*first*	nanuka	*seventh*
tsuitachi		yōka (VIII, 36)	*eighth*
futsuka	*second*	kokonoka	*ninth*
mikka	*third*	tōka	*tenth*
yokka	*fourth*	jū ichi nichi	*eleventh*
itsuka	*fifth*	jū ni nichi	*twelfth*

Shōwa jū nen no Nigatsu jū go nichi ni   *Showa of the tenth year February fifteenth*
    Tōkiō e kimashita (VIII, 31)   *day to Tokio he came, i. e., He came to*
                                             Tokio February 15th, 1935.

The customer, not realizing that 1926 is counted the first year of Shōwa, has miscalculated. The tenth year of Shōwa is 1935, not 1936 as she says on line 34. To get the Christian year from the Shōwa year, add 1925. To get the year of Shōwa from the Christian year, subtract 1925.

The days of the month (except tsuitachi) are also used for *one day, two days, twenty-five days*, etc. Jū ichi nichi means *eleven days* as well as *the eleventh day;* futsuka may mean *two days*, and ni jū go nichi may mean *twenty-five days*.

However, with months the situation is different. Nigatsu means *February*, but to express *two months* the numeral auxiliary ka followed by getsu *month* must be used thus: ni ka getsu *two months;* san ka getsu (XIV, 36) *three months*. The numbers of Japanese origin may also be used in this way, e. g., hito tsuki *one month;* futa tsuki *two months;* mi tsuki *three months*, etc. After tō tsuki *ten months*, the number is used without any auxiliary, e. g., jū ichi tsuki *eleven months* (see sections 113, 114 and 115).

iru, oru, AND aru

71. When used alone to mean *there is* or *there are* (see section 49) or to express location, etc. iru and oru are used when the subject is animate or active, while aru is used when the subject is considered in a passive or inactive condition. Thus rickshaws, being movable, are thought of as active objects. Iru and oru are used with the gerundial form of the verb (see section 31) to express the progressive tenses while aru is used with the gerund to express the passive voice in a perfect sense.

Jinrikisha ga san dai imasu (VIII, 62)	*There are three jinrikshaws.*
yogorete iru sentaku mono (XI, 7)	*soiled laundry*
ni kai ni aru . . . sentaku mono (XI, 7)	*the laundry which is upstairs*
kaite arimashita (XI, 36)	*was written*
Bangō wa fusagatte imasu (XIII, 18)	*The line is occupied.*
Burajiru ni imasu (XIV, 36)	*He is in Brazil.*

Oru is more formal than iru.

O-machi shite orimasu (XIII, 41)	*We are awaiting you.*
Komatte orimasu (XIII, 49)	*I am suffering.*

INTENTION

72. The attributive form of the verb (see section **26**) before the word **tsumori** *intention, expectation* expresses intention to do something. **Tsumori** is followed by the verb **be.** The negative of this phrase is **tsumori ja arimasen.** The noun form of the verb preceded by the honorific **o** may be used to modify **tsumori** and it is then connected to **tsumori** by means of the postposition **no.**

iku tsumori desu (IX, 1)	*intend to go*
Mugiwara-bōshi wa suteru tsumori desu (X, 26)	*I intend to throw away my straw hat.*
o-tomari no tsumori (XII, 38)	*the staying intention,* i. e., *intend to stop.*

INTERROGATIVE ADJECTIVES AND PRONOUNS

73. The **i** of **nani** *what* is often elided. **Donata** and **dare** are both used for *who,* and **dochira** and **doko** for *where.* **Donata** and **dochira** are considered the more polite forms. **Donata** has a plural form **donatagata** (XI, 15) which may be used when referring to more than one person. Both **dochira** and **dono** mean *which,* but **dochira** is used to mean *which of two,* while dono refers to *which of more than two.*

Dono depāto e ikimashō ka? (IX, 4)	*To which department store shall we go?* (More than two stores are being considered.)
Dochira no depāto e ikimashō ka?	*To which department store shall we go?* (Only two stores are being considered.)
Dono yado-ya ga ichiban ii ka? (XII, 1)	*Which inn is the best?* (considering more than two inns)

Doko is also used for *which,* e. g., **doko no ryōriya** (XI, 21) *which restaurant.* **Dochira** is used for *where* as well as *which,* e. g., **Dochira e desu ka?** (XIV, 27) *To which place is it?,* i. e., *Where are you going?*

Dō and **ikaga** both mean *how.* **Ikaga** is, however, more formal than **dō** and its use is restricted to certain expressions. **Ikaga** is frequently used to mean *how about, what do you think about?*

Dō sareta n' deshō ka? (XIII, 6)	*How was probably done?,* i. e., *What was done with it? I wonder what happened to it.*
O-kagen wa ikaga de gozaimasu ka? (XII, 52)	*How is the temperature?*
O-sake wa ikaga desu ka? (XI, 49)	*How about some sake? What do you say to some drinks?*
Nihon shoku wa ikaga desu ka? (XI, 23)	*How would you like Japanese food?*

Dono kurai or **dono gurai** means *about how far, about how long,* but does not necessarily refer to approximate quantity only, e. g., **Dono gurai o-tomari no tsumori desu ka?** (XII, 38) *(About) how long do you intend to stay?*

How much referring to price is **ikura,** e. g., **Kono gyūniku wa ikura desu ka?** (VII, 37) *How much does this beef cost?*

How much or *how many* referring to quantity is **iku, ikutsu,** or **nan. Iku** or **nan** are used with a numeral auxiliary, but **ikutsu** where the noun has no special auxiliary (for the auxiliary **tsu,** see section **64**). The final **n** of **nan** causes the same changes in the initial consonant of a following numeral auxiliary as does the **n** of **san** (see section **61, e**).

Ano ko wa iku sai desu ka? (VII, 18)	*How many years old is that child? How old is she?*
Ōkisa wa ikutsu de gozaimasu ka? (X, 2)	*The size, how much is it?*, i. e., *What is the size?*
O-kazoku wa nan nin de gozaimasu ka? (VIII, 44)	*How many people are there in your family?*

Iku, ikutsu, and nan usually follow the noun modified, but they may precede it, in which case they are connected to it by the postposition no.

Hako wo ikutsu motte imasu ka? Ikutsu no hako wo motte imasu ka?	*How many boxes have you?*
Empitsu wo nambon motte imasu ka? Nambon no empitsu wo motte imasu ka? Empitsu wo iku hon motte imasu ka? Iku hon no empitsu wo motte imasu ka?	*How many pencils do you have?*

Donna and dō iu mean *what kind of, what sort of.*

Donna mise desu ka? (VIII, 6)	*What sort of shop is it?*
Donna bōshi ga o-nozomi de gozaimasu ka? (X, 22)	*What kind of hat do you desire?*
Dō iu ambai desu ka? (XIII, 42)	*What kind of condition is it?*, i. e., *How is your condition?*
Kotoba wa dō iu imi desu ka? (XVI, 41)	*The word, what kind of meaning is it?*, i. e., *What does the word mean?*

See section 106.

THE SUFFIX tara

74. The verb has a conditional meaning when the suffix **tara** is added. **Tara** is affixed to the continuative stem of the verb (see section 27) and when added to verbs of class II, the same phonetic changes take place as do when **-te** is added to form the gerund (see section 30). The form in -tara expresses the idea of *if* in asking whether something is correct or not; do not confuse with *if* in asking permission (see section 35). It may also express the idea of *when* referring to the future.

Doko de nottara yoroshiū gozaimasu ka? (IX, 16)	*Where is it all right to board?*; i. e., *Where should I board?*
Doko de norikaetara ii ka? (IX, 29)	*Where should I change?*
okutte morattara (IX, 54)	*if I receive (them) sending;* i. e., *if I have them sent*
dempō wo uchimashitara (XIV, 63)	*when I send a telegram*

DIRECT DISCOURSE

75. Japanese employs direct discourse where English has indirect discourse.

Doko de Kyōbashi-yuki e norikaetara ii ka? shashō ni o-kiki nasai (IX, 20)	*Please ask the conductor, "Where should we take the Kyobashi bound car?"*
Itsu dekiru ka? kiite kudasai (XI, 13)	*Please ask, "When will it be ready?"*, i. e., *Please ask when it will be ready.*
Dono yado-ya ga ichiban ii ka? go-zonji desu ka? (XII, 1)	*Which inn is the best? Do you know?*, i. e., *Do you know which inn is the best?*
Dono hen ga ichiban itai n' desu ka? misete kudasai (XIII, 50)	*Which part hurts the most? please show me,* i. e., *Please show me which part hurts the most.*

MORAU

76. The verb **morau** *receive* is used to express English *take* meaning *purchase*. This verb is used for the receiving of the first person. For the second person, the polite form of **toru** is used.

San jū go roppiki moraimashō (VIII, 47)	*I'll take thirty-five or thirty-six (shrimp).*
San mai morau koto ga dekimasu ka? (IX, 49)	*May I take three shirts?*
Bīru wo ni hon moraimashō (XI, 50)	*We'll take two bottles of beer.*
Ryōhō tomo o-tori ni narimasu ka? (X, 37)	*Will you take both?*

After a verb in the **te** form (see section **30**), **morau** indicates that the action of the preceding verb is performed for the sake of the speaker and therefore it is often equivalent to the English *have* or *get a thing done*.

okutte morattara (IX, 54)	*if I have it sent*
Watakushi no tokei wo naoshite moratte . . . (X, 40)	*I (want to) have my watch fixed. . .*
Fuku wo koshiraete moraitai desu (X, 45)	*I want to have a suit made.*
Kogitte wa genkin ni kaete morau koto ga dekimasu ka? (XIV, 5)	*Can you cash a check for me?*

WEAR

77. There are three different ways to express the act of putting on or wearing articles, depending upon how they are worn. **Haku** means *put something on the legs or feet,* **kaburu** *put on the head,* and **kiru** *put on suits, shirts,* etc. Note that the gerund of both **kuru** *come* and **kiru** *put on* is **kite.** The verb **nugu** *take off,* however, may be used of all articles of clothing.

Kore wo haite mite kudasai (X, 5)	*Please try these (shoes) on.*
Bōshi wo kabutte kudasai	*Please put on your hat.*
Uwagi wo kite kudasai	*Please put on your jacket.*
Kutsu wo nuide kudasai	*Please take off your shoes.*

These verbs are compounded with the verb **kaeru** (a first class verb meaning *change,* not to be confused with **kaeru,** a second class verb, meaning *return*) to express the idea of changing wearing apparel.

Kutsu wo hakikaete . . . kudasai (XII, 24)	*Please change your shoes.*
o-kikae ni natte (XII, 51)	*changing your (clothes)*

sugiru

78. The verb **sugiru** *exceed* is added to the stem of adjectives (see section **43**) and to the continuative stem of verbs to express the concept *too much.*

hiro-sugiru (X, 7)	*too wide*
hade-sugiru (X, 50)	*too flashy*
atsu-sugiru (XII, 54)	*too hot*
omo-sugiru (XIV, 49)	*too heavy*
Ano hito wa nomi-sugimasu	*He drinks too much.*

ONLY

79. The postpositions **dake** or **bakari,** replacing either the nominative or accusative postpositions, mean *only, just.* **Shika** may also be so used, but when it is, the verb must be in the negative. **Shika** (not **dake**) is used to mean *only* after a number or a word denoting quantity.

Nakaore-bōshi dake moraimashō (X, 38)   *I'll take the felt hat only.*

Shindai wa ue shika nokotte imasen (XV,   *There do (not) remain butup per berths,*
28)   *i. e., There are only upper berths left.*

hitsuyō na mono bakari (XV, 51)   *just useful things*

TEMPORAL CONJUNCTIONS

80. *Before* indicating a time relation between events is expressed by **mae** or **mae ni,** and the verb preceding it may be in the simple present form (conclusive) whether referring to the present, past, or future, e. g., **kaeru mae ni** (X, 40) *before I return.* **Mae ni** also means *ago,* e. g., **ni shūkan mae ni** *two weeks ago.*

When may be expressed by **toki** followed by **ni** or **de. Toki** *time* or *occasion* is used at the end of a dependent clause, e. g., **o-kane wa dekiagarimashita toki ni, yoroshiū gozaimasu** (X, 63) *as for the money, at the finished time it's all right,* i. e., *You may pay when it is finished.*

After is expressed by the gerundial form of the verb followed by **kara,** e. g., **Tegami wo kaite kara, motte kite kudasai** *After you have written the letter, please bring it to me.*

While or *during* may be expressed by the continuative form of the verb followed by **nagara,** e. g., **Sō ii-nagara, heya kara dete ikimashita.** *While he was saying that, he went out of the room.* However, if the subject of the dependent clause differs from that of the independent clause, the attributive form of the verb followed by **aida ni** is used.

THE VERB oku

81. The verb **oku** *put, place, deposit* following a verb in **-te** means *leave in a state of.*

Uchikin wo okimashō ka? (X, 61)   *Shall I leave a deposit?*

Jū go sen ni shite okimasu (VIII, 53)   *I'll let you have it for fifteen sen.*

Chūmon shite okitai desu (X, 42)   *I want to leave an order.*

Chokin shite okitai n' desu (XIV, 19)   *I want to leave a deposit.*

hai AND iie

82. **Hai** in response to a negative question may often correspond to *no* and **iie** to *yes.* **Hai** then implies *yes, you have said the truth* and **iie,** *no, you have not said it correctly.*

Chūmon shite okitai desu ga kamaimasen   *I want to leave an order, so don't you mind?*
ka? Hai, yoroshiū gozaimasu tomo (X,   *Yes, (you have said it correctly, I don't mind)*
42)   *it's perfectly all right, i.e., No, it's all right.*

THE POSTPOSITION ya

83. The postposition **ya** is used as is **to** (see section 15) to mean *and so forth, and,* or *or.* It usually implies that more than the objects enumerated could be mentioned.

Kutsushita ya zubonshita wo kaimashō   *Let's buy socks and drawers and things of*
(X, 65)   *that kind.*

takusan no hana ya ki (XII, 28)   *many flowers and trees and such*

sekken ya tenugui (XII, 48)   *soap and towels and other such toilet*
                                             articles

mune ya kata ya ude ya (XIII, 48)   *chest and shoulder and arms and so forth*

Both . . . and may be expressed by **mo . . . mo . . .** or by **ya . . . mo** (see section 12), e.g.,

Watakushi wa Furansu go mo Eigo mo wakarimasu *I understand both French and English.*
Hagaki ya kitte mo kaitai desu (XIV, 46) *I want to buy both postcards and stamps.*

RELATIVE CLAUSES

84. As Sansom says (HGJ, p. 81) relative pronouns do not exist in Japanese. Therefore, a whole relative clause such as exists in English will in Japanese modify a following noun. The verb of the clause will usually be in the simple past or present form (the attributive) and will modify the following noun as if the verb were an adjective (see sections 18 and 26). The subject of the verb is usually governed by the postposition ga or no.

The English expression *never to be forgotten* in *He was present at that never to be forgotten event* (used as *that event which is never to be forgotten*) is similar to the Japanese construction.

anata ga hanashite ita hito (XI, 1)   *the you-were-talking-to man, i. e., the man to whom you were talking*

senshū okutta sentaku mono (XI, 4)   *the last-week-sent wash, i. e., the wash which we sent last week*

ni kai ni aru yogorete iru sentaku mono (XI, 7)   *the on-the-second-floor-soiled laundry, i. e., the soiled laundry which is upstairs*

takusan no yūmei na hito ga yoku yuku ryōriya (XI, 26)   *a many-famous-people-often-go restaurant, i. e., a restaurant to which many famous people often go*

tomodachi ga watakushi ni tegami de hana-shita ryōriya (XI, 31)   *my-friend-to-me-in-a-letter-spoken restaurant, i. e., a restaurant which my friend wrote to me about*

michi ni mukatte i-nai heya (XII, 20)   *a-not-facing-the-street room, i. e., a room which does not face the street*

Burajiru ni iru ototo (XIV, 30)   *my-is-in-Brazil-younger-brother, i. e., my younger brother who is in Brazil*

Watakushi no sunde iru ie wa ginkō no soba ni arimasu.   *The house in which I live is near the bank.*

A noun followed by no or na (see section 43) may form an adjectival subordinate phrase, e. g., kono Kōbe-yuki no tegami (XIV, 48) *this-going-to-Kobe letter, i. e., this letter which is going to Kobe.*

iru be necessary

85. The verb iru *be necessary* is a verb of the second class and consequently the **r** appears in the continuative form (see sections 26, 27 and 116). This verb should not be confused with iru *be*, a verb of the first class, the continuative stem of which is i.

The verb iru corresponds more to *be necessary* than *need* and consequently the object needed is followed by ga or wa. If the person who needs the object is expressed, the person is followed by ga or wa also. When both the person who needs something and the object needed are expressed, the one emphasized takes ga and the other wa (see section 5).

Shatsu ga shi-go mai irimasu (IX, 7)   *I need four or five shirts.*
Watakushi wa kane ga hyaku yen irimasu   *I need one hundred yen.*

GIVE

86. There are several verbs which express the concept of giving. Different verbs are employed according to the social status of the donor and the recipient. However, the verb

watasu *hand over* may be used to express the giving of anyone to anyone else, but this verb, as its meaning indicates, does not necessarily imply donation, e. g., **Sentaku mono wo watashite kudasai** (XI, 7) *Please give him the laundry.*

Ageru and, in very polite speech, **sashiageru** are used for the giving of the first person or of the giving of the second person to the third person or the third to the second person. **Ageru** means *raise up* (see section **91**) and therefore its use by the first person indicates humility or politeness (compare section **41**). If preceded by a gerund **ageru** indicates that the action of the preceding verb is performed in favor of someone else, i. e., for his benefit, and in this usage it is the opposite of **morau** (see section **76**).

Nani wo sashiagemashō ka? (XI, 41)	*What may I give you?*, i. e., *What can I do for you?*
Kusuri wo agemasu (XIII, 61)	*I'll give you some medicine.*
Sugu itte mite agemashō (XIII, 40)	*I'll try to come soon for your sake.*
Hakatte mite agemashō (XIV, 51)	*I'll see how much it weighs for you, i. e., I'll weigh it for you.*

Kudasaru or **kureru** is used of the giving of the second or third person to the first person (see section **32**). **Kudasaru** is more polite than **kureru**.

Ni hon kudasai (VIII, 5)	*Please give me two loaves.*
watakushi ni kozutsumi wo okutte kureta hito (XI, 37)	*the man who sent and gave the package to me, i. e., the man who gave me the package*

The verb **negau** *request* (see section **40**) may be used as is *please give me, please let me have* in English.

Sukiyaki wo futari mae negaimasu (XI, 43)	*We request two portions of sukiyaki, i. e., Please give us two portions of sukiyaki.*
Budōshu mo ippon negaimasu (XI, 51)	*I request a bottle of beer also, i. e., I'd like a bottle of beer also.*
Sangai no hō wo negaimasu (XII, 19)	*I'd like to have one on the third floor.*

When the person who is giving is in a superior position, the verb **yaru** is used. Thus the father says of his giving to his son **Kane wo okutte yarō to omotte iru tokoro desu** (XIV, 31) *I am thinking of giving him some money by sending, i. e., I am thinking of sending him some money.*

mō

87. Before a numeral **mō** is used to indicate *more, in addition*, e. g., **Mizu wo mō ni hai motte kite kudasai** (XI, 61) *Please bring us two more glasses of water.* (See section **47**.)

yo

88. **Yo** is an interjection added to a verb at the end of a sentence to emphasize the truth of the statement.

O-tsuri wa anata e no kokorozashi desu yo (XI, 65)	*The change is a tip for you!*
Ima iremasu yo (XIII, 22)	*I'm putting it in now, i. e., Here it goes!*

CONDITIONAL

89. The conditional may be formed by placing **nareba** or **naraba** *if it is* after the verb. The negative conditional may be formed in the same manner, except that the negative form of the verb is used and is followed by **nakereba** or **nai nareba** (see sectlon 57). The noun form of the verb followed by **de nakereba** may also be employed. The word **moshi** *if* may be used or it may be omitted at the beginning of the clause. The *if* clause always precedes the result clause, and the subject of the *if* clause is usually governed by the postposition **ga**.

moshi anata ga seiyō fū no hoteru ga o-suki nareba (XII, 4)	*if you would like a western style hotel*
moshi anata ga seiyō fū no yado-ya wo o-konomi de nakereba (XII, 6)	*if you don't like a western style inn*
moshi o-tsukare nareba (XII, 48)	*if you are tired*
takushi de oide ni nareba (XII, 11)	*if you go by taxi*

The ending **ba** may be omitted in **naraba** giving the word **nara** *if, if it is, in case.*

isshūkan nara (XII, 36)	*if one week*
sayō-nara (VI, 60)	*if it is so (then, unfortunately it must be),* i. e., *goodbye*

Nareba is composed of the perfect of **naru**, that is, **nare** plus the voiced form of **wa**. (**Wa** is written **ha** in the Japanese syllabaries; see section 61.) The conditional of verbs may be formed (in addition to the way shown above) by changing the final **u** of the conclusive form to the perfect ending **e** and adding **ba**, e. g., **ikeba** *if I go;* **yomeba** *if I read;* **mireba** *if I see;* **tabereba** *if I eat;* **sureba** (XIII, 63) *if you do;* **koseba** (XVI, 9) *if one crosses.* However, the conditional of the ending **masu** is **masureba**.

Historically, the perfect termination may be **re** rather than **e**, coming from the verb **aru** *be*, but the development is very obscure (see HGJ, p. 143).

The negative base plus **ba** is used only in **nara(ba)**. In the spoken language this is a somewhat isolated form. In the literary style, however, the conditional is expressed by the negative base and not by the perfect base. The perfect in the literary style expresses a realized or assumed condition which may be rendered by *since, as, when,* etc., but in the colloquial the perfect plus **ba** serves both uses and the negative base hardly appears in forming the conditional (see HGJ, p. 197-198).

See sections 116 and 117.

POTENTIAL

90. Many second class transitive verbs are made into first class verbs by adding **eru** *get, acquire, be able* to the base, i. e., to the conclusive form without the final **u** (verbs ending in **tsu** drop the **su**). Verbs so made are intransitive and potential. What in English is the object of a potential verb is in Japanese governed by **ga**. First class verbs in **-eru** have no potential form and to express ability they may be used with **dekiru** (see section 25) or in the passive (see section 92). Nevertheless, **mieru** is formed from the negative stem of **miru** plus **eru**.

toru	*take*
toreru	*be able to take*
toremashō (XII, 47)	*can take*
mairu	*go*
maireru	*be able to go*
mairemashō (XII, 13)	*can probably go*
however, **miru** (first class verb)	*see*
mieru (XII, 11)	*can see*
miemasu (XII, 29)	*can see*

Kanda eki kara noremasu ka? (XV, 15)	*Can I take it from the Kanda station?*
Furo ga toremashō ka? (XII, 47)	*Can I take a bath?*

TRANSITIVE AND INTRANSITIVE VERBS

91. Some intransitive verbs of the second class have corresponding transitive verbs of the first class formed by adding **eru** *get, acquire* to the base (see section **90**).

aku	*be open* (intransitive)
akeru	*open* (transitive)
Daidokoro wa mada aite imasu ka? (XII, 43)	*Is the kitchen still open?*
Mado wo akete mo ii n' desu ka? (V, 27)	*May I open the window?*
shimaru	*be closed, shut* (intransitive)
shimeru	*close, shut* (transitive)
Ima wa mō shimatte imasu (XII, 44)	*It's already closed.*
To wo shimete wa ikemasen (V, 28)	*You must not close the door.*
agaru	*go up*
ageru	*give* (literally, *raise to a high personage*)
O-agari kudasai (XII, 25)	*Please go up.*
Kusuri wo agemasu (XIII, 61)	*I'll give you medicine.*
kakaru	*hang* (intransitive)
kakeru	*hang* (transitive)
Hajimete o-me ni kakarimasu (VI, 12)	*For the first time I hang on your honorable eyes,* i. e., *I'm glad to meet you.*
Ima o-me ni kakemasu (XII, 23)	*Now I'll hang it on your honorable eyes,* i. e., *Now I'll show it to you.*

PASSIVE FORM OF THE VERB

92. The passive voice is formed by adding **areru** to the base (the conclusive without the final u) of both classes of verbs. Verbs ending in **tsu,** however, drop the **su,** and verbs ending in a vowel plus u change the **u** to **w** before adding **areru** (compare section **56**). This **-areru** is probably the verb **aru** *be* plus the verb **eru** *get* (see HGJ, p. 160, 161). These passive verbs may have the same tense endings as their active forms.

kowasu	*break*
kowasareru	*be broken*
Kusuri no bin wa kowasaremashita ka? (XIII, 1)	*Was the medicine bottle broken?*
taberu	*eat*
taberareru	*be eaten*
Ano niku wa imōto ni taberaremashita	*That meat was eaten by my younger sister.*
Sekai ni shirarete imasu (XVI, 35)	*It is known throughout the world.*

Some grammarians give the passive endings **rareru** for the first class verbs and **reru** for second class verbs, these endings being added to the negative stem.

The passive form has other uses besides expressing passive voice. Probably because of the presence of **eru** *get, obtain,* it has a potential use also (see HGJ, p. 161). Most of the examples cited below show this potential use because the passive voice is not much used in Japanese and an active construction is usually preferable especially when speaking of inanimate objects.

neru	*sleep*
nerareru	*be able to sleep*
Neraremasen deshita (XIII, 44)	*I couldn't sleep.*
okiru	*get up, rise*
okirareru	*be able to get up*
Nedoko kara okiraremasen (XIII, 45)	*I can't get out of bed.*
Amari takai tatemono wa tateraremasen (XVI, 27)	*Very high buildings can't be built.*

Mitsukaru *be discovered, be found* is compounded from **miru** *see* and **tsuku** *apply*. **Mitsukeru** is its transitive form (see section **91**).

| Denwachō ga mitsukaremasen (XIII, 6) | *I can't find the phone book.* |

The verb **suru** *do* forms its passive from its classical form **su**, thus **sareru**. The passive of **kuru** is **korareru**. In Japanese intransitive verbs may have passive forms and verbs in the passive can have an object governed by **wo**.

| Tennin sareru sō desu (XIV, 37) | *I hear he was done a transfer,* i. e., *I hear he was transferred.* |
| Dō sareta n' deshō ka? (XIII, 6) | *How was probably done with it?,* i. e., *What became of it?* |

The person or thing that receives or suffers the action of a passive verb is governed by the postposition **wa** or **ga**, and the person or thing by whom or by which someone receives or suffers the action of the passive verb is governed by the postposition **ni** or **kara**.

Bin wa kowasaremashita (XIII, 1)	*The bottle was broken.*
Denwachō ga mitsukaremasen (XIII, 6)	*I can't find the telephone book.*
(Watakushi wa) neraremasen deshita (XIII, 44)	*I could not sleep.*
Heishi ga shikan ni miraremashita	*The soldier was seen by the officer.*

The passive form may be used without expressing the passive voice or the potential at all, but simply to make a verb more polite and formal. Sansom says (HGJ, p. 163), "This usually is explained as an extension of the 'potential' significance of these forms, it being thought more respectful to say that a superior person is able to do a thing if he chooses than that he actually condescends to do it." When the verb is so used, the subjects and objects are governed by the same postpositions as would govern them if the verb were in the active form, e. g., **Ano yūmei na hito wa kono hon wo kakaremashita.** *That famous man wrote this book.*

Although in English only transitive verbs can be made passive, in Japanese intransitive verbs also may be made passive. The meaning of the verb is then to have something done or get something done to one; e.g., **Watakushi wa tokei wo nusumaremashita.** *I had my watch stolen.* Nusumu is *steal,* **nusumareru** *be stolen,* so that the above sentence is literally *I was stolen a watch* (see HGJ, p. 160).

CAUSATIVE FORM OF THE VERB

93. A verb is made causative by affixing **saseru** to the negative stem (see section **56**) of verbs of the first class and **seru** to that of verbs of the second class. The person who is made to do or let do something is governed by the postposition **ni**.

| Ane San ni denwa wo kakesasete kudasai (XIII, 10) | *Please cause telephoning by my elder sister,* i. e., *Please have my elder sister phone.* |
| Watakushi ni hanasasete kudasai (XIII, 30) | *Please cause talking by me,* i. e., *Please let me talk.* |

A passive causative is formed by the addition of **sareru,** the passive of **suru** (see section

92), to the negative stem, e. g., **nomu** *drink,* **nomaseru** *cause to drink,* **nomareru** *be drunk,* **nomasareru** *be caused to drink.*

Ane San ni ano kusuri wo nomasarema- **shita** (XIII, 46)	*I was caused to drink that medicine by my elder sister,* i. e., *I was made to drink that medicine by my elder sister.*

Sansom says of the origin of the causative ending, "There can be little doubt that -su is cognate with the verb su-ru 'to do,' but it is not quite clear how verbs like yukasu have come to bear their present meanings. In the very earliest writings the suffix -su seems to have an honorific and not a causative force." (HGJ, p. 164.)

THE SUFFIX ju

94. The suffix **jū,** usually added to words of native origin, means *through, throughout, in the course of, the whole.*

hitoban-jū (XIII, 12)	*throughout the whole night*
karada-jū (XIII, 48)	*throughout my whole body*

no ni

95. No ni after verbs in the past form indicates the concessive *although, in spite of,* e. g., **Kaze wo hiite ita no ni** (XIII, 59) *although (in spite of the fact that) you had a cold.*

THE PRESENT TENSE TO INDICATE FUTURE TIME

96. The present tense is often used to indicate an action which is to happen in the future.

Motte o-kaeri ni narimasu ka? (IX, 52)	*Do you take it with you? Are you going to take it back with you?,* i. e., *Will you take it with you?*
Raishū made ni wa kari-nui ga dekimasu (X, 59)	*The preliminary sewing will be done by next week.*
Itsu dekiru ka kiite kudasai (XI, 13)	*Please ask when it will be done.*
Toranku wo azukete kimasu (XV, 37)	*I'll check the trunk.*

The present is used where English has the perfect to express an action begun in the past and which is still going on, e. g., **Ni-san ka getsu Burajiru ni imasu** (XIV, 36) *He has been in Brazil for two or three months.*

THE VERB shimau

97. Shimau after verbs in the gerundial form indicates the final completion of the action expressed by the gerund, e. g., **Kyō no yōji wa sunde shimaimasu.** (XIV, 64) *The business for to-day is all finished.*

The past of shimau is often used after the gerund to indicate a past perfect, e. g., **Ano hito ga kimashita mae ni Matsumoto San wa dekakete shimaimashita** *Before he came, Mr. Matsumoto had left.*

WITHOUT

98. The idea of *without* before verbs in English may be expressed in Japanese by the suffix **zu** added to the negative stem of verbs (see section **56**). This form in **-zu** is usually followed by the postposition **ni**.

you	*be seasick, be drunk*

yowazu ni (XV, 58)	*without being seasick*
au	*meet*
awazu ni (XV, 61)	*without meeting*
ai (continuative stem of au) plus kawaru *change, transform*	
aikawarazu (II, 3)	*without change*

THE VERB au

99. The verb au *meet* requires the thing or person encountered to be governed by the postposition ni, e. g., **nami ni wa awazu ni** (XV, 61) *without meeting any waves.*

STEREOTYPED EXPRESSIONS

100. There are some verbal expressions which often are used as postpositions are. Thus, *on, about,* meaning *in reference to* or *concerning* is expressed by **ni tsuite.** As tsuite is the gerundial form of **tsuku** meaning both *adhere* and *follow,* ni tsuite may also mean *following* (see section 37).

Nippon no koto ni tsuite (XVI, 2)	*concerning Japanese things*
Tōkiō ni tsuite (XVI, 24)	*following Tokio*

Two other expressions of this type are **to shite** *concerning, by way of* and **(ni) itaru made** *up to, down to, until.*

omo na sambutsu to shite (XVI, 34)	*concerning the principal product,* i. e., *as its principal product*
daigaku ni itaru made (XVI, 46)	*up to arrival at the university,* i. e., *up to the university*

THE PREFIX ma

101. The prefix **ma** meaning *truth* is placed before the stem of an adjective (see section **43**) to indicate *very* or *truly.* When used with adjectives denoting color, it often means *pure* or *bright.* An initial consonant of a word to which **ma** is prefixed is lengthened. **Ma** is added to the noun **naka** *inside, interior* to mean *the very center.*

masshiroi	*pure white, snow white*
makkuroi	*pitch black*
mannaka (XVI, 17)	*the very center*

THE FORMER, THE LATTER

102. When referring to two subjects previously mentioned, it is understood that the first statement made refers to the former one and the second statement to the latter one. Thus it is clear that **mottomo yūmei na no** (XVI, 30) *the most famous one* refers to mountains and not to rivers.

THE SUFFIX rashii

103. The adjectival suffix **rashii** is added to the conclusive form of verbs, the stem of adjectives (see section **43**), and to nouns to mean *appearance, likelihood,* or *probability.* With adjectives it often has the force of the suffix *ish* in English.

asonde iru-rashii (XVI, 52)	*most likely play*
bakarashii (baka *fool* plus rashii)	*foolish*
otoko-rashii	*manly*

104. PERSONAL PRONOUNS

	SINGULAR	PLURAL	
FIRST PERSON	watakushi watashi washi boku (used by young men in familiar speech)	watakushidomo watashidomo ware-ware (familiar)	watakushitachi watashitachi bokura bokutachi
SECOND PERSON	anata . omae (not very polite) kimi (used by young men in familiar speech to other young men)	anatagata anatatachi kimira kimitachi	

THIRD PERSON	ano (kono, sono) kata
	  ano otoko no kata (M)
	  ano onna no kata (F)
	ano (kono, sono) hito
	  ano otoko no hito (M)
	  ano onna no hito (F)
	ano ko (youth)
	  ano otoko no ko (M)
	  ano onna no ko (F)
	ano otoko (M)
	ano onna (F)
	ano fujin (F)
	ano ojōsan (youth) (F)
	kare (M or F)
		ano (kono, sono) katatachi (katagata)
		  ano otoko no katatachi (M)
		  ano onna no katatachi (F)
		ano (kono, sono) hitotachi
		  ano otoko no hitotachi (M)
		  ano onna no hitotachi (F)
		
		karera (M or F) (M and F)	

105. DEMONSTRATIVES

ADJECTIVES			
kono kochi(ra) no }*this, these*		konna kō iu }*this kind of*	
sono sochi(ra) no }*that, those*		sonna sō iu }*that kind of*	
ano achi(ra) no }*that, those*		anna ā iu }*that kind of, such as that*	

PRONOUNS		ADVERBS	
kore kochi(ra) }*this, this one*	kō konna ni }*like this, thus*	koko kochi(ra) }*here*	
sore sochi(ra) }*that, that one*	sō sonna ni }*like that, thus*	soko sochi(ra) }*there*	
are achi(ra) }*that, that one*	ā anna ni }*like that, thus*	asoko achi(ra) }*there*	

106. INTERROGATIVE AND INDEFINITE PRONOUNS, ADJECTIVES, AND ADVERBS

INTERROGATIVE	INDEFINITE	NEGATIVE OR INCLUSIVE	ADJECTIVAL OR POSSESSIVE
dare *who*	**dare ka** *someone or other* **dare de mo** *anybody, everybody*	**dare mo** (with negative verb) *nobody*	**dare no** *whose*
donata *who* (polite)	**donata ka** **donata de mo**	**donata mo**	**donata no**
dō *how*	**dō ka** *somehow or other* **dō de mo** *anyhow*	**dō mo** *somehow*	**dō iu** *which*
doko *where*	**doko ka** *somewhere or other* **doko de mo** *anywhere, everywhere*	**doko mo** (with neg. verb) *nowhere*	**doko no** *which*
dochi(ra) *where, which*	**dochi ka** *one or the other* **dochi de mo** *anywhere, anyone*	**dochi mo** *both,* (with negative verb) *neither*	**dochira no** *which*
dore *which*	**dore ka** *one or another, something* **dore de mo** *either one, anyone*	**dore mo** *everyone,* (with negative verb) *none*	**dono** *which* **donna** *what kind of*
nani *what*	**nani ka** *something or other* **nani de mo** *anything, everything*	**nani mo** (with negative verb) *nothing*	**nan no** *what kind of*
iku}*how many* **nan**}	**nani ka** *something or other* **iku de mo**}*any number whatever* **nan de mo**}	**nan mo** *any number*	
ikura *how much*	**ikura ka** *a certain amount* **ikura de mo** *any amount whatever*	**ikura mo** *any amount*	**ikura no** *how much*
ikutsu *how many*	**ikutsu de mo** *any number whatever*	**ikutsu mo** *any number*	**ikutsu no** *how many*
itsu *when*	**itsu ka** *some time or other* **itsu de mo** *any time whatever, always*	**itsu mo** *any time, always*	**itsu no** *of when, of what date*

107. PRINCIPAL PARTS OF ADJECTIVES

ADJECTIVE	STEM	ATTRIBUTIVE	PREDICATE
chiisai *small*	chiisa	chiisai chiisa na	chiisai (affirmative) chiisaku (negative)*
ōkii *large*	ōki	ōkii ōki na	ōkii (affirmative) ōkiku (negative)*
yoi *good*	yo	yoi yo na	yoi (affirmative) yoku (negative)*
atsui *hot*	atsu	atsui atsu na	atsui (affirmative) atsuku (negative)*

* Also used affirmatively as predicate of verbs other than desu and gozaru.

108. TENSE AND MOOD OF ADJECTIVES

	PRESENT	PROBABLE PRESENT AND FUTURE	PAST
AFFIRMATIVE	chiisai *small*	chiisai{ deshō / darō chiisakarō	chiisakatta
NEGATIVE	chiisaku{ nai / arimasen	chiisaku{ nai deshō / nai darō / nakarō / arumai †	chiisaku nakatta
AFFIRMATIVE	ōkii *large*	ōkii{ deshō / darō ōkikarō	ōkikatta
NEGATIVE	ōkiku{ nai / arimasen	ōkiku{ nai deshō / nai darō / nakarō / arumai	ōkiku nakatta
AFFIRMATIVE	yoi *good*	yoi{ deshō / darō yokarō	yokatta
NEGATIVE	yoku{ nai / arimasen	yoku{ nai deshō / nai darō / nakarō / arumai	yoku nakatta
AFFIRMATIVE	atsui *hot*	atsui{ deshō / darō atsukarō	atsukatta
NEGATIVE	atsuku{ nai / arimasen	atsuku{ nai deshō / nai darō / nakarō / arumai	atsuku nakatta

† See footnote‡, p. 191.

PREDICATE WITH gozaru	ADVERBIAL FORM
chiisō (affirmative or negative)	chiisaku
ōkiū	ōkiku
yō	yoku *well*
atsū	atsuku

PROBABLE PAST	CONDITIONAL PRESENT	CONDITIONAL PAST	GERUND
chiisakattarō chiisakatta {deshō / darō}	chiisakereba chiisai nara(ba)	chiisakattara	chiisakute chiisakutte*
chiisaku nakattarō chiisaku nakatta {deshō / darō}	chiisaku nakereba chiisaku nai nara(ba)	chiisaku {nakattara / arimasen deshitara}	chiisaku nakute chiisaku nakutte*
ōkikattarō ōkikatta {deshō / darō}	ōkikereba ōkii nara(ba)	ōkikattara	ōkikute ōkikutte*
ōkiku nakattarō ōkiku nakatta {deshō / darō}	ōkiku nakereba ōkiku nai nara(ba)	ōkiku {nakattara / arimasen deshitara}	ōkiku nakute ōkiku nakutte*
yokattarō yokatta {deshō / darō}	yokereba yoi nara(ba)	yokattara	yokute yokutte*
yoku nakattarō yoku nakatta {deshō / darō}	yoku nakereba yoku nai nara(ba)	yoku {nakattara / arimasen deshitara}	yoku nakute yoku nakutte*
atsukattarō atsukatta {deshō / darō}	atsukereba atsui nara(ba)	atsukattara	atsukute atsukutte*
atsuku nakattarō atsuku nakatta {deshō / darō}	atsuku nakereba atsuku nai nara(ba)	atsuku {nakattara / arimasen deshitara}	atsuku nakute atsuku nakutte*

* Colloquial.

109. PLAIN AND POLITE VERBS

	PLAIN OR HUMBLE VERBS		POLITE AND HONORIFIC VERBS
be	iru oru	~	o-ide nasaru* irassharu
come	agaru mairu† kuru	~	o-ide nasaru‡ irassharu‡
do	itasu† suru		nasaru
drink	itadaku† chōdai suru† nomu	~	meshi-agaru agaru
eat	itadaku† chōdai suru† taberu kuu (among friends)	~	meshi-agaru agaru
give	ageru yaru (to an inferior)		kudasaru } (to the first person) kureru o-yari nasaru (not to the first person)
go	mairu† iku	~	o-ide nasaru‡ irassharu‡

inquire	tazuneru kiku	⎰ o-tazune nasaru ⎱ o-kiki nasaru
know	zonjiru† shiru	⎰ go-zonji ⎰de gozaru ⎱ ⎱de aru desu
meet	o-me ni kakaru† au	⎰ o-ai nasaru
receive	itadaku† chōdai suru† morau ukeru (catch) uketoru	⎰ o-morai nasaru§
see or look	haiken suru† miru	⎰ goran nasaru
show	o-me ni kakeru† miseru	⎰ o-mise ⎱nasaru (to me) ⎰kudasaru (to me) haiken saseru (to me)
speak	mōsu mōshi-ageru† hanasu iu	⎰ mōsu ossharu
visit	agaru tazuneru ukagau†	⎰ o-tazune nasaru

* The verb forms ni naru, de gozaru, de aru, or desu as well as nasaru may be used after the noun form of the verb.
† Humble.
‡ Used with kara means *come*; used with e means *go*.
§ Mostly used to mean *receive as a gift or purchase*. Uketoru is used for *receiving otherwise*.

110. NUMERALS

CARDINAL NUMERALS OF CHINESE ORIGIN.

1. ichi	11. jū ichi	21. ni jū ichi
2. ni	12. jū ni	22. ni jū ni
3. san	13. jū san	23. ni jū san
4. shi (yo or yon)	14. jū shi	24. ni jū shi
5. go	15. jū go	25. ni jū go
6. roku	16. jū roku	26. ni jū roku
7. hichi (or shichi)	17. jū hichi	27. ni jū hichi
8. hachi	18. jū hachi	28. ni jū hachi
9. ku	19. jū ku	29. ni jū ku

33. san jū san		
44. shi jū shi		
55. go jū go		
66. roku jū roku		
78. hichi jū hachi		
89. hachi jū ku		

10. jū	20. ni jū	30. san jū
50. go jū	60. roku jū	70. hichi jū
90. ku jū		

40. shi jū (or yon jū)	
80. hachi jū	

100. hyaku	101. hyaku ichi	102. hyaku ni
200. ni hyaku	254. ni hyaku go jū shi	
300. sambyaku		
400. shi hyaku		
500. go hyaku		
600. roppyaku		
700. hichi hyaku		
800. happyaku		
900. ku hyaku		

1000	sen
2000	ni sen
3000	san zen
4000	shi sen
5000	go sen
6000	roku sen
7000	hichi sen
8000	hachi sen
9000	ku sen
10,000	ichi man
20,000	ni man
100,000	jū man
1,000,000	hyaku man
100,000,000	oku
0	rei

CARDINAL NUMBERS OF NATIVE ORIGIN

1. hitotsu 2. futatsu 3. mittsu (or **mitsu**) 4. yottsu (or **yotsu**) 5. itsutsu 6. muttsu (or **mutsu**) 7. nanatsu 8. yattsu (or **yatsu**) 9. kokonotsu 10. tō

ORDINAL NUMBERS

first ichiban hajime no		ichiban hajime no
second ni bamme		futatsu me
third sam bamme		mittsu me
fourth yo bamme		yottsu me
fifth go bamme		itsutsu me
sixth roku bamme		muttsu me
seventh hichi bamme		nanatsu me
eighth hachi bamme		yattsu me
ninth ku bamme		kokonotsu me
tenth jū bamme		tō me

eleventh   jū ichi bamme
twelfth   jū ni bamme
thirteenth jū sam bamme
etc.
twentieth   ni jū bamme

FRACTIONS

$\frac{1}{2}$ hambun $\frac{3}{4}$ sam bun no shi
$\frac{1}{4}$ shi bun no ichi $\frac{3}{30}$ san jū bun no san

PERCENTAGE

The Japanese often compute *per ten* instead of *per hundred*. Ichi wari is *one per ten*, ni wari *two per ten*, etc. A tenth of a wari is called a bu and it corresponds therefore to per cent. Thus ichi bu is 1%, ni bu 2%, etc.

111. FREQUENTLY USED NUMERAL AUXILIARIES

chō for things with handles such as knives, tools, etc.

dai for vehicles

fuku for whiffs of tobacco or packages of medicine

hai glassfuls, cupfuls

hiki for animals

hon for long narrow objects such as pencils, pens, bottles, etc.

ken for houses and buildings

ko (ka) for various things having no special numeral auxiliary such as bundles, parcels, etc.

mai for flat things such as shirts, sheets, blankets, etc.

nin for people

satsu for books, magazines, etc.

sō for boats and ships

soku for footwear that come in pairs such as boots, shoes, socks, etc.

tsui for things that come in pairs such as vases

wa for birds

112. PHONETIC CHANGES OF NUMERAL AND NUMERAL AUXILIARY

	before ch or t **	before f or h* (or w)	before k†	before m or b	before s or sh‡
ichi *one*	it	ip	ik		is
san *three* **sen** *thousand*		sam sem		sam sem	
roku *six* **hyaku** *hundred*		rop hyap	rok hyak		
hachi *eight*	hat		hak (*infrequent*)		has
jū *ten*	jit	jip	jik		jis

* The f or h of the auxiliary becomes **p**, but after **san** or **sen** it usually becomes **b**.
** Before ts, ichi becomes **i**.
† The **k** of the auxiliary generally becomes **g** after **san** or **sen**.
‡ The **s** of the auxiliary usually becomes **z**, and **sh** becomes **j** after **san** or **sen**.

113. DAYS OF THE WEEK AND OF THE MONTH

Sunday	**Nichiyōbi**	(sun day)	*Thursday*	**Mokuyōbi**	(tree day)
Monday	**Getsuyōbi**	(moon day)	*Friday*	**Kinyōbi**	(metal day)
Tuesday	**K(w)ayōbi**	(fire day)	*Saturday*	**Doyōbi**	(earth day)
Wednesday	**Suiyōbi**	(water day)			

1st	tsuitachi	*11th*	jū ichi nichi	*21st*	ni jū ichi nichi
2nd	futsuka	*12th*	jū ni nichi	*22nd*	ni jū ni nichi
3rd	mikka	*13th*	jū san nichi	*23rd*	ni jū san nichi
4th	yokka	*14th*	jū yokka	*24th*	ni jū yokka
5th	itsuka	*15th*	jū go nichi	*25th*	ni jū go nichi
6th	muika	*16th*	jū roku nichi	*26th*	ni jū roku nichi
7th	nanuka	*17th*	jū hichi nichi	*27th*	ni jū hichi nichi
8th	yōka	*18th*	jū hachi nichi	*28th*	ni jū hachi nichi
9th	kokonoka	*19th*	jū ku nichi	*29th*	ni jū ku nichi
10th	tōka	*20th*	hatsuka or ni jū nichi	*30th*	san jū nichi
				31st	san jū ichi nichi

The word **misoka** is used for *the last day of the month* whether it be the thirtieth, thirty-first, twenty-eighth or twenty-ninth. The last day of the year is called **ō-misoka.** The days of the month with the exception of **tsuitachi** are used also to mean *one day, two days, twenty-five days,* etc. Thus **jū ichi nichi** means *eleven days* as well as *the eleventh day,* **futsuka** means *two days* as well as *the second of the month,* and **ni jū go nichi** means either *the twenty-fifth* or *twenty-five days.* Ichi nichi is used for *one day.*

Not referring to the day of the month, *the first day, second day,* etc. are **ichi bamme no hi, ni bamme no hi,** etc.; *the first month, the second month,* etc. are **ichi bamme no tsuki, ni bamme no tsuki,** etc., and *the first year, the second year,* etc. not referring to dates are **ichi bamme no toshi, ni bamme no toshi,** etc., e.g., **watakushi no byōki no hichi bamme no hi** *the seventh day of my illness.*

The first year of a year period is usually called **gannen.**

114. MONTHS OF THE YEAR AND PERIODS OF MONTHS

January	Ichi gatsu or Shōgatsu	*one month*	ikka getsu or	hito tsuki
February	Ni gatsu	*two months*	ni ka getsu	futa tsuki
March	San gatsu	*three months*	san ka getsu	mi tsuki
April	Shi gatsu	*four months*	shi ka getsu	yo tsuki
May	Go gatsu	*five months*	go ka getsu	itsu tsuki
June	Roku gatsu	*six months*	rokka getsu	mu tsuki
July	Hichi gatsu	*seven months*	hichi ka getsu	nana tsuki
August	Hachi gatsu	*eight months*	hakka getsu	ya tsuki
September	Ku gatsu	*nine months*	ku ka getsu	kokono tsuki
October	Jū gatsu	*ten months*	jikka getsu	tō tsuki
November	Jū ichi gatsu	*eleven months*	jū ikka getsu	
December	Jū ni gatsu	*twelve months*	jū ni ka getsu	
		twenty-five months	ni jū go ka getsu	
		etc.		

115. YEAR PERIODS AND PERIODS OF YEARS

Meiji	*1868–1912*	*one year*	ichi nen or	ikka nen
Taishō	*1912–1926*	*two years*	ni nen	ni ka nen
Shōwa	*1926 to the present*	*three years*	san nen	san ka nen
		twenty-five years	ni jū go nen	ni jū go ka nen
		etc.		

116. PRINCIPAL PARTS OF VERBS

IRREGULAR VERBS **kuru** AND **suru**

	kuru	suru
CONCLUSIVE, ATTRIBUTIVE, AND SIMPLE PRESENT	kuru	suru
CONTINUATIVE STEM	ki	shi
GERUND	kite	shite
NEGATIVE STEM	ko or ki	se or shi

FIRST CLASS

	-eru	-iru
CONCLUSIVE, ATTRIBUTIVE, AND SIMPLE PRESENT	taberu	miru
CONTINUATIVE AND NEGATIVE STEM; NOUN FORM	tabe	mi
GERUND	tabete	mite

SECOND CLASS

	*au	**bu	†gu	*iu	†ku	**mu	**nu	*ou	ru	su	tsu	*uu
CONCLUSIVE, ATTRIVUTIVE, AND SIMPLE PRESENT	harau	yobu	nugu	iu	kaku	yomu	shinu	omou	naru kaeru (return) shiru noru uru	hanasu	motsu	suu
CONTINUATIVE STEM	harai	yobi	nugi	ii	kaki	yomi	shini	omoi	nari kaeri shiri nori uri	hanashi	mochi	sui
GERUND	haratte	yonde	nuide	itte	kaite	yonde	shinde	omotte	natte kaette shifte notte utte	hanashite	motte	sutte
NEGATIVE STEM	harawa	yoba	nuga	iwa	kaka	yoma	shina	omowa	nara kaera shira nora ura	hanasa	mota	suwa

*, **, and † indicate that the verbs so marked are related in form; i. e., verbs with a vowel before the u ending are marked with one asterisk because their gerund and negative forms are similarly formed; verbs marked with a double asterisk show a nasal sound in the gerund, etc.

117. TENSE, MOOD, AND VOICE OF VERBS

FIRST CLASS VERBS
ACTIVE VOICE

			tabERU		mIRU	
			AFFIRMATIVE	NEGATIVE	AFFIRMATIVE	NEGATIVE
PRESENT	SIMPLE FORM	GENERAL	taberu	tabe-nai	miru	mi-nai
		PROGRESSIVE	tabete iru	tabete i-nai	mite iru	mite i-nai
	POLITE FORM	GENERAL	tabemasu	tabemasen	mimasu	mimasen
		PROGRESSIVE	tabete imasu*	tabete imasen	mite imasu*	mite imasen
PROBABLE PRESENT AND FUTURE	SIMPLE FORM	GENERAL	tabeyō / taberu deshō†	tabe-mai† / tabe-nai deshō	miyō / miru deshō†	mi-mai† / mi-nai deshō
		PROGRESSIVE	tabete iru deshō	tabete i-nai deshō	mite iru deshō	mite i-nai deshō
	POLITE FORM	GENERAL	tabemashō** / tabemasu deshō	tabemasu-mai / tabemasen deshō	mimashō** / mimasu deshō	mimasu-mai** / mimasen deshō
		PROGRESSIVE	tabete imashō	tabete imasu-mai	mite imashō	mite imasu-mai
PAST*	SIMPLE FORM	GENERAL	tabeta	tabe-nakatta	mita	mi-nakatta
		PROGRESSIVE	tabete ita	tabete i-nakatta	mite ita	mite i-nakatta
	POLITE FORM	GENERAL	tabemashita	tabemasen deshita	mimashita	mimasen deshita
		PROGRESSIVE	tabete imashita	tabete imasen deshita	mite imashita	mite imasen deshita
PROBABLE PAST	SIMPLE FORM	GENERAL	tabetarō / tabeta deshō	tabe-nakattarō / tabe-nakatta deshō	mitarō / mita deshō	mi-nakattarō / mi-nakatta deshō
		PROGRESSIVE	tabete itarō / tabete ita deshō	tabetei-nakattarō / tabetei-nakatta deshō	mite itarō / mite ita deshō	mite i-nakattarō / mite i-nakatta deshō
	POLITE FORM	GENERAL	tabemashitarō	tabemasen deshitarō	mimashitarō	mimasen deshitarō
		PROGRESSIVE	tabete imashitarō	tabete imasen deshitarō	mite imashitarō	mite imasen deshitarō

			taberu (affirmative)	taberu (negative)	miru (affirmative)	miru (negative)
PRESENT CONDITIONAL	SIMPLE FORM	GENERAL	tabereba	tabe-nakereba	mireba	mi-nakereba
		PROGRESSIVE	tabete ireba	tabete i-nakereba	mite ireba	mite i-nakereba
	POLITE FORM	GENERAL	tabemasureba	tabemasen nareba	mimasureba	mimasen nareba
		PROGRESSIVE	tabete imasureba	tabete imasen nareba	mite imasureba	mite imasen nareba
PAST CONDITIONAL	SIMPLE FORM	GENERAL	tabetara	tabe-nakattara	mitara	mi-nakattara
		PROGRESSIVE	tabete itara	tabete i-nakattara	mite itara	mite i-nakattara
	POLITE FORM	GENERAL	tabemashitara	tabemasen deshitara	mimashitara	mimasen deshitara
		PROGRESSIVE	tabete imashitara	tabete imasen deshitara	mite imashitara	mite imasen deshitara
CONJUNCTIVE (gerundial form)	SIMPLE FORM	GENERAL	tabete	tabe-nai de / tabe-nakute	mite	mi-nai de / mi-nakute
		PROGRESSIVE	tabete ite	tabete i-nai de	mite ite	mite i-nai de
	POLITE FORM	GENERAL	tabemashite	tabemasen de	mimashite	mimasen de
		PROGRESSIVE	tabete imashite	tabete imasen de	mite imashite	mite imasen de
IMPERATIVE	ARMY COMMAND OR LOW LANGUAGE		tabel / taberol / tabenal	taberu na! (to inferiors or intimates)	mi! / miro! / mina!	miru na!
	POLITE FORM (from least to most polite)		tabete (o)-kure / (o)-tabe nasai / o-tabe kudasai	tabe-nai de o-kure / tabete wa ike nai / tabe-nai de ii / tabe-nai de kudasai / o-tabe kudasaimasen na	mite (o)-kure / goran nasai§ / mite kudasai / goran kudasai§	mi-nai de o-kure / mite wa ike nai / mi-nai de ii / mi-nai de kudasai / goran kudasaimasen na§

* These forms are also used for the perfect tenses; e. g., tabemashita may mean *have eaten*; tabete imasu may mean *have been eating*; tabete imashō *probably have been eating, will have been eating*; tabete imashita *had been eating*; tabete imashita may mean *had been eating*. The past progressive form is often used to indicate the present perfect in the first person; e. g., haratte imashita may mean *have been paying* as well as *had been paying*.

** These forms in –ō, –mashō and –masumai also may mean *let us* and *let us not* respectively; e. g., tabemashō *let us eat*; tabemasumai *let us not eat*.

† Deshō may be substituted throughout the paradigm by darō which, however, is less polite. The forms with deshō followed or not by ni may be used to translate *should* or *would* in result clauses after a conditional; e. g., Ano hito ga kane wo motte ireba, kanjō wo harau deshō ni. *If he had the money, he would pay the bill*; Ano hito ga kane wo motte itara, kanjō wo haratta deshō ni. *If he had had money, he would have paid the bill.*

‡ The suffix mai is added to the conclusive form of second class verbs, but to the continuative form of first class verbs; e. g., Tegami wo kakumai. *I don't think I'll write a letter*; Gohan wo tabemai. *I don't think I'll eat dinner.*

§ The verb miru has the special honorific form goran (see section 109). The corresponding forms of kiru *put on* are o-kiri nasai, o-kiri kudasai, and o-kiri kudasaimasen na.

VERBS OF THE SECOND CLASS
ACTIVE VOICE

			harAU		yoBU	
			AFFIRMATIVE	NEGATIVE	AFFIRMATIVE	NEGATIVE
PRESENT	SIMPLE FORM	GENERAL	harau	harawa-nai	yobu	yoba-nai
		PROGRESSIVE	haratte iru	haratte i-nai	yonde iru	yonde i-nai
	POLITE FORM	GENERAL	haraimasu	haraimasen	yobimasu	yobimasen
		PROGRESSIVE	haratte imasu*	haratte imasen	yonde imasu	yonde imasen
PROBABLE PRESENT AND FUTURE	SIMPLE FORM	GENERAL	haraō / harau deshō†	harau-mai‡ / harawa-nai deshō	yobō / yobu deshō	yobu-mai / yoba-nai deshō
		PROGRESSIVE	haratte iru deshō	haratte i-nai deshō / haratte i-mai	yonde iru deshō	yonde i-nai deshō / yonde i-mai
	POLITE FORM	GENERAL	haraimashō** / haraimasu deshō	haraimasu-mai** / haraimasen deshō	yobimashō / yobimasu deshō	yobimasu-mai / yobimasen deshō
		PROGRESSIVE	haratte imashō	haratte imasu-mai	yonde imashō	yonde imasu-mai
PAST*	SIMPLE FORM	GENERAL	haratta	harawa-nakatta	yonda	yoba-nakatta
		PROGRESSIVE	haratte ita	haratte i-nakatta	yonde ita	yonde i-nakatta
	POLITE FORM	GENERAL	haraimashita	haraimasen deshita	yobimashita	yobimasen deshita
		PROGRESSIVE	haratte imashita	haratte imasen deshita	yonde imashita	yonde imasen deshita
PROBABLE PAST	SIMPLE FORM	GENERAL	harattarō / haratta deshō	harawa-nakattarō / harawa-nakatta deshō	yonda darō / yonda deshō	yoba-nakattarō / yoba-nakatta deshō
		PROGRESSIVE	haratte itarō / haratte ita deshō	haratte i-nakattarō / haratte i-nakatta deshō	yonde itarō / yonde ita deshō	yonde i-nakattarō / yonde i-nakatta deshō
	POLITE FORM	GENERAL	haraimashitarō	haraimasen deshitarō	yobimashitarō	yobimasen deshitarō
		PROGRESSIVE	haratte imashitarō	haratte imasen deshitarō	yonde imashitarō	yonde imasen deshitarō

PRESENT CONDITIONAL	SIMPLE FORM	GENERAL	haraeba	harawa-nakereba	yobeba	yoba-nakereba
		PROGRESSIVE	haratte ireba	haratte i-nakereba	yonde ireba	yonde i-nakereba
	POLITE FORM	GENERAL	haraimasureba	haraimasen nareba	yobimasureba	yobimasen nareba
		PROGRESSIVE	haratte imasureba	haratte imasen nareba	yonde imasureba	yonde imasen nareba
PAST CONDITIONAL	SIMPLE FORM	GENERAL	harattara	harawa-nakattara	yondara	yoba-nakattara
		PROGRESSIVE	haratte itara	haratte i-nakattara	yonde itara	yonde i-nakattara
	POLITE FORM	GENERAL	haraimashitara	haraimasen deshitara	yobimashitara	yobimasen deshitara
		PROGRESSIVE	haratte imashitara	haratte imasen deshitara	yonde imashitara	yonde imasen deshitara
CONJUNCTIVE	SIMPLE FORM	GENERAL	haratte	harawa-nai de / harawa-nakute	yonde	yoba-nai de / yoba-nakute
		PROGRESSIVE	haratte ite	haratte i-nai de	yonde ite	yonde i-nai de
	POLITE FORM	GENERAL	haraimashite	haraimasen de	yobimashite	yobimasen de
		PROGRESSIVE	haratte imashite	haratte imasen de	yonde imashite	yonde imasen de
IMPERATIVE		ARMY COMMAND OR LOW LANGUAGE	harae! / harae yo!	harawa-nai! (to inferiors or intimates)	yobe! / yobe yo!	yobu na!
		POLITE FORM (from least to most polite)	haratte (o)-kure / (o)-harai nasai / haratte kudasai / o-harai kudasai	harawa-nai de o-kure / haratte wa ike-nai / harawa-nai de ii / harawa-nai de kudasai / o-harai kudasaimasu na	yonde (o)-kure / (o)-yobi nasai / yonde kudasai / o-yobi kudasai	yoba-nai de o-kure / yonde wa ike-nai / yoba-nai de ii / yoba-nai de kudasai / o-yobi kudasaimasu na

VERBS OF THE SECOND CLASS—*Continued*
ACTIVE VOICE

			nuGU		IU	
			AFFIRMATIVE	NEGATIVE	AFFIRMATIVE	NEGATIVE
PRESENT	SIMPLE FORM	GENERAL	nugu	nuga-nai	iu	iwa-nai
		PROGRESSIVE	nuide iru	nuide i-nai	itte iru	itte i-nai
	POLITE FORM	GENERAL	nugimasu	nugimasen	iimasu	iimasen
		PROGRESSIVE	nuide imasu	nuide imasen	itte imasu	itte imasen
PROBABLE PRESENT AND FUTURE	SIMPLE FORM	GENERAL	nugō / nugu deshō	nugu-mai / nuga-nai deshō	iō / iu deshō	iu-mai / iwa-nai deshō
		PROGRESSIVE	nuide iru deshō	nuide i-nai deshō / nuide i-mai	itte iru deshō	itte i-nai deshō / itte i-mai
	POLITE FORM	GENERAL	nugimashō / nugimasu deshō	nugimasu-mai / nugimasen deshō	iimashō / iimasu deshō	iimasu-mai / iimasen deshō
		PROGRESSIVE	nuide imashō	nuide imasu-mai	itte imashō	itte imasu-mai
PAST*	SIMPLE FORM	GENERAL	nuida	nuga-nakatta	itta	iwa-nakatta
		PROGRESSIVE	nuide ita	nuide i-nakatta	itte ita	itte i-nakatta
	POLITE FORM	GENERAL	nugimashita	nugimasen deshita	iimashita	iimasen deshita
		PROGRESSIVE	nuide imashita	nuide imasen deshita	itte imashita	itte imasen deshita
PROBABLE PAST	SIMPLE FORM	GENERAL	nuida darō / nuide deshō	nuga-nakattarō / nuga-nakatta deshō	ittarō / itta deshō	iwa-nakattarō / iwa-nakata deshō
		PROGRESSIVE	nuide itarō / nuide ita deshō	nuide i-nakattarō / nuide i-nakatta deshō	itte itarō / itte ita deshō	itte i-nakattarō / itte i-nakatta deshō
	POLITE FORM	GENERAL	nugimashitarō	nugimasen deshitarō	iimashitarō	iimasen deshitarō
		PROGRESSIVE	nuide imashitarō	nuide imasen deshitarō	itte imashitarō	itte imasen deshitarō

PRESENT CONDITIONAL	SIMPLE FORM	GENERAL	nugeba	nuga-nakereba	ieba	iwa-nakereba
		PROGRESSIVE	nuide ireba	nuide i-nakereba	itte ireba	itte i-nakereba
	POLITE FORM	GENERAL	nugimasureba	nugimasen nareba	iimasureba	iimasen nareba
		PROGRESSIVE	nuide imasureba	nuide imasen nareba	itte imasureba	itte imasen nareba
PAST CONDITIONAL	SIMPLE FORM	GENERAL	nuidara	nuga-nakattara	ittara	iwa-nakattara
		PROGRESSIVE	nuide itara	nuide i-nakattara	itte itara	itte i-nakattara
	POLITE FORM	GENERAL	nugimashitara	nugimasen deshitara	iimashitara	iimasen deshitara
		PROGRESSIVE	nuide imashitara	nuide imasen deshitara	itte imashitara	itte imasen deshitara
CONJUNCTIVE	SIMPLE FORM	GENERAL	nuide	nuga-nai de / nuga-nakute	itte	iwa-nai de / iwa-nakute
		PROGRESSIVE	nuide ite	nuide i-nai de	itte ite	itte i-nai de
	POLITE FORM	GENERAL	nugimashite	nugimasen de	iimashite	iimasen de
		PROGRESSIVE	nuide imashite	nuide imasen de	itte imashite	itte imasen de
IMPERATIVE	ARMY COMMAND OR LOW LANGUAGE		nuge! / nuge yo!	nugu nai!	ie! / ie yo!	iu na!
	POLITE FORM (from least to most polite)		nuide (o)-kure / (o)-nugi nasai / nuide kudasai / o-nugi kudasai	nuga-nai de o-kure / nuide wa ike-nai / nuga-nai de ii / nuga-nai de kudasaimasu na	itte (o)-kure / (o)-ii nasai / itte kudasai / o-ii kudasai	iwa-nai de o-kure / itte wa ike-nai / iwa-nai de ii / iwa-nai de kudasai / o-ii kudasaimasu na

VERBS OF THE SECOND CLASS—*Continued*

ACTIVE VOICE

			kaKU		yoMU	
			AFFIRMATIVE	NEGATIVE	AFFIRMATIVE	NEGATIVE
PRESENT	SIMPLE FORM	GENERAL	kaku	kaka-nai	yomu	yoma-nai
		PROGRESSIVE	kaite iru	kaite i-nai	yonde iru	yonde i-nai
	POLITE FORM	GENERAL	kakimasu	kakimasen	yomimasu	yomimasen
		PROGRESSIVE	kaite imasu	kaite imasen	yonde imasu	yonde imasen
PROBABLE PRESENT AND FUTURE	SIMPLE FORM	GENERAL	kakō / kaku deshō	kaku-mai / kaku-nai deshō	yomō / yomu deshō	yomu-mai / yoma-nai deshō
		PROGRESSIVE	kaite iru deshō	kaite i-nai deshō / kaite i-mai	yonde iru deshō	yonde i-nai deshō / yonde i-mai
	POLITE FORM	GENERAL	kakimashō / kakimasu deshō	kakimasu-mai / kakimasen deshō	yomimashō / yomimasu deshō	yomimasu-mai / yomimasen deshō
		PROGRESSIVE	kaite imashō	kaite imasu-mai	yonde imashō	yonde imasu-mai
PAST*	SIMPLE FORM	GENERAL	kaita	kaka-nakatta	yonda	yoma-nakatta
		PROGRESSIVE	kaite ita	kaite i-nakatta	yonde ita	yonde i-nakatta
	POLITE FORM	GENERAL	kakimashita	kakimasen deshita	yomimashita	yomimasen deshita
		PROGRESSIVE	kaite imashita	kaite imasen deshita	yonde imashita	yonde imasen deshita
PROBABLE PAST	SIMPLE FORM	GENERAL	kaitarō / kaita deshō	kaka-nakattarō / kaka-nakatta deshō	yonda darō / yonda deshō	yoma-nakattarō / yoma-nakatta deshō
		PROGRESSIVE	kaite itarō / kaite ita deshō	kaite i-nakattarō / kaite i-nakatta deshō	yonde itarō / yonde ita deshō	yonde i-nakattarō / yonde i-nakatta deshō
	POLITE FORM	GENERAL	kakimashitarō	kakimasen deshitarō	yomimashitarō	yomimasen deshitarō
		PROGRESSIVE	kaite imashitarō	kaite imasen deshitarō	yonde imashitarō	yonde imasen deshitarō

PRESENT CONDITIONAL	SIMPLE FORM	GENERAL	kakeba	kaka-nakereba	yomeba	yoma-nakereba
		PROGRESSIVE	kaite ireba	kaite i-nakereba	yonde ireba	yonde i-nakereba
	POLITE FORM	GENERAL	kakimasureba	kakimasen nareba	yomimasureba	yomimasen nareba
		PROGRESSIVE	kaite imasureba	kaite imasen nareba	yonde imasureba	yonde imasen nareba
PAST CONDITIONAL	SIMPLE FORM	GENERAL	kaitara	kaka-nakattara	yondara	yoma-nakattara
		PROGRESSIVE	kaite itara	kaite i-nakattara	yonde itara	yonde i-nakattara
	POLITE FORM	GENERAL	kakimashitara	kakimasen deshitara	yomimashitara	yomimasen deshitara
		PROGRESSIVE	kaite imashitara	kaite imasen deshitara	yonde imashitara	yonde imasen deshitara
CONJUNCTIVE	SIMPLE FORM	GENERAL	kaite	kaka-nai de kaka-nakute	yonde	yoma-nai de yoma-nakute
		PROGRESSIVE	kaite ite	kaite i-nai de	yonde ite	yonde i-nai de
	POLITE FORM	GENERAL	kakimashite	kakimasen de	yomimashite	yomimasen de
		PROGRESSIVE	kaite imashite	kaite imasen de	yonde imashite	yonde imasen de
IMPERATIVE	ARMY COMMAND OR LOW LANGUAGE		kake! kake yo! kaki na!	kaku na!	yome! yome yo!	yomu na!
	POLITE FORM (from least to most polite)		kaite (o)-kure (o)-kaki nasai kaite kudasai o-kaki kudasai	kaka-nai de o-kure kaite wa ike-nai kaka-nai de ii kaka-nai de kudasai o-kaki kudasaimasu na	yonde (o)-kure (o)-yomi nasai yonde kudasai o-yomi kudasai	yoma-nai de o-kure yonde wa ike-nai yoma-nai de ii yoma-nai de kudasai o-yomi kudasaimasu na

VERBS OF THE SECOND CLASS—*Continued*

ACTIVE VOICE

			shiNU		omOU	
			AFFIRMATIVE	NEGATIVE	AFFIRMATIVE	NEGATIVE
PRESENT	SIMPLE FORM	GENERAL	shinu	shina-nai	omou	omowa-nai
		PROGRESSIVE	shinde iru	shinde i-nai	omotte iru	omotte i-nai
	POLITE FORM	GENERAL	shinimasu	shinimasen	omoimasu	omoimasen
		PROGRESSIVE	shinde imasu	shinde imasen	omotte imasu	omotte imasen
PROBABLE PRESENT AND FUTURE	SIMPLE FORM	GENERAL	shinô shinu deshô	shinu-mai shina-nai deshô	omô omou deshô	omou-mai omowa-nai deshô
		PROGRESSIVE	shinde iru deshô	shinde i-nai deshô shinde i-mai	omotte iru deshô	omotte i-nai deshô omotte i-mai
	POLITE FORM	GENERAL	shinimashô shinimasu deshô	shinimasu-mai shinimasen deshô	omoimashô omoimasu deshô	omoimasu-mai omoimasen deshô
		PROGRESSIVE	shinde imashô	shinde imasu-mai	omotte imashô	omotte imasu-mai
PAST*	SIMPLE FORM	GENERAL	shinda	shina-nakatta	omotta	omowa-nakatta
		PROGRESSIVE	shinde ita	shinde i-nakatta	omotte ita	omotte i-nakatta
	POLITE FORM	GENERAL	shinimashita	shinimasen deshita	omoimashita	omoimasen deshita
		PROGRESSIVE	shinde imashita	shinde imasen deshita	omotte imashita	omotte imasen deshita
PROBABLE PAST	SIMPLE FORM	GENERAL	shinda darô shinda deshô	shina-nakattarô shina-nakatta deshô	omottarô omotta deshô	omowa-nakattarô omowa-nakatta deshô
		PROGRESSIVE	shinde itarô shinde ita deshô	shinde i-nakattarô shinde i-nakatta deshô	omotte itarô omotte ita deshô	omotte i-nakattarô omotte i-nakata deshô
	POLITE FORM	GENERAL	shinimashitarô	shinimasen deshitarô	omoimashitarô	omoimasen deshitarô
		PROGRESSIVE	shinde imashitarô	shinde imasen deshitarô	omotte imashitarô	omotte imasen deshitarô

PRESENT CONDI- TIONAL	SIMPLE FORM	GENERAL	shineba	shina-nakereba	omoeba	omowa-nakereba
		PROGRESSIVE	shinde ireba	shinde i-nakereba	omotte ireba	omotte i-nakereba
	POLITE FORM	GENERAL	shinimasureba	shimasen nareba	omoimasureba	omoimasen nareba
		PROGRESSIVE	shinde imasureba	shinde imasen nareba	omotte imasureba	omotte imasen nareba
PAST CONDI- TIONAL	SIMPLE FORM	GENERAL	shindara	shina-nakattara	omottara	omowa-nakattara
		PROGRESSIVE	shinde itara	shinde i-nakattara	omotte itara	omotte i-nakattara
	POLITE FORM	GENERAL	shinimashitara	shimasen deshitara	omoimashitara	omoimasen deshitara
		PROGRESSIVE	shinde imashitara	shinde imasen deshitara	omotte imashitara	omotte imasen deshitara
CONJUNC- TIVE	SIMPLE FORM	GENERAL	shinde	shina-nai de shina-nakute	omotte	omowa-nai de omowa-nakute
		PROGRESSIVE	shinde ite	shinde i-nai de	omotte ite	omotte i-nai de
	POLITE FORM	GENERAL	shinimashite	shinimasen de	omoimashite	omoimasen de
		PROGRESSIVE	shinde imashite	shinde imasen de	omotte imashite	omotte imasen de
IMPERA- TIVE	ARMY COM- MAND OR LOW LAN- GUAGE		shine! shine yo!	shinu na!	omoe! omoe yo!	omou na!
	POLITE FORM (from least to most polite)		shinde (o)-kure (o)-shini nasai shinde kudasai o-shini kudasai	shina-nai de o-kure shinde wa ike-nai shina-nai de ii shina-nai de kudasai o-shini kudasaimasu na	omotte (o)-kure (o)-omoi nasai omotte kudasai o-omoi kudasai	omowa-nai de o-kure omotte wa ike-nai omowa-nai de ii omowa-nai de kudasai o-omoi kudasaimasu na

VERBS OF THE SECOND CLASS—*Continued*
ACTIVE VOICE

			naRU		hanaSU	
			AFFIRMATIVE	NEGATIVE	AFFIRMATIVE	NEGATIVE
PRESENT	SIMPLE FORM	GENERAL	naru	nara-nai	hanasu	hanasa-nai
		PROGRESSIVE	natte iru	natte i-nai	hanashite iru	hanashite i-nai
	POLITE FORM	GENERAL	narimasu	narimasen	hanashimasu	hanashimasen
		PROGRESSIVE	natte imasu	natte imasen	hanashite imasu	hanashite imasen
PROBABLE PRESENT AND FUTURE	SIMPLE FORM	GENERAL	narō / naru deshō	naru-mai / nara-nai deshō	hanasō / hanasu deshō	hanasu-mai / hanasa-nai deshō
		PROGRESSIVE	natte iru deshō	natte i-nai deshō / natte i-mai	hanashite iru deshō	hanashite i-nai deshō / hanashite i-mai
	POLITE FORM	GENERAL	narimashō / narimasu deshō	narimasu-mai / narimasen deshō	hanashimashō / hanashimasu deshō	hanashimasu-mai / hanashimasen deshō
		PROGRESSIVE	natte imashō	natte imasu-mai	hanashite imashō	hanashie imasu-mai
PAST*	SIMPLE FORM	GENERAL	natta	nara-nakatta	hanashita	hanasa-nakatta
		PROGRESSIVE	natte ita	natte i-nakatta	hanashite ita	hanashite i-nakatta
	POLITE FORM	GENERAL	narimashita	narimasen deshita	hanashimashita	hanashimasen deshita
		PROGRESSIVE	natte imashita	natte imasen deshita	hanashite imashita	hanashite imasen deshita
PROBABLE PAST	SIMPLE FORM	GENERAL	nattarō / natta deshō	nara-nakattarō / nara-nakatta deshō	hanashitarō / hanashita deshō	hanasa-nakattarō / hanasa-nakatta deshō
		PROGRESSIVE	natte itarō / natte ita deshō	natte i-nakattarō / natte i-nakatta deshō	hanashite itarō / hanashite ita deshō	hanashite i-nakattarō / hanashite i-nakatta deshō
	POLITE FORM	GENERAL	narimashitarō	narimasen deshitarō	hanashimashitarō	hanashimasen deshitarō
		PROGRESSIVE	natte imashitarō	natte imasen deshitarō	hanashite imashitarō	hanashite imasen deshitarō

PRESENT CONDITIONAL	SIMPLE FORM	GENERAL	hanasa-nakereba	hanaseba	nara-nakereba	nareba
		PROGRESSIVE	hanashite i-nakereba	hanashite ireba	natte i-nakereba	natte ireba
	POLITE FORM	GENERAL	hanashimasen nareba	hanashimasureba	narimasen nareba	narimasureba
		PROGRESSIVE	hanashite imasen nareba	hanashite imasureba	natte imasen nareba	natte imasureba
PAST CONDITIONAL	SIMPLE FORM	GENERAL	hanasa-nakattara	hanashitara	nara-nakattara	nattara
		PROGRESSIVE	hanashite i-nakattara	hanashite itara	natte i-nakattara	natte itara
	POLITE FORM	GENERAL	hanashimasen deshitara	hanashimashitara	narimasen deshitara	narimashitara
		PROGRESSIVE	hanashite imasen deshitara	hanashite imashitara	natte imasen deshitara	natte imashitara
CONJUNCTIVE	SIMPLE FORM	GENERAL	hanasa-nai de hanasa-nakute	hanashite	nara-nai de nara-nakute	natte
		PROGRESSIVE	hanashite i-nai de	hanashite ite	natte i-nai de	natte ite
	POLITE FORM	GENERAL	hanashimasen de	hanashimashite	narimasen de	narimashite
		PROGRESSIVE	hanashite imasen de	hanashite imashite	natte imasen de	natte imashite
IMPERATIVE	ARMY COMMAND OR LOW LANGUAGE		hanasu na!	hanase! hanase yo!	naru na!	nare! nare yo!
	POLITE FORM (from least to most polite)		hanasa-nai de o-kure hanashite wa ike-nai hanasa-nai de ii hanasa-nai de kudasai o-hanashi kudasai masu na	hanashite (o)-kure (o)-hanashi nasai hanashite kudasai o-hanashi kudasai	nara-nai de o-kure natte wa ike-nai nara-nai de ii nara-nai de kudasaimasu na o-nari kudasaimasu na	natte (o)-kure (o)-nari nasai natte kudasai o-nari kudasai

VERBS OF THE SECOND CLASS—*Continued*
ACTIVE VOICE

			moTSU AFFIRMATIVE	moTSU NEGATIVE	sUU AFFIRMATIVE	sUU NEGATIVE
PRESENT	SIMPLE FORM	GENERAL	motsu	mota-nai	suu	suwa-nai
		PROGRESSIVE	motte iru	motte i-nai	sutte iru	sutte i-nai
	POLITE FORM	GENERAL	mochimasu	mochimasen	suimasu	suimasen
		PROGRESSIVE	motte imaşu	motte imasen	sutte imasu	sutte imasen
PROBABLE PRESENT AND FUTURE	SIMPLE FORM	GENERAL	motō / motsu deshō	motsu-mai / mota-nai deshō	suō / suu deshō	suu-mai / suwa-nai deshō
		PROGRESSIVE	motte iru deshō	motte i-nai deshō / motte i-mai	sutte iru deshō	sutte i-nai deshō / sutte i-mai
	POLITE FORM	GENERAL	mochimashō / mochimasu deshō	mochimasu-mai / mochimasen deshō	suimashō / suimasu deshō	suimasu-mai / suimasen deshō
		PROGRESSIVE	motte imashō	motte imasu-mai	sutte imashō	sutte imasu-mai
PAST*	SIMPLE FORM	GENERAL	motta	mota-nakatta	sutta	suwa-nakatta
		PROGRESSIVE	motte ita	motte i-nakatta	sutte ita	sutte i-nakatta
	POLITE FORM	GENERAL	mochimashita	mochimasen deshita	suimashita	suimasen deshita
		PROGRESSIVE	motte imashita	motte imasen deshita	sutte imashita	sutte imasen deshita
PROBABLE PAST	SIMPLE FORM	GENERAL	mottarō / motta deshō	mota-nakattarō / mota-nakatta deshō	suttarō / sutta deshō	suwa-nakattarō / suwa-nakatta deshō
		PROGRESSIVE	motte itarō / motte ita deshō	motte i-nakattarō / mottei-nakatta deshō	sutte itarō / sutte ita deshō	sutte i-nakattarō / sutte i-nakatta deshō
	POLITE FORM	GENERAL	mochimashitarō	mochimasen deshitarō	suimashitarō	suimasen deshitarō
		PROGRESSIVE	motte imashitarō	motte imasen deshitarō	sutte imashitarō	sutte imasen deshitarō

PRESENT CONDITIONAL	SIMPLE FORM	GENERAL	moteba	mota-nakereba	sueba	suwa-nakereba
		PROGRESSIVE	motte ireba	motte i-nakereba	sutte ireba	sutte i-nakereba
	POLITE FORM	GENERAL	mochimasureba	mochimasen nareba	suimasureba	suimasen nareba
		PROGRESSIVE	motte imasureba	motte imasen nareba	sutte imasureba	sutte imasen nareba
PAST CONDITIONAL	SIMPLE FORM	GENERAL	mottara	mota-nakattara	suttara	suwa-nakattara
		PROGRESSIVE	motte itara	motte i-nakattara	sutte itara	sutte i-nakattara
	POLITE FORM	GENERAL	mochimashitara	mochimasen deshitara	suimashitara	suimasen deshitara
		PROGRESSIVE	motte imashitara	motte imasen deshitara	sutte imashitara	sutte imasen deshitara
CONJUNCTIVE	SIMPLE FORM	GENERAL	motte	mota-nai de mota-nakute	sutte	suwa-nai de suwa-nakute
		PROGRESSIVE	motte ite	motte i-nai de	sutte ite	sutte i-nai de
	POLITE FORM	GENERAL	mochimashite	mochimasen de	suimashite	suimasen de
		PROGRESSIVE	motte imashite	inotte imasen de	sutte imashite	sutte imasen de
IMPERATIVE	ARMY COMMAND OR LOW LANGUAGE		mote! mote yo!	motsu na!	sue! sue yo!	suu na!
	POLITE FORM (from least to most polite)		motte (o)-kure (o)-mochi nasai motte kudasai o-mochi kudasai	mota-nai de o-kure motte wa ike-nai mota-nai de ii mota-nai de kudasai o-mochi kudasaimasu na	sutte (o)-kure (o)-sui nasai sutte kudasai o-sui kudasai	suwa-nai de o-kure sutte wa ike ii suwa-nai de ii suwa-nai de kudasai o-sui kudasaimasu na

PASSIVE VOICE
(POTENTIAL AND POLITE ACTIVE)

			taberareru		mirareru	
			AFFIRMATIVE	NEGATIVE	AFFIRMATIVE	NEGATIVE
PRESENT	SIMPLE FORM	GENERAL	taberareru	taberare-nai	mirareru	mirare-nai
		PROGRESSIVE	taberarete iru	taberarete i-nai	mirarete iru	mirarete i-nai
	POLITE FORM	GENERAL	taberaremasu	taberaremasen	miraremasu	miraremasen
		PROGRESSIVE	taberarete imasu	taberarete imasen	mirarete imasu	mirarete imasen
PROBABLE PRESENT AND FUTURE	SIMPLE FORM	GENERAL	taberareyô taberareru deshô	taberare-mai taberare-nai deshô	mirareyô mirareru deshô	mirare-mai mirare-nai deshô
		PROGRESSIVE	taberarete iru deshô	taberarete i-nai deshô taberarete i-mai	mirarete iru deshô	mirarete i-nai deshô mirarete i-mai
	POLITE FORM	GENERAL	taberaremashô taberaremasu deshô	taberaremasu-mai taberaremasen deshô	miraremashô miraremasu deshô	miraremasu-mai miraremasen deshô
		PROGRESSIVE	taberarete imashô	taberarete imasu-mai	mirarete imashô	mirarete imasu-mai
PAST	SIMPLE FORM	GENERAL	taberareta	taberare-nakatta	mirareta	mirare-nakatta
		PROGRESSIVE	taberarete ita	taberarete i-nakatta	mirarete ita	mirarete i-nakatta
	POLITE FORM	GENERAL	taberaremashita	taberaremasen deshita	miraremashita	miraremasen deshita
		PROGRESSIVE	taberarete imashita	taberarete imasen deshita	mirarete imashita	mirarete imasen deshita

Tense	Form	Aspect				
PROBABLE PAST	SIMPLE FORM	GENERAL	taberaretarô taberareta deshô	taberare-nakattarô taberare-nakatta deshô	miraretarô mirareta deshô	mirare-nakattarô mirare-nakatta deshô
		PROGRESSIVE	taberarete itarô taberarete ita deshô	taberarete i-nakattarô taberarete i-nakatta deshô	mirarete itarô mirarete ita deshô	mirarete i-nakattarô mirarete i-nakatta deshô
	POLITE FORM	GENERAL	taberaremashitarô	taberaremasen deshitarô	miraremashitarô	miraremasen deshitarô
		PROGRESSIVE	taberarete imashitarô	taberarete imasen deshitarô	mirarete imashitarô	mirarete imasen deshitarô
PRESENT CONDITIONAL	SIMPLE FORM	GENERAL	taberarereba	taberare-nakereba	mirareba	mirare-nakereba
		PROGRESSIVE	taberarete ireba	taberarete i-nakereba	mirarete ireba	mirarete i-nakereba
	POLITE FORM	GENERAL	taberaremasureba	taberaremasen nareba	miraremasureba	miraremasen nareba
		PROGRESSIVE	taberarete imasureba	taberarete imasen nareba	mirarete imasureba	mirarete imasen nareba
PAST CONDITIONAL	SIMPLE FORM	GENERAL	taberaretara	taberare-nakattara	miraretara	mirare-nakattara
		PROGRESSIVE	taberarete itara	taberarete i-nakattara	mirarete itara	mirarete i-nakattara
	POLITE FORM	GENERAL	taberaremashitara	taberaremasen deshitara	miraremashitara	miraremasen deshitara
		PROGRESSIVE	taberarete imashitara	taberarete imasen deshitara	mirarete imashitara	mirarete imasen deshitara
CONJUNCTIVE	SIMPLE FORM	GENERAL	taberarete	taberare-nai de taberare-nakute	mirarete	mirare-nai de mirare-nakute
		PROGRESSIVE	taberarete ite	taberarete i-nai de	mirarete ite	mirarete i-nai de
	POLITE FORM	GENERAL	taberaremashite	taberaremasen de	miraremashite	miraremasen de
		PROGRESSIVE	taberarete imashite	taberarete imasen de	mirarete imashite	mirarete imasen de

PASSIVE VOICE
(POTENTIAL AND POLITE ACTIVE)

			harawareru*	
			AFFIRMATIVE	NEGATIVE
PRESENT	SIMPLE FORM	GENERAL	harawareru	haraware-nai
		PROGRESSIVE	harawarete iru	harawarete i-nai
	POLITE FORM	GENERAL	harawaremasu	harawaremasen
		PROGRESSIVE	harawarete imasu	harawarete imasen
PROBABLE PRESENT AND FUTURE	SIMPLE FORM	GENERAL	harawareyō / harawareru deshō	haraware-mai / haraware-nai deshō
		PROGRESSIVE	harawarete iru deshō	harawarete i-mai / harawarete i-nai deshō
	POLITE FORM	GENERAL	harawaremashō / harawaremasu deshō	harawaremasu-mai / harawaremasen deshō
		PROGRESSIVE	harawarete-imashō	harawarete imasu-mai
PAST	SIMPLE FORM	GENERAL	harawareta	haraware-nakatta
		PROGRESSIVE	harawarete ita	harawarete i-nakatta
	POLITE FORM	GENERAL	harawaremashita	harawaremasen deshita
		PROGRESSIVE	harawarete imashita	harawarete imasen deshita

PROBABLE PAST	SIMPLE FORM	GENERAL	harawaretarō harawareta deshō	haraware-nakattarō haraware-nakatta deshō
		PROGRESSIVE	harawarete itarō harawarete ita deshō	harawarete i-nakattarō harawarete i-nakatta deshō
	POLITE FORM	GENERAL	harawaremashitarō	harawaremasen deshitarō
		PROGRESSIVE	harawarete imashitarō	harawarete imasen deshitarō
PRESENT CONDITIONAL	SIMPLE FORM	GENERAL	harawarereba	haraware-nakereba
		PROGRESSIVE	harawarete ireba	harawarete i-nakereba
	POLITE FORM	GENERAL	harawaremasureba	harawaremasen nareba
		PROGRESSIVE	harawarete imasureba	harawarete imasen nareba
PAST CONDITIONAL	SIMPLE FORM	GENERAL	harawaretara	haraware-nakattara
		PROGRESSIVE	harawarete itara	harawarete i-nakattara
	POLITE FORM	GENERAL	harawaremashitara	harawaremasen deshitara
		PROGRESSIVE	harawarete imashitara	harawarete imasen deshitara
CONJUNCTIVE	SIMPLE FORM	GENERAL	harawarete	haraware-nai de haraware-nakute
		PROGRESSIVE	harawarete ite	harawarete i-nai de
	POLITE FORM	GENERAL	harawaremashite	harawaremasen de
		PROGRESSIVE	harawarete imashite	harawarete imasen de

* The passive forms of the preceding model verbs are yobareru, nugareru, iwareru, kakareru, yomareru, shinareru, omowareru, narareru, hanasareru, motareru, and suwareru. Their various forms are made in the same manner as those of harawareru.

IRREGULAR VERBS kuru AND suru
ACTIVE VOICE

			kuru		suru	
			AFFIRMATIVE	NEGATIVE	AFFIRMATIVE	NEGATIVE
PRESENT	SIMPLE FORM	GENERAL	kuru	ko-nai	suru	shi-nai
		PROGRESSIVE	kite iru	kite i-nai	shite iru	shite i-nai
	POLITE FORM	GENERAL	kimasu	kimasen	shimasu	shimasen
		PROGRESSIVE	kite imasu	kite imasen	shite imasu	shite imasen
PROBABLE PRESENT AND FUTURE	SIMPLE FORM	GENERAL	kiyō / kuru deshō	kuru-mai / ko-nai deshō	shiyō / suru deshō	suru-mai / shi-nai deshō
		PROGRESSIVE	kite iru deshō	kite i-nai deshō	shite iru deshō	shite i-nai deshō
	POLITE FORM	GENERAL	kimashō	kimasu-mai	shimashō	shimasu-mai
		PROGRESSIVE	kite imashō	kite imasu-mai	shite imashō	shite imasu-mai
PAST	SIMPLE FORM	GENERAL	kita	ko-nakatta	shita	shi-nakatta
		PROGRESSIVE	kite ita	kite i-nakatta	shite ita	shite i-nakatta
	POLITE FORM	GENERAL	kimashita	kimasen deshita	shimashita	shimasen deshita
		PROGRESSIVE	kite imashita	kite imasen deshita	shite imashita	shite imasen deshita
PROBABLE PAST	SIMPLE FORM	GENERAL	kitarō / kita deshō	ko-nakattarō / ko-nakatta deshō	shitarō / shita deshō	shi-nakattarō / se-nakattarō / shi-nakatta deshō / se-nakatta deshō
		PROGRESSIVE	kite itarō / kite ita deshō	kite i-nakattarō / kite i-nakatta deshō	shite itarō / shite ita deshō	shite i-nakattarō / shite i-nakatta deshō
	POLITE FORM	GENERAL	kimashitarō	kimasen deshitarō	shimashitarō	shimasen deshitarō
		PROGRESSIVE	kite imashitarō	kite imasen deshitarō	shite imashitarō	shite imasen deshitarō

PRESENT CONDITIONAL	SIMPLE FORM	GENERAL	kureba	ko-nakereba	sureba	shi-nakereba
		PROGRESSIVE	kite ireba	kite i-nakereba	shite ireba	shite i-nakereba
	POLITE FORM	GENERAL	kimasureba	kimasen nareba	shimasureba	shimasen nareba
		PROGRESSIVE	kite imasureba	kite imasen nareba	shite imasureba	shite imasen nareba
PAST CONDITIONAL	SIMPLE FORM	GENERAL	kitara	ko-nakattara	shitara	shi-nakattara se-nakattara
		PROGRESSIVE	kite itara	kite i-nakattara	shite itara	shite i-nakattara
	POLITE FORM	GENERAL	kimashitara	kimasen deshitara	shimashitara	shimasen deshitara
		PROGRESSIVE	kite imashitara	kite imasen deshitara	shite imashitara	shite imasen deshitara
CONJUNCTIVE	SIMPLE FORM	GENERAL	kite	ko-nai de ko-nakute	shite	shi-nai de se-nai de shi-nakute se-nakute
		PROGRESSIVE	kite ite	kite i-nai de	shite ite	shite i-nai de
	POLITE FORM	GENERAL	kimashite	kimasen de	shimashite	shimasen de
		PROGRESSIVE	kite imashite	kite imasen de	shite imashite	shite imasen de
IMPERATIVE	ARMY COMMAND OR LOW LANGUAGE		ko! koi!	kuru na!	se! seyo!	suru na!
	POLITE FORM		kite (o)-ki nasai (o)-ki kudasai kite kudasai o-ide kudasai	ko-nai de o-kure kite wa ike-nai ko-nai de ii ko-nai de kudasaimasu na o-ide kudasaimasu na	shite (o)-kure (o)-shi nasai shite kudasai o-nasatte kudasai	shi-nai de o-kure se-nai de o-kure shite wa ike-nai shi-nai de ii shi-nai de kudasai se-nai de kudasai o-shi kudasaimasu na o-nasatte kudasaimasu na

PASSIVE VOICE
(POTENTIAL AND POLITE ACTIVE)

			korareru		sareru	
			AFFIRMATIVE	NEGATIVE	AFFIRMATIVE	NEGATIVE
PRESENT	SIMPLE FORM	GENERAL	korareru	korare-nai	sareru	sare-nai
		PROGRESSIVE	korarete iru	korarete i-nai	sarete iru	sarete i-nai
	POLITE FORM	GENERAL	koraremasu	koraremasen	saremasu	saremasen
		PROGRESSIVE	korarete imasu	korarete imasen	sarete imasu	sarete imasen
PROBABLE PRESENT AND FUTURE	SIMPLE FORM	GENERAL	korareyō / korareru deshō	korare-mai / korare-nai deshō	sareyō / sareru deshō	sare-mai / sare-nai deshō
		PROGRESSIVE	korarete iru deshō	korarete i-mai / korarete i-nai deshō	sarete iru deshō	sarete i-mai / sarete i-nai deshō
	POLITE FORM	GENERAL	koraremashō / koraremasu deshō	koraremasu-mai / koraremasen deshō	saremashō / saremasu deshō	saremasu-mai / saremasen deshō
		PROGRESSIVE	korarete imashō	korarete imasu-mai	sarete imashō	sarete imasu-mai
PAST	SIMPLE FORM	GENERAL	korareta	korare-nakatta	sareta	sare-nakatta
		PROGRESSIVE	korarete ita	korarete i-nakatta	sarete ita	sarete i-nakatta
	POLITE FORM	GENERAL	koraremashita	koraremasen deshita	saremashita	saremasen deshita
		PROGRESSIVE	korarete imashita	korarete imasen deshita	sarete imashita	sarete imasen deshita

PROBABLE PAST	SIMPLE FORM	GENERAL	koraretarō / korareta deshō	korare-nakattarō / korare-nakatta deshō	saretarō / sareta deshō	sare-nakattarō / sare-nakatta deshō
		PROGRESSIVE	korarete itarō / korarete ita deshō	korarete i-nakattarō / korarete i-nakatta deshō	sarete itarō / sareta ita deshō	sarete i-nakattarō / sarete i-nakatta deshō
	POLITE FORM	GENERAL	koraremashitarō	koraremasen deshitarō	saremashitarō	saremasen deshitarō
		PROGRESSIVE	korarete imashitarō	korarete imasen deshitarō	sarete imashitarō	sarete imasen deshitarō
PRESENT CONDITIONAL	SIMPLE FORM	GENERAL	korarereba	korare-nakereba	sarereba	sare-nakereba
		PROGRESSIVE	korarete ireba	korarete i-nakereba	sarete ireba	sarete i-nakereba
	POLITE FORM	GENERAL	koraremasureba	koraremasen nareba	saremasureba	saremasen nareba
		PROGRESSIVE	korarete imasureba	korarete imasen nareba	sarete imasureba	sarete imasen nareba
PAST CONDITIONAL	SIMPLE FORM	GENERAL	koraretara	korare-nakattara	saretara	sare-nakattara
		PROGRESSIVE	korarete itara	korarete i-nakattara	sarete itara	sarete i-nakattara
	POLITE FORM	GENERAL	koraremashitara	koraremasen deshitara	saremashitara	saremasen deshitara
		PROGRESSIVE	korarete imashitara	korarete imasen deshitara	sarete imashitara	sarete imasen deshitara
CONJUNCTIVE	SIMPLE FORM	GENERAL	korarete	korare-nai de / korare-nakute	sarete	sare-nai de / sare-nakute
		PROGRESSIVE	korarete ite	korarete i-nai de	sarete ite	sarete i-nai de
	POLITE FORM	GENERAL	koraremashite	koraremasen de	saremashite	saremasen de
		PROGRESSIVE	korarete imashite	korarete imasen de	sarete imashite	sarete imasen de

APPENDIX

KATAKANA SYLLABARY

Vowels	B	D	G	H	K	M	N	P	R	S	T	V	W	Y	Z
a	ア	バ	ダ	ガ	ハ	カ	マ	ナ	パ	ラ	サ	タ		ワ	ヤ	ザ
e	エ	ベ	デ	ゲ	ヘ	ケ	メ	ネ	ペ	レ	セ	テ		ヱ		ゼ
i	イ	ビ	ヂ ji	ギ	ヒ	キ	ミ	ニ	ピ	リ	シ shi	チ chi		ヰ		ジ ji
o	オ	ボ	ド	ゴ	ホ	コ	モ	ノ	ポ	ロ	ソ	ト		ヲ	ヨ	ゾ
u	ウ	ブ	ズ zu	グ	フ fu	ク	ム	ヌ	プ	ル	ス	ツ tsu	ヴ		ユ	ズ

ン FINAL No'M

KATAKANA SYLLABARY

Although the Japanese usually use the Chinese characters in writing, they all know this syllabary. Japanese is usually written from top to bottom and from right to left. The words are written by syllables and not by letters. Note that **fu** is in column **H; ch** or **chi** in **T;** and **J** or **Ji** in columns **D** and **Z.**

However, spelling is not completely phonetic. The following are the more important of the irregularities:

1. **tsu** ツ may be used to indicate that the initial consonant of the following syllable is doubled, in which case it is often written small and slightly to the right; e. g., **matte** マテ. Compare **futatsu** フタツ.

2. Long vowels are usually made by placing **u** ウ (sometimes **wa** or **fu**) after the vowel, e. g., **teppō** *gun* テッポウ or by a dash after the lengthened sound, e. g., **iie** イー.

3. Long o (ō) is sometimes written **au**, e. g., **dō** ダウ.

4. After **k** or **g**, **e** plus **u** or plus **fu** are read **yō**, e. g., **ke** plus **u** is pronounced **kyō**.

5. There is a special letter for **n** or **m** when either occurs at the end of a word or syllable; e. g., **sutensho** ステンショ **ken** ケン **sambun** サンブン.

6. A consonant followed by **y** is written with two characters, e. g., **byu** is written **bi** plus **yu**, and **kyo** is written **ki** plus **yo**. Before **yū** a consonant in the **i** line plus **u** may be used.

7. The postposition **wa** is written ハ (ha) and the postposition (**w**)**o** is written ヲ (wo).

8. The letters **a, o, u** after **ch, j,** or **sh** are usually written **ya, yo, yu,** e.g., **sha** is written **shi ya.**

With a knowledge of these rules, words and sentences can be written which will be understood by all Japanese. The spelling may not be absolutely correct, for as Sansom says (HGJ, p. 49) ". . . the correct *kana* spelling of many compound sounds is a matter of considerable difficulty, and indeed is often the subject of controversy." However, if the sounds are written as shown, the words will be recognized.

A study of the chart and the rules should enable the student also to read notes written in *katakana*.

EXAMPLES

1. hon	ホン	6. tokei	トケイ		
2. tama	タマ	7 empitsu	エンピツ	11. jidōsha	ヂドウツャ
3. kami	カミ	8. kōhī	コーヒー	12. jōbu *strength*	ヂョウブ
4. fune	フネ	9. ikura	イクラ	13. chūbu *tube*	チュウブ
5. takai	タカイ	10. gyūnyū	ギュウニュウ	14. jū	ヂウ

The numbers are very easy to learn and will be most useful.

NUMBERS

WRITING CHART

Vowels		B	D	G	H	K	M	N	P	R	S	T	V	W	Y	Z
a	ア	バ	ダ	ガ	ハ	カ	マ	ナ	パ	ラ	サ	タ		ワ	ヤ	ザ
e	エ	ベ	デ	ゲ	ヘ	ケ	メ	ネ	ペ	レ	セ	テ		ヱ		ゼ
i	イ	ビ	ヂ Ji	ギ	ヒ	キ	ミ	ニ	ピ	リ	シ SH SHi	チ CH CHi		ヰ		ジ J Ji
o	オ	ボ	ド	ゴ	ホ	コ	モ	ノ	ポ	ロ	ソ	ト		ヲ	ヨ	ゾ
u	ウ	ブ	ヅ ZU	グ	フ FU	ク	ム	ヌ	プ	ル	ズ	ツ TSU	ヴ		ユ	ズ
								ン FINAL N or M								

This chart shows the order in which the strokes of the katakana syllabary are made. The strokes are numbered in the order made and the number is placed where the stroke begins. All strokes are made from top to bottom except final **n** or **m** and shi and ji which are made from bottom to top. Arrows have been placed in these three characters to indicate the direction of the stroke. The shape ┐ is made as one stroke.

ABBREVIATIONS

adj. adjective
adv. adverb, adverbial form
caus. causative
c. f. continuative form
cond. conditional
des. desiderative
f. form
fut. future
ger. gerundial form
hon. honorific
imp. imperative
interj. interjection
irreg. irregular
n. noun

n.f. noun form
neg. negative
num. aux. numeral auxiliary
pl. plural
post. postposition
pot. potential
pres. present
prob. pres. probable present
pron. pronoun
sg. singular
var. variant
v. i. intransitive verb
v. t. transitive verb

JAPANESE-ENGLISH DICTIONARY

All the words of the lessons and exercises are given here with their meanings and their etymology (where this will help the student learn the word or aid him to understand Japanese word formation). An accent mark indicates that the syllable over which it appears has higher pitch. Words with a preceding asterisk have level pitch throughout. The pitch of other words is not given. Homonyms represented in writing by different characters are listed separately. The Roman numerals and Arabic numerals in parentheses refer to lessons and lines respectively.

A

ā (X, 24) oh! good heavens!

abunai (XIII, 4) dangerous

achira (VII, 44) that, there, over there

ágari (VI, 9) *n. f.* of agaru

agarimasu (XII, 50) *pres.* of agaru

agaru go up, come up, enter, be offered, be completed

agemashō (XI, 28) *prob. pres.* of ageru

agemasu (XIII, 61) *pres.* of ageru

ageru offer, give (to a superior), raise; see sashiageru

agomuki face up

*aida (XI, 36) interval; between, among, during, while; kono — recently

*aikawarazu (II, 3) as usual, without change

*ainiku (X, 10) unfortunately

aite (XII, 43) *ger.* of aku

*Ajiya (XVI, 4) Asia

*akabō (XV, 32) porter, redcap

*akarui bright

akaru-sō (XII, 35) bright-looking; see akarui

*akeru *v. t.* open

akete (V, 27) *ger.* of akeru

áki (X, 26) autumn

*aku *v. i.* open, be vacant

*Amanoya (XII, 8) *name of a hotel*

ámari (VI, 29) too, too much; very (with negative form of verb); see taihen

ámbái (XIII, 42) condition, state

*Amerika (VI, 17) America, the United States

Amerika-jin (II, 16) American (person)

ammari *var.* of amari

anáta (II, 5) *sg.* you

*anatagata (II, 30) *pl.* you

*ane (XIII, 10) elder sister

*ano (II, 12) *adj.* that, those (distant from the person spoken to)

anō I say, if you please

arai (XV, 61) rough, rude, wild

Arasuka Alaska

aratte (V, 33) *ger.* of arau

*arau *verb* wash

*are (II, 27) *pron.* that, those (distant from the person spoken to)

ari (XVI, 13) *c. f.* of aru

arígatō (I, 3) thank you; — gozaimashita thank you

arimasen (I, 27) *pres. neg.* of aru; am not, is not, are not

arimashita (XI, 36) *past* of aru

arimashō (IX, 13) *prob. pres.* of aru

arimasu (VI, 43) *pres.* of aru

áru (VIII, 10) be, have, there is, there are

aruite (XI, 14) *ger.* of aruku

arúku *verb* walk

Aruzenchin (XIV, 37) Argentina

ása (I, 32) morning

*asahan (III, 1) breakfast

*asobu play, enjoy oneself

*asoko (VIII, 8) *adv.* there, that place

219

asonde (XVI, 52) *ger.* of asobu

asú (VIII, 18) tomorrow; — no asa tomorrow morning

atáráshíi (VIII, 37) new, fresh

atarashikute (XII, 5) *ger.* of atarashii

atsúi hot, warm

*atsukai (XV, 47) treatment, dealing

*atsusa heat

atsu-sugiru (XII, 54) too hot; see atsúi

áu meet, see

awazu (XV, 61) without meeting; see áu

azúkéru deposit, entrust

azukete (XIV, 22) *ger.* of azukeru

B

bakari (XV, 52) only, just, about

*ban (I, 36) evening

bán (VIII, 64) number

*banchi (IX, 59) house number, street number

bángó (XIII, 18) number, mark, numerical order

*bantō (IX, 35) clerk, salesman

basu (IX, 8) bus

*Beikoku (XI, 36) America, United States

Beikokú-jin (VIII, 12) American (person)

-beki (XV, 52) should, ought to

benjó (V, 35) washroom, W. C., latrine

Bentendōri *name of a street in Yokohama*

Berugi Belgium

bēsu-bōru (XVI, 49) baseball

-biki (VIII, 41) *sonant form* of hiki

bín (XIII, 1) bottle, flask

bíru (XI, 50) beer

*Biwa-ko (XVI, 32) Lake Biwa

*bōshi (X, 18) hat, cap, head-gear

Bosuton Boston

bótsu-botsu (XIV, 26) so, so; little by little, leisurely; — to slowly

bu percent, part, rate

budóshu (XI, 51) wine, grape wine

Buenosu Airesu Buenos Aires

Búkkyō (XVI, 36) Buddhism

bun part; shi — no san three quarters; hyaku — no ichi one hundredth, one per cent

Buraun (VI, 10) Brown

Burajiru (XIV, 36) Brazil

byóbu folding screen; — (w)o tatemawasu set up a screen around something

*byōki (XIII, 36) illness, disease

C

*cha (III, 9) tea

*cha-iro (X, 11) light brown color, tan

chaku *num. aux.* suits of clothing

chigatte *ger.* of chigau

chigau differ

chiísái (VI, 36) small, little

chíisaku (VI, 41) *adv. and neg. form* of chiisai

chikái (VI, 59) near, early

chikki (XV, 32) check

-chín (VIII, 68) charge, fare

chō (IX, 19) street, city block

chokin (XIV, 19) *n.* savings, deposit

*chokki (X, 58) vest, waistcoat

chōme (IX, 56) combination of chō and me, an ordinal suffix

Chōsen (XVI, 12) Korea

*chótto (IX, 46) a little, just a minute, hey there!

chú-gákkō (XVI, .45) high school, middle school

chúmon (X, 42) *n.* order

D

dá (XI, 64) am, is, are; *simple pres.* of desu

dai *prefix* largeness, greatness; — sansei (XI, 21) complete agreement

dái (I, 0) order, succession; an ordinal prefix; — ichi first

dái (VIII, 62) *num. aux.* for vehicles, chairs, tables

daibutsu the great statue of Buddha

*daidokoro (XII, 43) kitchen

*daigaku (XIV, 41) university, college

dake (X, 38) only, alone, no more

damé (XI, 56) no good, uselessness, impossibility

danna sama master, sir

dáre (II, 8) who; — ka somebody

dashi (XIV, 45) *c. f.* of dasu

dashimashita (XIV, 29) *past* of dasu

dashite (XIII, 54) *ger.* of dasu

dasu put out, take out, send, publish, begin to do, post

dásu (VII, 46) dozen

de (IV, 3) *post.* by means of, in, at, on, with, for

de *c. f.* of both desu and deru

de (XI, 49) and, and so; — wa if that's the case

dekake (VII, 33) *neg. f.* of dekakeru

dekakemashō (VII, 31) *prob. pres.* of dekakeru

*dekakeru go out, set out

deki (XI, 46) *neg. stem* of
dekiru

dekiagarimashita (X, 63) *past* of dekiagaru

*dekiagaru be completed, be ready

dekimasen (IV, 30) *neg. pres.* of dekiru

dekimashita (IV, 34) *past* of dekiru

dekimasu (IV, 33) *pres.* of dekiru

dekíru (XI, 13) be able, can, be done, be ready, be completed, be skilled in, produce

demasu (XV, 6) *pres.* of deru

dé mo (IV, 18) even; de mo — de mo either — or

*dempō (XIV, 63) telegram, wire, cable, radiogram; — (w)o utsu *verb* wire, send a telegram

dénki (XIV, 35) electricity, electric light

dénsha (VIII, 60) street-car, trolley, electric car, tram

denshín (XIV, 63) telegraph, telegram

dénwa (XIII, 10) telephone, phone

denwachō· (XIII, 9) telephone directory

depáto (IX, 1) department store

déru (XIV, 42) come out, go out, appear, leave, be graduated from

déshita (III, 16) *past* of desu

deshō (VII, 21) *prob. pres.* of desu

désu (I, 5) *contraction* of de arimasu; be; — kara therefore, in that case

*do (V, 22) time, degree, measure; ichi — once, ni — twice

dō (XIII, 42) how, what; —

iu what kind of, what sort of, who

dóchira (VI, 21) which (of two), where

Doitsu Germany

dóko (IV, 9) where; — no which

dokú (X, 10) poison; o-ki-no-doku Sama I'm very sorry for you

dónata (VI, 3) *sg.* who

donatagata (XI, 15) *pl.* who

dónna (VIII, 6) what kind of, what sort of

dóno (IX, 4) which (of more than two), what

dóno-gurai (IX, 11) how far, how long, how much, how many, how large, how deep, how high, etc.

doru (XIV, 4) dollar

Doyōbi (VIII, 17) Sunday

dózo (V, 37) please

E

e (V, 12) *post.* to, in, into, on

ē yes, oh yes

*ebi (VIII, 40) shrimp

*Eigo (IV, 37) English (language)

Eikoku (XI, 17) England

éki (XV, 17) train station, depot

*empitsu (I, 22) pencil

erebētā (LX, 36) elevator

F

fú (XVI, 21) urban prefecture

fú (XII, 30) style, appearance, manner, custom, air

*fude (I, 17) (writing) brush

Fúji-san (XVI, 31) Mount Fuji, Fujiyama; see -san

fukai deep, intense, thick

fukaku (XIII, 57) *adv. and neg. f.* of fukai

fukú (X, 45) clothes, suit

fun (XII, 13) minute

funá-chin (XV, 63) compound of fune and chin; boat fare; passage fare

fúne (XV, 57) ship, boat

funkazan volcano

furanku franc

Furansu (XI, 17) France

furó (XII, 51) bath, bathtub

furóba (XII, 49) bathroom

furugi (XV, 51) old clothes; see furui and ki *n. f.* of kiru

furúi (XII, 8) old, aged, ancient

fusagaru fill, shut, be closed, be stopped up, be engaged, be occupied

fusagatte (XIII, 18) *ger.* of fusagaru

futárí (VIII, 47) two persons, a couple, a pair

futátsú (VII, 44) two

fūto-bōru football

*futsū (XIV, 54) ordinary, normal, regular, common

fuyú (X, 30) winter

G

ga (I, 26) *post. used like* wa, *but emphasizing the subject;* as for

gai *sonant form* of kai

*gaikokŭ (XVI, 54) foreign country, foreign land; — go foreign language; — jin foreigner

*gakkō (VII, 14) school; — wo deru be graduated from school

-gawa (XVI, 32) *sonant form* of kawa river

génki (II, 3) health; spirits; — na healthy

genkín (XIV, 5) cash, ready money

Getsuyōbi (VIII, 15) Monday

gín (VII, 40) *sonant f.* of kin

ginka (XIV, 16) silver coin

*ginkō (XIV, 7) bank; Dai Ichi — First Bank

Ginza *a main street in Tokio*

gíshi (XIV, 35) engineer

gó (I, 37) language

go- (XIII, 39) *an honorific prefix*

*go (VII, 3) five

*gō (XV, 35) number, an ordinal suffix

goban (X, 25) checked, checker-board

gógo (VII, 24) afternoon; P.M.; kono — this afternoon

góhan (III, 6) rice, meal, breakfast, dinner, supper

go-issho (IX, 4) *hon.* of issho; together with you

go-kazoku (VIII, 44) *hon.* of kazoku; your family

*gomen (VI, 1) *n.* pardon, excuse

*goran (IX, 38) *hon.* you see

góro about (in point of time)

kono — recent (XV, 47); see gurai

gorufu (XVI, 51) golf

go-shinsatsu (XIII, 37) *hon.* of shinsatsu; a medical examination (for you)

go-shujin (VI, 1) *hon.* of shujín master of your house, your husband, your employer

-góto (XIII, 62) each, every

go-tsugō (XIII, 39) *hon.* of tsugō; your convenience

gozaimasen (VI, 35) *neg. pres.* of gozaru

gozaimashita (VIII, 18) *past* of gozaru

gozaimashite (IX, 42) *ger.* of gozaru

gozaimashō (VIII, 8) *prob. pres.* of gozaru

gozáimasu (VI, 4) *pres.* of gozaru

gōzen (VII, 23) A.M., the forenoon, morning

go-zónji (XII, 2) *hon.* and *n. f.* of zonjiru or zonzuru know, be acquainted with; you know

-gumi (X, 53) sonant form of kumi class, group, pack

*gunjin military man, soldier, sailor

gunjintachi (XI, 15) *pl.* military men; soldiers and sailors, soldiers, sailors

*gurai (VII, 36) *sonant form* of kurai; about (referring to duration of time)

Gurando Hoteru (XII, 5) Grand Hotel

gyūniku (VII, 37) beef

*gyūnyū (III, 7) milk

H

hā (XII, 19) *interj.* well, I see, yes, indeed

hachí (VII, 4) eight

hadé-sugiru (X, 50) *composed of* hade gaiety, showiness and sugiru; too showy, too gaudy

*hagaki (XIV, 46) postcard

hái (I, 19) yes, no (in response to a negative question)

hái *num. aux.* for cupfuls and glassfuls

*haien (XIII, 60) pneumonia, grippe

hairi (X, 21) *c. f.* of hairu

hairimasu (XVI, 11) *pres.* of hairu

háiru enter, get into

haite (X, 6) *ger.* of haku

haitte (V, 40) *ger.* of hairu

hajimaru *v. i.* begin, commence

*hajime (VIII, 3) beginning, first, opening

hajimeru *v. t.* begin, commence

hajímete (VI, 12) *ger.* of hajimeru

hakáru measure, gauge, weigh

hakatte (XIII, 55) *ger.* of hakaru

haki-dáshite (XIII, 58) *c. f.* of haku spew, vomit, and *ger.* of dasu; expel, send forth, vomit

hakikaete (XII, 25) *c. f.* of haku put on and *ger.* of kaeru change

*hako (VI, 51) *n.* box; *aux. num.* boxfuls

haku put on (shoes, boots, trousers), wear

*hakurai (X, 31) imported

*hamaki (XI, 60) cigar

*hámbún (VII, 60) *n.* half

hámu (III, 3) ham

hán (VII, 24) half-past, half

hana nose

haná (XII, 28) flower

Hanako (VI, 49) *a girl's given name*

hanasasete (XIII, 30) *caus. ger.* of hanasu

hánashi (XIII, 21) *c. f.* of hanasu

hanashita (XI, 32) *past* of hanasu

hanashitai (IV, 1) *des.* of hanasu; want to speak, want to say

hanashitaku (IV, 5) *des. neg.* of hanasu; do not want to speak, do not want to say

hanashite (V, 6) *ger.* of hanasu

hanásu (IV, 37) speak, say, converse, chat

*hantō (XVI, 12) peninsula

hara- (XIV, 50) *neg. stem* of haru

haratte (XI, 65) *ger.* of harau
*harau (XV, 52) *verb* pay
haru *verb* affix, stick, paste
háru (X, 30) spring
*hashi (XIII, 4) edge
háshi (XI, 45) chopstick
hashí bridge
hássun (IX, 49) *combination*
of hachi and sun; eight
inches
hatte (XIV, 55) *ger.* of haru
hayái quick, fast, early,
prompt
háyaku (VII, 48) *adv. form* of
hayai; quickly, fast, soon;
iki ga — naru get out of
breath
hayaru be early
*hazu (XIII, 3) should, ought
to, be bound to, be ex-
pected to
heishi (XI, 17) soldier
*hen (XIII, 50) part, side,
neighborhood
heyá (XII, 26) room, apartment
hi (VIII, 13) day, time, date,
sun
hichí (VII, 4) *var.* of shichi;
seven
*hidari (IX, 36) left
*higáshi (IX, 24) east
*hige (XV, 2) beard, whiskers
hiite (XIII, 59) *ger.* of hiku
hiki (VIII, 23) *num. aux.* for
animals, fishes, and insects
hikidashi drawer; composed of
hiku and dasu take out
hikóki (IV, 25) airplane
hikōyūbin (XIV, 52) airmail
hiku draw, pull, attract; kaze
(w)o — catch a cold
hikúi (VI, 47) short, low
hikuku (VI, 48) *adv. and neg.*
of hikui
hima leisure time — desu be
free, have leisure
Hiraderuhiya Philadelphia

hirói wide, broad
hiro-sugiru (X, 7) *stem* of
hiroi and sugiru; too wide
hiruhan (III, 5) lunch
*hito (II, 12) person; kono
—, sono —, ano — he, she
hito- one
hitóban (XII, 36) one night,
all night, overnight
hitóban-jū (XIII,12) throughout the whole night
hitoma (XII, 16) *combination*
of hito one and ma a *num.
aux. for rooms*
hitóri (VIII, 46) one person;
— no single, alone, only;
— de alone, by one's self,
voluntarily
hitótachi (II, 32) people;
kono —, sono —, ano —:
they
hitótsu (VII, 6) one
*hitsuyō (XV, 51) necessity,
need; — na necessary, re-
quired
hō (IX, 24) side, direction,
part
*hōchō (XI, 47) kitchen-
knife, table-knife
*hodo (VI, 48) extent, de-
gree, limit, as, like
*hoka (X, 54) some other
place; — ni (de) elsewhere;
— no other, another (dif-
ferent one)
*hoken (XIV, 60) insurance;
— tsukeru insure; — ni
hairu be insured; — kakeru
take out insurance
Hokkáidō (XVI, 19) *the
northern island of the Japanese homeland*
homéru *verb* praise, com-
mend, admire
homete (VIII, 21) *ger.* of
homeru
hón (I, 9) book, origin; —
-ya bookstore

hon *num. aux.* for long narrow objects, such as pen-
cils, pens, bottles, trees, etc.
hondóri main street
hóngoku (XVI, 10) one's own
country, the fatherland;
composed of hon origin
and koku nation
Hónshū (XVI, 17) *the central island of the Japanese
homeland*
Horutogaru Portugal
hoshíi (VI, 37) want, desire,
care for
hóteru (XII, 4) hotel
hotóndo (XVI, 6) almost, approximately
hyakú (VII, 8) hundred, one
hundred
hyappiki (VIII, 43) *contraction* of hyaku and hiki; one
hundred 'animals,' one
hundred 'fishes'

I

i- (XII, 21) *neg. stem.* of iru
ichí (VII, 3) one; dai — first
ichíban (VI, 38) number one,
first, most, best (used to
form superlative)
*ichi-do (V, 22) once, one
time; mō — once more
Ichigatsu January
ide (VI, 59) o-ide *hon. ger.* of
iru, iku, kuru, etc.; you
are, you go, you come; etc.
ii (V, 34) good, pleasant,
proper, all right
*iie (I, 27) *adv.* no; yes (in response to a negative question)
iimasu (X, 30) *pres.* of iu
ika- (VII, 20) *neg. stem.* of
iku
ikága (I, 2) how, what
ikemasen (V, 29) *pot. pres.* of
iku; cannot go (used to
express prohibition)

íki (XIII, 57) breath, respiration

ikimasén (IX, 2) *pres.* of iku

ikimashō (VII, 13) *prob. pres.* of iku

ikiru *verb* live, be saved, revive

ikita (VIII, 52) *past* of ikiru live, animate

ikitai *des.* of iku; want to go

íkkin (VII, 39) *contraction* of ichi and kin; one *kin*

ikk(w)a (I, 0) *contraction* of ichi and k(w)a; one lesson, one section, one department

iku (IX, 1) go, proceed, frequent, attend

íkura (VII, 37) how much, how many, how far, how long

íkutsu (X, 2) how many, so many

íma (IV, 43) now, the present; — kara from now on, now (referring to the future)

imasen (V, 4) *neg. f.* of iru

imashita (V, 13) *past* of iru

imasu (V, 10) *pres.* of iru

ími (XVI, 42) *n.* meaning, import

imōtó (VII, 14) younger sister

ippai (XI, 58) *contraction* of ichi and hai; full, one glassful, one cupful

íppon (XI, 52) *contraction* of ichi and hon

irasshaimashita (XI, 41) *past* of irassharu

irasshaimasu (VI, 3) *pres.* of irassharu

irássháru *hon.* come, go, be, enter, be at home, be welcome

iremasu (XIII, 22) *pres.* of ireru

*ireru put in, insert, let in, admit

irete (XIII, 20) *ger.* of ireru

irimasu (IX, 7) *pres.* of iru need

iró (X, 11) color, sexual passion; — (w)o suru engage in sexual intercourse

*iro-iro (XVI, 48) various, several, all kinds

*iru (XI, 7) be, there is, there are, live, inhabit, stay

iru, be necessary, need, want

iru-rashii (XVI, 52) seem to be

*isha (XIII, 10) physician, doctor

isogimasu (IV, 21) *pres.* of isogu

isógu (IV, 45) hurry, hasten

isoide (V, 47) *ger.* of isogu

issai (VII, 19) *contraction* of ichi and sai; one year old

issen (VIII, 33) *contraction* of ichi and sen; one thousand; one sen

*issho (IV, 6) ni together, together with, with, in company with

isshūkan (VIII, 12) *contraction* of ichi and shūkan; one week, the week

issoku (X, 1) *contraction* of ichi and soku; one pair (of footwear)

*isu (I, 13) chair

ita (XI, 14) *past* of iru

itái (XIII, 50) painful, sore

itámu *verb* feel a pain, pain, hurt, ache

itande (XIII, 49) *ger.* of itamu

itáru (XVI, 46) go, come; — made up to, down to, until

itashimashita (VI, 8) *past* of itasu

itashimashō (VI, 11) *prob. pres.* of itasu

itashimasu (VI, 13) *pres.* of itasu

*itasu do, bring about, serve

itchaku (X, 41) *contraction* of ichi and chaku; one suit

itchōme (IX, 62) *contraction* of ichi and chōme; first block, first street

itóko (VIII, 25) cousin

ítsu (IX, 54) when, at what time; — ka some time or other; — mo always

itsútsu (VII, 6) five

itte (V, 16) *ger.* of iku

itte (V, 23) *ger.* of iu

*iu (XVI, 41) *verb.* (pronounced yū) say, tell, speak

iya *adv.* no, nay

J

*ja (I, 27) a contraction of de wa; used after nouns and pronouns before aru or gozaru in the negative

*ja (XI, 64) well, well then; see de wa

jagaimo (VII, 54) white potato

jaku *sonant form of* shaku

*jama (XII, 40) hindrance, impediment; — suru interfere with

*ji (VII, 22) o'clock, hour (in point of time); see jikan

jidósha (IV, 31) automobile, auto

jíkan (VII, 36) hours time, hour (extent of time), time; — goto (XIII, 62) every hour

jikk(w)a (X, 0) *contraction* of ju and k(w)a; dai — tenth lesson

jimusho office, place of business

-jin (II, 16) person, man

jingū a Shinto shrine

*jinjō (XVI, 45) ordinary, common, elementary

*jinkō (XVI, 7) population

*jinríkisha (VIII, 62) rickshaw

jippun (VII, 49) *contraction* of jū and fun; ten minutes

*Jirō (II, 5) *a man's given name*

jishin (XV, 51) one's own self

jishin (XVI, 27) earthquake

jissen (VII, 39) *contraction* of jū and sen; ten sen

jitchōme (VII, 29) *contraction* of jū and chōme; tenth block

*jochū (XII, 50) maidservant, housemaid

jōtō first class

-jū (XIII, 12) through, throughout, in the course of

jú (VII, 4) ten

júdō (XVI, 50) Japanese art of self-defense

jū go (XV, 0) fifteen

jún (XII, 30) pure, genuine, unmixed, sterling, unalloyed

jū ni (XII, 0) twelve

júnsa (IX, 13) policeman

jū rokk(w)a (XVI, 0) sixteenth lesson

jū san (XIII, 0) thirteen

jū shi (XIV, 0) fourteen

K

ká (I, 2) an interrogative particle placed after the verb to make the sentence a question

ka or

ka getsu (XIV, 36) *num. aux.* for months

*kaban (XV, 32) valise, suitcase

kádo (IX, 18) corner, angle

kaera- (VII, 25) *neg. stem* of kaeru return

kaeri (VIII, 60) *n. f.* of kaeru return

kaerimasu (X, 15) *pres.* of kaeru return

*kaeru (verb of the first class) change, exchange; genkin ni — cash

káeru (VII, 15) *v. i.* (verb of the second class) return, come back, go back, go home

kaete (XIV, 16) *ger.* of kaeru change

*kagen (XII, 52) degree, extent, measure, adjustment

Kagetsu (XI, 35) *name of a restaurant (literally Flower-Moon)*

kai (XI, 7) story, floor; ni — upstairs

kaigun navy, fleet; — no naval

kaikyō channel, strait, sound

kaimashō (VII, 65) *prob. pres.* of kau

*kaimono (VII, 12) *n.* purchase; — suru go shopping

kaitai (IV, 25) *des.* of kau; want to buy

kaitaku (IV, 26) *neg. des.* of kau; do not want to buy

kaite (V, 31) *ger.* of kaku

kaji conflagration, fire

*kakari (X, 20) *n.* charge, duty, business

kakarimashō (VII, 34) *prob. pres.* of kakaru

kakarimasu (VI, 12) *pres.* of kakaru

kakaru *v. i.* hang, be hanging, depend on, cost, take (time), need, require, be called up

kakemashō (IX, 38) *prob. pres.* of kakeru

kakemasu (IV, 49) *pres.* of kakeru

kakéru *v. t.* hang, sit (hang

the legs); see suwaru; denwa (w)o — telephone

kakesasete (XIII, 11) *caus.* of kakeru

kakete (XIV, 60) *ger.* of kakeru

kakimasen (I, 45) *pres. neg.* of kaku

kakimashita (III, 32) *past* of kaku

kakimasu (I, 44) *pres.* of kaku

kakitai (IV, 20) *des.* of kaku

*kakitome (XIV, 46) registration, registered letter

káku write, spell

kamaimasen (X, 42) *pres. neg.* of kamau

Kamakura *a city in Japan*

*kamáu *verb* mind, trouble oneself about, care about, take notice of

kámbi (XVI, 47) perfection, completion

kamí (I, 17) paper

*kampan (XV, 60) deck (of a ship)

*kan interval, period, duration, in the space of

Kanada Canada

kánai (VI, 10) (my) wife

kánari (VII, 32) *adv.* quite, fairly

*Kanda (IX, 61) *a district of Tokio*

*kane (X, 63) money, cash, gold, sum of money

kángáe (XI, 30) *n.* thought, idea

kánjō (XI, 62) *n.* account, bill, computation; — suru calculate

kara- (XV, 3) *neg. stem* of karu

kára (IV, 42) because, since, after; from, out of, through, at the hands of karä (IX, 47) shirt-collar, collar

*karada (XIII, 48) body, physique

káre-kore (XVI, 7) approximately, this and that, one thing and another

Kariforuniya California

kari-nui (X, 59) *composed of* kari *temporary* and the *n. f.* of nuu; basting, tacking; — suru baste, try, fit (a coat) on

karite (XIII, 9) *ger.* of kariru

*kariru borrow, have on loan, hire, rent (a house, land), lease

karu *verb* cut, clip, crop

kashi (VI, 49) confectionery, cake, sweets, candy

kashikomarimáshita (V, 7) all right, willingly (acceding to a request)

*kasu lend, give credit

kata (XIII, 48) shoulder

katá (XI,38) person; kono —, sono —, ano — he, she

katákana (V, 31) *one of the Japanese syllabaries*

kata-michi (XV, 24) one-way, single (ticket)

katsudō movie, cinema, film

katte (XV, 2) *ger.* of karu

*kau (IV, 29) *verb* buy, purchase

*kawa (VII, 26) *neg. stem* of kau

kawa (XVI, 31) river, stream, brook

kawáite (XI, 50) *ger.* of kawaku

kawaku be thirsty, feel thirsty; dry, be dry

*kawase (XIV, 30) money-order, exchange

*kaze (XIII,59) wind, breeze, draught; cold (disease); — (w)o hiku catch cold

kazoemasu (VII, 8) *pres.* of kazoeru

kazóéru (VII, 1) count, reckon, calculate

kázoku (VIII, 44) family, one's folks

keiki business (affairs)

Keijō *capital of Korea*

kékkō,(X, 61) splendid, good, fine; — na excellent, marvelous, delicious, beautiful

*kekkon (VI, 45) marriage, matrimony; — suru wed, be married to, get married, marry

*kembutsu (VI, 27) sightseeing; a visit; — suru do the sights, go sightseeing

kemme (VIII, 67) *combination* of ken and me, an ordinal suffix

kén *num. aux.* house, door

ken prefecture

kéredomo (IV, 26) but, although

késa (VIII, 40) this morning

késhiki (XVI, 53) scenery, landscape

kesu extinguish, put out

ki (X, 10) spirit, mind, feelings; see doku

ki *c. f.* of kuru

ki *c. f.* of kiru

kí (XII, 29) tree, wood

kíbun (XIII, 47) feeling, humor; — ni naru feel like, have a mind to

kiite (IX, 13) *ger.* of kiku

kíito (XVI, 34) raw silk

kíji (IX, 42) quality, material; plain, pure

*kikae (XII, 51) *c. f.* of kikaeru

kikaeru change clothes

kiki (IX, 21) *c. f.* of kiku

*kiku ask a question, inquire; hear, listen to

kimashita (VIII, 22) *past* of kuru

kimasu (XV, 38) *pres.* of kuru

kímben (XVI, 48) diligence, hard work

kimono *composed of the c. f.* of kiru *and* mono; clothes, garments, kimono

*Kimura (XIV, 24) *a Japanese family name*

kin (VII, 39) 1.32 pounds

kínjo (VII, 27) neighborhood, vicinity

kinô (IV, 34) yesterday

kínu (X, 53) silk, silk fabric; — no silken, silk

Kinyōbi (VIII, 9) Friday

*kippu (XV, 37) ticket

kirashite (X, 10) *ger.* of kirasu

kirasu run out of, be short of, be out of stock

kire *num. aux.* for slices of bread, meat, etc.

kirei (na) (VI, 33) beautiful

Kirisuto-kyō (XVI,36) Christianity, Christian religion

kiru put on, wear

kiru *verb* cut, break off

kiseru pipe (for smoking); — wo suu smoke a pipe

kishá (XV, 1) railway train

*kita (IX, 26) *n.* north

kite (V, 12) *ger.* of kuru

*kitte (XIV, 47) postage-stamp, check

ko- *neg. stem* of kuru

*ko (VII, 18) child; *a diminutive prefix;* onna no — girl; otoko no — boy

Kóbe (VI, 30) *a city in Japan*

Kóbe-yuki (XIV, 48) Kobe bound, bound for Kobe

*kochira (VII, 55) this place, here, this way, this, this one

kodomo child, children

kogane change (in the sense of small sum of money); see tsuri

kogítte (XIV, 5) cheque, check

kōhí (III, 4) coffee

*koko (V, 12) here, this place; — no this

kokónotsu (VII, 7) nine

kokórómóchí (XII, 26) feeling, sensation, mood, spirits

*kokorozashi (XI, 66) a kind offer, gift, kindness, gratuity

koku (XVI, 52) nation, country

*kokumin (XVI, 48) nation, people, nationality

kokyū breath, respiration

*komáru be suffering

Komatsu (XI, 55) *name of a restaurant* (literally small pine)

komatte (XIII, 49) *ger.* of komaru

kómban (II, 1) this evening

kome uncooked rice

kón (X, 51) navy-blue, dark blue

kóndo (XIII, 58) this time, now, lately; — no present, next, recent

*konna (XIII, 4) such, like this; — ni like this, thus, in this way, so, so much

konnen this year

kónnichi (I, 1) today, this day

*kono (II, 28) *adj.* this, these

*kono-goro (XV, 63) now, at present, nowadays; lately

konómí (XII, 7) *n.* liking, fondness, wish; — no favorite

konominasu (XVI, 49) *pres.* of konomu

konómu *verb* like, be fond of, be partial to

koppu drinking glass, tumbler

*kore (I, 18) *pron.* this, these; — kara now, from now on

korosu kill, murder, slaughter

koseba (XVI, 9) *cond.* of kosu

koshi (XV, 43) *n. f.* of kosu

koshiraeru *verb* manufacture, make, get ready

koshiraete (X, 56) *ger.* of koshiraeru

kosu *verb* cross, pass, go across

kotó (IV, 28) thing, matter (abstract), affair, fact, occurrence, case; anata no — abcut you

kōtō (XVI, 46) high-class, higher; — no advanced, high

kotóbá (XVI, 41) word, speech, language, term, phrase, dialect

kowasaremashita (XIII, 1) *past* of kowasu

kowásu break, break down, destroy, impair

kozutsumi (XI, 37) parcel, package; see ko and zutsumi

*ku (VII, 4) nine

*kuchi (XIII, 54) mouth

kuchi-hige mustache

kudaru *hon.* or oriru; come down, get down, descend

kudasái (V, 16) *imp.* of kudasaru please, please give me

kudasaimasen (XIV, 16) *pres. neg.* of kudasaru

kudasaru give, confer on, be so kind as to, condescend

*kuni (XVI, 16) nation, country, land, territory

*kurai (IX, 13) *surd form* of gurai

*kureru (XII, 42) give, let (a person) have

kureta (XI, 38) *past* of kureru

kúro (X, 24) *stem* of kuroi

kurói (X, 1) black, dark

kúru *irreg.* come, come up, come down, approach, be derived from

*kuruma (VIII, 68) rickshaw, wagon, cart, vehicle, automobile; kuruma-ya (VIII, 68) rickshaw man, rickshaw station

*kusuri (XIII, 61) medicine, drug

kutsú (X, 1) shoes, boots

kutsúshita (X, 65) socks, stockings, hosiery; see kutsu and shita under

-k(w)a (II, 0) lesson, section, department

Kwagetsu (XI, 35) *var.* of Kagetsu

k(w)ayóbi (VIII, 16) Tuesday

*kyaku (X, 22) customer, guest, visitor, passenger

kyó (VIII, 34) today, this day

*Kyobashi (IX, 16) a district in Tokio

Kyōbashi-yuki (IX, 31) Kyobashi-bound, bound for Kyobashi

*kyōiku (XVI, 40) education, instruction, training, bringing up; — no educational; — suru *verb* educate

kyóku (XIV, 29) office, bureau

Kyóto (XVI, 25) *a city in Japan*

k(y)u (VII, 4) *var.* of ku nine

kyúji (XI, 61) waiter, waitress, bell-boy, page, office boy, servant; — suru wait on at table, serve at dinner

Kyūkyō Catholic religion

*kyūkō (XV, 24) express train, fast train; — **suru** hasten, hurry, go posthaste

Kyúshū (XVI, 18) *one of the islands of Japan proper*

M

ma- *prefix* pure, genuine, just, right, due

-ma (XII, 16) *aux. num.* room, chamber, apartment, space

mā (XIV, 24) Well, I say, come, just do! oh, my!

machi (VI, 6) *c. f.* of **matsu**

machí (VIII, 27) town, city, street

máda (XII, 43) still, yet, moreover, only

máde (VII, 34) until, till, before, by, to, up to, down to, as far as; — **ni** by, not later than

mádo (V, 27) window

mae (XI, 43) *num. aux.* helping, portion

máe (VII, 49) front; — **no** front, fore, former; — **ni** ago, since, before, formerly

*magaru *v. i.* bend, curve, be bent, turn, make a turn

magatte (IX, 18) *ger.* of **magaru**

mageru *v. t.* bend, lean (forward, backward); **koshi** (w)o — bend the legs, bend over

magete *ger.* of **mageru**

*mai (I, 32) every, each

mai *num. aux.* for flat thin objects, such as paper, dishes, blankets

*maido (X, 39) each time, constantly; — **arigató** I am greatly indebted to you

mairemashō (XII, 13) *prob. pres. pot.* of **mairu**

mairimashita (VI, 53) *past of* **mairu**

mairimashō (VIII, 18) *prob. pres.* of **mairu**

mairimasu (XI, 63) *pres.* of **mairu**

máiru *humble* go, come, call

makeru reduce in price, make cheaper, be defeated

makete (VIII, 53) *ger.* of **makeru**

maki-tabako cigarette

mán (VIII, 40) ten thousand

manabimasen (I, 43) *pres. neg.* of **manabu**

manabimasu (I, 40) *pres.* of **manabu**

manabu study, take lessons in

Manira manila

*mannaka (XVI, 17) *n.* middle, center, heart; — **no** middle, central; see **ma-** and **naka**

maru *a word of unknown origin always added to names of ships*

*marui (VI, 53) round, circular

massúgu (IX, 33) straight, direct, straight on; — **na** straight; — **ni** in a straight line; see **ma-** and **sugu**

*mata (VI, 59) again, too, moreover

mata- (VII, 15) *neg. stem* of **matsu**

matase (VI, 8) *n. f. caus.* of **matsu**

matawa (IX, 52) or, either . . . or; see **mata** and **wa**

matchi match

mátsu wait, wait for, expect

*Matsumoto (II, 9) *a family name*

matte (V, 41) *ger.* of **matsu**

*mawasu (IV, 31) drive (a vehicle), turn, spin, refer, transfer

*me (XII, 29) eye, vision

-me (VIII, 67) *an ordinal suffix*

Meiji year period from 1868 to 1912

Mekishiko Mexico

mén (XII, 27) *n.* face, features, surface, front

ménseki (XVI, 5) area, square measure

meshí (XI, 24) food, meal, cooked rice, livelihood

*michi (XII, 20) road, street, highway, thoroughfare

miemasu (XII, 29) *pot. pres.* of **miru**

miéru (XII, 11) can see, be seen, be visible, seem, appear, look as if

miete (XIII, 60) *ger.* of **mieru**

*migi (IX, 25) right (direction); — **no** right, abovementioned

*mihon (X, 47) sample, specimen, pattern

mijíkái short, brief

mijikaku (XV, 3) *adv. form* of **mijikai**

mimasen (III, 20) *pres. neg.* of **miru**

mimashita (III, 17) *past of* **miru**

mimashō (IX, 14) *prob. pres.* of **miru**

mimasu *pres.* of **miru**

miná (II, 19) all, everybody, everything; — **de** in all, all together

*minami (IX, 25) south; — **no** southern; — **ni** in the south, to the south

Minámí-Ámerika (XIV, 42) South America

míru see, look at, try

misé (VIII, 7) shop, store

miséru show, display, let (a person) see

misete (IX, 40) *ger.* of miseru

mite (V, 3) *ger.* of miru; —
morau receive a visit

*mitsu-gumi (X, 53) suit of
western clothes, a set of
three

mitsukarimasen (XIII, 6)
pres. of mitsukaru

*mitsukaru *v. i.* be discovered,
be found (out)

*mitsukeru *v. t.* find (out),
discover, perceive

mittsú (VII, 6) three

miukemasu (XV, 42) *pres.* of
miukeru

miukeru look, appear (to be),
see

miya Shinto shrine

miyako capital city

*mizu (XI, 61) cold water;
see o-yu

mizúúmi (XVI, 32) lake,
pond

*mo (III, 41) *post.* also
either; ... mo ... mo both
... and; not ... either,
neither ... nor

mo even, if

*mō (VIII, 41) already, yet;
now; another, more, again;
—sukoshi a little more

*mochikomu bring in, carry
in, take to

mochikonde (XV, 34) *ger.* of
mochikomu

Mokuyōbi (VIII, 16) Thursday

monó (X, 20) thing (con-
crete), object, matter; see
tatemono and kimono; per-
son, fellow; kakari no —
person in charge; see koto

moraimashō (VII, 57) *prob.*
pres. of morau

moraitai (X, 45) *des.* of
morau

morattara (IX, 54) *cond.* of
morau

moratte (X, 41) *ger.* of morau

*morau (VII, 60) get, have,
receive, take, have (something) done, have (a per-
son) do

móshi-móshi (XIII,13) hello!,
are you there?, I say there,
excuse me

mōshimasu (VI, 5) *pres.* of
mōsu

mōsu *verb* say, tell, speak to,
declare, name

Motomachi (VIII, 63) *name
of a street in Tokio*

mótsu have, hold, own, possess, maintain

motte (V, 10) *ger.* of motsu;
motte iku take (literally,
go having); motte kuru
bring (literally, come having)

mótto (VI, 36) more, some
more, further

móttomo (XVI, 30) most,
extremely

mugíwárá (X, 26) straw;
mugiwara-bōshi straw hat

muite (IX, 24) *ger.* of muku

mukatte (XII, 21) *ger.* of
mukau; toward, against

*mukau *verb* face, front, be
opposite, look out on, op-
pose

mukeru *verb* face, turn, aim,
point, direct

mukete *ger.* of mukeru

muku *verb* face, turn, look,
be suitable for

muné (XIII, 48) chest,
breast, bosom, feelings

múri (XIII, 60) unreasona-
bleness, strain, force; — na
unjust, strenuous; — ni
forcibly, unreasonably

*musuko (VI, 44) son, boy

musūmé (VI, 44) daughter,
girl, young woman

muttsú (VII, 7) six

muzukashii hard, difficult,
troublesome, laborious

muzukashiku (XV, 53) *adj.*
and *neg. f.* of muzukashii

myōgó-jitsu (XV, 13) day
after tomorrow

myōgó-nichi day after to-
morrow

N

n' (XIII, 7) *contracted form*
of mono

na name, given name, fame

na (VI, 33) *post. which relates
two nouns*

nadákái (XVI, 31) famous,
well-known

nado (XVI, 37) and so forth,
and the like, et cetera

nagái (VI, 57) long

nagara (XVI, 2) while, as, at
the same time that, during

nágasa (IX, 48) length

Nagásaki (XIV, 56) *city in
Japan*

Nagasaki-yuki (XV, 5) bound
for Nagasaki

nagashi bath service (washing of people by the bath
attendant); scullery, sink

nái (VII, 20) is not, are not,
has (have) not, be lacking,
be missing, there is no ...

naka (XIV, 58) inside, interior, midway; — ni within, inside; — de within,
between, among; naka-
naka very, considerably,
quite

nakáóré-bōshi (X, 24) soft
hat, felt hat

nakatta (XV, 53) *past* of nai;
was not, were not

nakereba (VII, 25) *cond.* of
nai; if not, if there is not,
if there are not

nakute (VIII, 60) *ger.* of nai;
not, not being

*namae (VIII, 13) name; see
na name and mae front
námi (XV, 61) wave, surf
nán (VII, 22) *var.* of nani;
what; how many; — ji
what time; when; — no
what kind of; — nen how
many years; — nichi how
many days; — to what
nanátsu (VII, 7) seven, seven
years old
náni (I, 14) what, which,
whatever
náni ka (IV, 14) something,
anything, some, any
náni mo (III, 15) nothing
(*with negative verb*) no
*Nan-yo (XVI, 14) South
Seas
naorimashō (XIII, 64) *prob.*
pres. of naoru
naóru *v. i.* get well, be cured
(of a disease), be mended,
be repaired, be fixed
naoshite (X, 41) *ger.* of naosu
naosu *v. t.* mend, repair, cure,
restore, correct
nara (XII, 36) if, provided,
in case, if it is
nara- *neg. stem* of naru
naraba *var.* of nareba
narau learn, be taught, take
lessons in
nareba (XII, 4) *cond. stem* of
naru *plus* ba (wa); if, if it
is, since, as
narimasen (VII, 15) *pres.*
neg. of naru
narimáshita (VI, 19) *past* of
naru
narimashō (XII, 40) *prob.*
pres. of naru
narimásu (IX, 53) *pres.* of
naru
naritatsu consist of, be composed of, be effected
*naritatte (XVI, 16) *ger.* of
naritatsu

náru (VIII, 26) become, be,
get, come to, change into,
elapse
nasai (I, 49) *imp.* of násaru;
do
nasáru do, perform, accom-
plish
natsú (X, 30) summer
natta (XIII, 60) *past.* of naru
natte (XII, 51) *ger.* of naru
náze (IV, 39) why, how, for
what reason
ne cost, price
né (VIII, 61) isn't that right?,
you see, doesn't it?, don't
you, I believe, I dare say,
etc.
*nedan (IX, 43) cost, price,
terms
nedókó (XIII, 45) bed, cot,
berth, bunk
negái (VI, 13) *n. f.* of negau;
entreaty, petition, request,
desire, wish
negaimasu (XI, 52) *pres.* of
negau
negáu *verb* request, beg, be-
seech, petition, desire, wish,
hope for
nemuru *verb* sleep, fall asleep
nén (VIII, 31) year; — ni
yearly, per annum
neraremasen (XIII, 44) *pres.*
neg. pass. (pot.) of neru
neru lie down, go to bed, go
to sleep
netsú (XIII, 55) tempera-
ture, fever, heat, mania, fad
ní (VII, 3) two
*ni (III, 28) *post.* at, on, to,
in, into, from, for, in exchange for
*niai (X, 55) *n. f.* of niau
niáu match well, befit, suit,
become, be in keeping with
*nichi (VIII, 34) day; —
gogo; afternoon; — nichi
everyday, day after day

Nichi-Bei Japanese-Ameri-
can
Nichiyóbi (VIII, 15) Sunday
Nigatsu (VIII, 31) February
nigekomimasu *pres.* of nige-
komú
nigekomu *composed of c. f.* of
nigeru flee, run away and
komu be full; run into,
take refuge in
Nihon (IV, 3) *var.* of Nippon
Japan; — go Japanese lan-
guage; — no *adj.* Japanese
Níhon-fū (XII, 30) Japanese
style
Nikkō *city in Japan*
nikú (III, 13) meat, flesh
nikusashi (XI, 46) *n.* fork
nikú-ya (VII, 34) butcher-
shop, butcher
nímotsu (XII, 41) baggage,
luggage, load, burden, personal effects
*nin (VIII, 44) *num. aux.*
person, people
*ninjin (VII, 50) carrot
Níppón (I, 37) *var.* of Nihon
Japan; — go: Japanese
language; — no Japanese
Nippón-jín (II, 19) *n.* Japanese (person)
Nippon-Kai (XVI, 9) Sea of
Japan
ni-san (XIV, 36) two or
three
*nishi (IX, 26) west; — no
western, west
niru resemble, look like, take
after
niru boil, cook
nite (XVI, 39) *ger.* of niru
resemble
*niwa (XII, 27) garden,
courtyard; — shi gardener
*no (III, 17) *post.* enables the
preceding noun to function
as an adjective or indicates
that it is the possessor;

makes a pronoun of a preceding adjective; one; 's, of, in, at, on

no de (XIII, 44) because, on account of, owing to

nódo (XI, 50) throat, gullet; — no guttural, jugular

nokóru remain, be left over, be left behind, stay

nokotte (XV, 28) *ger.* of nokoru

nomasaremashita (XIII, 46) *caus. past* of nomu; caused to drink, had drunk, had taken (by mouth)

nomimasu (III, 4) *pres.* of nomu

nomitai (IV, 17) *des.* of nomu

nomitaku (IV, 19) *des. neg.* of nomu

nómu drink, taste, swallow; smoke (cigarette or cigar); see suu

nónde (XIII, 62) *ger.* of nomu

noremásu (XV, 15) *pot. pres.* of noru

nori (IX, 32) *n. f.* of noru

nori (XI, 11) starch, paste

norikáeru *composed of c. f.* of noru and kaeru change; change trains, cars, transfer

norikaetara (IX, 20) *cond.* of norikaeru

noru ride, get into, get on, go on board

Noruwěi Norway

nottara (IX, 16) *cond.* of noru

*nozomi (X, 22) *n. f.* of nozomu; desire, hope

nozómu *verb* desire, care for, hope, hope for

nugu take off (articles of clothing)

nuguu *verb* wipe, mop

núi (X, 60) *n. f.* of nuu

núu *verb* sew, stitch

nutte *ger.* of nuu

Nyū Yōku (IV, 10) New York

O

o- (VI, 33) *honorific prefix*

Ō-Bei (XVI, 38) Europe and America; — no occidental, western

*o-cha (III, 9) tea

*ōfuku (XV, 22) return trip, round trip, going and coming; — suru go and come back, carry on correspondence with, keep company with

o-hayō (XIV, 1) *composed of* o and *the form* of hayai used *with* gozaru; good morning (literally, [it is] early)

o-ide (VI, 18) *hon. c. f.* of kuru, iku and iru

oishíi (VII, 58) tasty, good to the taste, palatable

oishiku (VI, 54) *adv. and neg. f.* of oishii

oishiū (VII, 59) *form of* oishii used *with* gozaru

oite (XIII, 4) *ger.* of oku put

okásan (VI, 26) composed of o, kǎ, and san; mother

Okayama *city in Japan*

ōkíi (VI, 36) big, large, great, loud

ōkiku (VI, 41) *adv. and neg. f.* of ōkii

ōkikute (XII, 34) *ger.* of ōkii

okimashō (X, 61) *prob. pres.* (*fut.*) of oku put

okimásu (VIII, 54) *pres.* of oku put

o-ki-no-doku (X, 10) I am very sorry (literally, spirit poison)

okiraremasen (XIII, 45) *pass.* (*pot.*) *pres.* of okiru

*okíru get up, rise, get out of bed, awake

*ōkisa (IX, 48) size, dimen-

sions, magnitude, volume; see ōkii and -sa

okitai (X, 42) *des.* of oku

ōkiū (XII, 6) *form of* ōkii used *with* gozaru

okosan (VI, 42) *composed of* o, ko and san; children

oku one hundred million

oku put, place, leave; deposit; allow

okureru be late, be behind schedule; lose (time), go slow

okuri-dashi (XIV, 45) *c. f.* of okuridasu

okurídásu *c. f.* of okuru plus dasu send out, forward; see off

okurimasen (III, 46) *pres. neg.* of okuru

okurimashita (III, 44) *past* of okuru

okurimasu *pres.* of okuru

okuritai (XIV, 56) *des.* of okuru

*okuru send, forward, see off, escort

okusama (VI, 20) madam, wife, married lady; Mrs.; see okusan

okusan (VIII, 36) *composed* of óku interior and san; (your, his) wife

okutta (XI, 4) *past* of okuru

okutte (IX, 54) *ger.* of okuru

ō-misoka last day of the year; New Year's Eve

ómo (XVI, 34) principal, chief, surface, face, front

omoi heavy, weighty, serious

omoimasu (X, 50) *pres.* of omou

omosa weight

omóshirói *composed of* omo face and shiroi; funny, queer, interesting

omoshiro-sō (XIV, 39) *com-*

posed of stem of omoshiroi and sō

omo-sugiru (XIV, 49) *composed* of omoi and sugiru

omotte (XIV, 31) *ger.* of omou

omóu think, think of, think about, judge, believe, intend, hope, fear

omowaremasu (XIII, 61) *pres.* of omowareru

omowareru *pass. f.* of omou; seem, appear, impress (a person) as

onáji (X, 8) same, identical; — ni equally

o-naka *n.* (XI, 58) stomach, belly, inside

onná (II, 12) woman, female; — no women's, feminine; — no benjo women's toilet

onna no hitó (II, 12) woman; kono —, sono —, ano — she; see hito

onna no hitotachi (II, 34) women; kono —, sono —, ano — they (women); see hitotachi

orimasu (X, 11) *pres.* of oru

oríru go down, come down, descend, alight, disembark

orite (X, 65) *c. f.* of oriru

Ōsaka (VI, 30) *a city in Japan*

*oshieru teach, impart, show, give lessons in

oshiete (IX, 60) *ger.* of oshieru

osoi late, slow

osóréru fear, be afraid of

osorete (XV, 61) *ger.* of osoreru

Ōsutorariya Australia

otókó (II, 26) male, man; — no man's, gentlemen's, masculine; — no benjo men's toilet

otoko no hitó (II, 26) man; kono —, sono —, ano — he

otoko no hitotachi (II, 32) men; kono —, sono —, ano — they (men)

otósan (VI, 26) father

ototo *var.* of otōto

otōtó (XIV, 33) *var.* of ototo; younger brother

*ototoi (XI, 55) day before yesterday

o-tsuri; see tsuri

oya parent, parents

oyogimasu *pres.* of oyogu

oyogu *verb* swim, sail

o-yu hot water, hot bath

P

pán (VIII, 1) bread

pán-ya (VII, 64) baker, bakery

Pari Paris

*pen (I, 7) pen

Penshirubania Pennsylvania

pin *n.* pin, hairpin

pondo pound, £

R

rai- *prefix* next

ráigetsu (XIV, 37) next month

raimen next year

*raishū (X, 59) next week

-rashii (XVI, 52) *suffix* seem, appear, likely to, like, -ly

rei zero

*renshū (V, 31) exercise, practice, training; — suru *verb* practice, drill

*ri (IX, 13) ri (3.927 kilometers)

rikúgun (VI, 17) military service, army; — no army, military

rokkin (VII, 53) *contraction* of roku and kin

Rokkī-zan Rocky Mountains

rokk(w)a (VI, 0) *contraction*

of roku and kwa; six lessons; dai — sixth lesson

rokú (VII, 3) six

Rondon London

roppíki (VIII, 38) *contraction* of roku and hiki

roppyaku (XIII, 13) *contraction* of roku and hyaku

Róshya (XVI, 10) Russia; — no Russian

*ryōhō (X, 37) both, both sides, both directions; — no both, in two ways

*ryoken (XV, 49) passport

*ryōkin (XIII, 20) fee, charge, fare, rate

ryokò travelling; — suru *verb* travel, make a trip

ryōri cooking, cuisine; — suru *verb* cook; — nin *n.* cook

ryóríya (XI, 27) restaurant

S

-sa *a suffix which makes a noun from an adjective*

sā (XI, 39) come now, well, ah

sahodo (IX, 43) *adv.* so, so much, very

*sai (VII, 18) *num. aux.* year, age, years

sají (XI, 47) teaspoon; ōkii — tablespoon

saji-zutsu (XIII, 62) spoonful

*sakana (III, 6) fish

*sakana-ya (VIII, 6) fishstore, fish dealer, fish monger

*sake (XI, 49) (alcoholic) liquor, rice wine; — ni you get drunk

saki front, tip; — no previous, former; — ni forward, ahead; massugu — ni straight ahead

sakúban (XIII, 11) last night

sakunen last year

Samá (VI, 10) *var.* of San; Mr., Messrs., Master, Miss, Mrs.

samá (X, 10) *same as* Sama; a title of respect, often used with names of occupations and relatives of the second or third person

sambámmé (XIV, 22) *contraction* of san, ban, and me; third

*sambun (VII, 61) *contraction* of san and bun; third

*sambutsu (XVI, 34) product, production, result

sámbyaku (VIII, 63) *contraction* of san and hyaku; three hundred

*sampo (XVI, 1) *n.* walk, stroll; — (w)o suru take a walk

sámpu (XVI, 20) *contraction* of san and fu; the three chief urban prefectures

samúi cold, chilly

*San (II, 5) *var.* of Sama; Mr., Miss, Mrs.

san *var.* of sama

*san (III, 0) three; — chōme third street

-san mountain

*sangai (XII, 19) *contraction* of san and kai; third floor

sangen (XVI, 20) *contraction* of san and ken prefecture

*sansei (XI, 21) agreement, approval; — suru *verb* agree, approve of, support, vote for

*sareru (XIV, 37) *pres. pass.* of suru

sareta (XIII, 7) *past. pass.* of suru

sashiagemashō (XI, 42) *prob. pres. (fut.)* of sashiageru

*sashiageru offer, give (to a superior); life up; see ageru

sashímí (VIII, 49) raw fish slices

sáte (VII, 22) well, so, but, now, however

*satsu (XI, 64) *aux. num.* volume, copy (of books or magazines); note (money)

Saun Pauro São Paulo

sawara- (XIII, 52) *neg. stem* of sawaru

*sawaru *verb* touch, feel

*sayō (X, 47) so, yes, indeed

sayonára (I, 48) goodbye, so long; (literally, if so . . . [must be]; see sayō and nara)

sayōnara *var.* of sayonara

séi (VI, 47) stature, height; — no takasa height

séido (XVI, 40) system. organization, institution

*Seireki (VIII, 33) A.D., the Christian era

seito student, scholar

séiyō (XII, 4) *n.* the West, the Occident; — no occidental, western

sekái (XVI, 35) world, earth; — no international

sékken (XII, 48) soap; sentaku — laundry soap

semái (X, 8) narrow, limited, cramped

sembiki (VIII, 41) *combination* of sen and hiki

sén (VII, 43) 1/100 of a yen

sen thousand

sengetsu last month

sensei teacher, instructor

*senshū (XI, 4) last week

*sentaku (XI, 4) *n.* washing; — mono wash (articles to be washed or already washed); — suru *verb* wash, do washing

sentaku ya (XI, 10) laundry (place), laundry-man, laun-

dress, washerman, washer-woman

sha (XV, 35) vehicle, car, wagon

sháke (VIII, 37) salmon

*shaku (IX, 48) Japanese measure approximately a foot (10 sun = 1 shaku): .33140 yards

*shashin (VI, 24) photograph, picture; — ya photographer's shop

shashinki camera

*shashō (IX, 28) conductor, guard

shátsu (IX, 39) shirt

shi (XVI, 2) *c. f.* of suru

shi (XII, 28) and, besides, moreover

shí (VII, 3) four

shiai *n.* match, game; jūdō no — judo match; — suru play a match

shibai play, drama, theater, fake

shibáraku (XIV, 24) for a while, for a spell

*Shiberiya (XVI, 10) Siberia

shichí (VIII, 1) *var.* of hichi; seven

shi-go (IX, 7) four or five

*shigoto (XIV, 39) *n.* work, toil, business, job

*shika (XV, 28) only, but, no more than, barely

Shikago Chicago

shikákú (VI, 51) square

shikán (VI, 18) military officer

shikáshi (VII, 43) but, however

*shikata (X, 13) way, method, remedy

*shiki (X, 28) the four seasons

Shikóku (XVI, 18) *one of the islands of Japan proper*

shima (IX, 39) stripes; — no striped

shimá (XVI, 16) island
shimáguni (XVI, 5) composed of shima *island* and
kuni; island country
shimaimasu (XIV, 65) *pres.*
of shimau
shimashita (V, 21) *past* of
suru
shimásu (I, 32) *pres.* of suru
*shimau finish, conclude
shimaru *v. i.* be shut, be
closed
shimatte (XII, 45) *ger.* of
shimaru
*shimbun (I, 15) newspaper
shiméru *v. t.* shut, close
shímete (V, 29)*ger.* of shimeru
shímpo (XVI, 39) *n.* progress,
advance, improvement; —
suru progress, advance
Shína (XVI, 13) China; — no
Chinese
Shinagawa *a district in Tokio*
shinamono article, goods,
wares
Shiná-jin (II, 21) Chinese
person
Shinánó-gawa (XVI, 32) the
Shinano river; see -gawa
*shindai (XII, 31) bed, couch,
sleeping berth; — sha sleeping car
Shinkyō Protestant religion
*shinsatsu (XIII, 37) medical examination, diagnosis;
— suru examine a patient
*shinshitsu (XII, 16) bedroom, stateroom
Shíntō (XVI, 37) Shintoism,
the Shinto religion
shinu die, pass away
shirarete (XVI, 35) *pass. ger.*
of shiru
shiraseru *caus.* of shiru; inform, let know, report
shirasete *caus. ger.* of shiru;
see shiraseru

shirimasén (XII, 3) *pres. neg.*
of shiru
shiro (X, 24) *stem* of shiroi
shirói white, blank
shiru know
*shita (X, 65) lower part,
downstairs, first floor,
under, below, beneath
shita (XIII, 60) *past* of suru
shita (XIII, 54) tongue
shitai (IV, 12) *des.* of suru
shitaku (IV, 13) *des. neg.* of
suru
shitara *cond.* of suru; ni-san
nichi — after two or three
days
*shite (V, 8) *ger.* of suru
shitsúrei (V, 21) discourtesy,
impoliteness, rudeness; —
suru beg pardon
shitte *ger.* of shiru
shízuka (XII, 20) — na still,
quiet, silent; — ni *adv.* still,
calmly, quietly
shō-gakkō (XVI, 45) elementary school
*Shōgatsu (VIII, 36) January, the new year
shōji sliding screen
*shōkai (VI, 11) introduction, presentation; — suru
introduce, present, recommend
shōkin specie, cash
*shoku (XI, 23) food, eating,
meal, fare
shokúgyō (XIV, 35) occupation, profession
shōsū (XVI, 51) a small number, minority
*Shōwa (VIII, 29) year period from 1926 to the present
shú master, employer, chief,
the Lord
shú (XVI, 6) state, country,
province, continent
shū week

shufu mistress of the house,
housewife, landlady
shúfu (XVI, 22) capital city,
metropolis; — no metropolitan
shújin (VI, 1) *composed of*
shu and jin; master of the
house, husband, landlord
shúkan (XV, 45) week, week's
extent; see shū week and
kan extent
shúkyō (XVI, 36) religion,
creed
shu-to-shite(XVI,36)mainly,
chiefly; see shu, to and shite
sō (I, 25) thus, so; — desu
that's right, so it is
sō *num. aux.* for ships and
boats
sō *num. aux.* for folding
screens
-sō (XII, 35) looking, appearing, seeming; — desu people say, it is said, I hear
that, it seems
sóba (XIII, 3) side, vicinity;
— no neighboring; — ni by
the side of, alongside, beside
*sochira (VII, 43) there, that,
those
*sode (IX, 48) sleeve
*soko (VIII, 36) that place,
there; — no that, that one;
— ni (de) in that place,
there
soku (X, 1) *num. aux.* for
pairs of footwear
sókutatsu (XIV, 52) express
delivery, special delivery,
urgent
sonna such, like that, that
sort of; — ni in that way
*sono (II, 26) *adj.* that, those
(near the person spoken
to); — uchi among the
rest, of the number; — ue
moreover, besides

*sore (II, 24)*pron.* that, that one, those (near the person spoken to); — **de wa** in that case, then; — **kara** after that, since then

soru *verb* shave

soshite (III, 4) and (connecting clauses)

sōshite *var.* of soshite

sotte (XV, 3) *ger.* of soru

su, do; see suru

sugíru (X, 50) exceed, pass, be over, be more than; pass by, pass through, elapse

súgu (VI, 6) soon, at once, immediately, in a moment

*suiei (XVI, 50) swimming, bathing; — suru *verb* swim, bathe

súihei (XI, 17) sailor, seaman

*suika (VII, 58) watermelon

*suimono (XI, 44) soup

Suiyóbi (VIII, 16) Wednesday

sukí (VIII, 49) *n.* liking, fondness; — desu *verb* like, be fond of; dai — *n.* love; dai — desu *verb* love, be enamoured of; — na likeable, enjoyable

sukimasen (VIII, 51) *pres. neg.* of suku like

sukimáshita (XI, 19) *past* of suku become empty; o-naka ga — I am hungry (my stomach got empty)

sukiyaki (XI, 43) sukiyaki (beef slices cooked in Japanese fashion)

suku *verb* like, love, be fond of

suku become empty, become vacant

sukóshi (IV, 38) little, few, somewhat; — mo not in the least

Sumisu (VII, 12) Smith

sumitai (IV, 7) *des.* of sumu want to live

sumitaku (IV, 11) *des. neg.* of sumu

*sumō (XVI, 50) *n.* wrestling, wrestling-match

*sumpō (X, 58) measure, dimensions; —(w)o toru take one's measure for clothes

súmu *verb* live, dwell, reside, occupy

sumu *verb* end, finish, be completed

sun (IX, 49) about 1.19 inches (the Japanese inch)

súnde (V, 43) *ger.* of sumu dwell

sunde (XIV, 64) *ger.* of sumu end, finish

Supein Spain; — go Spanish language; — no Spanish

súreba (XIII, 63) *cond.* of suru

*suru (IV, 43) *verb* do, try, act, make, cost

*suteru (X, 27) throw away, cast aside

sutte (XIII, 57) *ger.* of suu

*suu *verb* suck, draw in, inhale; smoke (pipe or cigar)

suwaritai (IV, 22) *des.* of suwaru

suwaritaku (IV, 24) *des. neg.* of suwaru

*suwaru (IV, 47) sit down (Japanese fashion, i. e., squat), see kakeru

suwatte (V, 30) *ger.* of suwaru

T

tába (VII, 51) bundle, bunch, faggot

*tabako (XI, 59) tobacco, cigarette; — ya cigar store

tabemasen (III, 15) *pres. neg.* of taberu

tabemáshita (III, 14) *past* of taberu

tabemasu (III, 2) *pres.* of taberu

tabemóno food

tabéru (IV, 34) eat, have to eat

tábeta (XI, 56) *past* of taberu

tabetai (IV, 14) *des.* of taberu

tabetaku (IV, 16) *des. neg.* of taberu

tábete (V, 1) *ger.* of taberu

tabeyō (XI, 20) *fut.* of taberu

tábun (IX, 57) probably, perhaps, maybe

tachimasu (XV, 10) *pres.* of tatsu

tachitai (IV, 22) *des.* of tatsu

tada free of charge, gratis

Taſhéiyō (XVI, 4) Pacific Ocean (tai is the surd form of dai large)

*taihen (VI, 57) very, serious, awful; — ni very, exceedingly

Taiseiyō Atlantic Ocean; — no Atlantic

táishita (XV, 66) many, much, a great deal (tai is the surd form of dai large)

Taishō year period from 1912 to 1925 inclusive

táisō (VIII, 8) great many, good deal, a lot of, very much

*Taiwan (XVI, 13) Formosa

Taiyō Maru S. S. Oceanic

Takagi (XIII, 24) *family name*

takai tall, high, eminent, expensive

Takáhashi (II, 5) *family name*

takaku (IX, 43) *adv.* and *neg. form* of takai

Takashima (IX, 6) *a family name;* — ya (IX, 11) Takashima's store

take bamboo

takeyabu bamboo grove, clump of bamboos

takō (VII, 56) *form* of takai used *with* gozaru

*taku (VI, 1) house, home, residence

takusán (V, 18) a large quantity; — no much, many, abundant; — ni plentifully

takushí(XII, 11) taxi, taxicab

tamágo (III, 3) egg

tamé (XVI, 27) good, advantage, profit; — ni because of, on account of, to, in order to, for the sake of, for

Tanaka *a family name*

Tarō *a man's given name*

táshika (X, 4) I think, I suppose, if I am not mistaken

tashite (XII, 55) *ger.* of tasu

*tasu *verb* add

tasú (XVI, 54) a large number, majority; — no many, a number of

tatémono (XII, 12) building, architecture

tateraremasen (XVI, 28) *pass. neg.* of tateru

tatéru *verb* build, erect, establish, set up

tátsu (IV, 44) *verb* stand, stand up, come forward, depart

tatte (V, 5) *ger.* of tatsu

té (V, 10) *n.* hand

*tegami (I, 11) *composed* of te and the sonant form of kami; letter(epistle)

teishaba railway station, depot

teki drop, drops of liquid

teki enemy, foe

Tekisasu (XVI, 6) Texas

tempura fried shrimp

*tenisu (XVI, 50) tennis

ténki (XVI, 1) weather

*tennin (XIV, 37) change of post; — suru *verb* change one's position, transfer (position)

*tenugui (XII, 49) *composed* of te and the *n. f.* of nuguu

*to (I, 13) *post* and (connecting nouns and pronouns), with; if, when; that, as

*to (V, 28) door

tō the said

tố (VII, 7) ten

tō (XV, 24) class, grade; ittō first class; san tō third class

tóbi-iró (X, 11) brown

tobitai (IV, 27) *des.* of tobu

*tobu (IV, 28) *verb* fly, jump, skip, hop

todokemashō (IX, 52) *prob. pres. (fut.)* of todokeru

todókéru forward, send, report, notify

*tōfu (XI, 44) bean-curds

*tōi (VI, 28) far, distant

*tokai (XVI, 24) city, town; — no urban

*tokei (X, 40) watch, clock

tokí (X, 64) time, occasion, opportunity

*Tōkiō (IV, 10) Tokio

tokkyū (XV, 8) limited express train

*tokoro (VII, 30) place, locality, one's house, thing, thing that, what, time, while, occasion, but, on the contrary

*toko-ya (XV, 1) barber, hair-dresser, barber shop

tōku (VI, 32) *adv.* and *neg. f.* of tōi

tomari (XII, 38) *n. f.* of tomaru

tomarimasen (XV, 17)

*tomaru *v. i.* lodge, stop, stop at, stop in

tomeru *v. t.* give lodging, put (a person) up, stop

tómo (X, 37) both, together with, as well as

*tomodachi (III, 24) friend, companion; *originally a*

plural; *composed* of tomo and dachi, *the sonant form* of tachi

*tonari (VIII, 20) *n.* neighbor; —no next-door, neighboring

tonde (VII, 9) *ger.* of tobu

toranku (XV, 37) trunk, suitcase, valise

toremashō (XII, 47) *prob. pres. pot.* of toru

tori bird, fowl, chicken

tori (X, 37) *n. f.* of toru

tōri (XII, 30) road, street, as, like, in the manner of; see tōru

*tori-atsukai (XV, 47) treatment, dealing, handling; see tori-atsukau

tori-atsukau *verb* treat, deal with, transact

*torihiki (XIV, 7) transactions, dealings; — suru *verb* do business with, deal with, have an account with

toritai (XV, 2) *des.* of toru

toríúchí (X, 25) fowling, shooting; — bōshi cap

tóru take, hold, get, receive, engage, buy

tốru go through, pass through, get through

tsugí (V, 31) next, following

*tsugố (XIII, 39) convenience, circumstances, arrangement

*tsuide (VIII, 11) next, secondly; — ni incidentally, by the way, while, when

tsuite (V, 38) *ger.* of tsuku follow; concerning, about, following; — iku follow (there); — kuru follow (here)

tsukare (XII, 48) *n. f.* of tsukareru

tsukárete (XII, 46) *ger.* of tsukareru

tsukaréru get tired, grow weary, become fatigued

*tsukau (XI, 46) *verb* use, handle, employ

tsuke- (XI, 11) *neg. stem* of tsukeru

tsukemasu (X, 53) *pres.* of tsukeru

tsukéru attach, sew on, apply, put in, put on

tsukete (XI, 10) *ger.* of tsukeru

tsukí (VIII, 3) month, moon; — ni per month

tsukimashita (VIII, 40) *past* of tsuku

tsukimashō (IX, 55) *prob. pres. (fut.)* of tsuku

tsukimasu (XV, 11) *pres.* of tsuku

ts kú arrive, accompany, wait on, follow

*tsukue (I, 13) desk, table

*tsumetai (XII, 54) cold, chilly, freezing

*tsumori (IX, 2) intention, thought, purpose

*tsureru be attended by, take with, bring with

tsurete (V, 35) *ger.* of tsureru; accompanying; —iku: take (conduct); — kuru bring (a person)

*tsuri (X, 17) change (remainder from money given); see kogane

tsutsumi bundle, package

tsutsúmu *verb* wrap, pack goods

tsutsunde (X, 14) *ger.* of tsutsumu

tsuzuite (XVI, 10) *ger.* of tsuzuku

tsuzuku *verb* continue, follow, appear in succession, be adjacent to

U

uchí (VI, 35) house, home; among, during, within, while; — ni (de) inside, indoors

uchikin (X, 61) deposit (money paid on account)

uchimashitara (XIV, 64) *cond.* of utsu

udé (XIII, 48) arm, skill

*ue (XV, 28) upper part, upside, surface; — no upper, higher, more than; besides, in addition to; after, on, when, since; sono — moreover, besides

Ueda (XVI, 1) *a family name*

*umareru be born

umarete (VIII, 26) *ger.* of umareru

úmi (XV, 55) sea, ocean

*unagi eel; — ya eel restaurant

unagi-meshi (XI, 24) *composed* of unagi and meshi; eel and rice

*undō (XVI, 49) physical exercise, athletic sports, motion; — suru move, be in motion, take exercise

urá (X, 53) *n.* lining, reverse side, inside

urágákí (XIV, 10) *composed* of ura and the *n. f.* of kaku; endorsement

urikiremashita (XV, 29)

uríkíréru *composed* of c. f. of uru and kireru cut well, be cut off, be out of stock (compare kiru cut) be sold out

*uriko (X, 27) *composed* of *n. f.* of uru and ko child; salesman, saleswoman, shop-boy, shop-girl

urimashita (VIII, 41) *past* of uru

*uru sell

*ushiro (IX, 26) back, rear; — ni (de, e) behind, at the rear of

utarimashita *past pass.* of utsu

utte (X, 18) *ger.* of uru

*utsu strike, beat, wound, hit, shoot; dempō (w)o — send a wire; niwa ni mizu (w)o — water the garden; go (w)o — play the game of *go*

utsumuki face down

*uwagi (X, 58) coat, jacket; *compare* ue and ki, the *n. f.* of kiru wear

uwázóri (XII, 23) slippers, indoor sandals; see ue and zōri

W

*wa (I, 18) *post.* indicating that the preceding word is the logical subject of the sentence; may be translated by *as for*

*waishatsu (IX, 39) white shirt

wakarimasén (V, 19) *pres. neg.* of wakaru

wakarimáshita (XVI, 44) *past* of wakaru

wakáru *verb* understand, be clear, recognize, distinguish, divide

wari per ten (instead of per cent)

warúi (XIII, 37) bad, immoral, malicious, roguish

wasure- (XI, 47) *neg. stem* of wasureru

wasureru forget, dismiss from the mind

*watakushi (II, 9) I; — no mine, my

watákúshídomo (II, 31) we; — no our, ours

watáshídómo (VI, 45) *var.* of watakushidomo

watashimashita (III, 29) *past* of watasu

watashimasu *pres.* of watasu

watashite (XI, 8) *ger.* of watasu

watasu hand over, give, pass over, carry across

*(w)o (I, 32) *post.* usually indicates the preceding word as the object of the verb; has no English equivalent

Y

-ya (VII, 30) *suffix* store, house, merchant

ya .(XII, 29) and so forth, and

yabu bamboo thicket, grove

yado house, home, lodgings; — chin hotel bill; — chō; hotel register book

*yado-ya (XII, 7) inn, hotel, tavern

yamá (XVI, 29) mountain, peak

*Yamada (XIII, 27) *a family name*

*Yamamoto *a family name*

*yao-ya (VII, 48) grocer, grocery shop

yarō (XIV, 31) *fut.* of yaru

yaru give (to an intimate or inferior), present, perform, hold (a meeting), do

*yasai (III, 13) vegetable

yasashii easy, simple

yasashikatta (XV, 49) *adj. past* of yasashii

yasúi (VII, 54) cheap, moderately priced

yasui easy, simple

yasumi (I, 49) *n. f.* of yasumu rest, vacation

yasumu *verb* rest, repose, lay off, be absent from, cut (class)

yatte (XIV, 26) *ger.* of yaru

yattsú (VII, 7) eight

yawárákái (XI, 57) soft, tender, limp

yén (VII, 39) yen (Japanese standard of money)

yo (VII, 24) four

yo (XI, 66) *a particle added to verbs to give emphasis;* I say, I tell you

yō (XI, 11) manner, way; — na like, as; — ni so as to, in order to, to

yô *n.* ocean, sea; — no foreign

yobi (VI, 6) *n. f.* of yobu

*yobu call, hail, summon, send for

*yōfuku (X, 41) composed of yō foreign and fuku; foreign clothes, occidental dress; — ya tailor, tailor shop

yogoreru become dirty, be soiled

yogorete (XI, 7) *ger.* of yogoreru

yói (XVI, 53) *adj.* good, fine, agreeable, fitting, desirable, all right

*yōji (XIII, 35) business affairs, errand, engagement

yōka (VIII, 36) eighth day; eight days

yokatta (XV, 58) *adj. past* of yoi

yokka four days, the fourth day

*yoko (XIII, 56) *n.* side, flank; — no cross, sidelong; — ni across, sideways, horizontally

yokochō (XI, 28) *composed of* yoko and chō; side street

*Yokohama (XV, 45) *city in* Japan

yóku (X, 55) *adv. form* of yoi; well, right, ably; often, much, usually

yomimasen (III, 23) *neg. pres.* of yomu

yomimashita (III, 22) *past* of yomu

yomimásu (I, 38) *pres.* of yomu

yomitaku (IV, 39) *des. neg.* of yomu

yómu (IV, 41) *verb* read, peruse, recite

yón (XV, 23) four

yonde (V, 19) *ger.* of yomu

yonde *ger.* of yobu

yori (VI, 30) than, from, since, out of, in

Yōroppa Europe

*yoroshii (IV, 18) good, all right

*yoroshiku (VI, 13) *adv. form* of yoroshii; well, properly; Dōzo — o-negai itashimasu Pleased to meet you (literally, Please think well of me, I beg you); Matsumoto San ni — Best regards to Mr. Matsumoto

yoroshiū (VII, 62) *form* of yoroshii used with gozaru

yoru turn. twist

yōshoku western food

yōsu (XIII, 36) state of affairs, condition, circumstances, symptom

yottari four persons

yotte *ger.* of yoru

yotte accordingly, on account of, in response to

yóttsú (VII, 6) four

yóu get seasick, get drunk

yowazu (XV, 58) *neg. stem* of you

*yu (XII, 52) hot water, hot bath, bath-house, hot spring

yúbín (XIV, 30) mail, post; — -bako post-box, letter box (bako is the sonant form of hako); — kyoku post office

Yudaya Judea; — no Jewish; — jin Jew

Yudaya-kyō Jewish religion
*yūhan (III, 8) supper, dinner
*yukata (XII, 49) bath robe, dressing gown
-yuki (IX, 28) *n. f.* of yuku; bound, destined for
yukimashō (VII, 48) *prob. pres. (fut.)* of yuku
yukitai (IX, 15) *des.* of yuku
yukkúri (V, 22) deliberately, slowly, gently; — suru *verb* take one's time
*yuku (VI, 32) *var.* of iku go
*yūmei (XI, 26) famous, notorius

Z

-zan *sonant form* of san mountain
zashíkí (XII, 16) parlor, room, apartment
*zasshi (I, 15) magazine, journal
zéhi (XI, 35) by all means, without fail, certainly
*zeikan (XV, 47) customhouse, customs
*zeikin (XV, 52) tax, duty, charge
zémbu (XII, 27) all, the whole; — no all, entire; — de in full, in toto, altogether

zen *sonant form* of sen
zonji (XII, 2) *n. f.* of zonjiru
zonjiru *verb; colloquial form* of zonzuru (zuru is the sonant form of suru); know, be acquainted with
zubón (X, 58) trousers, pants
*zubonshita (X, 65) *composed* of zubon and shita under; drawers, underwear
-zun *sonant form* of sun
-zutsu (VII, 9) by, apiece, per
zutsū (XIII, 44) headache
-zutsumí *sonant form* of tsutsumi

ENGLISH-JAPANESE DICTIONARY

A

A. D. Seireki
able: be — dekiru
about goro
abuse *n.* muri
accompany tsuku
add tasu
after kara, ue
afternoon gogo, nichigogo
again mata
agreement sansei
ah sā
airmail hikōyūbin
airplane hikōki
Alaska Arasuka
all mina, zembu; in — mina de
all right kashikomarimashita
almost hotondo
alone hitori de
already mō
also mo
although keredomo
America Amerika, Beikoku
American Amerika-jin, Beikoku-jin

among aida, uchi
and soshite, shi, to; — so de; — so forth nado, ya
anything nani ka
approximately kare-kore
area menseki
Argentina Aruzenchin
arm ude
army rikugun
arrive tsuku
article (goods, thing) shina-mono
as hodo, to; — for ga, wa
Asia Ajiya
ask (inquire) kiku; (request) negau
at de, ni
Atlantic Ocean Taiseiyō
attach tsukeru
Australia Ōsutorariya
automobile jidōsha
autumn aki

B

back *n.* senaka
bad warui

baker pan-ya
bamboo take; — grove take-yabu
bank ginkō
barber toko-ya
baseball bēsu-bōru
bath furo, — robe yukata, — room furoba, — service nagashi
bathe suiei suru
be aru, desu, iru, naru
bean-curds tōfu
beard hige
beautiful kirei (na)
because kara, no de; — of tame
become naru
bed nedoko, shindai; — room shinshitsu
become naru
beef gyūniku
beer bíru
before mae (ni)
begin *v. i.* hajimaru; *v. t.* hajimeru; — to ... -dasu
beginning hajime

behind ushiro
Belgium Berugi
bend magaru, mageru
beside (no) soba (ni)
besides sono ue
between aida, naka de
bill *n.* kanjō
bird tori
black kuroi
blue aoi; navy — kon
boat fare funa-chin
body karada
book hon; — store hon-ya
born: be — umareru
borrow kariru
both ryōhō, tomo; — ... and mo ... mo ...
bottle bin
bound (for) -yuki
box hako
boy otoko no ko
Brazil Burajiru
bread pan
break kowasu
breakfast asahan
breath iki, kokyū
bridge hashi
bright akarui; — looking akaru-sō (na)
bring motte kuru; — in mochikomu
brother: older —ani; younger — otōto
brown tobi-iro
Buddha's Great Statue Daibutsu
Buddhism Bukkyō
Buenos Aires Buenosu Airesu
build *verb* tateru
building tatemono; *num. aux.* ken
bunch taba
bus basu
business (affairs) yōji
busy: be — (telephone connection) fusagaru; *adj.* isogashii
but keredomo, shikashi, ga

butcher niku-ya; — shop niku-ya
buy kau
by de, made, zutsu; — means of de; — the way tsuide ni

C

cake kashi
California Kariforuniya
call yobu
camera shashin-ki
can *verb* dekiru
candy kashi
capital (city) shufu
carrot ninjin
cash *n.* genkin; *verb* genkin ni kaeru
certainly zehi
chair isu
change *n.* kogane, tsuri; *verb* kaeru; — clothes kikaeru
channel kaikyō
charge: — money ryōkin; person in — kakari
cheap yasui
check *n.* kitte, kogitte; *verb* chikki suru
checked (design) goban
chest mune
child ko, kodomo, okosan
China Shina
Chinese (person) Shina-jin
chopstick hashi
Christian religion Kirisuto-kyō
cigar hamaki
cigarette maki-tabako, tabako
city machi
class (kind) tō; first — ittō
clerk bantō
clock tokei
close shimeru
clothes fuku, yōfuku, kimono; old — furugi
coffee kōhī
cold tsumetai: (weather)

samui; (disease) kaze; catch — kaze wo hiku
collar karā
color iro
come kuru, mairu; — up agaru
completed: be — dekiru, dekiagaru
completion kambi
concerning tsuite
condition ambai, yōsu
conductor shashō
consist naritatsu
continent shū
continue tsuzuku
convenience tsugō
cooking ryōri
corner kado
cost *verb* kakaru
count *verb* kazoeru
country kuni, -koku
cousin itoko
cross (over) kosu
cure *verb* naosu
custom fū
customer kyaku
customs zeikan
cut *verb* (crop) karu; kiru

D

dangerous abunai
daughter musume
day hi, nichi; — after tomorrow myōgo-nichi, myōgo-jitsu; — before yesterday ototoi, issakujitsu
dealings torihiki
deck (of ship) kampan
deep fukai
degree do, kagen
department store depāto
deposit *n.* chokin; (advance payment) uchikin: *verb* azukeru
descend kudaru, oriru
desire *n.* nozomi; *verb* nozomu, hoshii desu
desirous hoshii

desk tsukue
die shinu
difficult muzukashii
direction hō
disease byōki
do itasu, nasaru, suru, yaru
doctor isha
dollar doru
door to
downstairs shita
dozen dāsu
drink *verb* nomu
drive mawasu
drop *n.* teki
drunk: get — you
during aida

E

each -goto
early hayai
earthquake jishin
east higashi
easy yasashii
eat taberu, agaru
edge hashi
education kyōiku
eel unagi; — and rice unagi-
meshi
egg tamago
eight hachi, yattsu; — inches
hassun
either: — ... or de mo ... de
mo
electricity denki
elementary jinjō
elevator erebētā
endorsement uragaki
engineer gishi
England Eikoku
English (language) Eigo
enjoy oneself asobu
enter hairu, agaru
et cetera nado
Europe Yōroppa; — and
America Ō-Bei
even *adv.* de mo
evening ban; this — komban
every mai, -goto

examination shinsatsu
exceed sugiru
exercise *n.* (lesson) renshū;
(physical) undō
expensive takai
extent hodo
eye me

F

face *verb* mukau, muku,
mukeru, men suru
fact koto
family kazoku
famous nadakai, yūmei
far tōi; as — as itaru
fare chin
fast *adj.* hayai
father otōsan
favorite konomi no
fear *verb* osoreru
February Nigatsu
fee ryōkin
feminine onna no
fever netsu
few sukoshi (no)
fifteen jū go
find *v. t.* mitsukeru; *v. i.*
mitsukaru
finish dekiru, dekiagaru, shimau, sumu
fire (conflagration) kaji
first dai ichi, hajime no, ichiban
fish sakana; raw — slices
sashimi; — seller sakana-
ya; — store sakana-ya
five go, itsutsu
floor (story) kai; third —
sangai
flower hana
fly *verb* tobu
follow tsuite iku, tsuite kuru,
tsuzuku
following tsugi
food shokumotsu, tabemono,
meshi
football fūto-bōru
foreign land gaikoku

forget wasureru
fork nikusashi
Formosa Taiwan
four yo, yon, yottsu, shi; —
or five shi-go
fourteen jū shi
France Furansu
free (time) hima
fresh atarashii
Friday Kinyōbi
friend tomodachi
from kara, ni; — now on ima
kara
full ippai

G

garden niwa
Germany Doitsu
get: — on noru, — out of
breath iki ga hayaku naru,
— up okiru, — well naoru
girl onna no ko, musume
give (to a superior) ageru;
(to an inferior) yaru; (to
me) kudasaru, kureru;
(hand over) watasu
glass koppu
glassful hai
go iku, yuku, mairu; — out
dekakeru, deru; — through
tōru; — up agaru
golf gorufu
good ii, yoi, yoroshii; —
morning o-hayō; no —
dame
goodbye sayonara
Grand Hotel Gurando Hoteru
graduated: be — from deru
gratis tada
grocer yao-ya

H

half hambun, han
ham hamu
hand *n.* te; *verb* watasu
hat bōshi; felt — nakaore-
bōshi; straw — mugiwara-
bōshi

have aru, gozaru, motsu
he (kono, sono, ano) otoko no
   hito, otoko no kata
headache zutsū
health genki
hear kiku
heavy omoi
hello moshi-moshi
help *verb* tasukeru; it can't be
   —ed shikata ga nai
here kochira, koko
high (advanced) kōtō
hindrance jama
hit *verb* utsu
hot atsui; too — atsu-sugiru
hotel hoteru, yado-ya
hour ji, jikan; every — jikan-
   goto
house ie, taku, uchi
how do, do iu, ikaga; about
   — much dono gurai, (cost)
   ikura; — many iku, ikutsu,
   nan
hundred hyaku
hurry *verb* isogu
hurt *verb* itamu

I

I watakushi, watashi
idea kangae
if moshi, nara
illness byōki
immediately sugu
imported hakurai
in de, ni, naka ni
industrious kimben na
inhale iki wo suu
insert ireru
inside naka, uchi (de, ni)
insurance hoken
intend tsumori desu
interesting omoshiroi
interval aida, -kan
into e, ni, no naka e
introduce shōkai suru
island shima; — country
   shimaguni

J

jacket uwagi
January Shōgatsu, Ichigatsu
Japan Nihon, Nippon
Japanese Nihon no; (person)
   Nihon-jin, Nippon-jin;
   (language) Nihon go, Nip-
   pon go; — American Nichi-
   Bei
Jewish Yudaya no; (person)
   Yudaya-jin

K

kill korosu
kimono kimono
kitchen daidokoro
knife hōchō
know shiru, zonjiru
Korea Chōsen

L

lady of the house shufu
lake mizuumi
language go
large ōkii, dai-
late osoi; be — okureru
latrine benjo
laundress sentaku-ya
learn narau
leave v. i. deru, dekakeru
left (direction) hidari
lend kasu
length nagasa
lesson gakk(w)a, -k(w)a
letter tegami; — box yūbin-
   bako
lie (down) neru
like *verb* konomu, suku
lining ura
little *adj.* chiisai; *adv.* sukoshi;
   — by — botsu-botsu
live *adj.* ikita; *verb* sumu
London Rondon
long nagai
loud (flashy) hade na
love *verb* dai suki desu
low hikui

luggage nimotsu
lunch hiruhan

M

madam okusama
magazine zasshi
mail yūbin
mainland hongoku
male otoko
man otoko, -jin, -ya
Manila Manira
manufacture koshiraeru
many takusan no
marry kekkon suru
master of the house shujin
match matchi
meal gohan
meaning imi
measurement sumpō; take —
   sumpō wo toru
meat niku
medicine kusuri
meet au
merchant -ya
Mexico Mekishiko
middle mannaka
military man gunjin
milk gyūnyū
mind *verb* (trouble oneself)
   kamau
mine *pron.* watakushi no
minute fun; ten — s jippun;
   just a — chotto
Miss San, Sama
missing: be — nakusuru
Monday Getsuyōbi
money kane; — order kawase
month tsuki; last — sengetsu;
   next — raigetsu
more motto, mō; a little —
   mō sukoshi
morning asa, gozen; this —
   kesa
most ichiban, mottomo
mother okāsan
mountain yama, -san
mouth kuchi
movie katsudō

Mr. San, Sama
Mrs. San, Sama
mustache kuchi-hige
my watakushi no

N

name na, namae
narrow semai
nation kuni, koku
naval kaigun no
navy kaigun
near chikai
necessary hitsuyō na; be — iru
need *verb* iru
neighbor tonari
neighborhood kinjo
neither: — . . . nor mo . . . mo
new atarashii
newspaper shimbun
New Year's Eve o-misoka
New York Nyū Yōku
next tsugi, rai-
night ban; last night sakuban; one — hitoban; throughout the — hitoban-jū
nine ku, kokonotsu
no iie, iya, hai
north kita
Norway Noruwĕi
nose hana
nothing nani mo (with negative verb)
now ima, ima kara
number ban, bangō, gō, dai-; large — tasū; small — shōsū

O

Occident Seiyō, Ō-Bei
occidental seiyō no; (person) seiyō-jin
occupation shokugyō
occupied: be — (filled up) fusagaru
ocean umi
o'clock ji
of no

offer ageru, sashiageru; be —ed agaru
office jimusho, -kyoku
officer (military) shikan
often yoku
oh ā
old furui; (age) toshiyori
on de, e, ni
once ichi do; — more mō ichi do
one ichi, hitotsu, hito
only bakari, dake, shika
open *v. t.* akeru; *v. i.* aku
or matawa, ka
order (for goods) chūmon
ordinary futsū
Orient Tōyō
Oriental tōyō no; (person) tōyō-jin
other (different one) hoka no
ought to hazu, -beki
our watakushidomo no, watashidomo no

P

Pacific Ocean Taiheiyō
package tsutsumi, kozutsumi
pain *verb* itamu
painful itai
pair soku; one — issoku
paper kami
pardon gomen, shitsurei
parents oya
Paris Pari
parlor zashiki
part (section) hen
pass over kosu
passport ryoken
paste *verb* haru
pay *verb* harau
pen pen
pencil empitsu
peninsula hantō
Pennsylvania Penshirubania
people hitotachi; (citizens) kokumin; two — futari
percent bu; one — hyaku bun no ichi; (per ten) wari

perhaps tabun
person hito, kata, mono, -jin, -sha; one — hitori
personal jishin no
Philadelphia Hiraderuhiya
Philippines Hirippin
photograph shashin
pin pin
pipe (smoking) kiseru
place tokoro
plain *adj.* kiji
play *verb* asobu
pleasant kokoromochi no, ii
please dōzo, kudasai; — give me kudasai
pleased to meet you dōzo yoroshiku o-negai itashimasu
pneumonia haien
poison doku
policeman junsa
population jinkō
porter akabō
Portugal Horutogaru
post office yūbin-kyoku
postcard hagaki
potato (white) jagaimo
praise *verb* homeru
prefecture fu
present *adj.* kondo no
price ne, nedan
principal *adj.* ōmo na; —ly sbu-to-shite
probably tabun, tashika
product sambutsu
progress *n.* shimpo; *verb* shimpo suru
publish dasu
pure ma-, jun-
put oku; — on haku, kaburu, kiru

Q

quality kiji
quickly hayaku
quiet shizuka na
quite kanari

R

read yomu
ready: be — dekiru, dekia-garu
really *interj.* ne
receive morau
recent kono goro; —ly kono aida
reduce (in price) makeru
registered kakitome
regular futsū
religion shūkyō
remain (be left over) nokoru
repair naosu
request *n.* negai; *verb* negau
resemble niru
rest *n.* yasumi; *verb* yasumu
restaurant ryōriya
return *v. i.* kaeru
rice (cooked) gohan; (un-cooked) kome
rickshaw jinrikisha, kuruma; —man, —station kuruma-ya
ride *verb* noru
right (direction) migi
river kawa
road michi, tōri
Rocky Mountains Rokkī-zan
room heya
rough arai
round marui; — trip ōfuku
rudeness shitsurei
run out (of stock) kirasu
run (away to) nigekomu
Russia Roshya

S

sailor suihei
salesgirl uriko
salmon shake
same onaji
sample mihon
São Paulo Saun Pauro
Saturday Doyōbi
say *verb* iu, hanasu, mōsu
scenery keshiki
school gakkō; elementary —

shō-gakkō; high — chū-gakkō
screen: folding — byobu; sliding — shōji
Sea of Japan Nippon-Kai
seasick: get — you
seasons shiki
see miru
seem mieru, miukeru; — to be iru-rashii; it —s sō desu; —ing -sō
sell uru
sen sen; one — issen; ten — jissen
send okuru, todokeru; — out dasu, okuridasu
servant (maid) jochū
seven hichi, shichi, nanatsu
several iro-iro
sew nuu; preliminary —ing kari-nui
shave *verb* soru
she (kono, sono, ano) onna no hito, (kono, sono, ano) onna no kata
ship fune
shirt shatsu; white — wai-shatsu
shoe kutsu
shoot *verb* utsu
shopping: go — kaimono ni iku
short (in stature) hikui, (in length) mijikai
should hazu, -beki, hazu-beki
shoulder kata
show *verb* miseru
shrimp ebi
Siberia Shiberiya
side hō, yoko
sightseeing kembutsu; go — kembutsu suru
silk kinu; raw — kiito; —en kinu no
sister: elder — ane; younger — imōto
sit kakeru, suwaru

six roku, muttsu; —teen jū roku
size ōkisa
sleep nemuru, neru
sleeve sode
slippers uwazōri
slow osoi, yukkuri
small chiisai
smoke *verb* nomu, suu
so *adj.* sayō, sō; *adv.* sahodo; *interj.* sate; so, so botsu-botsu
soap sekken
soil *verb* yogoreru
soldier heishi, heitai
something nani ka
son musuko
soon sugu
sore *adj.* itai
sorry: I am — o-ki-no-doku sama
soup suimono
south minami; — America Minami-Amerika
South Seas Nan-yō
Spain Supein
speak hanasu
special delivery sokutatsu
splendid kekkō na
spoon saji; —ful saji-zutsu; table — ōkii saji
sport undō
spring haru
square shikaku
squat suwaru
stamp (postage) kitte
stand *verb* tatsu
starch *n.* nori
state (geographical) shū
stateroom shinshitsu
station (railway) teishaba; eki
stature sei
stock: be out of — urikireru
stocking kutsushita
stomach o-naka, hara
stop tomaru, tomeru
store mise, -ya

straight (directly) massugu
street tōri, chō; first — it-chōme; main — hondōri; side — yokochō; — car densha
stripe shima
student seito
study manabu, benkyō suru
style fū
such konna, sonna
suit fuku, yōfuku; *aux. num.* chaku; one — itchaku
suitcase kaban
summer natsu
Sunday Nichiyōbi
supper yūhan
swim *verb* oyogu
system seido

T

table taberu, tsukue
tailor yōfuku-ya, shita-ya
take (carry) motte iku; (seize) toru; — out dasu
tall takai
tan cha-iro
tasty oishii
tax zeikin
taxicab takushī
tea cha, o-cha
teach oshieru
teacher sensei
telegram denshin, dempō
telegraph *verb* dempō wo utsu
telephone *n.* denwa; — directory denwachō; *verb* denwa wo kakeru
tell iu
temperature kagen
ten jū, tō; — thousand man
tender yawarakai
tennis tenisu
Texas Tekisasu
than yori
thank you arigatō (gozaimasu) (gozaimashita)
that sono, sore, sochira, ano, are, achira

theater shibai
there soko, asoko; sochira, achira; — is ga aru; ga gozaru
therefore desu kara, sore de wa
they (kono, sono, ano) hito-tachi
thing koto, mono
think *verb* omou, omowareru
third (of a series) sambamme; (fraction) sambun
thirsty: become — nodo ga kawaku
thirteen jū san
this kono, koko no, kochira, kore
those sono, ano, soko no, sore, are, ano
thousand sen
three san, mittsu; — quarters shi hun no san
throat nodo
through kara; —out -jū
throw away suteru
Thursday Mokuyōbi
thus sō, konna ni
ticket kippu
time toki, ji, jikan, do; long — shibaraku; many —s maido; one — ichi do; two —s ni do
tip kokorozashi
tired: be — tsukareru
to e, ni; up — itaru; itaru made
tobacco tabako
today kyō, konnichi
together issho ni
tomorrow asa, asu
tongue shita
too (excessive) amari; (also) mo
top ue; on — of no ue ni
touch ataru, sawaru
train (railroad) kisha; express — kyūkō; limited — tokkyū

transact tori-atsukai
transfer *n.* tennin; *v. t.* tennin suru; (change cars) nori-kaeru
travel ryokō suru
treatment atsukai, tori-atsukai
tree ki
trousers zubon
trunk toranku
try miru
Tuesday K(w)ayōbi
turn *v. i.* magaru
twelve jū ni
two ni, futatsu; — people futari; — or three ni-san

U

under no shita ni
under-drawers zubonshita
understand wakaru
unfortunately ainiku
United States Amerika, Bei-koku
university daigaku
until itaru made, made
upstairs ni kai
use *verb* tsukau
usual: as — aikawarazu

V

various iro-iro
vegetable yasai
very taihen, taishita, taisō, naka-naka; (with negative verb) amari
vest chokki
volcano funkazan
vomit haku
vote: — for sansei suru

W

wait matsu
waiter kyūji
walk *n.* sampo; *verb* aruku; take a — sampo wo suru
want ga hoshii, -tai
warm atatakai

wash *n.* sentaku; *verb* arau, sentaku suru
washroom benjo
water mizu; hot — o-yu; — a garden niwa ni mizu wo utsu
watermelon suika
wave nami
way (manner) shikata, yō; one — kata-michi
we watakushidomo, watashi-domo
wear haku, kaburu, kiru
weather tenki
Wednesday Suiyōbi
week shūkan, shū; last — senshū; next — raishū; one — isshūkan
weigh hakaru
well *adv.* yoku, yoroshiku
well *interj.* mā, ja, hā, sā, sate

west nishi
what nani, nan, dō; — kind of donna, dō iu
when itsu, nan ji; toki
where doko, dochira
which dono, dochira, doko, no
while aida, nagara
white shiroi
who dare, donata; *pl.* donatagata
why naze
wide hiroi
wife: (my) kanai; (your or his) okusan, okusama
willingly (acceding to a request) kashikomarimashita
wind *n.* kaze
window mado
wine budōshu
winter fuyu
wipe nugu

wish *verb.* -tai, negau, ga iru
with de, issho, to
woman onna, onna no hito, onna no kata
word kotoba
work *n.* shigoto; *verb* hataraku
world sekai
wrap *verb* tsutsumu
wrestling sumō
write kaku

Y

year nen; last — sakunen; next — rainen; one — old issai
yes hai, ē, iie
yesterday kinō
yet mada
you *sg.* anata; *pl.* anatagata
young wakai

INDEX

Numbers refer to sections of the grammar.

A

accompaniment, 46
adjectives, 21, 43, 47, 78, 101, 103, 105, 106, 107, 108
adverbs, 14, 28, 106
after, 44, 80
agaru, 41
age, 58
alternative questions, 24
and, 15, 83
articles, 2
aru, 8, 31, 71
attributive form of the verb, 25, 26, 72
au, 99

B

base of the verb, 30, 56, 90
because, 29, 44
before, 80
begin, 27
beki, 68
better, 59
bring, 37

C

capability, 25, 90, 92
causative form of the verb, 93
come and *go* with the gerundial form of the verb, 37
comparison of adjectives and adverbs, 47
compound words, 61
conclusive form of the verb, 26
conditional, 57, 89
continuative form of the verb, 14 18, 21, 26, 40, 44, 56 74, 85
coordination and subordination, 44
correlatives, 24

D

dake, 79
dasu, 27
dates, 70, 113, 114, 115
days of the week, 67
de (postposition), 14, 22, 39
demonstratives, 2, 10, 73
desire, 14, 21
direct discourse, 75

E

e, 14, 33

F

family relationships, 38
former and latter, 102
future, 54, 96

G

ga, 5, 21, 58, 59, 84, 85, 89, 90, 92
gerundial form of the verb, 28, 30, 31, 32, 35, 36, 44, 66, 71, 74, 76, 80, 81, 97
give, 86
go, 37
gohan, 17

H

hai and iie, 82
hazu, 68
honorifics, 30, 32, 38, 66, 86

I

indefinite pronouns, 23, 106
intention, 72
interrogative pronouns and adjectives, 73, 106
iru (be necessary), 85
iru, 31, 71

J

ja, 6, 39
-jū, 94

K

ka, 1, 23, 24, 106
kakaru and kakeru, 42
kan (suffix), 62
kara (postposition), 29, 45, 92
kuru, 26, 27, 30, 37, 56, 116, 117

M

ma- (prefix), 10¹
made, 51
masu, 7
miru, 66
mo (postposition), 12, 19, 83
mō, 87
morau, 76
must, 57

N

na, 43
nagara, 80
names, 9
naru, 38, 43, 69
ne, 48
negative of -masu, 8, 18
negative pronouns, 19, 106
negative stem of the verb, 32, 54, 56, 57, 93, 98
negau, 40, 86
ni, 14, 28, 92, 93, 98, 99
no, 13, 43, 55, 73, 84
no ni, 95
nouns, 4, 43
noun form of the verb, 27, 32, 38, 40
numerals, 52, 58, 61, 64, 70, 110, 112, 113, 114, 115
numeral auxiliaries, 58, 64, 70, 73, 110, 111

O

obligation, 57
oku (verb), 81

only, 79
order: *in — to*, **14**
oru, 31, 71

P

passive form of the verb, 92, 117
past tense, 18, 117
past perfect, 97, 117
permission, 35
personal pronouns, 11, 38, 104
phonetic changes, 18, 30, 61, 63, 67, 73, 101, 112
please, 32, 86
plurals, 4
possession, 13, 49
possessive case, 13
postpositions, 16, 100
potential form of the verb, 36, 90
preference, 59
present perfect, 31, 96, 117
present tense, 7, 26, 96, 117
probable present, 54, 117
progressive form of the verb, 31, 117
prohibition, 36

R

-rashii, 103
relative clauses, 84

S

shika, 79
shimau, 97
shiru, 31
should, 68
so, 5, 29
-sō, sō desu, 65
stereotyped expressions, 100
sugiru, 78
superlative of adjectives, 47
suru, 26, 27, 40, 50, 56, 89, 93, 106, 107

T

take, 37; — *off*, 77
-tara, 74
-te, 30
temporal conjunctions, 80
there is, there are, 49
time, 63
to, 15, 28, 46, 83
transitive and intransitive verbs, 34, 42, 91, 92

try, 66
tsumori, 72

V

verbs, 7, 18, 26, 27, 31, 109, 116, 117

W

wa and wo, 3, 5, 20, 21, 85, 92
wakaru, 34, 91
wear, put on, 77
when, 15, 70, 74, 80
which, 73
while, 80
without, 98

Y

ya (postposition), 83
-ya, 60
year periods, 70, 115
yo (final particle), 88
yō desu, yō ni, 65

Z

-zu, 98
-zutsu, 53